CREATIVE TRANSFORMATIONS

SUNY series in Latin American and Iberian Thought and Culture

Rosemary G. Feal, editor
Jorge J. E. Gracia, founding editor

CREATIVE TRANSFORMATIONS

Travels and Translations of
Brazil in the Americas

KRISTA BRUNE

Cover image courtesy of the Free Library of Philadelphia, Print and Picture Department. Text at the bottom reads "Our Centennial - President Grant and Dom Pedro II starting the Corliss Engine. From a sketch by Theo R. Davis."

Published by State University of New York Press, Albany

© 2020 State University of New York

All rights reserved

No part of this book may be used or reproduced in any manner whatsoever without written permission. No part of this book may be stored in a retrieval system or transmitted in any form or by any means including electronic, electrostatic, magnetic tape, mechanical, photocopying, recording, or otherwise without the prior permission in writing of the publisher.

For information, contact State University of New York Press, Albany, NY
www.sunypress.edu

Library of Congress Cataloging-in-Publication Data

Names: Brune, Krista, 1984– author.
Title: Creative transformations : travels and translations of Brazil in the Americas / Krista Brune.
Description: Albany : State University of New York, 2020. | Series: SUNY series in Latin American and Iberian thought and culture | Includes bibliographical references and index.
Identifiers: LCCN 2020023195 (print) | LCCN 2020023196 (ebook) | ISBN 9781438480619 (hardcover : alk. paper) | ISBN 9781438480626 (pbk. : alk. paper) | ISBN 9781438480633 (ebook)
Subjects: LCSH: Travelers' writings, Brazilian—History and criticism. | Travel in literature. | Brazilian prose literature—Translations—History and criticism. | Portuguese literature—Translations into English—History and criticism. | Translating and interpreting—Brazil. | Brazil—Relations—United States. | United States—Relations—Brazil.
Classification: LCC PQ9607.T73 B78 2020 (print) | LCC PQ9607.T73 (ebook) | DDC 869.09/3281—dc23
LC record available at https://lccn.loc.gov/2020023195
LC ebook record available at https://lccn.loc.gov/2020023196

10 9 8 7 6 5 4 3 2 1

CONTENTS

List of Illustrations		vii
Acknowledgments		ix
Introduction	Theorizing Travels and Translations of Brazil in the Americas	1
Chapter 1	The New World Travels and Translations of *O Novo Mundo*	27
Chapter 2	Modernism for Export: The Translational Origins and Afterlives of *Macunaíma*	67
Chapter 3	Silviano Santiago's Translational Criticism and Fiction	105
Chapter 4	Testing Translatability: Adriana Lisboa's Hemispheric Brazilian Novels	141
Conclusion	Translating Brazil Today: Retranslations and Untranslatability	175
Notes		193
Bibliography		229
Index		253

ILLUSTRATIONS

1.1 The opening page of the first issue of *O Novo Mundo*   35

1.2 The Agricultural Hall and the Memorial Building plans for the Centennial Exposition published in *O Novo Mundo*   45

1.3 Photograph of "Main Building—Brazil," Centennial Exhibition   49

1.4 Illustration in *O Novo Mundo* of Brazil's section in the Main Building   49

1.5 Photograph of "Agricultural Hall—Brazil," Centennial Exhibition   51

1.6 Illustration in *O Novo Mundo* of Brazil's section in the agricultural hall   51

2.1 Excerpt of *Macunaíma* published in *Revista de Antopofagia*   69

2.2 Grande Otelo as Macunaíma in the 1969 film *Macunaíma*   94

ACKNOWLEDGMENTS

Fitting for a study about travel and translation, this book has developed out of travels, exchanges, and dialogues that traverse languages and transcend national and cultural borders. Thanks to Pedro Meira Monteiro's inspiring classes that sparked my interest in Brazil as an undergraduate, I began this journey of considering Brazil's place in the Americas. I have benefited from Pedro's ongoing mentorship since those *primeiras aulas*. Natalia Brizuela, Candace Slater, and Scott Saul deepened my understanding of Brazilian literature and culture in connection to the hemispheric Americas and provided insightful comments on an earlier version of this project. I am grateful to Natalia for her continued guidance from afar. Support from the Tinker Foundation and the Department of Spanish and Portuguese at the University of California, Berkeley allowed me to conduct initial archival research in Brazil and the United States. Conversations during the National Endowment for the Humanities summer institute on the Centrality of Translation to the Humanities, directed by Elizabeth Lowe and Christopher Higgins, proved fundamental to my thinking about translation.

All of my colleagues in the Department of Spanish, Italian, and Portuguese at Pennsylvania State University have welcomed me and supported my research. In particular, I thank my department head Paola Giuli Dussias, for her unwavering commitment to my work and to the Portuguese program; my faculty mentor Sherry Roush, for her invaluable advice on writing a first book; and my fellow Latin Americanists John Ochoa, Judith Sierra-Rivera, Marco Martínez, and Sarah J. Townsend, for reading my drafts and collaborating to build a lively intellectual community. A semester-long residency at Penn State Humanities Institute granted me the necessary time to think, write, and complete this manuscript. Exchanges with the institute's director John Christman, associate director Lauren Kooistra, and my fellow residents Anna Ziajka Stanton, Jessamyn Abel, and Nicolai Volland helped refine my ideas. Conversations with Magalí Armillas-Tiseyra, Thomas Beebee, Dayse Bedê, Kristina Douglass, Martha Few, Chris Heaney, Zachary Morgan, Manuel Rosaldo, and Rebecca Tarlau have enriched my teaching and research on Brazil and Latin America. Discussions with graduate students in seminars on translation, politics, and the Americas at both Penn State and Universidade de São Paulo have deepened my understanding of translation as a theory and a practice. It was a pleasure to coteach in São Paulo with Marcelo Pen Parreira and to embark on hemispheric exchanges together and in dialogue with his colleagues, especially Lenita Maria Rimoli Pisetta and Marcos Natali.

I am indebted to colleagues and friends across the United States and Brazil for contributing to my thinking and for providing continuous support. Leila Lehnen, Bruno Carvalho, and Luciano Tosta kindly read drafts of the proposal and provided useful suggestions on how to frame the argument and structure the project. I am grateful to Adriana Johnson, Jens Andermann, Marília Librandi Rocha, and Sergio Waisman for traveling to central Pennsylvania to share their insights on writing about Brazil and translation. Katrina Dodson, Adam Morris, and Magdalena Edwards have shed light on life as a working translator today. Exchanges with Cristiano Aguiar, Thayse Lima, Marcelo Lotufo, Alfredo Cesar Melo, José Luiz Passos, Pedro Schact Pereira, Ty West, Isabel Gómez, and Adriana Amante have contributed to my thinking. The friendships, steadfast support, and perceptive reading of Manuel Cuellar, Julie Ward, Ashley Brock, and Julia Chang have made our writing group a lifeline over the years. Sebastião Edson Macedo is a critical interlocutor who has always listened with care and read with attention to deepen my engagement with Brazilian literature and culture.

At State University of New York Press, I have in Rebecca Colesworthy an ideal editor whose enthusiasm for my work and guidance through the publishing process have been instrumental. I thank series editors Rosemary G. Feal and Jorge J. E. Gracia for their interest in this book and for their commitment to publishing scholarship on Brazil as an integral part of Latin American and Iberian thought. I am grateful to the two anonymous reviewers for carefully reading my manuscript and providing invaluable suggestions that have improved the book. A shorter and earlier version of chapter 1 was originally published in *Journal of Lusophone Studies*. An earlier version of the discussions in chapter 4 and the conclusion on contemporary trends in translation was published in *Comparative Critical Studies*. Reproductions of images in chapters 1 and 2 come from Free Library of Philadelphia, Print and Picture Collection; Library of Congress; and Biblioteca Brasiliana Guita e José Mindlin–PRCEU/USP.

Writing this book would not have been possible without the love and support of friends and family who bring joy to my life and remind me of what truly matters. I am lucky to count Lori Piranian Mulcare, Liliane and Luciane Costa da Silva, Kelly Sanabria, and Dan-el Padilla Peralta as dear friends who have welcomed me into their homes and families over the years as travels have taken me to New York and São Paulo. My parents, Linda and Gary Brune, instilled in me a love of reading and a deep appreciation for nature. I am indebted to their model of a balanced life and a supportive partnership. My deepest gratitude to Ian Thompson, for filling our home with music, laughter, and love, and for always being up for a walk.

Introduction

Theorizing Travels and Translations of Brazil in the Americas

Brazilian emperor Dom Pedro II (1825–1891) traveled by steamship from his native Rio de Janeiro to New York in 1876, the centennial of independence of the United States. After his arrival in mid-April, the emperor spent the next three months traversing the nation's continental span via railroads and river steamships.[1] Traveling as Pedro de Alcântara, the emperor enjoyed a freedom of movement that he lacked within the hierarchical confines of the Brazilian monarchy (Barman 285). Along the way, he met political leaders, most notably President Ulysses S. Grant, and intellectual and cultural elites, including scientist and Harvard professor Louis Agassiz and writer Henry Wadsworth Longfellow. The emperor accessed privileged realms reserved for nineteenth-century elites whose political status, wealth, and education allowed them to intermingle within cosmopolitan circles. His interactions when discussing literature with Longfellow or marveling at the industrial capacity of new technologies at the Centennial Exhibition alongside Grant unfolded in a learned language of English, rather than his native Portuguese. Pedro II's mobility across the United States and adeptness among accomplished scientists, artists, politicians, and business leaders depended upon his linguistic abilities and intellectual curiosity.

The emperor expressed in his diary an affinity for his encounters with Longfellow by describing the writer as an "excelente amigo em todo o sentido" (excellent friend in the complete sense; Pedro vol. 17, 49).[2] One evening, after a dinner at Longfellow's house, the two men retired to the patio for a more intimate conversation that built on their knowledge of the other's work and shared interests in the literatures and cultures of the Americas. Before physically traveling to the United States, Pedro II journeyed metaphorically among its peoples and geography by reading Longfellow's verses, specifically his 1847 epic *Evangeline*. Pedro commissioned Franklin Dória to translate the poem into Portuguese, which was published in Brazil in 1870. The poem connected with readers throughout the Americas with its tale of a young woman searching for her lost love and longing to return to the primeval forest of Acadia. With frequent translations into Spanish and Portuguese, the epic modeled how to craft a national poem by celebrating the distinct nature of the Americas.[3] On that June evening at Longfellow's Cambridge home, the writer gave the emperor two books and asked various questions about Brazil in an exchange indicative of the emerging inter-American project that has foregrounded literary and political ties between the United States and Brazil since the nineteenth century. The encounter between the Brazilian emperor and the North American poet exemplifies the dynamics of hemispheric travel and translation at stake in this study. On his figurative and physical travels throughout the United States, Pedro II explored cultures and geographies that differed from those of his native Brazil and thus generated feelings of displacement. From his privileged position, the emperor navigated unfamiliar political and cultural realms with relative ease given his aptitude as a linguistic and cultural translator.

A renowned polymath and autodidact coronated as emperor at the age of fourteen, Pedro II had long engaged in processes of travel and translation when adapting and combining elements from European monarchies and the industrializing United States in order to build a modern Brazilian nation. For historian and anthropologist Lilia Moritz Schwarcz, Dom Pedro crafted Brazil as "an 'original copy': a culture constructed on continual borrowing that it incorporated, adapted, and redefined" (*The Emperor's Beard* xx). Her vision of Brazil as an "original copy," whereby it modeled itself on other nations' systems and practices but adapted them to local specificities, resonates with how the Brazilian artists and intellectuals that I study in this book approach translation as a theoretical concept and a necessary practice. Rather than dismiss it as derivative, they showcase translation's creative potential and utility in communicating across languages and cultures, even when efforts at cross-cultural exchange generate misunderstanding. Translation, I argue, is essential to negotiating the contradictory impulses that shape Brazil's position in the Americas. By translation, I refer to literal translations unfolding in spoken and written language in multiple directions between Portuguese, English, Spanish, and indigenous languages and to the associated cultural encounters and exchanges. In a broader sense, translation also denotes processes of interpretation, explication, and transformation critical to navigating Brazil's place within the hemispheric Americas and, in particular, in relationship to the United States. Since the 1870s, when Dom Pedro II traversed the United States and journalist José Carlos Rodrigues (1844–1922) published the Portuguese-language periodical *O Novo Mundo* (The new world) from New York, Brazilians traveling to and living in the United States have felt displacements that demand personal acts of translation to facilitate movement within circles of North American elites and to render foreign ideas and experiences for their compatriots living in Brazil.

Move forward nearly 150 years to 2018, a moment when migration in the Americas has emerged as a humanitarian crisis further instigated by the inflammatory rhetoric and actions of far-right politicians Donald Trump and Jair Bolsonaro. Whereas Brazilian intellectual and artistic elites, whose works I study in the following chapters, continue to travel with relative ease throughout the hemisphere and beyond, other migrants and refugees embark on arduous journeys from Central America and, to a lesser extent, Brazil and other South American nations through Mexico to the United States or from Venezuela to neighboring Colombia and Brazil. They attempt to migrate without the required visas and other documentation that allow contemporary Brazilian writers like Silviano Santiago and Adriana Lisboa to study, work, and live in the United States. Disparities in education, socioeconomic backgrounds, and linguistic abilities contribute to these differentiated experiences of travel and migration as undocumented migrants and refugees confront draconian policies that close borders and authorize the separation of children from their parents.[4] Language further marginalizes these migrants, especially when their native tongue is Portuguese or an indigenous language rather than the Spanish more frequently spoken by translators and authorities at the border.

The story of Jaene Silva de Miranda, a Brazilian mother separated from her three children at the US-Mexico border in June 2018, exemplifies how inabilities to translate between national languages and, thus, to navigate distinct cultural contexts hinder the mobility of travelers and migrants in the Americas.[5] Miranda and her children traveled from the interior of Minas Gerais for five days, with four flights and a three-hour walk in the desert, to reach the southern border of the United States in a trajectory that parallels the journey of other undocumented Brazilian immigrants, including the character Luiz in Lisboa's 2013 novel *Hanói*. In the fictional narrative, Luiz crossed illegally into the United States without apprehension by border patrol. In real life, Miranda did not encounter the same good fortune as Immigration and Customs Enforcement agents arrested her and separated her from her children. Negotiating the labyrinths of US immigration law without knowing Spanish and English further isolated Miranda and complicated her situation. After forty-four days, she was reunited with her children, thanks to the help of relatives living in the United States who hired a Brazilian immigration attorney.

The absence of Portuguese-language translators at the border and in the judicial system indicates that demands for linguistic and cultural translation, even when unfulfilled, continue to structure the lives of Brazilians who circulate with varying ease throughout the Americas. Undocumented migrants like Jaene Silva de Miranda and the fictional Luiz confront linguistic, legal, socioeconomic, and cultural barriers that impede their mobility between nations. After traversing these obstacles to arrive in the United States, they suffer a more radical sense of displacement than their elite counterparts in earlier eras and the current moment. Attempting to understand the experiences of Brazilians in the United States requires hearing the stories of both the privileged artists and intellectuals who document their own journeys and the struggling migrants who often lack the educational and financial resources to narrate their life stories. While my analysis in the subsequent chapters focuses on works by Brazilian elites who have lived in the United States or traveled metaphorically through the Americas, I recognize the critical need to include voices of undocumented migrants and other underrepresented peoples often elided in efforts to write and translate Brazil. Their stories tend to reach reading publics in Brazil and throughout the Americas via processes of translation that first occur between different socioeconomic and cultural milieus within the shared language of Brazilian Portuguese and, subsequently, between national languages. Writers like Santiago and Lisboa serve as these intralingual translators who convey tales of a migrant underclass in the United States to an educated readership in Brazil.

Since the nineteenth century, Brazilian intellectuals and artists who have spent time in the United States have integrated personal encounters and societal observations from abroad into their creative works. In doing so, they have facilitated the transfer and exchange of ideas, images, and experiences in both directions between Brazil and the United States. To complement these hemispheric journeys, other Brazilians, including modernist Mário de Andrade, traveled within their native country to discover popular, Amerindian, and Afro-descendant oralities, cultural practices, and folkloric traditions, which they translated for educated Brazilians by integrating and transforming them into their writings. For the Brazilian artists and intellectuals that I study here, travels generate dislocations and discoveries, which they process through linguistic and cultural translations that serve to communicate their knowledge and experiences to others. These travelers, whether privileged writers or the marginalized migrants that they represent, share a desire for the world, which Mariano Siskind identifies as the epistemological structure at the heart of cosmopolitan discourses (1). Whereas nineteenth-century journalists, twentieth-century modernists, and twenty-first-century global novelists exude an elite cosmopolitanism, the migrants and refugees that appear in select contemporary literature point to what Silviano Santiago terms the cosmopolitanism of the poor.[6] Across this temporal span, the hemispheric travels of Brazilians reveal cross-cultural conflicts, connections, and contradictions that necessitate translation in its multiple meanings.

Creative Transformations: Travels and Translations of Brazil in the Americas contends that translation is essential to Brazil's standing in the Americas, even when it does not seem like translation is explicitly or directly at stake. The book asks: To what extent is it possible to "translate Brazil"? What are the political implications of such a project? Who are these translators of Brazil, and how do they contribute to representations and interpretations of the nation? How does a focus on translation's role in hemispheric exchanges contribute to our understanding of Brazil's place in the Americas? *Creative Transformations* argues that travels of Brazilian artists and intellectuals since the nineteenth century have resulted in displacements and encounters that demand linguistic, cultural, and epistemological translations. Travels unfold both geographically, as Brazilians leave their homes for the United States or distant regions of Brazil, and intellectually, as they read travel narratives and dialogue intertextually with Spanish American writers and theoretical concepts from abroad. During their journeys, these Brazilians comprehend foreign ideas and expressions via forms of creative translation that, in turn, shape Brazil's image abroad, especially in the Americas, as a nation of contradictions.

My approach to the topic of Brazil in the Americas is, by necessity, limited in its scope. I foreground the relationship between Brazil and the United States that develops through creative and critical works primarily in Portuguese and English. At times, intersections with Spanish American texts and the Spanish language emerge within the Portuguese-language writings of Brazilians who have lived and studied in the United States. With allusions to Spanish American writers and multilingual conversations in Portuguese, Spanish, and English, these Brazilian texts establish connections to Spanish America that are often triangulated through the United States. In other instances, intertextual dialogues develop between narratives in Portuguese from Brazil and in English from Guyana and their inspirations in the languages and oral cultures of Amazonian Amerindians. The languages, nations, and cultures that I privilege in this book account for only a portion of the diverse linguistic and literary traditions of the Americas. To understand more fully the literatures of the Americas, it is necessary to consider texts from throughout the "New World" written in Spanish, Portuguese, and French, as well as indigenous and creole languages. With his 1991 study *Rediscovering the New World: Inter-American Literature in a Comparative Context*, Earl Fitz argued for such a comprehensive vision of inter-American literature.[7] This method establishes inter-relations between literatures of the Americas on the basis of historical, geographic, and cultural affinities, most notably encounters between indigenous peoples and European colonial forces, histories of slavery, myths of national origin and expansion, and ongoing experiences of immigration.

In the intervening decades, Inter-American studies has emerged as a discrete field closely connected to Comparative Literature, Hemispheric American studies, and Latin American studies.[8] Fitz addresses the current state of Inter-American literary studies and related disciplines in his 2017 tome *Inter-American Literary History: Six Critical Periods*. He recognizes advances in Americanist scholarship that emphasize comparisons between the United States, Spanish America, and the Caribbean yet fail to account for Canada and Brazil.[9] "Giant, Portuguese-speaking Brazil," Fitz laments, "so unique, as an American nation, in so many ways, is routinely ignored, rendered invisible" (*Inter-American* 382). This commentary on Brazil's relative obscurity within comparative inter-American approaches points to ideas of Brazilian exceptionalism on the basis of its language and size. Linguistic, cultural, and intellectual barriers between Latin American nations tended to reinforce the divisions that the Treaty of Tordesillas established in 1494 as it split the Americas between Spain and Portugal. With his 1993 essay "Abaixo Tordesilhas!" (Down with Tordesillas), Jorge Schwartz joined Fitz and other scholars of Latin America in a call for more comparative work between the literatures, cultures, and intellectual histories of Brazil and Spanish America.[10]

Studies comparing Brazil to Spanish-speaking Latin American and Caribbean nations, most notably Cuba, Mexico, and Argentina, have become more common in the last two decades.[11] These scholars examine similarities and inter-relations between literary and cultural works from different languages and contexts in order to reveal affinities across Latin American aesthetic grammars, thematic interests, and historical contexts. Other recent books advance a more explicitly inter-American perspective in comparisons between Brazil, Spanish America, and the United States. With their focus on poetry and poetics, Justin Read's *Modern Poetics and Hemispheric American Cultural Studies* (2009), Charles Perrone's *Brazil, Lyric, and the Americas* (2010), and Harris Feinsod's *The Poetry of the Americas: From Good Neighbors to Countercultures* (2017) recognize that hemispheric dialogues and creativity flourish in literary genres other than narrative. Perrone identifies a "transamerican verse" as an inextricable trait of poetic works that travel in the Americas (36). Read further elaborates on hemispheric links between travel, translation, and poetry: "The foundation of American culture is migration. The original language of the Americas is only ever translation. The poem is the process by which the language of migration—*translation*—materializes in its own right" (xxvii). I similarly regard translation and migration as central to the experiences of the Americas but do so without confining their literary and artistic expressions to poetry.

Within this burgeoning corpus of inter-American literary and cultural studies, I must acknowledge the contributions of Zita Nunes's *Cannibal Democracy: Race and Representation in the Literature of the Americas* (2008) and Antonio Luciano Andrade de Tosta's *Confluence Narratives: Ethnicity, History, and Nation-Making in the Americas* (2016). Their comparative readings prioritize the critical role of Brazil within hemispheric histories, artistic movements, and racial and ethnic constructs. Nunes analyzes discursive and artistic representations of race with a focus on Brazilian modernism and the Harlem Renaissance. In addition to stressing affinities and inter-relations between Brazil and the United States, she draws parallels to contemporary literary works from other parts of the Americas. Tosta likewise privileges Brazil in his analysis of contemporary narratives of historical confluence, which pairs a Brazilian novel with one from Mexico, the United States, Argentina, or Canada per chapter to illuminate Amerindian, Afro-descendant, Jewish, and Asian experiences in the Americas. In thinking of Brazil in the Americas, I look toward works by Perrone, Nunes, and Tosta as examples of how to recognize hemispheric inter-relations of languages, literatures, and cultures and, at the same time, emphasize the prominence of Brazil as a territorial giant comparable to the United States. Rather than restrict my analysis to a specific literary genre or to a schematic comparative framework, I examine a varied archive that elucidates how travels of Brazilian artists and intellectuals inflect their creative and critical works with an ethos of translation. While my study favors narrative and the relationship of Brazil and the United States, I acknowledge that the hemispheric Americas constitutes a more encompassing idea.

The following chapters bring together periodicals, material and visual culture, essays, short stories, and novels from the late nineteenth through the early twenty-first centuries to reveal how linguistic, cultural, and epistemological translations shape Brazil's profile in the Americas. Exploring the hemispheric exchanges of Brazilian artists and intellectuals across this temporal span illuminates the critical role of translation in uncovering how politics and economics shape intersections of language, culture, and belonging. Translation serves as a fruitful theoretical and methodological approach to question Brazil's assumed marginality vis-à-vis the United States. My study suggests that ideas and examples from Brazil can enrich discussions of translation and cosmopolitanism in the US-based disciplines of Comparative Literature and Inter-American studies.[12] By drawing attention to the oft-overlooked presence of Brazilians among Latin American communities in the United States since the nineteenth century, the book proposes a more expansive and nuanced vision of Latinx identities and hemispheric connections.

My examination of Brazilians in the United States begins by situating *O Novo Mundo* as the creation of Brazilians living in New York in the 1870s. The periodical's cautious interest in establishing hemispheric connections resonates with the dual impulses of intrigue and disdain that Spanish American writers, most notably José Martí, expressed toward the United States while living in the country in the late nineteenth century.[13] Encounters between Brazilians and Spanish Americans in the United States continue in the late twentieth and early twenty-first centuries, as Silviano Santiago and Adriana Lisboa depict in their contemporary fictions. Their interactions pose a challenge to ideas of Brazilian exceptionalism on the basis of language, history, and culture. To a certain extent, they point to the potential for a more inclusive form of Latinidad that accounts for Portuguese-speaking Brazilians and Spanish-speaking Caribbean and Latin American residents of the United States. Intellectual and artistic dialogues between Brazilians and Spanish Americans facilitate the construction of a hemispheric project that US geopolitical and socioeconomic interests in Pan-Americanism do not govern.[14]

Creative Transformations proposes a genealogy of key moments in the translation of Brazil within the hemispheric Americas since the late nineteenth century. A genealogy, as Lisa Lowe reminds us in her reading of Michel Foucault's concept, is a mode of creating a history of the present that uncovers how categories are established as given (3). To craft this history of the present, I trace how travel and translation have intersected to result in transcreation as a practice critical to the experiences and representations of Brazil in the Americas. By transcreation, I refer to the neologism that Haroldo de Campos developed for processes of experimental poetic and literary translation that require creative transposition. I employ the term more capaciously to characterize how languages, cultures, and ideas creatively transform as people and texts travel. My study begins with the second half of the nineteenth century as a moment when literal and figurative forms of translation emerged as key to elite constructs of Brazil. In particular, the 1870s marked a period of transition for Brazil and the United States as these two hemispheric giants attempted to define and project their nations on a global stage.[15] Translation allowed Brazilian elites to embrace the nation's contradictions as an emerging modern nation whose place in the global system of early industrial capitalism depended upon its tropical resources. They argued for creatively adapting North American and European forms of modernity and modernization to Brazil's geographic, political, economic, and sociocultural specificities. Throughout the twentieth century and into the twenty-first, translation as a linguistic, cultural, and epistemological endeavor has facilitated negotiations and critiques of apparent binaries of local and global, national and cosmopolitan, and tropical and modern.

Crafting this genealogy reveals how acts of translation render transnational experiences of Brazilian travelers and migrants into national literary works. This approach also underscores continuities from the late nineteenth century through the early twenty-first, including a continued presence of Brazilians in the United States and a persistent desire for global recognition and prominence of a modern Brazil. My readings of a nineteenth-century periodical *O Novo Mundo* and its depictions of the

Centennial Exhibition, Mário de Andrade's modernist *Macunaíma* and its afterlives in film and fiction, Silviano Santiago's idea of the space in-between and its manifestations in fiction, and Adriana Lisboa's contemporary hemispheric Brazilian novels underscore how translation fosters cross-cultural exchanges yet generates misunderstandings. I examine translation as a thematic thread and a theoretical concern that weaves together these varied works. In this sense, I am not primarily addressing translation as literal textual rendering of a literary work from one national language to another. My analysis instead considers the personal forms of linguistic, cultural, and epistemological translation that develop as these writers and their characters travel and migrate. Translation facilitates linguistic and cultural dialogues, but it also confronts limitations as misinterpretations and other errors point to the potential of a politics of untranslatability that allows for the circulation of diverse voices and texts without flattening them into a homogeneous aesthetic.

Brazilian artists and intellectuals have often commented on their travels throughout the Americas in periodicals, diaries, essays, and fictional tales that reach mainly a readership in Brazil. These traveling peoples, ideas, and texts have contributed to the transnational process of constructing Brazil as a modern nation, seemingly despite its unruly tropical nature but actually due to its natural resources. Understanding Brazil as, in Benedict Anderson's concept, an "imagined community" draws attention to how periodicals, literary texts, and visual and material cultures craft the nation as a task of imagination that involves translations. In studying works since the late nineteenth century, I concentrate on periods of what Ottmar Ette terms "accelerated globalization" that also represent key moments in Brazil's negotiation of its global position. Ette outlines four phases of accelerated globalization: first, Spanish and Portuguese colonial expansion in the early modern era; second, British and French scientific explorations of the mid-eighteenth to early nineteenth centuries; third, neocolonial ambitions of the United States and Europe in the late nineteenth to early twentieth centuries; and, finally, the current phase of rapidly globalizing financial networks and communication systems. My book's first two chapters examine an 1870s periodical of "progress" and a 1928 modernist novel to coincide with what Ette identifies as the third phase of accelerated globalization. The other two chapters analyze essays, short stories, and novels from the 1970s through the 2010s, which roughly correspond to the final phase of heightened globalization.

The temporal framework of this study represents key developments in the history of Brazil and the United States. This overview of historical events from the 1870s to the 2010s serves to contextualize the literary and artistic works that I analyze in the following chapters.[16] For both nations, the 1870s represented a period of transition in the aftermath of Brazil's defeat of Paraguay in the War of the Triple Alliance (1864–1870) and the Union's victory over the Confederacy in the US Civil War (1861–1865).[17] In the post–Civil War years, especially before Reconstruction ended in 1876, the United States provided a potential path for how Brazil could transition from an empire where slavery remained legal to a republic that had abolished slavery. Moreover, with the United States replacing Europe as a center of capital and industrial growth in the late nineteenth century, Brazilian elites looked toward the United States as a new locus of production that could guide their nation's future direction.[18] Following the abolition of slavery in 1888, Brazil became the last nation in the Americas to proclaim itself a republic in 1889. Though its new official name, Estados Unidos do Brasil, expressed an affinity with the United States of America, ideas from France inspired the republicanism of Brazil's urban intellectuals, but without a revolution. As historian Leslie Bethell explains, "Like the transition from colony to empire, the transition from empire to republic was marked more by fundamental social and economic continuity than change" (151).

The 1920s represented another period of transition for the young democracy of Brazil as the final decade of the first republic, which ended with the military coup of the Revolution of 1930 that brought Getúlio Vargas to power. Cultural revolutions were under way in São Paulo alongside these political ones as modernists attempted to rethink Brazilian literature and art and to rupture institutional structures with their Week of Modern Art in 1922.[19] Mário de Andrade and his fellow modernists proposed visions of the nation that complicated romantic glorifications of indigenous peoples by recognizing cultural mixtures and slippages as constitutive of Brazilian identities. These years also saw the emergence of "racial democracy" as a construct and a myth central to perceptions of Brazilian national identity.[20] In contrast, Jim Crow laws and other forms of institutionalized racism dictated social norms in the southern United States. Different concepts and lived experiences of race in Brazil and the United States led Mário de Andrade to assert in his 1944 poem "Canção de Dixie" (Dixieland song), in English, "No, I'll never be / In Colour

Line Land."[21] True to his word, the modernist never visited the United States, but he learned via textual travels about the importance of African rhythms and instruments to popular music in the United States and the lack of recognition for African American musicians. During this period, the United States intervened in Latin America by occupying Cuba, the Dominican Republic, Haiti, Nicaragua, and Honduras prior to implementing the Good Neighbor Policy in 1934. The 1929 stock market crash sent global economies reeling, resulting in the Great Depression in the United States. Against this economic backdrop, *Macunaíma*, as I analyze in the second chapter, struggled to reach an audience in translation given the constriction in the publishing market.

Roughly forty years later, Brazil faced another political crisis with the 1964 military coup and the subsequent dictatorship that lasted until 1985. After the decree of the Fifth Institutional Act (AI-5) in December 1968, which tightened the regime's authoritarian control by suspending indefinitely all legislative bodies, ending habeas corpus, and heightening censorship, Brazilian leftists and dissidents entered into voluntary or forced exile.[22] The late 1960s and early 1970s saw Tropicália musicians Caetano Veloso and Gilberto Gil living in London, singer-songwriter Chico Buarque staying in Italy, and visual artist Hélio Oiticica and intellectual Silviano Santiago residing in New York.[23] Santiago's fiction explores migration and exile, while his theory of the space in-between responded to geopolitical hierarchies that marginalized Latin Americans, as I discuss in the third chapter. In the context of the Cold War, the United States exerted influence in Latin America and throughout the Global South via cultural and economic imperialism and, at times, direct political intervention. Cold War cultural politics contributed to the Latin American Boom as an editorial phenomenon of translation in an effort to garner interest in countries deemed politically relevant to the United States through literary and artistic expressions.[24] Heightened concern in the United States with Brazil and Spanish America during this period influenced Santiago's professional and personal trajectory as he taught Portuguese at the University of New Mexico and interacted with other Latin American migrants and exiles in the United States.

The first decades of the twenty-first century are emerging as another critical transition for the global position of Brazil and its relationship to the United States. The election of Luiz Inácio Lula da Silva in 2002 inaugurated a period of optimism in Brazil as political and social change seemed possible under the leadership of the Workers' Party (PT). Increased global prominence as one of the BRIC nations coincided with these domestic developments.[25] In 2013, historian Marshall Eakin echoed this enthusiasm by proclaiming, "The time has come to recognize that the country of the future has become the country of the present" ("The Emergence" 230). This assessment of Brazil as a global political and economic leader has proved premature. In the wake of its moment in the international spotlight as the host of the 2014 World Cup and the 2016 Olympic Games, Brazil has entered a deepening crisis, with the impeachment and conviction of Dilma Rousseff, economic instability, increasing inequality and violence, and the rise of the far-right culminating in Bolsonaro's election in October 2018 and his disastrous first year in office. Similar to the case of Trump in the United States, the electoral success of Bolsonaro responds, in part, to frustrations among segments of Brazil with the political and socioeconomic gains of Afro-descendants, women, LGBTQ+ communities, and other underrepresented minorities. In particular, racial animosity and xenophobia have fueled the support of these far-right leaders.

The movement of migrants and travelers between Brazil and the United States continues, though not as freely as it once had. In the wake of the terrorist attacks of September 11, 2001, the United States sought greater control over the entry of foreign nationals into the country by increasing border security and tightening visa requirements. The demand for inexpensive, immigrant labor persisted in the United States, even as entering the country and remaining there legally became more difficult. As a result, the population of undocumented immigrants continued to grow until it peaked in 2007.[26] Due to the constraints on immigration and the contraction of the US economy following the 2008 financial crisis, Brazilian immigrants in the United States returned to Brazil, where the economy was fairing comparatively well.[27] The hemispheric Brazilian novels by Adriana Lisboa that I analyze in the fourth chapter exist in this landscape where political and economic fortunes link Brazil and the United States and shape migratory flows between the nations. With its broad temporal scope, *Creative Transformations* draws parallels and recognizes differences between distinct historical moments. Geopolitical and socioeconomic contexts ground my analysis of textual relationships and intellectual networks that develop as Brazilian artists and intellectuals embark on hemispheric travels. By exploring how their experiences of displacement affect their personal negotiations between distinct languages, cultures, and ideas, I assert that literal and figurative processes of translation are central to representing and understanding Brazil's place in the Americas.

Toward a Latin American Theory of Translation

My interest in the intersections of travel and translation builds upon two seminal studies from the 1990s: *Routes: Travel and Translation in the Late Twentieth Century*, by James Clifford, and *Imperial Eyes: Travel Writing and Transculturation*, by Mary Louise Pratt. They interrogate the imperial and colonial practices underlying naturalist and ethnographic travels to document the "otherness" of the non-Western world. For anthropologist Clifford, travel is a "translation term," or, in other words, a comparative concept (11). This figurative understanding emphasizes that movement and transformation structure both travel and translation. Literary scholar Lydia H. Liu similarly notes that "comparative scholarship that aims to cross cultures can do nothing but translate" (1). In framing translation as essential to the critical work of comparison, both Clifford and Liu engage with and build upon Edward Said's 1983 essay on "Traveling Theory." Said identifies four stages in the travel of a particular theory, beginning with the origin; continuing with, second, the distance traversed; third, the conditions that allow for the introduction of the idea to another context; and ending with the incorporation of a transformed version of the idea in this new realm (227). Liu notes, however, that the traveling part of this equation becomes lost as subsequent scholars, including Clifford, take up Said's concept. The idea of traveling theory, Liu argues, tends to prioritize theory by granting it mobility, while it "fails to account for the vehicle of translation" (21). Overlooking translation's role in this process renders travel an abstraction that does not recognize how the movement of theory unfolds in specific directions and languages for distinct purposes and publics. Liu's analysis corrects this oversight by paying attention to how texts and ideas travel to China in the early twentieth century. Though I focus on a different context of Brazil in the Americas, I similarly aim to examine how the spatial and temporal dimensions of travel generate what Liu terms the "condition of translation" (26). Rather than consider translation as a neutral aesthetic act, I stress its enmeshment in geopolitical, socioeconomic, cultural, epistemological, and ideological realms.

As Brazilians have traveled in the Americas, their displacements have resulted in cross-cultural exchanges that invite personal gestures of translation. For Pratt, the contact zone denotes these contentious spaces of encounter. Hierarchical relationships of colonialism, imperialism, and slavery governed the dynamics between European naturalists who traveled to Latin America in the eighteenth and nineteenth centuries and the indigenous, Afro-descendant, and creole peoples who lived there. Without explicitly linking travel and translation, Pratt proposes transculturation to describe the transfers and transformations between cultures that occur in these contact zones.[28] According to Fernando Ortiz in *Cuban Counterpoint: Tobacco and Sugar* (1940), transculturation refers to a reciprocal process whereby cultures transform each other to create a new distinctive form. Ortiz contrasted transculturation with acculturation, which consisted of one culture adapting and assimilating into the more dominant culture. Ángel Rama later adapted this anthropological concept of transculturation to literature to characterize the interactions of autochthonous Latin American cultures and European influences that result in Latin American narratives' distinctive language, literary structures, and cosmovisions. Drawing on Rama's work, Pratt employs transculturation to account for the transformations central to the imperial gaze of European naturalists and the self-fashioning of Latin American creoles. By emphasizing how language and culture change with travel, Pratt constructs a theoretical concept that resembles my vision of translation, in its varied manifestations, as creative transformation.

With translation as my critical lens, I explore how travels and migrations of people and texts produce linguistic and cultural transformations that, in turn, extend the reach of a given work, image, or idea. Circulation emerges as a key concept in recent studies of translation, most notably Ignacio Infante's *After Translation: The Transfer and Circulation of Modern Poetics Across the Atlantic*.[29] Infante builds on an anthropological conceptualization of circulation to analyze the role of translation in the creation and transmission of modern transatlantic poetry. For Benjamin Lee and Edward LiPuma, "cultures of circulation" refer to processes of transmission that involve performative and constitutive elements of culture (192–93). Envisioning circulation in this manner invites us to consider how cultures constitute and project themselves within a global capitalist market. In identifying transformation and circulation as critical processes, I draw attention to how travels of peoples, texts, and ideas create displacements and unexpected encounters that require linguistic, literary, and cultural translations.

Literary studies often view translation as a mode of travel in the sense of *translatio* or carrying across that entails spatial and temporal dimensions. This focus on travel has, according to Rebecca Walkowitz, "tended to emphasize the distinction between literature's beginnings and its afterlives" (29). This comment recalls Walter Benjamin's view of translation as the afterlife or continuation of a text into another language, place, and time. In his 1923 essay "The Translator's Task," Benjamin contends that translation "develops into a linguistic sphere that is both higher and purer" as it proceeds from the original (79). He frames translation as a form determined by a text's translatability, by which he refers to the distinctiveness and quality of the original's language. His ideas contrast with commonplace definitions within the publishing market that equate relative ease of translating a text with its translatability. Benjamin's concept of translatability dialogues with the philosophical construct of the untranslatable.[30] For Barbara Cassin and Emily Apter, the untranslatable does not denote the impossibility of rendering a word into another language but rather indicates a word or an idea that, on a conceptual level, demands recurrent interpretations and attempts at translation. Although Walkowitz alludes to Benjamin's ideas, her comment on differentiating literary origins and afterlives refers specifically to studies by David Damrosch and Pascale Casanova that feature translation as essential to world literature as a category, method, and theory. For Damrosch, positioning translation as an institution of world literature elucidates how a text transcends its linguistic and contextual origins when circulating within global networks and markets (281). Casanova's Francocentric vision of world literature contends that "critical recognition and translation are weapons in the struggle by and for literary capital" (23). According to Casanova, critics and translators grant cultural capital and prestige to literary and cultural works as they circulate within a global market.

Circulations of literary and cultural texts respond to market demands and depend upon the actions of "agents of translation." John Milton and Paul Bandia conceive of an "agent" in translation as a producer, editor, patron, writer, or literary agent who mediates between a translator and the final translation (1). These agents function as gatekeepers who determine which works circulate and influence the shape of the resulting translations. The artists and intellectuals that I study in the following chapters serve as agents of translation in a more expansive sense. While at times they mediate between an individual translator and a final translation, they also navigate more figurative and conceptual realms by rendering ideas of the nation and explicating dense theories. *O Novo Mundo*'s editor José Carlos Rodrigues facilitated the publication of a serialized and abridged translation into Portuguese of Harriet Beecher Stowe's *My Wife and I*. In the 1930s and 1940s, Mário de Andrade's correspondence with North American and German translators revealed efforts to enable *Macunaíma*'s publication in translation. With their interpretations in *Glossário de Derrida*, Silviano Santiago and his students aimed to make Jacques Derrida's ideas more accessible to readers of Brazilian Portuguese in the 1970s. Adriana Lisboa's background as a literary translator informs how she interacts with the translators of her novels. Recognizing these artists and intellectuals as agents of translation, who also engage in individual acts of linguistic and cultural translation while traveling in and beyond Brazil, draws attention to networks of people and texts that shape Brazil's place in the Americas.

Poets, critics, and translators Haroldo and Augusto de Campos embrace the role of agents of translation by promoting unknown foreign writers and forgotten figures in Brazilian letters, experimenting with verbivocovisual poetics in their own verse and translations, and positing new methods of translation.[31] The *paulista* brothers brought translation to the forefront of literary activity in Brazil with their critical essays and their translations of key literary figures such as James Joyce, e. e. cummings, Ezra Pound, Paul Valéry, Stéphane Mallarmé, Arnaut Daniel, Octavio Paz, Dante, Goethe, and Vladimir Mayakovsky from a range of languages, including English, French, Occitan, Spanish, Italian, German, and Russian.[32] They also traveled to the United States as visiting scholars and writers at the University of Texas at Austin in the 1980s, which contributed to their inter-American poetic and intellectual dialogues. In analyzing the Campos brothers as agents of translation, Thelma Médici Nóbrega and John Milton stress that especially Haroldo "has had considerable influence on attitudes towards translation; he has put forward a complex theory of translation that emphasizes the aural and visual aspects of the translation of literature" (258). His 1962 essay "Da tradução como criação e como crítica" ("Translation as Creation and Criticism") proposes a semiotic approach to translation's creative and critical potential without citing a wide range of theoretical works. Rather than assume the impossibility of translating works by experimental writers like Pound, Mayakovsky, and Joyce, Haroldo posits that "every translation of a creative text will always be a 're-creation,' a parallel and autonomous, although reciprocal, translation—'transcreation'" (*Novas* 315). This formulation differentiates literal, word-for-word translations from a creative process of re-creation governed by an isomorphic relationship, reminiscent of a Poundian ideogram, between a text and its translation. A translation is one work among a constellation of texts that recreate the sign and the signified in another language to contribute to the overall meaning of the original.

Over the next two decades, Haroldo de Campos read touchstones of translation theory, including "The Translator's Task" and Roman Jakobson's 1959 essay "On Linguistic Aspects of Translation," and refined his theorizing of transcreation. Frustrated with the focus on literalness in translation, he proposed new terms that characterized translation as a creative process, as he outlined in his 1985 essay "Da transcriação: poética e semiótica da operação tradutora" (Transcreation: poetics and semiotics of translative operations). These neologisms include, in addition to the previously cited re-creation (*re-criação*) and transcreation (*transcriação*), reimagination (*reimaginação*), transtextualization (*transtextualização*), transparadization (*transparadisação*), and transluciferation (*transluciferação*). Transcreation has emerged as the term with the most critical weight and staying power. At a semiotic level, transcreation operates as a practice that misconfigures and, at the same time, transfigures (*Transcriação* 101). In Jakobson's formulation of poetic translation as "creative transposition," which emphasizes movements within and between languages, Haroldo de Campos identifies a concept primed for further analysis in disciplines of literature, history, and anthropology.

The essay also invokes Benjamin's metaphysical concept of translation, which serves to liberate pure language through a process of transpoetization (98). Given their approach to theorizing translation as critics, writers, and translators, both Campos and Benjamin tended to valorize the translator's creative agency and to dismiss readings of translations as mere copies. To illustrate this point, Haroldo de Campos cites Benjamin's metaphor of a vessel, broken into pieces and then reconstructed. The translator must divide the original text, which the vase represents, into component parts and reconstitute it in another language, resulting in a work that approximates the original but is not a perfect copy. This image of breaking apart and recreating a work in another context underscores the craft involved in processes of translation. Moreover, with his interests in semiotics and the philosophy of language, the Brazilian poet-critic recognizes the slippages that occur between the sign and the signified in a given language. Translation, therefore, can never function as a mechanical reproduction resulting in an exact duplicate of the original in another language. Literary and cultural translators must embark on a creative practice that involves reading and interpreting the work, breaking it down into structures of meaning, and then reassembling it in a different context.

In line with these theoretical interventions from Brazil, I frame translation as a critical tool for questioning the supposedly peripheral positions of Brazil and the rest of Latin America in the hemisphere and beyond. My approach to theorizing translation with Latin American and, in particular, Brazilian texts expands upon Sergio Waisman's compelling study of how creative infidelities in translation contest established hierarchies and allow writers from peripheries to exert irreverence with respect to dominant North American or European literature. In focusing his analysis on Argentine writer Jorge Luis Borges and translation, Waisman emphasizes the spatial and temporal specificity of translation to posit the distinct role of the translator in Argentine and, more generally, Latin American culture. Waisman astutely places Borges's thoughts on translation in dialogue with prominent twentieth-century theorists Benjamin, Jakobson, and Derrida. He contends that Borges's playful approach to translation questions concepts of the definitive text and fidelity, which anticipates recent trends in translation studies (Waisman 72). Beginning with his 1926 text "Las dos maneras de traducir" ("Two Ways to Translate"), Borges insisted on how spatial and temporal contexts impact the meaning of words, an idea further fleshed out in his renowned 1939 piece "Pierre Menard, autor del *Quijote*" ("Pierre Menard, Author of the *Quixote*"). Comparisons of Miguel de Cervantes's seventeenth-century masterpiece and Pierre Menard's twentieth-century rewriting of the novel emphasize that a text's significance can vary based on the conditions of its creation and reception, even when its contents remain identical. In pieces on the Homeric versions and the translators of *One Thousand and One Nights*, Borges similarly stressed the impossibility of a definitive text and its faithful translation by framing translations as versions that add to the meaning of a given work. Placing the works of Borges and the Campos brothers in dialogue underscores similarities in their visions of translation as creative rewriting that questions ideas of the definitive text and the perfect copy.[33] Comparing Argentine and Brazilian writers and translators establishes translation theories and practices that contest allocating ideas from Latin America to a peripheral realm.

For modernist Oswald de Andrade, Brazilians needed to engage in *antropofagia*, a form of digesting foreign cultures and ideas and transforming them into original works. In the 1960s, Haroldo and Augusto de Campos evoked a modernist ethos of making it new again to define translation with neologisms transcreation, translation-art, and intranslation. Literary and translation studies scholars, including Else R. P. Vieira, K. David Jackson, and Edwin Gentzler, link modernism's cultural cannibalism to the Campos brothers' translation theory.[34] These critics identify in Brazilian thought and culture a recurrent devouring of texts, languages, ideas, and cultural practices in order to create something new. This process involves interpretative analysis and creative transformation, as I illustrate in the following chapters by exploring how Brazilian artists and intellectuals negotiate cross-cultural encounters during hemispheric travels. Akin to Borges's view of translation, transcreations require the creative agency of the translator, who interprets the text and contributes to its meaning by transforming it and reconstituting it in a new context. Latin American theories of literary translation establish a critical grammar to analyze the travels, linguistic encounters, cultural exchanges, and creative transformations that have defined Brazil's position in the Americas since the nineteenth century.

The approach of Brazilian and Spanish American writers to translation invites attention to geopolitical, economic, linguistic, and cultural dynamics of the global production and circulation of literature, which Emily Apter studies with her concepts of the translation zone and the politics of untranslatability. Apter proposes the translation zone as one of "critical engagement that connects the 'l' and 'n' of transLation and transNation" (*The Translation Zone* 5). Literature and art created in this zone do not belong to a single nation, nor do they exist in an amorphous realm of postnationalism. Instead, as I demonstrate in this study, literary and cultural works of translation zones reveal an entanglement of the national and the transnational. The construction of a modern Brazil unfolded in the nineteenth century as a transnational process foregrounding ties to the United States due to emerging networks of capital, industry, and higher education. Throughout the twentieth century and into the twenty-first, the nation persists as an imagined community and as a cultural construct that contributes to how individuals position themselves in the world, even as scholars like Apter advance a more radical questioning of categories related to the national.

Brazil's hemispheric and global prominence depends upon and shifts through travels and translations, as I examine in the second half of this book. Engaging with the idea of the nation in the twenty-first century requires critical self-awareness, as Benedict Anderson exemplifies with his 2006 afterword to *Imagined Communities*. Anderson examines how the translation and global circulation of his study transformed the text and his own view of the nation. This reflection complicates his earlier argument about the key role of print-capitalism to nineteenth-century nationalism. Expanding upon the link that Anderson draws between nation and translation, Walkowitz reads *Imagined Communities* as an example of a "born-translated" book, given that "Anderson argues translation can contribute to the imagination of national communities. But as Anderson demonstrates, translation puts pressure on the conceptual boundaries between one community and another and may spur the perception of new communities altogether" (29). As I turn my attention in the third and fourth chapters to recent literary representations of Brazilians living in the United States, I analyze translational aesthetics and transnational exchanges that expand and transform ideas of what it means to be Brazilian. These connections between nation and translation that Anderson theorizes and that I address in the context of literary representations center on ideas of community and cultural difference that also inform Homi Bhabha's work.

The travels and translations of Brazilian artists and intellectuals that I study in the following chapters epitomize the metaphorical and physical movement that Bhabha identifies within migrant and marginal communities living and writing the nation. These writings require "doubleness" in terms of temporal and spatial representation, a form of textual travel, rewriting, and transformation also known as translation (Bhabha 202–03). Although Bhabha focuses on cultural translation to examine how difference shapes understandings of postcolonial space within boundaries of the nation, he dialogues with ideas of linguistic and literary translation by citing Benjamin's "The Translator's Task." Analyzing Benjamin's ideas about the foreignness of language and the untranslatable in relation to cultural difference showcases the potential of studying literature, art, cultural policies, and social dynamics through the lens of translation. Bhabha points to possible limitations of translation for facilitating cross-cultural understanding, which he, in turn, frames as an opportunity for people on the margins and the borders "to translate the differences between them into a kind of solidarity" (244). This call to action positions the challenges of translating and narrating the nation in the face of cultural difference as the basis for a new form of transnational solidarity between those living on the peripheries of the nation, a gesture reminiscent of Santiago's idea of the cosmopolitanism of the poor. Though I recognize the value of such marginalized peoples and their expressions, I privilege elite cultural figures in my study, given their critical and ongoing role in curating Brazil's hemispheric profile.

Chapter Organization: Case Studies of Travels and Translations

The book's first chapter, "The New World Travels and Translations of *O Novo Mundo*," analyzes how *O Novo Mundo* engaged in literal and figurative translations as it traveled between Brazil and the United States during the 1870s. Published in New York from 1870 to 1879, the periodical conveyed the anti-imperial and abolitionist ideals of its editor José Carlos Rodrigues to a readership primarily in Brazil. Its articles celebrated Brazil's natural resources and urged elites to transforms models of modernization seen in the United States to the specificities of Brazil, rather than merely copying them. By documenting the travels of North American scientists in Brazil and Pedro II in the United States, the periodical articulated a hemispheric outlook grounded in bilateral exchanges and shared investments in political, socioeconomic, cultural, and technological modernization. The 1876 Centennial Exhibition in Philadelphia with its interest in "progress" received significant coverage in *O Novo Mundo* in articles portraying for Brazilian readers how the nation projected itself as modern-yet-tropical on a global stage.

To further examine hemispheric underpinnings of Brazilian culture in the nineteenth century, I turn my attention to the periodical's sections on literature. By publishing an 1873 essay by renowned Brazilian writer Joaquim Maria Machado de Assis (1838–1908) on the "instinct of nationality," which argues that authors do not need to depict local color to be considered Brazilian, the periodical stressed the need to approach the idea of the nation from a hemispheric perspective. Poet Joaquim de Sousa Andrade (1833–1902), better known by his pen name Sousândrade, contributed to the periodical while living in New York from 1871 to 1885, illustrating that the role of Brazilians in the United States dates to at least the nineteenth century. *O Novo Mundo*'s literary translations, paired with its linguistic and cultural ones, indicate the centrality of translation to the periodical's hemispheric travels and connections in the late nineteenth century.

Chapter 2, "Modernism for Export: The Translational Origins and Afterlives of *Macunaíma*," focuses on Mário de Andrade's 1928 modernist masterpiece to explore how translation continued to facilitate negotiations and critiques of Brazil's contradictions in the early twentieth century. Reading the novel in conjunction with debates about its translations, adaptations, and intertextual dialogues highlights travel and translation as essential to the creation and circulation of Macunaíma as a character and a text in the Americas. *Macunaíma* emerged out of travels of peoples, tales, and ideas that invited creative transformations, which resulted in one of the most innovative works of Brazilian literature. The chapter opens by reading *Macunaíma* as an exemplary transcreation due to Andrade's transformations of Theodor Koch-Grünberg's documentation of indigenous myths and legends. Translating the novel into English proved difficult for Margaret Richardson Hollingsworth, as she expressed in letters to Mário de Andrade about her unpublished North American version in the 1930s, and for E. A. Goodland, who published a widely criticized English-language version in 1984.

Later attempts at circulating the novel beyond national and linguistic borders revealed the need for creative adaptations to reach a broader public. I contend that the afterlife of *Macunaíma* in the Anglo-American context has unfolded primarily through Joaquim Pedro de Andrade's 1969 film and Pauline Melville's 1997 novel *The Ventriloquist's Tale*. Analyzing the film as an intersemiotic translation of the novel and *The Ventriloquist's Tale* as a fictional reimagination of Macunaíma in the narrator's role frames these more recent works as creative transformations of Mário de Andrade's *Macunaíma* that extend the reach of the original novel and contribute to the visibility of Macunaíma in the Americas. This textual trajectory points to translation's centrality for the creation and circulation of literatures of the Americas, while also revealing that the need for linguistic and cultural translations emerges even with travels that exist primarily within Brazil.

The third chapter, "Silviano Santiago's Translational Criticism and Fiction," opens by analyzing how Santiago's essay, "O entre-lugar do discurso latino-americano" ("Latin American Discourse: The Space In-between"), developed as a product of travel and translation. First presented in 1971 as a lecture in French in Montreal, the essay was translated into English and expanded in a Portuguese version. Its trajectory between languages and nations parallels Santiago's travels between Brazil, France, and the rest of the Americas. Applying French theory to Latin American works, Santiago proposed the space in-between as a discursive realm from which Latin Americans always speak or write back to the United States and Europe. He supports his theorization with literary examples from Jorge Luis Borges and Julio Cortázar that illuminate the possibilities of creative infidelity in translation. Discussing the space in-between through the lens of translation reveals the concept's political potential for questioning and subverting hierarchies that tend to prioritize the original over the copy.

After situating Santiago's essay in the realm of translation studies, the chapter considers how travel and translation intersect in his fictional works about Brazilians in the United States: the 1985 novel *Stella Manhattan* and the short story collections *Keith Jarrett no Blue Note* (Keith Jarrett at the Blue Note, 1996) and *Histórias mal contadas* (Poorly told stories, 2005). To capture the linguistic and cultural in-between of Brazilians and other Latin Americans in the United States, Santiago integrates specific allusions and Spanish and English phrases into his Portuguese prose. Attempts at communication by Brazilians in the United States can generate mistranslations and misunderstandings. The story "O Borrão" ("Blot"), for example, captures how constructs of race do not translate smoothly from Brazil to the United States. Codeswitching and cultural references of Santiago's translational prose resist facile translation and point to barriers that impede cross-cultural understandings.

The fourth and final chapter, "Testing Translatability: Adriana Lisboa's Hemispheric Brazilian Novels," situates Lisboa as Santiago's literary descendant given the intersections of travel and translation in her narratives. Translation is a particularly useful mode to analyze Lisboa due to her experience as a translator from French and English, her thematic explorations, and her work's relative success in translation. With prose that captures how travelers and migrants move between languages and cultures, her novels serve as a case study of the possibilities and limitations of translation in contemporary Brazilian literature. Lisboa creates fictional characters whose displacements require their exploration of unfamiliar settings via forms of linguistic and cultural translation. My analysis focuses on depictions of Brazilians living in the United States in her novels *Azul-corvo* (2010; *Crow Blue*, 2013) and *Hanói* (2013). Attention to the oft-overlooked role of Brazilians in the United States, especially in connection to other Latin American and Latinx communities, sheds light on how translations facilitate hemispheric encounters across languages, cultures, races, and nations.

Lisboa's recent novels suggest a preference for market translatability, since her narrative style is fairly accessible and easy to translate, and the need for a politics of untranslatability, which can resist homogenizing language and identity. *Azul-corvo* and *Hanói* depict linguistic, cultural, and racial differences that Brazilians face in the United States by integrating English and Spanish words and cultural references to create a sense of displacement for Brazilian readers that allows them to better empathize with characters' experiences as migrants, exiles, and travelers. Her prose captures misunderstandings across languages and cultures that resist translation and thus point to the need for a politics of untranslatability that rejects commodifying narratives for the global literary market. As a political gesture, this approach to representing migrant lives recognizes that there are lived experiences, cultural references, and forms of codeswitching that cannot be flattened into homogeneous narratives of world literature.

The conclusion, "Translating Brazil Today: Retranslations and Untranslatability," examines broader concerns of what it means to translate Brazil now by considering how the market shapes which voices remain excluded from this partial process of translation. I address other dilemmas of translation that impact the literary profile and cultural prominence of Brazil in the Americas, namely, retranslation and untranslatability. By retranslation, I refer to new translations of previously translated works, such as the recent New Directions translations of Clarice Lispector's novels and short stories. Examining retranslation sheds light on the global literary market, which opts for seemingly translatable works, and, more importantly, the creative agency of translators. Rather than accept translatability as the dominant aesthetic, I consider what a politics of untranslatability would look like for Brazilian literature in the Americas. Embracing untranslatability would involve maintaining the linguistic strangeness and cultural specificities of texts, words, and ideas often deemed untranslatable by continuing to attempt to interpret their strangeness and render it into another language without minimizing or erasing the distinctiveness.

Creative Transformations creates awareness of the politics of translation in the context of Brazil by focusing on travels and translations, with their creative infidelities, from the nineteenth century to the present. The concepts of retranslation and untranslatability point to future research opportunities of analyzing how Brazilian literary and cultural texts challenge dominant politics of translation that demand either flattening difference or celebrating the exotic. Permitting spaces of untranslatability would complement translation by allowing for a broader range of Brazilian voices, aesthetic forms, and critical practices to circulate within the Americas. In recent years, small presses and alternative venues have begun to embark on such a necessary and challenging task. For now, let us turn our attention to the elite voices from Brazil that embarked on these hemispheric travels and translations, beginning in the nineteenth century.

Chapter 1

The New World Travels and Translations of O Novo Mundo

During the second half of the nineteenth century, Brazilian elites traveled and engaged in acts of translation as they sought new models of political and economic development in the United States and the rest of the Americas. In parallel to these travels north by Brazilians, North American naturalists traversed Brazil in search of scientific discoveries. *O Novo Mundo*, a Portuguese-language periodical edited by Brazilian José Carlos Rodrigues and published in New York from 1870 to 1879, documented these hemispheric travels for readers primarily in Brazil. As it traveled from New York to Brazil, this "new world" newspaper translated scientific, industrial, educational, and cultural developments unfolding in the United States for an elite Brazilian readership. *O Novo Mundo* also featured representations of Brazil that appeared in travelogues and international exhibitions. The periodical captured exchanges unfolding in both directions as North American scientists traveled to Brazil, Brazilian politicians traversed the United States, and Brazilian men of letters lived in New York. Through forms of translation and retranslation, *O Novo Mundo* projected a hemispheric vision of "progress" that blinded it to future dangers posed by capitalist extraction and neocolonial ambitions of the United States.

Scientists, writers, and other elites featured in *O Novo Mundo* desired to foster greater knowledge of and within the Americas. Their trajectories contrasted with those of late eighteenth-century and early nineteenth-century naturalists, whose travel books about non-European places gave European readers an investment in the imperial project, according to

Mary Louise Pratt. The artists and intellectuals that I examine here aimed to share discoveries with readers and to inspire further interest in Brazil among North Americans and in the United States among Brazilians, even as they failed to safeguard the nation from future exploitation. A desire to construct a modern Brazil informed *O Novo Mundo*'s editorial outlook as it critiqued both nations and advocated for greater hemispheric dialogue. This chapter situates *O Novo Mundo* in a translation zone to highlight how its travels and translations produced creative transformations and potential misunderstandings. Emily Apter conceives of the translation zone as a realm of possible conflict and reciprocal exchanges, which contrasts with Pratt's vision of the contact zone resulting from colonial and imperial hierarchies that result in "social spaces where disparate cultures meet, clash, and grapple with each other" (7). Though Apter proposes this concept to account for contemporary geopolitical, social, and psychological ramifications of translation, her idea provides a useful tool for analyzing the exchanges between Brazil and the United States in *O Novo Mundo*. In its role as translator, the periodical transferred ideas, images, and experiences between nations of the Americas and, thus, suggested a shift in foreign influence among Brazil's elites away from Europe and toward the United States.

O Novo Mundo's editor Rodrigues and other proponents of this hemispheric vision did not fully foresee the implications of a close relationship between Brazil and the United States.[1] Instead, as indicated by the journal's documentation of the 1876 Centennial Exhibition in Philadelphia, it seemed possible to establish mutually beneficial connections between Brazil and the United States. At the fair's inauguration on May 10, 1876, President Ulysses S. Grant and Emperor Dom Pedro II toured the grounds together. Accompanied by four thousand invited guests, they examined national displays as they made their way to the fair's industrial centerpiece, the Corliss engine. Turning the wheels on the enormous machine, the two heads of state started the generator that powered the other displays in machinery hall.[2] With this symbolic act, Grant and Dom Pedro affirmed their belief in Eurocentric visions of progress as a teleological ideal that could help their nations achieve global prominence. While the United States would soon emerge as a global force of industrial capitalism, Brazil would remain on the political and economic margins as a nation of primitive accumulation.

Touring the Centennial Exhibition together allowed the president and the emperor to envision possibilities for their nations during difficult periods of transition. They faced similar challenges of governing an expansive territory, grappling with legacies and burdens of colonialism and slavery, and establishing unified national identities. The two countries were also worlds apart, with the United States a democracy recovering from a devastating Civil War and Brazil a tropical monarchy holding on to the vestiges of slavery.[3] Being the only nation in the Americas with a monarch contributed to Brazil's isolation and exceptionalism, especially in relationship to its Spanish American neighbors, so it instead looked toward the United States for potential points of dialogue.[4] The encounter between the president and the emperor provides an entrance into exploring the shared desires for and distinct claims to modernity of the United States and Brazil. Political and labor reforms over the next decades would facilitate the embrace of industrial capitalism to varying degrees in the two countries as the Americas increasingly became a center of global capital. The Philadelphia exhibition suggested this shift spatially and visually with the prominence of the United States and Brazil in the displays where they translated curated visions of national identity and economic potential for a foreign public.

O Novo Mundo dedicated significant coverage to the Centennial Exhibition, since it represented a material expression of Rodrigues's hemispheric visions of industrial modernization that aimed to connect a print community across the Americas. With *O Novo Mundo* as my focal point, this chapter analyzes forms of travel and translation initially mentioned in the periodical, such as scientific writings, exhibition displays, Pedro II's travels, and literary texts. *O Novo Mundo* provided subtle critiques of both the United States and Brazil that echoed Rodrigues's views. Articles on the post–Civil War United States and translated excerpts of a novel by abolitionist Harriet Beecher Stowe served to condemn the continued legality of slavery in Brazil. To complement its symbolic function as a hemispheric translator, the periodical published pieces on literary translation. Reading *O Novo Mundo* as integral to the archive underscores the centrality of translation to hemispheric relationships and the long-standing presence of Brazilians in the United States to reveal the transnational underpinnings of a modern Brazil.

A Hemispheric Turn:
The Historical Context of *O Novo Mundo*

While efforts to strengthen connections between Brazil and the United States had previously manifested during struggles for independence, such exchanges took on heightened relevance in the late nineteenth century as slavery came to an end in both nations through a series of protracted measures.[5] In the United States, the 1863 Emancipation Proclamation freed most remaining slaves, around three million people, without comprehensively abolishing slavery. President Abraham Lincoln's decree did not apply to the nearly half-million slaves living in Union border states. Congress passed the Thirteenth Amendment in December 1865 to abolish slavery throughout the United States.[6] The Reconstruction Act of 1867 proposed a political, economic, and social vision for the New South. Most radically, the Fourteenth Amendment guaranteed black suffrage and national equality before the law. Reforms emphasized a concept of national citizenry and attempted to address regional inequities. While the plan's architects envisioned an infusion of Northern and foreign capital to promote Southern industry, this economic growth failed to develop. By 1876, Reconstruction's experiment of an interracial democracy had ended due to racial violence, corruption, and unmet promises.[7]

Abolition in the United States served as a model for Brazil's struggle against slavery, which remained legal until 1888 and threatened Pedro II's desires to modernize his nation in the model of western Europe and the United States. He longed to implement political, industrial, and educational forms observed during his travels to Portugal, France, Germany, Italy, Palestine, and Egypt in 1871 and the United States, London, Brussels, Rome, Vienna, Paris, the Baltic countries, and the Middle East in 1876.[8] The Brazilian emperor had to address slavery after freeing a limited number of slaves to fight in the War of the Triple Alliance (1864–1870) as Brazil, Argentina, and Uruguay struggled to eventual victory over Paraguay.[9] Brazil's slow process of abolition began with the September 28, 1871, passage of the Rio Branco Law, or the Law of the Free Womb, which freed all children, known as *ingênuos* or "innocents," born after the law's signing. This step functioned as a half-measure akin to the Emancipation Proclamation. During this period, Brazilian elites observed effects of abolition in the United States and considered how a similar transition would impact Brazil. By conveying abolitionist ideas for his limited readership in Brazil, Rodrigues contributed in a minor way to discussions of slavery. International influence and changing economic structures further swayed attitudes toward slavery in Brazil. In 1883 in *O abolicionismo* (*Abolitionism: The Brazilian Antislavery Struggle*), writer, lawyer, and diplomat Joaquim Nabuco (1849–1910) argued for complete abolition by critiquing the 1871 Rio Branco Law.[10] Since the law was not retroactive, slavery would persist as a limited legal practice in Brazil until the death of every person born a slave prior to its passage. Nabuco claimed that Brazil could not wait for fifty years or more to abolish slavery, given that the institution impeded industrial and economic growth. Pressure for abolition grew until the passage of the Abolition Law, the *Lei Áurea*, on May 13, 1888.[11]

Rodrigues's *O Novo Mundo* similarly posited that the continued legality of slavery would hinder Brazil's development. This self-proclaimed, according to its subtitle, "periódico ilustrado do progresso da edade" (illustrated periodical of the progress of the era) framed Brazil's trajectory as a modern nation in terms of political, economic, and industrial progress. Without fully examining the contradictions between the realities of the Brazil's racial composition and the preferences for whiteness in the period's dominant positivist ideologies, *O Novo Mundo* presented the United States as a model of how Brazil could transition from an agrarian, slave state to a modern, industrialized nation.[12] Rodrigues's position between Brazil and the United States allowed him to draw parallels in the periodical between the two countries and correct misunderstandings that Brazilian readers had about daily life in the United States. Born in the interior of Rio de Janeiro, Rodrigues received a formal education at the best schools in imperial Brazil: Colégio Dom Pedro II in Rio de Janeiro and the Law School of São Paulo. In 1863, while still a student, he published an interpretation of Brazil's Imperial Constitution that previewed the republican and Protestant beliefs, specifically a concern with freedoms of religion and the press, that guided *O Novo Mundo*'s editorial outlook.[13] After completing his legal studies in 1864, he worked as a journalist but soon became involved in an embezzlement scandal that forced him to leave Brazil in 1867. He settled in Lowell, Massachusetts, before moving to New York, where he lived for the next fifteen years. Rodrigues wrote articles about Latin America for *The Nation* and served as a correspondent for *Diário Oficial* and *Jornal de Comércio* until he founded *O Novo Mundo* in October 1870.[14]

Among the 378 foreign-language journals estimated to exist in the United States in 1872, Rodrigues's periodical was the only one published in Portuguese, a language spoken by about one hundred people in the United States (*O Novo Mundo* 2.21, 162). Other Portuguese-language publications appeared later in the decade, including the *Aurora Brasileira*, published by Brazilian students at Cornell from 1873 to 1875, and *Revista Industrial Ilustrada*, published by Rodrigues and André de Rebouças from 1877 to 1879. *O Novo Mundo* and *Revista Industrial Ilustrada* aimed to interpret the United States for readers in Brazil, instead of addressing needs of Brazilians or other Portuguese-speakers in the United States as part of the ethnic or immigrant press.[15] Existing scholarship on *O Novo Mundo* focuses on its historical or literary merits without situating it in a broader framework. George Boehrer's 1967 article provides a well-researched, historical-biographical study of Rodrigues that stresses the periodical's inter-American outlook. More recent work by Brazilian scholars concentrates on *O Novo Mundo*'s literary value, with Mônica Maria Rinaldi Asciutti framing the periodical in terms of Brazilian literature's shift from romanticism to realism and Gabriela Vieira de Campos analyzing how scientific literature interacted with literary texts in the periodical. With a scope of analysis that expands beyond *O Novo Mundo*, I contend that it represents a late nineteenth-century entry into the genealogy of translating Brazil in the Americas. Its circulation illustrated how travels of people, ideas, and objects between Brazil and the United States required linguistic and cultural translations that helped to discursively construct a modern Brazil and to foster a hemispheric outlook.

O Novo Mundo accompanied its articles with high-quality reproductions of images originally published in *Harper's Magazine*, *Frank Leslie's Illustrated Newspaper*, or *The Graphic*. The journal depicted "popular, historical, artistic and other subjects, connected with the events of the day, by engravings executed in the best style of modern art and . . . printed with the utmost typographical neatness and skill" (*O Novo Mundo* 1.2, 31). The periodical captured the materiality of progress by facilitating the transnational circulation of lithographic images originally created in the United States and, thus, exposing readers in Brazil to more advanced visual technologies.[16] According to Maria Inez Turazzi, developments in visual technologies during the nineteenth century placed an emphasis on rendering everything visible, rather than legible ("Imagens da nação" 120). *O Novo Mundo* contributed to this regime of visibility with new printing technologies that engaged in forms of translation at visual and textual levels.

For Rodrigues, translation functioned as a relational practice of cultural exchange whereby *O Novo Mundo* traveled from New York to Brazil to reach up to eight thousand monthly subscribers.[17] Its monthly publication fell on the eve of the departure of the *S. Thomas and Brazil* ship, which carried the periodical to its readership in Brazil. To woo potential advertisers and investors in New York, *O Novo Mundo* emphasized the ties that it established:

> This paper furnishes the countries and colonies where Portuguese and Spanish are spoken, a most thorough digest of the course of events, particularly the political and industrial progress of the United States, describing the peculiar features of American advancement and civilization, as embodied in the Government, and treating the topics of the day in elaborate articles, having in view the object of uniting more closely the existing bonds of a political, commercial and friendly character among the several countries of the Western hemisphere. (1.2, 31)

One of the few uses of English in the periodical, this statement expressed a desire to strengthen hemispheric relations by reporting to Brazilians primarily on news from the United States.

Over the course of 108 issues from October 1870 until December 1879, *O Novo Mundo* commented on developments in the United States, Brazil, and, to a lesser extent, the rest of the Americas. Rodrigues was the periodical's sole proprietor until the incorporation of the Novo Mundo Association in 1875 as a joint stock company.[18] The association hoped to further its reach in the Americas beyond the sphere of periodicals by printing books for the Brazilian government or producing a Portuguese- or Spanish-language guide to the Centennial Exhibition. The company also supported the bimonthly *La América Ilustrada*, which was founded in 1872 and merged with *El Mundo Nuevo* to form "a J.C. Rodrigues publication" in 1875.[19] Directed at a Spanish American public, *La América Ilustrada* similarly aimed to promote hemispheric solidarity by keeping readers abreast of events in the United States (*La América Ilustrada* 1.1, 2). With the association, Rodrigues transformed his periodical's editorial vision into a commercial enterprise that furthered connections across the Americas. In July 1877, he launched the *Revista Industrial Ilustrada* as a companion dedicated to agriculture, mining, manufacturing, and transportation. The cover image of tropical fauna framing a moving freight train with a bucolic farmhouse in the background encapsulated the periodical's ethos of heralding industry, while suggesting that implementing such practices would not destroy Brazil's idyllic nature (*Revista Industrial Ilustrada* 1.1, 1). With the arrival of *Revista Industrial*, *O Novo Mundo* stopped reporting extensively on industry and introduced a women's page.

The Novo Mundo Association ceased to exist in 1880 when postal tariffs for printed materials entering Brazil increased. Rather than pay the tariff, which would have cost 500 *réis* or $6 per year for *O Novo Mundo*, Rodrigues decided to suspend his publications. Since the financial situation never improved, December 1879 marked the end of his periodicals.

Rodrigues continued to live in New York until 1882 and wrote articles for *The Nation*, *Jornal do Comércio*, and *New York World*. Despite his republican critiques of the empire, he often defended Brazil abroad. In letters exchanged with future US diplomat Caleb Cushing in the 1870s, Rodrigues promoted learning Portuguese and reading Brazilian literature.[20] While living in London from 1882 to 1890, Rodrigues responded to critiques of Brazil in editorial letters. For instance, in an August 15, 1884, letter to *The Times*, Rodrigues clarified Brazil's policy of slavery by reminding the British public that "the question in my country has long ago ceased being one of morality, it is simply a matter of complicated economic problems." These articles and letters provide insight into Rodrigues's view of Brazil and his periodical's role in strengthening hemispheric ties.[21]

Education and Exploration in O Novo Mundo

Rodrigues and his collaborators in *O Novo Mundo* expressed a fascination with the "progress of the era" as they proposed an inter-American outlook distinct from calls for Spanish American unity. Whereas Simón Bolívar (1783–1830) and José Martí (1853–1895) emphasized linguistic bonds and a shared colonial past in their view of the Americas, Rodrigues privileged political and economic ties between Brazil and the United States.[22] Rodrigues's observations of daily life in New York anticipated the work of Martí, who arrived in the United States in 1881. While Rodrigues praised North American progress, Martí expressed ambivalence toward the United States.[23] *O Novo Mundo* diverged from earlier periodicals *Correio Braziliense* (London, 1808–1822) and *Revista Nitheroy* (Paris, 1836), which had positioned Europe as the epitome of culture and progress, by framing New York as a center of industry, capital, and culture.[24] The periodical's title graphic visually depicted Rodrigues's "new world" perspective with a line on the globe linking New York and Rio de Janeiro to trace the paper's trajectory from its place of production to its readership in Brazil and, thus, suggest the spatial component of translation.

The first issue in October 1870 outlined the periodical's mission with an editorial letter from Rodrigues that invited readers to subscribe to learn more about life in the United States, while claiming that "não queremos, todavia, americanizar o Brasil nem país algum" (we do not want, however, to Americanize Brazil nor any other country; 1.1, 2). Despite the delay in the periodical's circulation caused by the steamship journey from New York to Rio de Janeiro, its articles remained relevant to Brazilian readers. The opening homage to Christopher Columbus for "discovering" the Americas hinted at the colonial underpinnings of this "new world"

Figure 1.1. The opening page of the first issue of *O Novo Mundo* (Library of Congress).

periodical, even as it distanced itself from celebratory discourses of Portuguese colonialism like Pero Vaz de Caminha's letter to king of Portugal Dom Manuel describing Pedro Álvares Cabral's "achamento" (finding) of Brazil in 1500 (see fig. 1.1).[25] *O Novo Mundo*'s identification of Europe as the "old world" and the Americas as the "new world" exemplifies how colonial geographies persisted in nineteenth-century Latin American lettered discourses with their teleological views of history and progress.[26] Another article in the first issue previewed the journal's abolitionist stance by comparing slavery in Brazil and Cuba to abolition in the United States. The periodical also drew parallels between Brazil and the United States via biographical articles about diplomats Domingos José Gonçalves de Magalhães (1811–1882) and Henry T. Blow (1817–1885). A piece portrayed Gonçalves de Magalhães as the embodiment of what Kirsten Silva Gruesz terms an "ambassador of culture" by recognizing his three-year service as Brazilian minister in Washington and his literary contributions to Brazilian romanticism.[27] The companion article on Blow, foreign minister of the United States in Rio de Janeiro, advocated for furthering trade between Brazil and the Missouri and Mississippi valleys as mutually beneficial.

Reforming education in Brazil was a critical issue for *O Novo Mundo*. The periodical claimed, "O verdadeiro progresso nacional consiste em educar o povo que temos" (True national progress consists of educating the people that we have; 1.1, 3). The article urged Brazil to base its educational system on the United States, where the 1862 Morrill Act legislated the creation of land grant institutions with technical programs, positing that agricultural and mechanical skills would prove more valuable in the Americas than degrees in philosophy or law.[28] The periodical mentioned that twelve Brazilian students were currently at institutions in the United States prioritizing technical study, including Cornell University. In conjunction with education, scientific expeditions emerged in the pages of *O Novo Mundo* as essential to fostering the exchange of knowledge across the Americas. To convey the fascination with the Amazon among scientists and other travel writers, the journal translated excerpts of English-language books about Brazilian geography, including James Orton's 1870 book *The Andes and the Amazon: Across the Continent of South America*. A professor of natural history at Vassar College, Orton traveled to South America in 1867 on a Smithsonian-funded expedition. He published his observations in the New York *Evening Post* and later in a book introduced by J. C. Fletcher, who wrote *Brazil and the Brazil-*

ians.²⁹ Orton rendered Brazilian geography, flora, and fauna into descriptive narratives in English that allowed readers in the United States to travel figuratively to the region. *O Novo Mundo*'s Portuguese version of Orton's account exposed its readers to a foreign representation of Brazil's land. The translated excerpt reduced the three-hundred-page book, which was reviewed elsewhere in the issue, to a two-column article that briefly described Brazil's land and water without maps or illustrations.

The inaugural issue reviewed another English-language account of Brazil published in 1870, *Geology and the Physical Geography of Brazil* by Charles Frederick Hartt. The periodical preferred Hartt's rigorous examination of Brazil's geological features over Orton's claims based on existing research.³⁰ The review nevertheless praised Orton's *The Andes and the Amazon* as a "livro ou roteiro de um viajante bem informado cujo estilo agrada tanto como seu assumpto" (book or itinerary of a well-informed traveler whose style is as pleasing as his topic; 1.1, 10). With its descriptive details and beautiful images, the book brought South American land closer to readers in the United States through what German philosopher Friedrich Schleiermacher would describe as a domesticating process. His 1813 essay "On the Different Methods of Translating" outlined as possible ways to translate either bringing the original closer to the language of translation or bringing readers closer to the original, which he preferred. In his 1995 study *The Translator's Invisibility*, Lawrence Venuti similarly argued against domestication due to its tendency to erase marks of foreignness and to render the translator invisible. While their concepts of domesticating and foreignizing focus on literary translation, they can also apply to linguistic and cultural translations, like Orton's travel narrative.

O Novo Mundo broadly admired Hartt's ability as a scientist and a writer: "Realmente o prof. Hartt põe a geologia do Brasil ao alcance da inteligência do comum dos leitores" (Professor Hartt actually places Brazil's geology within reach of readers' common intelligence; 1.1, 10). After first traveling to Brazil in 1865 to 1866 with the Thayer Expedition led by Swiss biologist, geologist, and Harvard professor Louis Agassiz, Hartt returned to Brazil in 1867 to research its coastal regions.³¹ He envisioned his book as a scientific companion to the Agassizes' *A Journey in Brazil* that made reefs and other features of Brazilian geography accessible to English-language readers through concise and vibrant descriptions. After becoming a Cornell professor in 1868, Hartt continued to translate Brazil for students and readers in the United States. *O Novo Mundo*, in turn, condensed, reviewed, and translated Hartt's work into Portuguese for Brazilian readers. The periodical's first issue reported on his visit to Pará preceding an expedition to Xingú. Placed next to bilingual ads for Rodrigues's English-language reader and Orton's travelogue, an announcement in Portuguese for Hartt's book appealed to Brazilians by characterizing his depiction of Brazil's geology and climate as "de mesmo interesse para homens de letras, viajantes e negociantes, e cada estante de brasileiro deve ser adornada com um exemplar dela" (of equal interest for men of letters, travelers, and businessmen, and the shelf of every Brazilian should be adorned with a copy of it; 1.1, 14).[32] Reading this book, as the ad claimed, would allow Brazilians to learn more about their country's distant regions through the eyes of a foreign, scientific traveler. The periodical depicted Hartt as a scientist committed to rigorous inquiry and furthering hemispheric knowledge of Brazilian geography.

After its first issue, *O Novo Mundo* frequently returned to topics of scientific exploration and education due to their relevance for discussions of hemispheric progress. Articles outlined pedagogical approaches in both countries and provided statistics on Brazilian schools, students, and government support. A piece on schools and teachers in New York claimed that "o estado das escolas era geralmente muito próspero" (the state of schools was generally very prosperous; 1.2, 22). Rather than advocate directly for reforms, the journal required readers to generate their own interpretations by piecing together comparisons between reported conditions of public schools in New York and Brazil. A piece about the lag in public education in regions where slavery remained strong in Brazil implied, based on observations in the United States, that abolishing slavery would improve instructional quality and help to expand access to public schools, which would consequently contribute to efforts to modernize Brazil (1.3, 34).[33] *O Novo Mundo* praised US higher education, namely, courses in mining, metallurgy, engineering, and agriculture offered to Brazilian students enrolled at Columbia, Cornell, and Lehigh, and suggested that Brazilian institutions should implement similar programs. An October 1874 article critiqued proposed reforms in Brazil for favoring humanistic disciplines and undervaluing science and technology. Given its limited circulation, the periodical's advocacy for certain educational models did not immediately nor directly affect policies and practices in Brazil.[34]

Colleges in the United States emerged as key sites of translation and hemispheric dialogue in the nineteenth century given that they educated Brazilian students and supported scholarship about Brazil. Cornell best exemplified this role of the university by training Brazilian students and facilitating Hartt's research in Brazil. *O Novo Mundo* highlighted Hartt's importance as a translator of Brazil for readers in the United States by noting that "o seu livro . . . trouxe à sua luz verdadeira a importância dos seus estudos sobre a geologia do Brasil" (his book . . . brought to its true light the importance of his studies of Brazilian geology; 1.4, 60). He shared observations about Brazilian life in journalistic writing, such as a letter to the editor in the *New York Tribune* that praised the complex originality of Brazilian popular music. *O Novo Mundo* published a translated excerpt of this piece accompanied with editorial comments that emphasized Hartt's importance as a transnational translator: "Ele crê que a música . . . deve-se grande parte daquela suavidade de maneiras e fino trato dos cavalheiros do Brasil e lástima que nos Estados Unidos não se cultive mais esta arte nas instituições do ensino público" (He believes that music . . . must be a large part of that suaveness of ways and fine behavior of Brazilian gentlemen and it is too bad that, in the United States, this art is not cultivated more in institutions of public education; 1.5, 75). Hartt's travels and writings exemplified how scientific and cultural ideas flowed bilaterally between Brazil and the United States during the 1870s.

When Hartt died at thirty-eight from yellow fever in Rio de Janeiro, *O Novo Mundo* emphasized his strong ties to both nations in an April 1878 obituary: "Rara vez os dois países unirão mais merecidamente as vozes da sua imprensa para lamentarem o passamento de um de seus homens notáveis, ligado a um pelo berço, ao outro pela sepultura, a ambos pelos serviços relevantes com que soube encher a sua breve, mas gloriosa existência" (Rarely will these two countries more deservedly unite the voices of the press to lament the passing of one of their notable men, linked to one by the cradle, to the other by the grave, to both by the relevant services that he learned to fill his brief, but glorious, existence; 8.88, 74). To further disseminate his scientific and ethnographic knowledge, Hartt directed the geological section of the Museu Nacional in 1876 and 1877 and advised Brazil's plans for the Centennial Exhibition. He also ensured that future generations in the United States would study Brazil by selecting students, like John Casper Branner (1850–1922), to participate in his scientific expeditions.

After assisting on Hartt's 1874 geological survey of Brazil, Branner strengthened ties between the two countries as he continued to study Brazil's lands and peoples. As a professor of geology at Stanford University and its second president, Branner led three expeditions to Brazil, published books, a geological map, and articles about the nation, and amassed a comprehensive library about Brazil that he later donated to Stanford's Green Library.[35] His letters to writer and diplomat Manuel de Oliveira Lima (1867–1928) expressed interest in Brazilian history and literature, and the Portuguese language.[36] Branner helped to organize Oliveira Lima's 1912 lecture series on Brazilian history at Stanford, Cornell, Harvard, and other elite US universities. He encouraged Oliveira Lima to publish the lectures as a textbook, which resulted in *The Evolution of Brazil Compared with that of Spanish and Anglo-Saxon America* (1914), by Oliveira Lima and Stanford historian Percy Alvin Martin.[37] Branner embodied the critical role of higher education to reciprocal intellectual exchanges between the United States and Brazil in the late nineteenth and early twentieth centuries.

Branner's contributions to the study of Brazil and to hemispheric educational exchange would not have been possible without Hartt's work in promoting research on Brazil in the US academy. At Hartt's home institution of Cornell, Brazilian undergraduates published the *Aurora Brasileira* from 1873 to 1875 with the mission of: "enviar, mensalmente, para o Brasil notícia de seus filhos, narrando os seus progressos e as fases da sua vida social e escolásticas; . . . estreitar cada vez mais os laços de amizade existentes entre o nosso país e os Estados Unidos" (sending, monthly, to Brazil news of its sons, narrating their progress and phases of their social and scholastic life; . . . tightening increasingly the existing bonds of friendship between our country and the United States; *Aurora Brasileira* 1.1, 1). Under the editorship of Herculano de Aquino, the periodical applauded Hartt and Ithaca's Clube Brasileiro for supporting Brazilian students. The periodical claimed, "A criação da *Aurora* é pois mais um triunfo para o *Novo Mundo*, que deve ver nela a companheira, embora pequena, mas leal, nessa propaganda eminentemente patriótica do bem do nosso país" (The creation of *Aurora* is thus a triumph for *O Novo Mundo*, which should see in it a companion, however small, but loyal, in this eminently patriotic propaganda of our country's good; 1.4, 28). The student paper followed Rodrigues's distribution model but reached an even more limited readership. As one would expect, its ideas of educational reform did not have concrete repercussions in Brazil.[38] Whereas *Aurora Brasileira* foregrounded the role of education, *O Novo Mundo* reported on schools as one part of its broader interest in political and societal progress.

Travels and Translations at the 1876 Centennial Exhibition

In the years leading up to the 1876 Centennial Exhibition, *O Novo Mundo* devoted articles and illustrations to other international exhibitions and to preparations for Philadelphia.[39] The fair's layout and events mirrored the global geopolitical and economic landscape of the second half of the nineteenth century as displays translated essentialized visions of participating nations for a foreign public. Visitors traveled figuratively to distant lands as they wandered through displays of raw materials, agricultural goods, new technologies, and artworks. Over the course of the nineteenth century, the physical size and public reach of world's fairs expanded to become popular celebrations of industry and technology.[40] Universal exhibitions, as Werner Plum accurately claims, served as "the popular self-portraits of the resourceful, creative industrial bourgeoisie" (6). Robert Rydell similarly notes that the "world's fairs performed a hegemonic function precisely because they propagated the ideas and values of the country's . . . leaders and offered these ideas as the proper interpretations of social and political reality" (3). These idealized visions reached a broader public via exhibition displays, which served as the nineteenth-century equivalent to today's televised global mega-events (Plum 64). Exhibitions generated what Jens Andermann terms "new forms of display and spectatorship [that] re-organized local systems of value" within the interconnected realm of global capital ("Tournaments of Value" 334).

With temporary displays of national wealth that subscribed to Eurocentric concepts of progress, international exhibitions exemplified what Francisco Foot Hardman describes as an "era of spectacle" (63). Underscoring this spectacular element, Lilia Moritz Schwarcz claims that "era como se fosse preciso teatralizar a realidade e construir cenários" (it was as if it were necessary to theatricalize reality and construct sceneries; "Os trópicos" 200). The exhibitions' invented architectural styles and temporary structures epitomized the material consumption and rapid disposability characteristic of late nineteenth-century modernity and industrial capitalism. While lacking physical permanence, exhibition structures continued to exist in the archive of official catalogs, books, newspapers, and photographs. These records captured displays and pavilions for historical posterity and for people unable to attend the fairs, including the readers of *O Novo Mundo*. Existing scholarship on international exhibitions only briefly touches on ways of communicating representations of Brazil abroad to a public at home.[41] To counter this oversight, I analyze in this section how *O Novo Mundo* represented the Centennial Exhibition for readers in Brazil. By reporting on visions of Brazil showcased at exhibitions, the periodical invited its readers to embrace new technology in efforts to modernize Brazil.

Beginning with the 1862 London fair, Brazil actively participated in universal exhibitions by strategically displaying agricultural products, indigenous cultures, and raw materials next to its "civilized" features. As Hardman astutely observes, Brazil crafted itself as modern at world's fairs through the comparative categorizing, cataloging, and displaying of natural resources (109). Universal exhibitions, like their contemporaneous scientific expeditions, organized the world based on nations' raw materials and economic potential, resulting in hierarchies corresponding to evolutionist views of modernity. According to Walter Mignolo, " 'modernity' is a complex narrative whose point of origination was Europe; a narrative that builds Western civilization by celebrating its achievements while hiding at the same time its darker side, 'coloniality' " (2–3). The Centennial Exhibition downplayed modernity's darker side, even as former colonies like Brazil showcased resources susceptible to extractive relations. Schwarcz illustrates the logic of coloniality undergirding the exhibition's categorization, which situated Western nations at the peak of civilization and African and indigenous cultures as the "past" of humanity ("Os trópicos" 199). Schwarcz convincingly argues that, despite Pedro II's desires to depict Brazil as modern, during the 1862 London Exhibition, "como sempre, para fora era o nosso lado exótico que estava em pauta e pouco se alterava a imagem do país" (as always, it was our exotic side that was at stake abroad and the country's image showed little change; 205). The image of an exotic Brazil with diverse flora, fauna, and natural resources persisted and served as the basis for its displays in subsequent exhibitions.

O Novo Mundo first dedicated coverage to international exhibitions with a March 24, 1873, article about the relative weakness of the Brazilian display at the Vienna Exhibition. The Vienna display would be worse than the Paris one due to a disinterest among Brazilian citizens (3.30, 103). This reliance on government planning and lack of involvement of private citizens and industry resulted in a Brazilian display that was "tão minguada e tão injusta a natureza e a já nascente indústria do país" (so scarce and so unjust to the country's nature and already nascent industry; 103).

With access to sources in Brazil, the United States, and Europe, *O Novo Mundo* could critique Brazil's preparations for the fairs and inform readers in Brazil of the nation's displays. The periodical suggested that national elites could correct Brazil's underrepresentation in Vienna by showcasing resources and industry during the next world's fair in Philadelphia. Further reporting on the Vienna Exhibition in November 1873 recognized the key role of these fairs in projecting an image of Brazil as modern for foreign audiences. One piece highlighted the industrial and commercial potential of Brazilian pine trees from Paraná. An accompanying image captured how the thirty-three-meter-tall *araucaria braziliense* had been divided into twenty pieces and, reassembled, towered over nearby buildings (4.38, 33). By stressing the quality of natural commodities on display, *O Novo Mundo* affirmed that Brazil's development relied on the circulation of its wood and other raw materials in a global, capitalist system.

As preparations for the Centennial Exhibition continued, *O Novo Mundo* increased its reporting on the exhibition's role in creating a modern Brazil without recognizing the underlying elements of coloniality that more recent scholars have emphasized. According to Rydell, the Centennial Exhibition "was intended to teach a lesson about progress. The lesson was far from benign, for the artifacts and people embodied in the 'world's epitome' at the fair were presented in hierarchical fashion and in the context of America's material growth and development" (15). The layout revealed what Rydell considers the racist ideology of a classification system that privileged Western nations. As architectural historian Bruno Giberti rightly contends, nationalist and imperialist projects accompanied the fair's organizational hierarchies (93). Dom Pedro II's belief that Brazil could gain prominence as modern through its role at the Centennial Exhibition led him to participate in commission preparations and opening day events in Philadelphia. Displays foregrounded Brazil's raw materials and commodities, even though the nation had entries in all areas of the exhibition: mining and metallurgy, manufacturing, education and science, art, machinery, agriculture, and horticulture. Yet, as Schwarcz astutely argues, the nation only seemed to convince itself, and thus the rest of the world, of its primary resources ("Os trópicos" 208). The exhibition's statistics confirm this claim as Brazil displayed a vast range of natural resources and only a token number of industrial, manufactured items.[42] Since national elites believed natural resources would facilitate Brazil's economic and industrial growth, displays at world's fairs reinforced images of Brazil as a tropical paradise.

Given its proximity to Philadelphia as a periodical based in New York, *O Novo Mundo* occupied a prominent position among written and visual records of the Centennial Exhibition for a Brazilian reading public. The periodical's coverage of the exhibition began over a year and a half before it opened with a December 1874 article that informed readers of the commission's work to procure funds, establish a budget, and plan Brazil's display, which would be larger than for any other Latin American nation (5.51, 71). Statistics of the layout allowed readers to visualize Brazil's prominence within the exhibition's spatial arrangement. *O Novo Mundo* followed the preparations for the Philadelphia fair more closely than its Brazilian counterparts with reports stressing the commission's ability to complete the ambitious plan on time and within budget.[43] A more detailed article on the exhibition's physical layout in March 1875 delineated the buildings' sizes and functions and noted that only the gallery of fine arts, with its durable materials of granite, iron, and glass, would exist permanently.

To provide readers in Brazil with a better sense of the exhibition, *O Novo Mundo* included illustrations of plans for the main hall, agricultural hall, and fine arts gallery with their extravagant architectural styles that echoed the arches, columns, and ornamentation of previous world's fairs (5.54, 160–01). By depicting exhibition buildings resembling European palaces, churches, and monuments with natural surroundings in the background, the images pointed to the supposed contradictions of containing both the exotic and the civilized in the United States and, by extension, other parts of the Americas (see fig. 1.2). A September 23, 1875, article about the main exhibition hall's final layout confirmed that only the United States, France, Great Britain, Germany, Austria, Canada, and Australia would occupy more space than Brazil. Unlike other South American nations who would share an area, Brazil received its own allotment near the center of the hall. *O Novo Mundo* emphasized Brazil's placement in the exhibition hall across from the United States as potentially indicative of future economic and political proximity between these hemispheric giants.

The fairgrounds would also feature national pavilions and other minor buildings that could still be proposed in 1875. *O Novo Mundo* expressed hope for a Brazilian contribution by wondering, "Não haverá no Brasil algum botequinista empreendedor que venha aqui fornecer café tal qual se bebe no Rio de Janeiro e que é uma perfeita *revelação* comparado com o que aqui se chama *café*? Não será este um meio excelente de anunciar aquele produto?" (Is there not in Brazil some entrepreneurial barkeep who can come here and provide coffee like they drink in Rio de Janeiro and that is a perfect revelation compared to what they call coffee here? Wouldn't this be an excellent way of announcing that product?; 5.60, 286). The journal's editors drew on their familiarity with consumer preferences in New York to posit that Brazilian coffee would merit attention at the fair. The planning commission seemed to heed this recommendation since the exhibition featured a Brazilian-style café. A September 1876 article claimed that the café served genuine Brazilian coffee, even though "a grande massa dos visitantes da Exposição não sabe discernir a qualidade dos diferentes

Figure 1.2. The Agricultural Hall and the Memorial Building for the 1876 Centennial Exposition, illustrations of plans published in March 1875 in *O Novo Mundo* (5.54, 161) (Library of Congress).

grãos do precioso arbusto, mas pode apreciar o que seja uma xícara de bom café" (the great majority of Exhibition visitors do not know how to discern the different beans of the precious shrub, but can appreciate what is a cup of good coffee; 6.72, 261). The periodical reinforced the idea of Brazil as a source of raw materials by noting that the nation provided nearly 80 percent of all coffee beans in the United States (6.64, 81). Another article stressed the quality of Brazilian coffee by dismissing the Dutch colonial product, claiming, "O que é muito inferior ao nosso . . . é o café de Java" (What is quite inferior to ours . . . is the coffee from Java; 6.68, 169). The periodical repeatedly positioned coffee as critical to Brazil's emerging commercial identity within a global capitalist system.

Leading up to opening day, *O Novo Mundo* commemorated the centennial anniversary of US independence with a January 1876 article praising the government as "o mais apropriado à civilização porque é o mais natural ao homem. Os Estados Unidos têm democratizado o mundo inteiro" (the most appropriate to civilization because it is the most natural to man. The United States has democratized the entire world; 6.64, 74). The periodical also highlighted the role of Dom Pedro II as a traveler and translator linking the two nations as they furthered their trade, cultural, and political relations. An article described the Centennial Exhibition as "um grande acontecimento industrial do século" (the great industrial event of the century) but questioned whether the Brazilian government would take heed of this industrial trend (6.64, 75). Lamenting what it perceived as the incomplete status of the planned displays, *O Novo Mundo* contended that Brazil should prominently feature Amazonian resources in its exhibition materials given the comparative familiarity of US residents with that region (6.64, 75). The periodical wanted Brazil to be seen as a site of industrial growth and a repository of natural resources, which supports Schwarcz's analysis that the nation's claim to being modern in the second half of the nineteenth century depended upon its raw materials and their extractive properties.

O Novo Mundo reported more thoroughly on Brazil at the Philadelphia fair than other newspapers in the United States or Brazil due to its vested interest in Brazil's hemispheric relations and its privileged access to information from both nations. After receiving complaints about Brazil's poor organization from Centennial Exhibition planners, the periodical consulted reports in Brazilian newspapers about the Brazilian commission in an effort to counter such claims. *O Novo Mundo* cynically suggested that the delays in planning resulted from the government remaining faithful to its maxim: "Não fazer hoje o que pode ser feito amanhã" (Don't do today what can be done tomorrow; 6.65, 95). Though occasionally criticizing Brazil's imperial government, the periodical longed for a favorable representation of the nation at the Centennial Exhibition. Detailed articles on Brazil's displays informed readers of foreign perceptions of Brazil and urged the commission to proceed with care.

The periodical dedicated particular attention to Dom Pedro II's travels across the United States as exemplifying a hemispheric outlook of industrial progress that coincided with its editorial perspective. A March 1876 article posited that the Brazilian emperor would bring prestige to the festivities in Philadelphia as the first monarch to visit the United States. As "obreiros humildes do desenvolvimento intelectual de nossa pátria" (humble workers for the intellectual development of our homeland), *O Novo Mundo*'s editors encouraged Pedro II to carefully observe the democratic practices, religious freedoms, educational models, and industrial developments of the United States (6.65, 118). The periodical envisioned creatively adapting these models to the specificities of Brazil, rather than directly copying them. Rodrigues and his collaborators hoped that the trip would help to revise potential misconceptions that the emperor and other Brazilians had of the United States (6.66, 142). Following a welcoming reception from the Brazilian community in New York, Pedro II would depart for San Francisco, St. Louis, New Orleans, and the Northeast. The article lamented the fast pace of his transcontinental travels but claimed that it would be impossible for him to overlook "as feições mais salientes do estupendo progresso desse povo" (the most salient features of the stupendous progress of these people; 6.66, 142). After outlining what the emperor would see on his journey, the article stated that "todo este espetáculo, e afinal, o da síntese do progresso americano na Exposição de Philadelphia vai de certo causar profunda impressão no ânimo imperial. . . . Oxalá que toda esta lição não seja perdida e que por amor da nossa pátria comum . . . ele anime realmente o espírito de iniciativa, a autonomia individual, base da grandeza de todo e qualquer país" (all this spectacle, and after all, that of the synthesis of American progress at the Philadelphia Exhibition will certainly make a profound impression on the imperial mood. . . . Hopefully this whole lesson is not lost and, for the love of our common homeland . . . it really animates the spirit of initiative, individual autonomy, basis of greatness of every and any country; 6.66, 142). *O Novo Mundo* lacked the enthusiasm of the *New York Herald*'s reporting on Pedro II's travels.[44] Instead, guided by an interest in Brazil's future, it focused on how the emperor's exposure to US politics, industry, and culture could inform policies.

Starting with the fair's opening in May 1876, *O Novo Mundo* devoted more attention to the proceedings of the Centennial Exhibition "como uma bela representação do estado atual das indústrias e artes" (as a beautiful representation of the current state of industry and the arts; 6.68, 166). Though not among the fair's ten million visitors, readers in Brazil could figuratively travel to and experience the Centennial Exhibition via *O Novo Mundo*'s lithographic prints and articles. Its May cover featured an illustration of the Brazilian pavilion with an accompanying article pondering the history of great nations and whether racial and political differences would matter more in the future, which allowed the piece to speculate about Brazil's position among the nations at the exhibition. The issue also included a map of the grounds and articles guiding readers through exhibition spaces and opening day events. The periodical's descriptions highlighted the elaborate displays of manufactured goods from the United States and the prominent position of Brazil next to France and the Netherlands. In rendering these displays into articles in Portuguese, *O Novo Mundo* echoed official catalog entries and also asserted its editorial outlook. For instance, the journal claimed that "o visitante do Sul fica surpreendido com o progresso do Canadá" (the visitor from the South is surprised with the progress of Canada; 6.68, 167). With manufactured sewing machines and chemical products, Canada impressed *O Novo Mundo* as an example of how Brazil's industry could develop. The periodical's references to European and other national displays prioritized Brazilian interests via comparisons that stressed the superiority of its natural resources.

O Novo Mundo also highlighted Brazil's displays in the main, agricultural, fine arts, and machinery halls, with attention to material details and colors. Designed by Philadelphia architect Frank Furness, the Brazilian pavilion blended Moorish and Victorian styles (Giberti 111). To add vibrancy to an accompanying black-and-white illustration, the periodical referenced the *New York Tribune*'s comparison of the structure to Arabic palaces: "O pavilhão brasileiro faz a gente lembrar-se dos palácios imaginários de ouro e pedras preciosas dos génios das Noites arábicas. . . . A fachada e as portas interiores são ornadas de azulejos de vidro transparente, atrás dos quais há desenhos de lindas cores. . . . As cores empregadas nos ornatos são o verde e o amarelo, o azul e o encarnado" (The Brazilian pavilion reminds us of the imaginary palaces of gold and precious stones of the genies from *Arabian Nights*. . . . The façade and the interior doors are ornamented with transparent glass tiles, behind which there are designs of beautiful colors. . . . The colors embedded in the ornaments are green and yellow, blue and scarlet; 6.68, 170). With its towering height, prominent columns and arches, glass tiles, and decorative painting in the imperial flag's colors, the structure did not draw on Portuguese or Brazilian architectural styles, but rather created an orientalist gesture that marked Brazil as exotic in an aesthetic form already familiar to exhibition visitors (see figs. 1.3 and 1.4).[45]

Figure 1.3. Photograph of "Main Building-Brazil," Centennial Exhibition (Free Library of Philadelphia, Print and Picture Collection).

Figure 1.4. Illustration of Brazil's Section in the Main Building in *O Novo Mundo*, 6.68, Supplement (Library of Congress).

In his 1877 unofficial account *The Century: Its Fruits and Its Festival*, Edward C. Bruce praised Brazil's structure in a comparative manner: "The Moorish colonnade of the Brazilian pavilion lifts its head in graceful rivalry of the lofty front reared by the other branch of the Iberian race" (98). Brazil strove to transcend its tropical identity at the exhibition by attracting visitors' attention with its structures' sizes, colors, and ornamentations. As the only Latin American country with its own building on the fairgrounds, Brazil occupied a more prominent position among the thirty-seven participating countries than the eleven Spanish American nations. They displayed Inca relics, silver, and other natural resources in a shared space to curate an exotic otherness prone to exploitation.[46]

After concentrating on Brazil's "civilized" side in the May 1876 edition with accounts of the nation's prominence in Philadelphia, *O Novo Mundo* focused its next issue on agricultural products and natural resources showcased in the nation's displays. By informing readers of the economic value of Brazilian coffee and rubber, the periodical underscored commodities' centrality to the project of a modern Brazil. A black-and-white image of Brazil's agricultural display captured the contrast between its exotic products and the refinement of exhibition visitors (6.69, 200). This illustration rendered a house-like cotton structure at the image's shadowy edge as plain and dark, especially in comparison to the distinctive texture and relative whiteness of the cotton building in photographs of the agricultural hall (see figs. 1.5 and 1.6). The image focused on the stretched-out animal carcasses hanging from the rafters, which accentuated Brazil's "savage" elements. With this visual juxtaposition, the periodical implicitly suggested that Brazil could not escape the logic of coloniality that reduced the former Portuguese colony to its essence of primary resources susceptible to extraction, even as it embraced forms of industrialization and modernization. Determined to portray Brazil as civilized, the exhibition organizers did not recognize the negative consequences of defining the nation solely in terms of natural resources. Similarly, *O Novo Mundo*'s belief in progress prevented it from expressly critiquing modern Brazil's dependency on extracting and exporting raw materials.

The periodical portrayed Brazil's role at the exhibition as extending beyond its natural resources by citing that Brazilian participants received 350 medals in a variety of categories won (6.71, 234).[47] Another article explained how Brazil aimed to further educate US residents by distributing the book *O Brazil na Exposição de Philadelphia* to universities and

Figure 1.5. Photograph of "Agricultural Hall-Brazil," Centennial Exhibition Digital Collection (Free Library of Philadelphia, Print and Picture Collection).

Figure 1.6. Illustration of Brazil's Section in Agricultural Hall in *O Novo Mundo* (6.69, 200) (Library of Congress).

libraries, which would grant greater permanence to Brazil's claims to modernity temporarily on display at the fair. Beatriz González Stephan argues that such written records "testified to these facts for the benefit of all those who had not been present at the expositions themselves. These catalogs became, in effect, a genre in themselves, as inventories of the merchandise on display, while quantifying, enumerating, imposing uniformity, and fitting Latin American products and ideas into a preexisting rhetoric" (231). The official catalog, along with *O Novo Mundo*'s reporting and other written records, inscribed Brazil into the classificatory logic of modernity that deemed industrial goods and new technologies as superior to raw materials.

The January 1877 issue of *O Novo Mundo* reflected on Brazil's experience at the Centennial Exhibition, which closed on November 10, 1876. While more visitors had attended the Philadelphia event than any previous universal exhibition, the periodical reported that few foreigners beyond the national commissions had visited the fair (7.73, 4). As a popular event attended by one-fifth of all residents in the United States, the exhibition allowed visitors to experience other nations without embarking on expensive travel abroad (Rydell 49). By pairing an article on attendance with images of Brazil's displays, *O Novo Mundo* reminded readers that the exhibition facilitated "travel" to Brazil by exposing primarily US residents to its natural resources, manufacturing, coffee, and art. The periodical noted that Brazilian paintings in the fine arts hall portrayed nationalistic sentiments by representing valiant Brazilian soldiers in the War of the Triple Alliance and bucolic foundational scenes, most notably Victor Meirelles's *Primeira missa no Brasil* (First mass in Brazil; 1860). This painting depicts what art historian Jorge Coli terms "o ato de batismo da nação brasileira" (the baptismal act of the Brazilian nation; 110). A cross and priest occupy the focal point from which light emanates to other priests and explorers to portray Catholicism and Portuguese colonialism as civilizing forces in Brazil. Mostly naked indigenous bodies, in shadows at the front and side of the painting, contrast the idealized background images of coastal Brazil with palm trees and lush foliage. With this romantic representation of the baptism of Brazil as a colonial entity, Brazil's artistic display echoed the Centennial Exhibition's celebration of progress that idealized modernity and relegated its dark underside of coloniality to the margins. *O Novo Mundo* did not critique the ideology encoded in the image nor provide a detailed description or reproduction of the painting. It instead mentioned the positive reception of Meirelles's work in English-language accounts by Frank

Leslie and Edward C. Bruce. These favorable responses indicated that the commission had successfully showcased Brazil's cultural promise to visitors via artistic works that recreated the intertwined logic of modernity and coloniality. The periodical concluded its coverage of the Centennial Exhibition by emphasizing how Brazil's displays underscored a symbiotic relationship between the modern and the exotic at the core of the nation.

Textual Translations and Treatises of a Modern, Literary Brazil

O Novo Mundo considered literature another realm for representing Brazil as modern and for fostering hemispheric exchanges as it examined the linguistic practices and cultural politics involved in translation and creative transformation. *O Novo Mundo* directly explored the role of translation in the dissemination of Brazilian literature abroad with a March 24, 1872, article about Sir Richard Francis Burton's February 19, 1872, lecture at London's Athenaeum Club. The periodical summarized Burton's lecture, previously reproduced in the club's newspaper on February 24, 1872. To establish Burton's credibility, the piece referenced his translations *1,001 Nights* from Arabic and *The Lusiads* from Portuguese and his two-volume study *Highlands of Brazil*. Burton's lecture emphasized the importance of translating Brazilian works into English. He proposed creating a translation fund in response to an editor who claimed that translations earned no money and thus refused to publish Burton's translation of eighteenth-century naturalist Francisco José de Lacerda e Almeida's letters.[48] Burton urged his British audience to translate Brazilian literature, which remained "virgin to the English labourer" as "still sealed books, written in 'bastard Latin' or in 'jargon of Spanish'" (242). *O Novo Mundo*'s article differentiated the languages and literatures of Brazil from related traditions by underscoring Burton's claim that "o português é 'certamente a mais difícil' das línguas neo-latinas" (Portuguese is "certainly the most difficult" of the Romance languages; 2.18, 95). His view that Brazilian and Anglo-American literatures merited comparisons aligned with the periodical's hemispheric outlook. Burton asserted that much work remained, even though he had already translated Basílio da Gama's *O Uruguai* (1769) and his wife had translated José de Alencar's *Iracema* (1865).[49] Per his assessment, nineteen Brazilian works most in need of translation to English included Tomás António Gonzaga's satirical *Cartas chilenas* (1799), Gonçalves de Magalhães's epic poem *A Confederação dos Tamaios* (1856), and seventeenth-century Jesuit priest António Vieira's letters. His advocacy, unfortunately, did not result in their translations. By reporting on Burton's lecture, *O Novo Mundo* framed translation as necessary for the ongoing circulation of Brazilian texts and ideas.

The periodical also examined translations into Portuguese of mainly English and French works. The April 23, 1874, review of Franklin Dória's translation of Henry Wadsworth Longfellow's *Evangeline* introduced the poet in relation to James Fenimore Cooper, the US writer best known in Brazil.[50] Longfellow gained recognition in the Americas as readers connected to his 1847 epic poem about Evangeline searching for her lost love Gabriel.[51] The poem challenged Latin American translators with its hexameter typical of Greek and Latin epics, but it nonetheless became one of the nineteenth-century Anglo-American poems most translated into Spanish and Portuguese.[52] The poem's expressed desire to return to the primeval forest of Acadia resonated with Brazilian romanticism's celebrations of nature. Longfellow enjoyed further renown in Brazil as one of Pedro II's favorite poets; the two men met during the emperor's travels to the United States.[53] Prior to this encounter, Pedro II had requested that Dória translate *Evangeline* into Portuguese.

To articulate the distinct approaches to translating poetry, *O Novo Mundo*'s review cited Dória's belief: "A tradução, sem degenerar em repetição servil, deve antes de tudo refletir o original" (Translation, without degenerating into servile repetition, should above all reflect the original; 4.43, 125). In attempting to remain faithful to the English original in his Portuguese translation, Dória embarked on what the review described as "uma tarefa não só difícil . . . mas até impossível de satisfatória execução" (not only a difficult task . . . but one with near impossible satisfactory execution; 4.43, 125). Based on a linguistic and cultural familiarity with the United States, the reviewer questioned syntactical and lexical choices of the translation. The review pointed to the limitations of literal translation by claiming that Dória sacrificed the poem's beauty by opting for word-for-word equivalents. After comparing specific verses in English to the Portuguese translation, the reviewer concluded, "Dória escolheu o pior método possível de traduzir a poesia inglesa. Ele propõe-se traduzir a *Evangelina* 1°, literalmente, e 2°, em verso, e ele não conseguiu fazer uma conciliação satisfatória destas duas condições. No sacrifício da primeira à segunda, ele não transladou fielmente Longfellow" (Dória selected the worst possible method of translating English-language poetry. He aims to translate *Evangeline*, first, literally, and second, in verse, and he did not achieve a satisfactory conciliation of these two conditions. In the sacrifice of the first to the second, he did not faithfully translate Longfellow; 4.23, 125).

This harsh review of Dória's translation subscribed to nineteenth-century preferences for fidelity in translation while recognizing the challenges of such a task. The review closed by proposing a more flexible and nuanced approach to translation: "A arte do tradutor não está em procurar traduzir palavra por palavra. . . . A dificuldade da arte de traduzir está em produzir nos que leem a tradução *os mesmos* efeitos causados pelo autor do original . . . ;—a dificuldade está na escolha e no bom uso dos melhores meios da produção destes efeitos" (The translator's art is not in seeking to translate word for word. . . . The difficulty of the art of translating is in producing in those who read the translation the same effects caused by the author of the original . . . ; the difficulty is in the selection and in the good use of the best modes of production of these effects; 4.23, 125). *O Novo Mundo* entered into a discussion about equivalence or function in translation that had existed since Jerome defended his sense-for-sense translation of a papal letter in 385.[54] The periodical indicated an awareness of the challenges of poetic translation and suggested how criticism could contribute to an awareness of Brazilian literature in relation to other national literatures and, in turn, facilitate ongoing exchanges of texts and ideas.

O Novo Mundo provided insight into life in the United States by analyzing and translating literary representations of admirable political, economic, and social structures. Most notably, the periodical applauded Harriet Beecher Stowe's literary work and abolitionist beliefs via a profile, translated excerpts of *My Wife and I*, and a review of a Portuguese-language translation of *Uncle Tom's Cabin*. To contextualize the 1852 novel *Uncle Tom's Cabin* as relevant to Brazilian readers, a January 23, 1875, article emphasized the contradictions due to slavery's continued legality. The piece praised Stowe's novel as "uma brilhante luz no horizonte que ia revelar os corações pelo mundo inteiro, mostrando os horrores da vida escrava, e a injustiça da instituição" (a brilliant light on the horizon that was going to lay bare hearts worldwide, showing the horrors of slave life and the injustice of the institution; 5.52, 101). Moreover, the article noted, "A humanidade tem esta grande dívida para a autora deste livro revolucionário. Não há mulher viva a quem mais deva liberdade do que a Sra. H. Beecher Stowe" (Humanity has this great debt to the author of this revolutionary book. There is not a living woman to whom liberty is more indebted than Mrs. H. Beecher Stowe; 5.52, 101). The accompanying lithographic portrait granted a female writer visual prominence usually reserved for male politicians and military heroes.

A brief March 1879 article further recognized Stowe by praising *Uncle Tom's Cabin* for "mostrar bem ao vivo quais são alguns dos tristes resultados do sistema da escravidão que então existia ainda nos Estados Unidos" (showing quite vividly what are some of the sad results of the system of slavery that then still existed in the United States; 9.99, 61). The article emphasized the novel's role in US resistance to slavery and its subsequent success as a global publishing phenomenon.[55] According to Afranio Peixoto, the novel "provoked tears and forwarded the abolition of slavery" in Brazil (127). More recently, critics have highlighted the novel's contested legacy in the United States and Brazil. G. Reginald Daniel draws on David Haberly's study of Brazilian abolitionist literature to explain that the "existence of the stereotype of the Noble, Faithful, or Pitiful Slave did not call into question the institution of slavery itself. Much of this stereotypical literature was written in response to Harriet Beecher Stowe's *Uncle Tom's Cabin* (1852), translated into Portuguese and published twice during the 1850s—no doubt because it was a foreign bestseller" (*Machado de Assis* 168). Whereas Daniel analyzes Stowe's reception in Brazil with historical distance to consider racialized constructs, *O Novo Mundo* favorably evaluated the ideological underpinnings of her novels from the perspective of relatively contemporaneous abolitionists searching for literary models. Commending the Portuguese translation for its fidelity to the original, the periodical explained that "os que não souberem o inglês e lerem essa tradução verão por si mesmos como é que esse livro pode tornar-se arma tão poderosa para a abolição da escravidão nos Estados Unidos" (those who do not know the English and read this translation will see for themselves how it is that this book could become such a powerful weapon for the abolition of slavery in the United States; 9.99, 61). In praising the novel as a tool in the struggle against slavery, the periodical noted that the book's emotional power transcended translation.

Beyond representing cultural manifestations against slavery, Stowe's writings, with their depictions of daily life in the United States, could help to broaden Brazilian readers' hemispheric perspectives. *O Novo Mundo* published an abridged version of Stowe's 1871 novel *My Wife and I*, translated as *Minha mulher e eu*, in a serialized format from August 23, 1872, to May 23, 1873. The journal characterized the novel as "uma série de quadros de costumes americanos, em que a autora discute algumas das questões sociais do dia; e é por isso mesmo que o *Novo Mundo* o escolheu, a sua missão principal sendo a de fazer este país mais conhecido no Brasil" (a series of pictures of American customs, in which the author discusses some of the current social questions; and that is why *O Novo Mundo* selected it, its principle mission being that of making this country better known in Brazil; 2.23, 201). This serialization granted Brazilian readers access to a novel never published in an unabridged Portuguese-language translation. With this foray into serialized novels, *O Novo Mundo* followed the era's publishing trends given that, according to Marlyse Meyer, the feuilleton gained importance in the nineteenth century with the rise of cities, flaneurs, and print culture. Tapping into a growing interest in melodrama, the periodical served as a transnational translator introducing readers to literary works from the United States and Europe.

O Novo Mundo further facilitated hemispheric literary connections through collaborations with Brazilians writers Sousândrade and Machado de Assis. A native of the northeastern state of Maranhão, Sousândrade studied at the Sorbonne before moving to New York in 1871 to oversee his daughter's education at the Sacred Heart Academy in Manhattanville (Price 82). Over the next fourteen years, while living in New York and working on his epic *O Guesa*, he contributed to *O Novo Mundo* and served as the Novo Mundo Association's vice president.[56] As a published poet of the 1857 collection *Harpas selvagens*, Sousândrade heightened the prestige of the periodical's literary reporting. He first contributed with a November 24, 1871, article signed J. de Souza Andrade that responded to a *New York Gazette* piece with an astute explanation of the emperor's position on slavery: "Dom Pedro merece aplausos não por ter alevantado a voz em favor da emancipação, mas por ter ouvido a voz da nação, que bradava forte" (Dom Pedro deserves applause for not having raised his voice in favor of emancipation, but for having heard the voice of the nation that shouted loudly; 2.14, 31). Sousândrade outlined the political, economic, and social forces resulting in the persistence of slavery in Brazil without explicitly supporting the institution. Writing from voluntary exile in New York, he recognized Brazil's faults but nevertheless opted to defend his home nation when necessary.[57]

Sousândrade's journalism tended to focus on events unfolding in Brazil. His March 23, 1872, article "O Estado dos Índios" (The state of the Indians) examined the possibility of creating an indigenous state in the Amazon, warning that resource exploitation and increased travel within the region would disrupt the lives of indigenous peoples. By referencing Hartt's claim that Amazonian natives were more intelligent than the Irish, Sousândrade challenged social hierarchies that tended to associate indigeneity with barbarity but failed to fully contest positivist categorizations of intellect on the basis of race and ethnicity (2.18, 102).[58] His praise of indigenous intelligence came at the expense of the Irish, who were the targets of xenophobic views after their mass migration to the United States in the nineteenth century.[59] Another piece by Sousândrade commented on literary representations of native peoples and iconic landscapes. In an unsigned October 1873 article that Campos attributed to the poet, Sousândrade praised Joaquim Serra's poems via comparison: "Como Gonçalves Dias nas *Americanas* mostrou-nos em todo o esplendor a poesia dos Índios selvagens, na primeira parte do seu livro o Sr. Serra vem revelar grande beleza da poesia dos sertões" (As Gonçalves Dias in the *Americanas* showed us the poetry of the savage Indians in all its splendor, in the first part of his book Mr. Serra comes to reveal the great beauty of the poetry of the backlands; 4.37, 10).[60] This parallel emphasized indigenous peoples and the *sertão* as central to constructs of the autochthonous within nationalist discourses and cultural imaginaries of Brazil.[61] By referencing European writers Lamartine, Milton, and Dante in balance with local particularities, Sousândrade situated Serra's poetry as Brazilian literature worthy of international recognition.

As a Brazilian poet living in New York with access to the literatures of the Americas, Sousândrade addressed with comparative authority the merits of Brazilian literary works. He characterized Luís Nicolau Fagundes Varela's *Anchieta, ou, o Evangelho na Selva* as an epic that, given its exploration of religious themes with pristine language, "continuaremos a ler . . . e iremos até o último canto, desejando que todos façam o mesmo" (we will continue to read . . . and we will go until the last canto, desiring that everyone does the same; 6.65, 103). An August 1877 piece celebrated the quality and diversity of new forms of Brazilian lyricism and indigenous representations. Sousândrade highlighted this innovative nature of Brazilian verse by claiming, "É um horror ao estrangeiro que deseja aprender o português, ver um novo modo de escrever em cada livro que abre" (It is a horror, to the foreigner who desires to learn Portuguese, to see a new mode of writing in each book that he opens; 7.80, 186). Though he related to the difficulties of learning a language that continues to evolve, he suggested that poetic experimentation would intrigue, rather than frustrate, readers.

Sousândrade embraced the periodical's hemispheric outlook by reporting on Spanish American literary developments in a September 1877 review of Venezuelan poet Juan Antonio Pérez Bonalde's *Estrofas*. To support his claim that *Estrofas* facilitated a better understanding of Venezuela's land and people, Sousândrade included select verses in Spanish to grant bilingual readers of his review more direct access to Bonalde's poems. Sousândrade compared *Estrofas* to "estes mimosos e gentis *Recuerdos de un Viajero*, que melhor falem por nós aos nossos leitores" (these sweet and gentle *Recuerdos de un Viajero*, which better speak for us to our readers; 7.81, 211). Bonalde, who lived in New York in the 1870s, captured travelers' peripatetic nature in poems that subsequently served to translate experiences abroad for Latin American readers. Sousândrade's review concluded that the interconnected themes of travel and translation in these poems would speak to *O Novo Mundo*'s readers.

While contributing to *O Novo Mundo* and living in New York, Sousândrade drafted and revised sections of *O Guesa*. His epic poem of thirteen cantos, which took him over forty years to complete, follows an errant Amerindian protagonist as he journeys throughout the hemispheric Americas from the Andes to the Amazon before heading north to New York. According to Earl Fitz's *Inter-American Literary History*, *O Guesa* "stands alone in the world of late nineteenth century American letters" in both form and content (217). Charles Perrone fittingly claims in *Brazil, Lyric, and the Americas* that "*O guesa* is wholly New World, as brief jumps to Africa and southern Europe are simply to explore what truly takes root after cross-Atlantic migration" (109).[62] Perrone characterizes *O Novo Mundo* as Sousândrade's "singular journalistic source" for allusions to current events that constitute the poem's societal critiques (113). Perhaps the poet relied on *O Novo Mundo* as a Portuguese-language publication that he supported financially and journalistically. The periodical, in turn, praised Sousândrade's work with a February 1877 article stressing his dedication "escrever o *Guesa*—o grande trabalho de sua vida" (to write the *Guesa*—the great work of his life) while living in Manhattanville (7.74, 39). The journal commended "nosso amigo" (our friend) for *Harpas selvagens* and the published cantos of *O Guesa*. The article also reprinted excerpts from a piece by J. M. Pereira da Silva published in Rio de Janeiro's *Reforma* that asked: "Quem é . . . Joaquim de Souza Andrade? Onde vive? O que faz? O que escreveu?" (Who is . . . Joaquim de Souza Andrade? Where does he live? What does he do? What has he written?; 7.74, 39).

By responding to these questions, *O Novo Mundo* elevated Sousândrade to a place of greater prominence within literatures of Brazil and the Americas. As *O Novo Mundo* posited and later critics have contended, Sousândrade deserved recognition for his stylistic invention, varied poetic and cultural influences, and insight into the hemispheric relations of Brazil, the rest of Latin America, and the United States.[63] The poet was a footnote in Brazilian literary history as a minor romantic until poets, translators, and critics Augusto and Haroldo de Campos celebrated his work in their 1964 *ReVisão de Sousândrade* (ReVision of Sousândrade).[64] Sousândrade's work was relatively inaccessible in Brazil until they praised him as a worthy contemporary of Baudelaire in their formalistic analysis of his innovative quasi-telegraphic style. In rehabilitating Sousândrade's legacy, the Campos brothers embarked on a critical project of rediscovering and reinterpreting canonical Brazilian writers that complemented their theoretical and practical interests in translation as a mode of criticism and creation. Their reading of Sousândrade's epic focused on a selection of 176 verses from the tenth canto that they termed "The Wall Street Inferno." With its experimental verse, the section exposes the speculative dangers of capitalism in the United States. However, as Perrone advises, the "Inferno" is best read contextualized within the rest of the canto in order to grasp how the poet's perception of the dark side of escalating capitalism in New York coexists with his admiration for the United States' political structure as a democratic republic. This balance between criticizing and praising the United States paralleled the editorial perspective of *O Novo Mundo*.

Relatively obscure references render *O Guesa* difficult to understand without knowledge of social, political, and economic contexts. The poet integrated expressions in foreign languages, advertising slogans, and newspaper headlines into his Portuguese to craft a verse that exhibits the varied discourses intermingling on Wall Street and in New York during the 1870s.[65] To convey the fanfare surrounding Pedro II's visit to the United States, the poem references press coverage: "(The Sun:) / —Agora a União é império; / Dom Pedro é nosso imperador: / 'Nominate him president'; / Resident . . . / Que povo ame muito a Senhor" (Sousândrade 366–67; "[The Sun:] / —The Union's become an empire; / Dom Pedro is Emperor now: / 'Nominate him President'; / Resident . . . / May the people love him, and how"; Sousa Andrade 94).[66] The poem criticizes rampant capitalism via allusions to robber barons and crooked politicians, and exchanges like "—*'Is there any hope for parvenu?*' / —Com certeza não,

Sir Burglár! . . ." (—'*Is there any hope for parvenu?*' / —Of course not, *Sir Burglar!* . . . ; Sousândrade 384). With its multilingual verse and plentiful references, *O Guesa* proves more difficult to access than Sousândrade's journalism. While *O Novo Mundo* advocated for progress almost blindly in its journalistic fervor, the epic criticized the dark underside of modernity as generating corruption and fueling speculative capitalism.[67]

Sousândrade's writings exemplified the importance of transnational perspectives for the development of a critical practice that, as *O Novo Mundo* implied, could enhance Brazil's cultural standing among modern nations. Machado de Assis compellingly argued for the necessity of criticism in "Notícia da atual literatura brasileira: Instinto de nacionalidade" ("Reflections on Brazilian Literature at the Present Moment: The National Instinct"). First published in *O Novo Mundo* in March 1873, the essay contributed to the journal's mission of fostering knowledge of Brazil in the Americas. To underscore the essay's initial materiality, I cite the version published in *O Novo Mundo* rather than the one included in Machado's *Obra Completa*. Even though Machado never left his home of Rio de Janeiro, his reflections on Brazilian national literature developed out of hemispheric exchanges of texts and ideas. In a letter on September 22, 1872, Rodrigues congratulated Machado on the "brilhante sucesso" (brilliant success) of his first novel *Ressurreição (Resurrection)* (Machado de Assis 78). A December 23, 1872, review in *O Novo Mundo* praised Machado's novel for accurately depicting life in Rio de Janeiro: "Quem conhece a complexidade da nossa sociedade não vê na *Ressurreição* mais do que uma boa fotografia de um de seus aspectos comuns" (One who knows the complexity of our society sees nothing more in *Resurrection* than a good photograph of one of its common aspects; 3.27, 46). The periodical praised this novel, often dismissed as a minor effort, for its astute representation of societal complexities.[68]

Rodrigues wanted to contribute to readers' knowledge about Brazilian literature by publishing an article by Machado de Assis, whom he considered an apt critic to convey the nuances of the national literary scene. In his 1872 letter to Machado, Rodrigues explained that his periodical "precisa de um bom estudo sobre o caráter geral da literatura brasileira contemporânea, criticando as suas boas ou más tendências, no aspecto literário e moral: um estudo que sendo traduzido e publicado aqui em inglês, dê uma boa ideia da fazenda literária que lá fabricamos, e da escola ou escolas do processo de fabricação" (needs a good study about the general character of contemporary Brazilian literature, critiquing its good or bad tendencies, in literary and moral terms: a study that, being translated and published here in English, gives a good idea of the literary work that we create there, and of the school or schools of the creative process; *Machado de Assis* 78–79) before asking "quererá o amigo escrever sobre isso?" (will you, friend, want to write about this?). Writing to Rodrigues on January 25, 1873, from Rio de Janeiro, Machado expressed gratitude for his review of *Ressurreição* before mentioning, "O nosso artigo está pronto há um mês. Guardei-me para dar-lhe hoje uma última demão; mas tão complicado e cheio foi o dia para mim, que prefiro demorá-lo para o seguinte vapor" (Our article has been ready for a month. I reserved today to give it a final look-over; but the day was so complicated and full for me that I prefer to wait for the next ship; 82). Machado approached this task of literary journalism with careful attention that would delay its scheduled publication.

His sole contribution to *O Novo Mundo* provided an extensive update on Brazilian literature that has continued to impact discussions of Brazil's national identity and literary traditions into the twenty-first century. For instance, Abel Barros Baptista cites Machado's essay as a foundational commentary on the coexisting impulses of nationality and cosmopolitanism in Brazilian literature (177). Critics tend to refer only in passing to the text's publication in *O Novo Mundo*.[69] A closer look at the material qualities of its initial printing in Rodrigues's periodical provides insight into the relevance of transnational print communities for articulating more critical visions of romanticized literary nationalism. The essay appeared next to an apparently unrelated image, a lithograph of a young girl posing in front of a mirror titled "Primeiros ensaios com o espelho" (First rehearsals with the mirror; 3.30, 108). The image of the girl lacked direct correspondence to literary discussions but resonated with the reflective project of constructing the nation as modern. Like the girl who practiced her self-presentation in front of a mirror, the essay's view of Brazilian literature published abroad was reflected back to readers in Brazil through the periodical's circulation from Rio de Janeiro to its place of publication in New York before returning to Brazil in the pages of *O Novo Mundo*.

Machado's text challenged romantic preferences for "local color" by proposing a personal instinct of nationality as the defining trait of being a Brazilian writer. The essay formed part of his broader engagement in fiction and criticism with questions of nationality via explorations of authorship, originality, and relationships of the particular and the universal. As

Efraín Kristal and José Luiz Passos rightly argue, "Machado's own writings clearly indicate that he was looking for a literary mode of expression that would transcend simplistic nationalistic pronouncements" (19). Claiming that literary works did not need to depict local specificities or celebrate national symbols to be considered Brazilian, Machado identified a "certo instinto de nacionalidade" (*O Novo Mundo* 3.30, 107; "certain national instinct," Newcomb, "Reflections" 404) as a key trait of poetry, prose, and other literary genres in Brazil. He critiqued Brazilian writers for seeking "vestir-se com as cores do país" (3.30, 107; "to clothe themselves in the nation's colors," 404) in efforts to distinguish their works from European literary traditions. Machado criticized Brazil's literary nationalism for manifesting itself primarily in indigenous themes in romantic works like Gonçalves Dias's poem *Os Timbiras* (1857). He contended that Brazilian writers could look beyond the specific to find inspiration in shared experiences of the Americas, including "os costumes civilizados, ou já do tempo colonial, ou já do tempo de hoje" (3.30, 107; "civilized customs, which we find in both the colonial period and the present time," 407) and "a natureza americana, cuja magnificência e esplendor naturalmente desafiam a poetas e prosadores" (3.30, 107; "American nature, the magnificence and splendor which naturally call out to and challenge poets and prose writers," 407). His analysis recognized the universal elements within national expressions and experiences.

Referring to *Hamlet* and *The Golden Legend*, Machado noted that Anglo-American writers did not limit their subjects to national land, people, or history. He concluded: "Não há dúvida que uma literatura, sobretudo uma literatura nascente, deve principalmente alimentar-se dos assuntos que lhe oferece a sua região; mas não estabeleçamos doutrinas tão absolutas que a empobreçam. O que se deve exigir do escritor antes de tudo, é certo sentimento íntimo, que o torne homem do seu tempo e do seu país, ainda quando trate de assuntos remotos no tempo e no espaço" (3.30, 107; "There is no doubt that a literature, and especially a literature that is still coming into being, should draw in the main on topics offered by its land. But let us not establish doctrines that are so absolute as to be impoverishing. What we should expect of the writer above all is a certain intimate feeling that renders him a man of his time and country, even when he addresses topics that are remote in time or space," 408). Brazilians possessed a personal sense of nationality that infused their poetry and prose regardless of topic and therefore must not limit their work to forms of local color.

Moreover, Machado posited that "a falta de uma crítica assim é um dos maiores males de que padece a nossa literatura" (3.30, 107; "the lack of this sort of criticism is one of the worst ills suffered by our literature," 409). He contended that stronger criticism would make literary works more accessible to readers and thus increase interest in Brazilian literature. His essay modeled how a critical practice could improve national and universal appreciation for Brazilian literature. Machado considered the novel the most fully realized literary genre in Brazil, even though novelists' tendency to search for local color often resulted in sentimental works. He envisioned critics urging novelists to explore topics not specifically linked to Brazil but cautioned that their guidance would have a more outsized effect in poetry than prose. Machado suggested that critics could help to rein in poetic grandiloquence and, in the process, transform Brazilian poetry by contesting superficial uses of local color and by preferring simple language to approximate nature's beauty.

At the end of his essay, Machado addressed language as key to the distinctiveness of Brazilian literature, a discussion that anticipated modernist Mário de Andrade's investment in writing in Brazilian Portuguese and documenting this distinct language, which I examine further in the next chapter. According to Machado, "entre os muitos méritos dos nossos livros nem sempre o da pureza da linguagem" (3.30, 108; "purity of language does not always figure among the many merits of our books," 415), given the influence of popular expressions and French terms in Brazilian Portuguese. Machado argued that Brazilian writers should embrace their linguistic specificities but warned that "a influência popular tem um limite" (3.30, 108; "the people's influence has its limits," 416). By highlighting Brazilian literature's strengths of "viva imaginação, delicadeza e força de sentimentos, graças de estilo, dotes de observação e análise" (3.30, 108; "lively imagination, delicacy and force of feeling, graceful style, talent for observation and analysis," 416), and weaknesses, like "carências às vezes de reflexão e pausa, língua nem sempre pura, nem sempre copiosa, muita cor local" (3.30, 108; "at times a lack of reflection and stillness, a language that is not always pure and not always plentiful, a great deal of local color," 416), Machado concluded that Brazilian literature would have a "certíssimo futuro" (3.30, 108; "a very secure future," 416).

Machado aimed to insert Brazilian literature more fully into the world republic of letters by distancing it from depictions of local customs and landscapes. Achieving this desired prominence of a modern Brazil within a more expansive literary market would necessitate linguistic, literary, and cultural forms of translation. *O Novo Mundo* provided an apt venue for Machado's essay as a periodical published in the United States for Brazilians and by Brazilians. The journal invited a more distanced view of Brazil, which allowed Machado to criticize Brazilian literature's preference for local color even as he defended the project of national literature. Machado's perspective of literature served as a precursor to Jorge Luis Borges's ideas about writers, tradition, and national literatures.[70] Negotiating national interests with cosmopolitan desires characterized *O Novo Mundo* as a periodical invested in a hemispheric project. From its position between Brazil and the United States, the periodical, on the one hand, embraced discourses of progress, and, on the other, hinted at potential dangers of Eurocentrism and incipient industrial capitalism. *O Novo Mundo*'s optimism about the possibilities of translation for cross-cultural exchange glossed over the limitations of understanding and intelligibility, which subsequent Brazilian creative and critical works would explore in more detail.

Chapter 2

Modernism for Export

The Translational Origins and Afterlives of Macunaíma

Nearly fifty years after imperial Brazil staked its claim to a tropical modernity at the 1876 Centennial Exhibition, polemic avant-garde writer Oswald de Andrade (1890–1954) proposed a new approach to Brazil's relationship with international culture and capital. His 1924 "Manifesto da Poesia Pau-Brasil" ("Manifesto of Pau-Brasil Poetry"), first published in *Correio da Manhã*, encouraged a reevaluation of cultural influence and artistic creation in Brazil. In an incipient articulation of *antropofagia*, the manifesto contrasted earlier practices of copying external, imported poetics with modes of assimilating foreign influence into a national aesthetic balancing Brazilian nature ("the forest") with lettered culture ("the school").[1] Oswald envisioned a Pau-Brasil poetry for exportation that would capture "a língua sem arcaísmos, sem erudição. Natural e neológica. A contribuição milionária de todos os erros. Como falamos. Como somos" (136; "language without archaisms, without erudition. Natural and neologic. The millionaire-contribution of all the errors. The way we speak. The way we are," "Manifesto of Pau-Brasil Poetry" 185).[2] With its ironic tone and telegraphic style, the manifesto urged Brazilians to break free from rigid confines in their writing to more closely approximate ways of speaking. Writer, critic, folklorist, musician, and ethnomusicologist Mário de Andrade (1893–1945) similarly articulated a vision of language that aimed to minimize the divide between written and spoken Portuguese in Brazil. He approached language in an ethnographic manner in an effort to create and follow a grammar of the specific vocabulary and syntax of spoken Brazilian Portuguese.[3]

For the more radical Oswald de Andrade, dynamics of language were connected to ongoing political and economic hierarchies between Brazil, Europe, and the United States. As long as Brazil imported cultural models and exported raw materials, like its famous *pau-brasil* or brazilwood, it would remain on artistic and geopolitical peripheries as a nation of primitive accumulation that grants minimal value to its creative agency and expression. Rather than maintain these binaries, Oswald advocated for "o trabalho contra o detalhe naturalista—pela *síntese*; contra a morbidez romântica—pelo *equilíbrio* geômetra e pelo *acabamento* técnico; contra a cópia, pela *invenção* e pela *surpresa*" (137; "the reaction against naturalistic detail—through *synthesis*; against romantic morbidity—through geometric *equilibrium* and technical *finish*; against copy, though *invention* and *surprise*," 187). This proclamation advanced a modernist ethos of critically consuming external influences as the basis for national artistic innovation that Oswald would further develop and radicalize in his "Manifesto Antropófago" ("Cannibalist Manifesto"), published in May 1928 in the first issue of the *Revista de Antropofagia* (1928–1929).[4] With his playful irreverence, metaphorical language, and humorous poetic prose, the renegade modernist posited an aesthetic and historical revolution that, in searching for synthesis, would invert established hierarchies between the colonizer and the colonized. In declaring, "Só a antropofagia nos une. Socialmente. Economicamente. Filosoficamente" (142; "Cannibalism alone unites us. Socially. Economically. Philosophically," 38), Oswald articulated a double meaning of cannibalism in Brazil as both a historical fact and a figurative act of "devouring" artistic and intellectual ideas and practices in order to transform and integrate them into national expressions of culture.[5]

Mário de Andrade crafted an experimental literary work that embraced the call of *antropofagia* to invert established hierarchies and to revolutionize national cultural expression with his 1928 masterpiece *Macunaíma: o herói sem nenhum caráter* (*Macunaíma: the Hero Without a Character*).[6] The *Revista de Antropofagia* published in its second issue in June 1928 an excerpt from the novel's opening opposite a short announcement that *Macunaíma (História)* would be available that month (see fig. 2.1). In its August and September issues, the *Revista* advertised that *Macunaíma*, no longer labeled as a history or story, was available to purchase. The promotion of Mário's text within the literary magazine of *antropografia* points to the deep affinity between Oswald's theoretical concepts and Mário's creative and scholarly endeavors in the late 1920s.

Ethnographic travels, musical and folkloric research, and voracious reading formed the basis for Mário's cultural cannibalism that generated an original text blending Amerindian myths, Afro-Brazilian traditions, and popular Brazilian cultures and expressions. With its linguistic playfulness and cultural specificity, *Macunaíma* resists translations that flatten its prose into homogenized world literature or a consumable vision of otherness. Instead the text demands translations that strive to recreate

Figure 2.1. Excerpt of *Macunaíma* published in *Revista de Antopofagia* (Biblioteca Brasiliana Guita e José Mindlin—PRCEU/USP).

its particularities in another context. Film and fictional adaptations introduce his protagonist's tale to a broader public in Brazil and the rest of the Americas to contribute to more nuanced visions of Brazil as a land of contradictions.

My analysis of *Macunaíma* underscores its origins in linguistic and cultural translations that defy interlingual translations mired in literalisms and rather invite transcreations and creative adaptations. Unlike his fellow *modernistas* Oswald de Andrade and painter Tarsila do Amaral (1886–1973), who rediscovered Brazilian cultures while in Paris, Mário de Andrade stayed relatively close to his native São Paulo, traveling within Brazil and to the Peruvian Amazon. According to Telê Porto Ancona Lopez in her introduction to the definitive critical edition, Mário's trip to the Amazon from May to July 1927, as documented in the posthumously published *O Turista Aprendiz*, informed the narrative of *Macunaíma* (xxxvi). He complemented his travels with readings of travelogues and ethnographic texts, most notably *Vom Roroima zum Orinoco 1911–1913* (From the Roraima to the Orinoco) by German anthropologist Theodor Koch-Grünberg (1872–1924).[7] Mário transformed Amerindian trickster tales and creation myths into a novel that, in balancing cultural references and narrative inventions, reflected his folkloric research, musical studies, and literary interests. The modernist masterpiece ironically comments on Brazilian national identity and culture through the tale of Macunaíma, a shapeshifting hero without any character, and his brothers' journey from their Amazonian home to São Paulo in search of the lost *muiraquitã*, a magical talisman given to the hero by the mother of the forest Ci. After recovering the amulet from Venceslau Pietro Pietra, also known as the human-eating giant Piaimã adapted from the Taulipang tale "Macunaíma and Piaimã," Macunaíma returns to his native region, dies, and becomes the constellation Ursa Major. Before his death, Macunaíma relays his story to a parrot, who then passes it on to a man who preserves the tale in writing.

Recent critics have characterized the text's subversive transformation of source materials as a postcolonial move. For Luís Madureira, *Macunaíma* embodies contradictions of primitivism and modernism since the protagonist both symbolizes the nation and represents fundamental difference. The hero carries the "trace of the suppressions and exclusions" that Brazil's marginalized peoples historically suffered and that persisted in the modernist project (Madureira 16). Fernando Rosenberg's geopolitically inflected analysis of *Macunaíma* identifies a temporal paradox between modernization and colonial origins that appears in the nation's geographic disjunctions. These contradictions point to the text's radical potential to critique Brazil's desire for and embrace of modernity by "expos[ing] the basic fault of the incorporative model of happy consumption" (Rosenberg 103–04). By focusing on these contradictions, Alfredo Cesar Melo reads Mário de Andrade as a transcultural narrator who blends avant-garde aesthetics with folkloric research to create a novel that simultaneously praises and critiques *antropofagia*.

Considering the politics at stake in *Macunaíma* in light of questions of translation helps to better understand nuances and contradictions inherent in Mário's project. He recognized the limits of *antropofagia* and expressed ambivalence toward triumphant discourses of modernity. Reading the 1928 text as a creative transformation of indigenous and popular tales contests the hierarchy of the original and the copy to underscore Mário's agency. The novel challenges translators who privilege literal meaning, like E. A. Goodland with his 1984 English translation, and thus has circulated more widely beyond Brazil when translators recognize the text's cultural specificities and aim to recreate them in another context without flattening or easily appropriating difference. The character and tales of Macunaíma establish cultural dialogues in the Americas via transmutations and fictional reinterpretations, most notably Joaquim Pedro de Andrade's 1969 film adaptation and Pauline Melville's 1997 novel *The Ventriloquist's Tale*.

Macunaíma as Translation: From Koch-Grünberg's Tales to Mário de Andrade's Masterpiece

According to Mário de Andrade's self-mythologizing in a May 19, 1928, letter to writer and critic Alceu Amoroso Lima, *Macunaíma* was "escrito em dezembro de 1926, inteirinho em seis dias, correto e aumentado em janeiro de 1927, e vai parecer inteiramente antropófago" (written in December 1926, all of it in six days, corrected and expanded in January 1927, and will seem entirely cannibalistic; Andrade, *Macunaíma* 400). Mário acknowledged that a variety of source materials shaped his literary creation, which he first labeled a novel on his 1926 draft before crossing it out and adding "história" (history or story; 359). He subsequently described the text as "um poema herói-cômico" (a heroic-comic poem) in a 1935 letter to philologist Souza da Silveira (416), before classifying it as a "rapsódia" (rhapsody) in its second edition published in 1937 (xxx). These distinct terms suggest the work's musicality, orality, storytelling, and humor that transcend the classificatory bounds of genres. *Macunaíma* puzzled readers upon its initial publication, with some critics responding favorably and others arriving at more tepid conclusions.[8] To facilitate the work's initial reception, Tristão de Ataíde, Lima's journalistic pseudonym, published a review in *O Jornal* that quoted from the two unpublished prefaces by Mário de Andrade in an attempt "não só para entender a intenção do autor, como para livrá-lo de qualquer insinuação de plagio" (not only to understand the author's intention, but also to free it from any insinuation of plagiarism; FBN—Periódicos). These prefaces provided insight into what initially inspired the work and how a desire to traverse geographic, generic, cultural, and linguistic borders guided Mário's textual efforts to examine Brazilian identity.[9]

A concern with perceived plagiarism also informed an entry in Raimundo Moraes's *Dicionário de Cousas da Amazônia*. Without identifying who accused Mário of plagiarism, Moraes defended the modernist's originality: "Os maldizentes afirmam que o livro *Macunaíma* do festejado escritor, Mário de Andrade, é todo inspirado no *Vom [sic] Roraima zum Orinoco* do sábio (Koch-Grünberg). Desconhecendo eu o livro do naturalista germânico, não creio nesse boato, pois o romanista patrício, com quem privei em Manaus, possui talento e imaginação que dispensam inspirações estranhas" (The detractors affirm that the book *Macunaíma* by the celebrated writer Mário de Andrade is entirely inspired in *Vom [sic] Roraima zum Orinoco* by the wise man (Koch-Grünberg). Not familiar with the German naturalist's book, I do not believe this rumor, since the elegant novelist, whom I got to know in Manaus, possesses talent and imagination that bestows strange inspirations; qtd. in Andrade, *Macunaíma* 427). Responding to Moraes in a September 20, 1931, letter published in the *Diário Nacional*, Mário rejected the defense and instead celebrated his "carnivorous" process of relating to various authors: "Copiei, sim, meu querido defensor. O que me espanta . . . é os maldizentes se esquecerem de tudo quanto sabem, restringindo a minha cópia a Koch-Grünberg, quando copiei todos" (Yes, I copied, my dear defender. What shocks me . . . is that my detractors forgot all they know, restricting my copying to Koch-Grünberg, when I copied them all; 427). He referenced folklorist and historian Carlos Teschauer, botanist João Barbosa Rodrigues, geologist Charles Frederick Hartt, and ethnologist Edgar Roquette-Pinto as contributing to his knowledge of the Amazon and Brazil.

Mário's assessment of his own practice anticipated critical studies by Manuel Cavalcanti Proença in 1955 and Telê Porto Ancona Lopez in 1974 that identified works by Koch-Grünberg, historian João Capistrano de Abreu, writer and ethnologist José Vieira Couto de Magalhães, and literary critic and folklorist Sílvio Romero as sources for the 1928 novel. For Cavalcanti Proença and Lopez, Mário transformed "raw materials" of indigenous and popular tales into art as a nonindigenous intellectual. In contrast, Lúcia Sá's 2004 reading appreciates the creative originality already present in the sources to frame his literary project as one of re-creation. She contends that "Mário aligns himself with several writers and theorists of the twentieth century—from Brecht and Borges to Kristeva and Derrida—who see literature as an intertextual practice. Unlike them, however, he is less concerned with intertextuality as such than with the possibilities of intercultural relations opened by the intertextual dialogue" (Sá 39). Interests in intertextuality led Mário and his Argentine contemporary Borges to challenge hierarchical concepts of the original and the copy and to assert creative agency as readers, writers, and translators.[10]

With its ethnographic awareness of Amazonian peoples and cultures, Mário's literary project paralleled the work of Guatemalan Miguel Ángel Asturias (1899–1974) and Cuban Alejo Carpentier (1904–1980), who drew on indigenous and popular sources when writing *Leyendas de Guatemala* (1930, *Legends of Guatemala*) and *Los pasos perdidos* (1953, *The Lost Steps*), respectively.[11] In creatively rendering popular oral expressions and ethnographic records into experimental narratives, these writers occupied an intermediary position analogous to a translator. Engaging in an intertextual and intercultural dialogue with Koch-Grünberg's work, Mário's marginalia in the second volume noted that he should "aproveitar bem esta lenda pra demonstrar falta de caráter . . . de Macunaíma" (make good use of this legend to demonstrate . . . Macunaíma's lack of character; 239). By selecting the verb "aproveitar," meaning to make good use of, to use, or, negatively, to exploit or profiteer, Mário indicated that he recognized his sources' value as discrete tales as he also transformed them to his advantage. Existing studies, however, have tended to underappreciate indigenous source materials by conceiving of the tales as raw materials in need of manipulation. Lopez's analysis of Mário's annotations of Koch-Grünberg's text underscores how the modernist transformed previously documented myths and legends and integrated them with elite forms and colloquial language to craft his rhapsodic narrative (*Macunaíma: a margem* 9). Her research draws on extensive archival work in Mário's personal library, which was donated to the University of São Paulo's Institute of Brazilian Studies in 1968, to identify relevant tales from Koch-Grünberg's text, summarize them, and analyze their use in the novel.[12] Gilda de Mello e Souza examines how variation and adaptation structure *Macunaíma*'s composition as a bricolage of European, indigenous, and African elements. She contends that the narrative relies on carnivalized Arthurian romances and, thus, remains essentially European (Souza 74–76, 89). As Sá rightly critiques, Souza arrives at this conclusion by focusing on the search for the *muiraquitã* (Sá 54). Haroldo de Campos similarly restricts his Proppian analysis of *Macunaíma* to this element of the narrative (*Morfologia* 31).

Approaching *Macunaíma* as a text with origins in translation facilitates a reevaluation of earlier scholarship. Like Sá, I recognize the value of indigenous texts as more than simply raw materials, but I also acknowledge, as do Lopez and Souza, Mário's role in rendering these tales into an original narrative. My analysis of *Macunaíma* as a transcreation, to evoke Haroldo de Campos's neologism for translation as creative transposition, resonates with Gayatri Spivak's vision of translation as "the most intimate act of reading" in which "the translator must surrender to the text" (Spivak 315).[13] Mário dedicated himself to his indigenous and popular sources while maintaining his creative agency to transform them into his masterpiece. He proposed a similar way of approaching translation in a 1945 *Diário de Notícias* article: "traduzir é necessariamente ato de amor. Ou de pragmática social—o que vale dizer sempre, amor. . . . Traduzir, afinal das contas, é criar" (translating is necessarily an act of love. Or of social etiquette—which is, more accurately, love. . . . Translating, after all, is creating; IEB-USP Archive, MA-MMA-112). Mário's view of translation brings to mind theories by, among others, Borges, Benjamin, and Spivak that frame the translator as an intimate reader, writer, and re-creator.[14]

In letters and interviews about composing *Macunaíma*, Mário recognized the work of translation at play in rendering spoken language into writing. His November 1928 letter to Rosário Fusco characterized *Macunaíma* as "escrito em língua artificial, como é de fato toda língua escrita" (written in artificial language, as all written language is in fact; Andrade, *Macunaíma* 407). This perspective anticipates Walter Ong's work on orality and literacy, which frames writing as an artificial technology in contrast to oral speech (81). Mário viewed his prose as "uma estilização lírica puramente individualista da fala brasileira" (a purely individualistic, lyrical stylization of Brazilian speech; Andrade, *Macunaíma* 407–08), or, in other terms, translation between what Macunaíma identifies as the "duas línguas da terra, o brasileiro falado e o português escrito" (two languages of the land, spoken Brazilian and written Portuguese; 87), rather than between two national languages.[15] Due to the heterogeneity of spoken language in Brazil, the text's written prose must integrate popular sayings, indigenous terms, and foreign words. As Mário explained in a 1944 interview, "quis escrever um livro em todos os linguajares do Brasil. O resultado foi que . . . me fiz incompreensível até para os brasileiros" (I wanted to write a book in all the dialects of Brazil. The result was that . . . I made myself incomprehensible even for Brazilians; 423). He contested Brazil's internal divisions by traversing linguistic and cultural regionalisms in a gesture that coincided with the intention of "desgeograficar" (ungeographizing) articulated in his second unpublished preface (xlv).

Understanding *Macunaíma* requires acts of translation even for readers of Portuguese. Mário claimed that, to make the text more intelligible for a potential English translator, he had "traduzir pro português as palavras brasileiras do livro, grifar em vermelho as que devem ficar como estão, porque a clareza não se perde com isso, grifar em azul as locuções, provérbios, costumes nacionais, etc. que carecerá mais transportar que traduzir" (to translate into Portuguese the book's Brazilian words, underlining in red those that must stay as they are, because clarity is not lost as such, underlining in blue the phrases, proverbs, national customs, etc. that will require more transporting than translating; 413). He commented that the annotated text was covered in blue given the many references and expressions that defied direct translation. These culturally specific terms required explanations and creative solutions to transport them into other spatial and temporal contexts. By creatively transposing Koch-Grünberg's German renderings of Amerindian tales along with other source materials and lived experiences into the written Brazilian Portuguese of *Macunaíma*, Mário introduced readers to relatively unknown indigenous tales, popular traditions, and modes of speech from comparatively remote regions of Brazil.[16]

For a novel that explored ideas of travel and translation, *Macunaíma* seemed to resist those very processes in terms of its circulation in national and international literary markets. The novel reached a relatively limited public in Brazil, especially in the fifteen years after its 1928 publication when only 1,800 copies of the novel circulated, and did not reach readers in translation until 1970, with the publication of the Italian version.[17] Its readers were mainly other elites of São Paulo and Rio de Janeiro who lacked familiarity with Amazonian languages and were unlikely to have the reading knowledge of German that would have granted them access to Koch-Grünberg's writings. It is worth considering, as Kimberle López does in her analysis of *Macunaíma*'s ethnographic basis, if Mário could adapt tales from Koch-Grünberg's text without adopting his gaze of Amerindians as other. She astutely responds by stating that Mário occupied "the same inside/outside position as the ethnographer: he is Brazilian, but the Brazil he describes is not his own urban South" (López 33). His work indicates how travel and translation intersected with dynamics of power as Brazil continued to negotiate its place as a nation whose claim to modernity depended upon its tropical nature. Mário expressed ambivalence toward modern Brazil, noting that "não aprecio a civilização, nem, muito menos, acredito nela" (I do not appreciate civilization, nor, much less, do I believe in it; IEB-USP Archive, MA-ESC-003).

By positioning Macunaíma as a hero who transforms as he travels, Mário de Andrade parodies romantic narratives idealizing indigenous peoples and celebrating foundational myths.[18] Born deep in the Amazon to indigenous peoples who move freely between northern Brazil, Venezuela, and Guyana, Macunaíma transcends the confines of a single nationality to declare, "Sou americano e meu lugar é na América. A civilização européia de-certo esculhamba a inteiriza do nosso caráter" (I am American and my place is in the Americas. European civilization surely ridicules the entirety of our character; Andrade, *Macunaíma* 114–15).[19] Though characterized as the "hero of our people," where "our" tends to be understood as Brazilian, Macunaíma never claims to be Brazilian and instead positions himself as American. Understanding him as transnational also requires recognition of indigenous and African concepts of tribe as nation. Macunaíma projects a sense of hemispheric belonging reminiscent of *O Novo Mundo*'s editorial outlook. He recalls another character with Amerindian origins who embarks on transnational travels: the errant protagonist of Sousândrade's *O Guesa*. These indigenous peripatetic tricksters embrace the Americas as they question Europe's supposed superiority.

Rather than conform to cosmopolitan itineraries of Brazilian elites that privileged Europe, Mário de Andrade traveled from São Paulo to the Amazon and the Brazilian Northeast to discover the interior of his own nation. Similarly, but in the reverse direction of the author and other scientific or ethnographic travelers, Macunaíma and his older brothers Maanape and Jiguê journeyed from north to south along the Araguaia River.[20] The text emphasizes the geographic pathways that move the brothers from one place to another: "Muitos casos sucederam nessa viagem por caatingas rios corredeiras, gerais, corgos, corredores de tabatinga matos-virgens e milagres do sertão. Macunaíma vinha com os dois manos pra São Paulo" (Many events happened on that trip through brush rivers rapids, commons, creeks, the tabatinga narrows virgin-forests and miracles of the *sertão*. Macunaíma came with his two brothers to São Paulo; 36). Framing travel as a transfer recalls the etymology of translation from the Latin verb *translatio*, meaning to carry across or to transfer. The absence of commas and the use of consonant alliteration generate an accumulative effect that approximates storytelling. The use of *corgos* for *córregos*, *manos* for *irmãos*, and *pra* for *para* more closely recreates popular pronunciation and terms.[21] With textual approximations of vernacular speech, Mário acted as an intralingual translator between written and spoken Brazilian Portuguese.[22]

In refusing to flatten his novel into a homogeneous style, Mário de Andrade anticipated Emily Apter's twenty-first-century warning against the potential dangers of world literature.[23] The text draws on folkloric sources and authorial invention to craft an oneiric and fantastical narrative of travels and transformations that contest temporal and spatial logic as the brothers' journey to recover the lost amulet.[24] The double identity of Macunaíma's antagonist as the Italian-Peruvian businessman Venceslau Pietro Pietra and the mythic cannibal Piaimã exemplifies how rural traditions and urban modernization, indigenous cultures and immigrant influences, and popular tales and avant-garde fiction coexist in a single narrative. Negotiating these apparent dichotomies in the text often involves rendering the unfamiliar into more accessible terms and common reference points. While these elements of cultural specificity are not unique to *Macunaíma*, such particularities and references are so heightened that the text is strange, even to Brazilian readers. *Macunaíma* suggests how rendering Amerindian tales into experimental prose can facilitate cross-cultural communication within Brazil and, at the same time, resist facile translatability within an international literary market. For instance, the novel reiterates that Maanape is a *feiticeiro* (19, 41), a sorcerer whose healing powers allow him to bring the hero back to life after his first encounter with Piaimã by wrapping his body parts together in banana leaves (45). The term *feiticeiro* lacks the negative connotations often associated with the words "witch" or "sorcerer" in English, a subtlety that would be lost in literal translation.[25] Moreover, comparing Macunaíma's reconfiguration to a *pamonha*, a sweet corn cake akin to a tamale, frames the magical process in more familiar terms for Brazilian readers while precluding foreigners without Brazilian culinary knowledge from completely understanding the reference.

Similarly, by alluding to an origin tale common throughout the Americas, the scene of the enchanted bath exemplifies the duality of communicating across cultures and maintaining a degree of particularism.[26] At the beginning of their journey to São Paulo, the brothers came across a pool of water. Macunaíma entered first and, "quando o herói saiu do banho estava branco louro e de olhos azuizinhos, água lavara o pretume dele" (when the hero left the bath, he was white blond and blue-eyed, the water had washed away his blackness; Andrade, *Macunaíma* 37). Bathing after Macunaíma, the middle brother Jiguê "só conseguiu ficar da cor do bronze novo" (only managed to become the color of new bronze; 37). As the last brother to enter the water, "Maanape conseguiu molhar só a palma dos pés e das mãos. Por isso ficou negro bem filho da tribo dos Tapanhumas. Só que as palmas das mãos e dos pés dele são vermelhas por terem se limpado na água santa" (Maanape managed to soak only the palms of his feet and hands. So, he stayed black, very much a son of the Tapanhuma tribe. Yet the palms of his hands and feet are red for having been cleaned in the sacred water; 37).

This passage contains localized knowledge of Amazonian tales of enchantment and race in Brazil without footnotes or explanatory asides that would make it more comprehensible to readers unfamiliar with the cultural context. As in other folktales about the distinct racial makeup of the Americas, "os três manos um louro um vermelho outro negro" (the three brothers one blond one red one black) represent the European, Amerindian, and African peoples of Brazil (38).[27] According to David Haberly's reading of race in *Macunaíma*, the transformation of the hero from a dark-skinned Amerindian to a white man means that he "is at once black and red and white" (*Three Sad Races* 153), a simultaneity of racial identities that Haberly suggests Mário de Andrade felt within himself (138). The narrative thus reveals the complicated relationship of Brazil to European "civilizing" discourses and ideas of race. Integrating elements of oral storytelling, such as simple sentence structures and the use of the diminutive, into written Brazilian Portuguese helps to establish the idea of a shared cultural inheritance across the Americas. However, without understanding Brazil's constructs of race that would give rise to the myth of racial democracy, the dynamics of racial identities and relations at play in this episode fall flat.

The use of travel as the narrative's organizing principle allows tensions between cross-cultural dialogue and resistance to translation to further unfold. After reaching São Paulo, Macunaíma's travels jump between distant parts of Brazil. He travels by train to Rio de Janeiro to attend a Macumba ceremony, where he asks Exu to make the giant Piaimã suffer (Andrade, *Macunaíma* 56–64). The text depicts the ceremony by integrating Afro-Brazilian *orixás* and rhythmic chants.[28] The scene refers to Tia Ciata, a key historical figure of Afro-Brazilian culture, and the "macumbeiros," consisting of avant-garde writers Raul Bopp and Manuel Bandeira (64).[29] This fictional ceremony opens up a space for communication between different peoples while preserving a degree of cultural difference. Readers must draw on personal knowledge or critical studies to understand fully the scene with its references to Afro-Brazilian deities and prominent Brazilian artists. After this ceremony, the hero travels in a single night via a series of surreal displacements from Rio de Janeiro to the island of Marajó in the north to the Paraná River in the south before returning to the Guanabara Bay (65–68). This dreamlike trajectory contrasts with earlier journeys of scientific exploration through contiguous geographies. Later in the novel, when escaping from Piaimã's wife, Macunaíma jumps on a horse that rapidly takes him to Manaus, then Mendoza in Argentina before heading north again to French Guyana. As the chase ensues, Macunaíma abandons the horse for a bird and then an airplane, fantastically passing through, among other geographies, the brush near Natal, the plateaus of Minas Gerais, and the São Francisco and Tietê Rivers, before returning to the São Paulo boarding house (106–09). These travels bring lands, languages, and peoples together textually to generate radical forms of dislocation that require linguistic and cultural translations in order for Macunaíma to comprehend differences between his Amazonian home and the modern metropolis of São Paulo.

The novel's ninth chapter, "Carta pras Icamiabas," in which Macunaíma deciphers São Paulo for the Amazonian women who finance his travels, exemplifies how displacement necessitates translation. The letter marks a stylistic shift as Macunaíma attempts to write in a formal manner that parodies Pero Vaz de Caminha's letter exclaiming the riches of Brazil to the Portuguese king Dom Manuel I in 1500. Macunaíma's letter exaggerates the conventions of formalized written Portuguese, specifically its use of *vós*, honorifics, and florid language, to describe, with humorous effect, the glories of modernizing São Paulo. Triumphant claims that "vivem e prosperam os paulistas na mais perfeita ordem e progresso"

(Paulistas live and prosper in the most perfect order and progress; 82) contrast with the confusion Macunaíma experiences in the city when he mistakes cars for cougars upon first seeing the unfamiliar machines (40). The letter glosses over the city's negative elements to portray it as a space worthy of investment by evoking, in a somewhat cynical manner, Brazil's national motto of "order and progress." In writing the letter, Macunaíma emerges as, per Melo's analysis, a transculturator who reframes urban culture that he encounters in terms of more familiar rural experiences ("*Macunaíma*" 210). As a process of cultural interaction that results in something new, transculturation parallels an idea of translation as re-creation rather than duplication. Both concepts recognize the impossibility of cultural assimilation and reproducibility, but to different ends. Whereas narrative transculturation in Ángel Rama's view aims to make cultural difference legible, translation in Mário de Andrade's practice allows for cross-cultural exchange that resists rendering particularities easily intelligible.

Reading Macunaíma's letter as an attempt to translate São Paulo for Amazonian women recalls José Luiz Passos's comparative analysis of the texts by Caminha and Macunaíma as spaces of encounter. According to Passos, "o texto de Caminha é ao mesmo tempo tradução da diferença e primeiro espelho da nação brasileira" (Caminha's text is at the same time translation of difference and the Brazilian nation's first mirror; 110). As a colonizing document, Caminha's letter represented the Americas by means of European terms in a dynamic of copy and original that Silviano Santiago explores with his concept of the space in-between, which I further examine in the next chapter. Given the parallels that Passos identifies in the two letters, Macunaíma's letter also gestures toward translating difference as a way to negotiate binaries of traditional and modern, rural and urban, popular and erudite, or national and foreign. Rather than meld together into a uniform nation, these contradictory realms coexist in Brazil. Passos concludes that Macunaíma's letter serves as "uma ação simbólica que denuncia um projeto histórico—e linguístico—de hegemonia cultural baseado na mistura" (a symbolic action that denounces a historic—and linguistic—project of cultural hegemony based on mixture; 121). The letter to the Icamiabas and *Macunaíma* illustrate both the possibilities and the limits of Mário's work as translator of diverse spoken languages and popular cultures.

Mário de Andrade's efforts to approximate orality in a written literary narrative would prove challenging to translate into other languages.

He aimed to depict common forms of pronouncing Brazilian Portuguese through orthographic changes, writing *faiz, rapaiz,* and *nóis* rather than *faz, rapaz,* and *nós* (Andrade, Macunaíma 17, 63) to capture diphthongization (Azevedo 51). To indicate the pronunciation of unstressed vowels in Brazilian Portuguese, Mário substituted /i/ for /e/ and /u/ for /o/, writing *si* for *se* and *enguliu* for *engoliu* (Andrade, Macunaíma 153).[30] Diminutives and abbreviations heighten the texture of orality in the prose, as evidenced with phrases "té-loguinho" (113), instead of *até logo* (until later), and "Vam'bora, gente!" (101), rather than "Vamos embora, gente!" (Let's go, people!). Placing the verb between the repetition of a nasalized no evokes rhythms of speech, as in Macunaíma "não chorou não" (no, he didn't cry; 17). Repetitions of entire phrases, such as "E Venceslau Pietro Pietra era o gigante Piaimã comedor de gente" (And Venceslau Pietro Pietra was the giant Piaimã eater of people; 42, 49), remind readers of key plot elements. Exclamations "É fome é fome!" (It's hunger it's hunger; 141) or reiterations "caminhou caminhou" (he walked he walked; 107) provide emphasis by accumulation. The sentences serve as refrains that indicate the tendency for repetition when telling a story.

Attempting to render oral expressions into written language raises questions about the limitations of literarily representing popular tales and ways of speaking. Near the novel's end, the repetition of the phrase "tem mais não" (ain't no more; 161, 168), which follows a typical form of negation in vernacular Brazilian Portuguese, points to the orality of the text and its finality.[31] This idea of nothing else reappears in the epilogue with "nenhum conhecido sobre a terra não sabia nem falar na fala da tribo" (no one known on earth knew even how to speak the tribe's speech; 167). Due to this disappearance of the indigenous language, the narrator ponders, "Quem que podia saber do herói?" (Who could know about the hero?; 167). The novel's existence implies that Macunaíma's tale was not forgotten among lost languages but rather transformed into a written narrative. Lamenting the loss of indigenous languages and recognizing the value of specific stories point to an awareness of what Doris Sommer describes as the need to proceed with caution when interacting with minority literatures. Heeding this warning, the novel relates Macunaíma's tale without resorting to world literature's tendency of "homogenizing difference, flattening forms, and minimizing cultural untranslatability" (Apter, *Against* 328). To depict the specificities of Brazilian and Amerindian experiences, the text engages in linguistic and cultural translations as it resists forms of appropriation and assimilation.

While the narrator's question hints at a resistance to facile communication of indigenous tales, the appearance of a parrot who hears and shares Macunaíma's story contests such limits. The novel ends with the parrot's transmission of the tale to the narrator: "Tudo ele contou pro homem. . . . E o homem sou eu, minha gente, e eu fiquei pra vos contar a história. Por isso vim aqui . . . ponteei na violinha e em toque rasgado botei a boca no mundo cantando na fala impura as frases e os casos de Macunaíma, herói de nossa gente. Tem mais não" (Everything he told to the man. . . . And the man is me, my people, and I hung around to tell you the story. That's why I'm here . . . I strummed my little guitar, and, in an open tuning, I cast my mouth into the world singing in impure language the phrases and events of Macunaíma, the hero of our people. Ain't no more; Andrade, *Macunaíma* 168). The parrot salvages Macunaíma's story, told in a language that no longer exists, by passing it on to a man who documents it in written Portuguese. This transfer features the parrot and the narrator as translators who move between indigenous languages and Portuguese, between species, and between spoken and written language to extend the reach of Macunaíma's story. The use of the first-person subject pronoun *eu* and the verb *contar* (to tell) highlight the narrator's key role in transmitting Macunaíma's tale as a storyteller and writer interested in the imperfections of popular expressions. The movement from Macunaíma to the parrot to the narrator is analogous to the text's trajectory from Amerindian tales to Koch-Grünberg's documentation to Mário de Andrade's masterpiece.[32] The avant-garde narrative that resulted from these textual transformations challenges subsequent translators of *Macunaíma* into other national languages, as I examine further in the next section.

Macunaíma in Translation: Limitations and Possibilities of Literary Transcreation

Debates about *Macunaíma*'s translatability have circulated since its publication in letters between Mário de Andrade and his contemporaries, critical studies, and reviews of existing translations. During his lifetime, Mário communicated with potential translators of *Macunaíma* into English, Spanish, and German, reading and commenting on translations that remained unpublished. Correspondence with English-language translator Margaret Richardson Hollingsworth from 1930 to 1936 discussed the difficulties of translating *Macunaíma* and the limitations of the publishing industry. Argentine artist Carybé with Raúl Brié completed their Spanish translation of the novel in 1944, but it was never published. Carybé's accompanying illustrations were included in later Brazilian editions.[33] German Brazilian translator Ignez Teltsche translated chapter 15 of *Macunaíma*, which appeared in her 1938 anthology of Brazilian literature *Von der brasilianischen Seele*. She also conversed with Mário about translation and Brazilian and German literatures. These exchanges underscored the difficulties of translating *Macunaíma* into other national languages and the constraints of the literary market but did not rule out the possibility of the novel's translation.

Critical studies and artistic adaptations of *Macunaíma*, most notably the 1969 film by Joaquim Pedro de Andrade, contributed to the novel's visibility in Brazil from the 1950s to 1980s. The film version, which I analyze further in the next section, helped the character Macunaíma reach a broader audience in Brazil and beyond its geographic and linguistic borders. It was only after the release of the film that the novel was first published in translation with Giuliana Segre Giorgi's 1970 Italian version. Translations into other Romance languages followed shortly thereafter, with Héctor Olea's 1977 Spanish transcreation and Jacques Thiériot's 1979 French translation.[34] Despite the delay in publishing translations of the novel and the difficulties that its translators continue to face, *Macunaíma* has become Mário de Andrade's most translated work. Translations were published in German (1982), Hungarian (1983), Polish (1983), English (1984), and Danish (1989). More recently, *Macunaíma* has been translated into Czech (1998), Korean (2016), and Japanese (2013 and 2017). With translations into eleven national languages, *Macunaíma* is not, despite David Haberly's assessment, "utterly untranslatable" (*Three Sad Races* 146). A closer look at Mário's thoughts on translating the novel and the translations' critical receptions reveals the potential and the limits of translating seemingly untranslatable works.

Mário questioned whether it would be possible to render *Macunaíma*'s tonal nuance and linguistic and cultural specificities into another national language. He also considered whether it would be a challenge to find a market for his works in translation in his response to D. B. Richardson's November 1930 inquiry about his daughter Margaret translating *Macunaíma*. Noting that his books would test her translation skills, Mário stated he was "quasi certo que a sra. Hollingsworth desistiria de traduzir 'Macunaíma'" (almost certain that Mrs. Hollingsworth would quit translating *Macunaíma*; IEB-USP Archive, MA-C-CAL518, 1). Despite this skepticism, he offered to help her by translating certain Brazilian phrases and reviewing translated chapters so that he could "auxiliá-la na perfeita transposição para o inglês, do espírito e carácter desse livro" (aid her in the perfect transposition to English, of this book's spirit and character; 3). While the idea of translation as a "perfect transposition" may seem to prioritize fidelity, Mário's emerging theory of translation resonates with Haroldo de Campos's concept of transcreation. Both writers recognized that translating involves creatively transposing and transforming words and sounds to render images and rhythms from one language into another. They approached this question from different angles: Mário as a writer advising possible translators, and Campos as a poet and critic exploring creative agency through translation.

Details of contracts, publishers, and payments often prevailed in the communication between Mário de Andrade, D. B. Richardson, and Margaret Richardson Hollingsworth, with translation as craft and theory mentioned only minimally. Hollingsworth discussed the translation of *Macunaíma* more openly early in her correspondence, before shifting her attention to legal and financial concerns in later letters. Her first letter outlined her domesticating approach to translation as she explained, "I have modified the book occasionally in places where I considered it might be a trifle Rabelaisian for the American taste and also where I thought that there were too many difficult words (Portuguese or Indian ones) for the public to pronounce" (IEB-USP Archive, MA-C-CPL3674). Hollingsworth viewed translation as a mechanism for stylistic and linguistic flattening that would allow narratives of distant others to circulate in the Anglophone market. In refusing to accept the slap of difference demanded by *Macunaíma*'s creative rendering of Amerindian tales, she created a translation that, at least initially, failed to meet Mário's hopes for a "perfect transposition" of the novel's spirit.

In contrast, Mário remained invested in the question of how to translate linguistic and cultural specificities into other languages in discussions with poet Manuel Bandeira about the novel's translatability. Bandeira urged his friend in an August 28, 1930, letter to use caution when negotiating a potential translation contract with Monteiro Lobato, a Brazilian writer best known for his children's books. Writing from New York on August 6, 1930, Lobato expressed interest in helping translate *Macunaíma* for publication in the United States. Given the self-importance of Lobato's claim that he would "sair da cova só para isso" (leave his cave only for this; IEB-USP Archive, MA-C-CPL, 4331), Bandeira was astute to warn Mário to approach the translation of *Macunaíma* with care. According to Bandeira, "Não é verdade que *Macunaíma* seja intraduzível. É intraduzível em toda a sua expressão tão gostosa, mas isso não é de longe o cerne da obra. . . . ele valerá para o estrangeiro como um formidável repositório de populário brasileiro apresentado . . . como matéria viva" (It is not true that *Macunaíma* is untranslatable. It is untranslatable in all its quite delightful expression, but this is not by far the kernel of the work. . . . It will be valuable abroad as a formidable repository of Brazilian folklore presented . . . as living matter; IEB-USP Archive, MA-C-CPL1114). For Bandeira, innovative expressions and cultural allusions impeded the text's accessibility, but did not make it entirely untranslatable. He posited that translation could help to remove excessive colloquialisms from the prose. Bandeira approached what he considered untranslatable in *Macunaíma* as a challenge that needed to be neutralized so that the novel could reach a broader readership. For Mário, however, the specificity of writing Brazilian by incorporating Tupi words, altering the lexicon, and otherwise innovating language was one of his key goals. Leaving unfamiliar words and references unexplained would force readers from southeastern Brazil to experience linguistic and cultural misunderstandings that result from displacement without traveling to the Amazon or the *sertão*.

When tasked with facilitating the translation of *Macunaíma* into another language, Mário acknowledged that the absence of explanatory notes could limit a translator's ability to capture the text's complexities. Writing to Bandeira on December 12, 1930, Mário expressed concerns about Hollingsworth's relative unfamiliarity with the languages and cultures of Brazil: "Não creio que ela consiga reproduzir a essência poema-herói-cômico, do livro" (I do not believe that she can manage to reproduce the book's comical-heroic-poetic essence; Andrade, *Macunaíma* 412). In an effort to alleviate his worries, he sent her extensive notes defining indigenous words and Brazilian phrases and suggesting how to translate certain expressions into English. The notes function mostly as a glossary of popular Brazilian sayings, localized vocabulary, and Amerindian myths.[35] Other entries reveal a philosophy of translation as Mário commented on whether an expression or a scene should be transposed, translated literally, or elided. He deemed certain expressions in Brazilian Portuguese untranslatable and recommended that they be transferred into an Anglo-American equivalent, as in the case of "dandar." After defining the verb as part of a popular Brazilian phrase that adults say to children to get them to walk, Mário noted that "a frase é intraduzível. Tem de ser transposta, pois só tem sentido como está, pra quem conhece o folclore luso-brasileiro" (the phrase is untranslatable. It has to be transposed, since it only makes sense as it is for those who know Luso-Brazilian folklore; 387). He posited transposition of culturally specific terms and references as a way to resolve supposed untranslatability.

The verb "transportar" (to transport, to carry, or to transfer) appears throughout the notes, usually in opposition to "traduzir" (to translate), to indicate when the translator should prioritize sense and sound over literal meanings. Mário encouraged the translator to aim for similar poetic effects and sonorities in English when transposing onomatopoetic or interjective phrases, series of household items, lists of geographic places, and dialogues with popular expressions (387, 388, 390). The notes identified scenes, like the Macumba ceremony, whose intense cultural specificity and linguistic innovation would prove difficult to translate, and urged the translator to parallel the original's inventiveness via re-creations and transformations (391). Mário thus anticipated Haroldo de Campos's approach to translation by recommending creative transposition, that is, transcreation, as the desired mode of translating *Macunaíma*. Other notes invited the translator to omit sexually explicit sections deemed too risqué and immoral for North American readers.[36] This view of Anglophone readers' sensibilities implies an awareness of the limits that publishers place on texts in translation, especially as the industry contracted due to global economic depression.

Hollingsworth thanked Mário for these translation notes in a February 12, 1931, letter, but her subsequent letters focused mostly on the contract and the financial strains in publishing. In a June 2, 1931, letter to Sebastião Sampaio, who mediated exchanges about the contract in his role as Brazilian consulate general of New York, Hollingsworth observed, "The book market has suffered from the depression and it is very difficult to get a book published even though the author be well-known" (IEB-USP Archive, MA-C-CTL42). Achieving editorial success by translating an experimental Brazilian writer during an economic depression was a daunting task. Hollingsworth received tepid interest after sharing her translations of *Macunaíma*'s first chapters with publishers who, according to her December 4, 1931, letter to Mário, "seem to think that, although the book is interesting, unusual and even poetic, that the sale at the present time would not be sufficient to warrant publication" (IEB-USP Archive, MA-C-CPL3681). Following publishing's preference for accessible narratives, Hollingsworth opted to translate Mário's more conventional 1927 novel *Amar, verbo intransitivo*, which Macaulay published as *Fräulein* in 1933. Motivated by the economic logic of the literary market, Hollingsworth opted to delay her translation of *Macunaíma* until after *Fräulein* had helped to establish Mário de Andrade as a recognizable name among Anglo-American readers. Her hope that the translation's success would establish a path toward publication for *Macunaíma* never came to fruition, given the dire state of the North American publishing industry in the 1930s and, more critically, the radical differences between the two novels and their potential readers.

Mário continued to underscore the challenges of translating *Macunaíma* in his letters to Hollingsworth. On October 25, 1931, he insisted that his novel "é uma obra tão fora dos limites comuns ou gerais da literatura, que naturalmente fica em mim uma curiosidade inquieta, tanto mais que tantos brasileiros como estrangeiros que o conhecem, o afirmam intraduzível. Não creio que seja intraduzível" (is a work so outside of the common or general limits of literature that naturally an uneasy curiosity remains in me, even more so since Brazilians, as well as foreigners familiar with it, say it's untranslatable. I do not believe that it is untranslatable; IEB-USP Archive, MA-C-CAL, 254). Mário echoed Bandeira's assessment that the text was not entirely untranslatable, but rather its originality created difficulties for potential translators. Given these challenges, Mário wanted to read a sample of Hollingsworth's translation to have a better sense of her abilities. He requested chapter 15 in order to compare her work to Ignez Teltscher's translation into German. Hollingsworth responded over a month later claiming that she would send a translated chapter, although not the requested one, on the next boat (IEB-USP Archive, MA-C-CPL3681). A translation of chapter 6 reached Mário over a year after he asked to see chapter 15.[37] Throughout their exchange, Hollingsworth tended to delay direct engagement with translation. At first, she attributed her shift of focus to *Amar, verbo intransitivo* to pressures of the market, only to acknowledge later the difficulties of translating *Macunaíma*. On March 17, 1933, she informed Mário that she had started to work on *Macunaíma* again since the Macaulay Company wanted to see it (IEB-USP Archive, MA-C-CPL3684). The next month, publication was no longer her main concern as she admitted that *Macunaíma* "is a very difficult book to translate" that would benefit from Mário's consultation (MA-C-CPL3685).

More interested in commerce than craft, Hollingsworth failed to develop a personal theory of translation. Her comments on the difficulty of translating *Macunaíma* tended to address its accessibility for readers in the United States. By equating a novel's translatability with its readability, Hollingsworth subscribed to a view of the global literary market that privileged universalisms and tended to flatten cultural particularisms. She domesticated texts in translation via what she characterized as small changes to make books more accessible and publishable in the United States (Andrade, *Macunaíma* 414). After reading reviews of her translation *Fräulein*, Mário lamented, "Parece porém que ela deformou muito certas coisas e isso me traz meio divertidamente assustado" (It seems, however, that she deformed many certain things, and this leaves me, somewhat amusingly, afraid; 414). The worries he conveyed in this August 6, 1933, letter to Bandeira extended to *Macunaíma*, especially since Hollingsworth appeared to prioritize market success over considering how best to convey in English the novel's tone and cultural specificities. Publishers nevertheless decided to pass on *Macunaíma* because, as she told Mário in an August 5, 1935, letter, they "felt that it was too unusual for the present" (IEB-USP Archive, MA-C-CPL3691). Their evaluation of *Macunaíma* as "too unusual" pointed to its originality as a text that did not conform to the modes of social realism or escapist romance that US publishers tended to prefer during the Depression.

Translators have not always respected the text's resistance to flattening difference, resulting in translations with varied editorial and critical success. The relative "boom" in translating *Macunaíma* during the 1970s and 1980s occurred after a renewed interest in the text due to its public rediscovery through artistic adaptations and critical interpretations.[38] It also coincided with the end of the Latin American Boom as a publishing phenomenon, which primarily manifested itself in the publication of translations of works by Spanish American writers Gabriel García Márquez, Mario Vargas Llosa, and Carlos Fuentes, among others. English-language translations of Brazilian writers Jorge Amado, Machado de Assis, and Clarice Lispector appeared in this period in a more limited fashion.[39] This publishing landscape unfolded in a geopolitical context of the Cold War where interventions of the United States in Latin America served to generate interest in the languages, cultures, and histories of Brazil and its neighboring countries among North Americans.

Against this backdrop, Héctor Olea and E. A. Goodland presented two divergent approaches to translating *Macunaíma* in the Americas. Whereas Olea's 1977 Spanish transcreation reveals a potential for subverting linguistic hierarchies by translating between Iberian languages rather than into more prominent western European languages, Goodland's 1984 English version underscores the dangers of translating the meanings of words literally without accounting for tone and cultural specificities. The differences between these translations exemplify distinct theories and methods of translation. With a preface from Haroldo de Campos, the Spanish version explicitly embraced transcreation as Olea experimented with language to capture the sonic and semiotic qualities of Mário's renderings of popular and indigenous expressions. Biblioteca Ayacucho's 1979 publication of Mário de Andrade's selected works included *Macunaíma* in its "transcreación al español de Héctor Olea" (transcreation to the Spanish by Héctor Olea; vi). Gilda de Mello e Souza compiled insights from previous scholarship and Mário's translation notes for an introduction to the Ayacucho edition that replaced Campos's preface and Olea's epilogue from the earlier Seix Barral edition. Isabel Gómez astutely claims that pairing these notes with Olea's version in the Ayacucho edition results in the coexistence of incompatible manuals of thick translation and transcreation, which correspond to the paradoxes of cultural hybridity inherent in *Macunaíma*.[40] Olea's transcreation successfully extended the reach of a Brazilian novel to a Spanish American readership by emphasizing Macunaíma's place in a shared geography and culture of the Americas with parallels between Afro-Brazilian Macumba and Cuban Santería or the *bumba-meu-boi* dance of the Brazilian *sertão* and the Mesoamerican *danza de torito*.

Unlike the Spanish translation, which benefits from cultural similarities and an effort to recover a shared Latin American past, Goodland's English-language translation suffers from his limited familiarity with the novel's linguistic and cultural context. His stay in Guyana shaped his knowledge of Amazonian peoples and cultures, resulting in an indirect and relatively limited exposure to Brazilian Portuguese and Amerindian languages. The resulting translation prioritizes literal meanings over the rhythms and connotations of popular expressions. At times, the translation aims to shock with vulgar language not included in the original, such as rendering Macunaíma's repeated lament of laziness "Ai! que preguiça!" as "Aw! What a fucking life!" (Andrade, *Macunaíma* 3). This phrase conveys a playful bilingual pleonasm, given that "ai" or "aig" means sloth in Tupi and "preguiça" denotes laziness or sloth in Portuguese.[41] "Ah, what laziness" is a literal rendering of the expression, but more idiomatic possibilities include Renata Wasserman's "I feel sooo lazy . . ." ("Preguiça and Power" 99), K. David Jackson's "Ai! I'm bushed!" ("Literary

Criticism" 331), and Albert Braz's "Ah, I'm pooped!" ("Traducing the Author"). None of these options capture the joke of the Tupi-Portuguese phrase, but they more accurately reflect the original's sensibility. With his unnecessary use of profanity, Goodland characterizes Macunaíma more crassly as an uncouth hero fed up with life in a tonal change that fails to account for nuances of irony and humor. He thus fell into traps that Mário de Andrade feared would mark Hollingsworth's translation into English. Goodland's English-language rendition exemplifies a mode of translating *Macunaíma* in the Americas that contrasts with Olea's Spanish transcreation and, moreover, reveals the limitations of literal translations over what Mário envisioned as the "perfect transposition" of the novel's spirit.[42] The critiques of Goodland's translation suggest the need for creative transformations for the circulation of Macunaíma as text and character in the Anglo-American context.

Transmutations of *Macunaíma* from Page to Screen

Macunaíma invites adaptations and rewritings to extend the tale's visibility beyond Amerindian and Brazilian cultures. Director Joaquim Pedro de Andrade's 1969 film exemplifies how adapting the text into another medium allows *Macunaíma* to reach a broader audience, especially outside of Brazil. In transforming Mário's narrative into film, Joaquim Pedro created an intersemiotic translation, or what Roman Jakobson terms a transmutation. Similarly, Haroldo de Campos envisioned breaking words into their linguistic parts and bringing those components into another language via creative transposition, which he terms re-creation or transcreation. This concept provides a bridge between Jakobson's linguistic approach to translation and Julio Plaza's discussions of intersemiotic translation from a Brazilian context in his 1987 study *Tradução intersemiótica*. For Plaza, intersemiotic translation attempts to understand how distinct sign systems work to better analyze the transmutations of forms that unfold when transferring between novels, films, or other media (84). His view of translation as a critical and creative practice between different semiotic systems proves useful to reading the film as an intersemiotic translation of the text.

Two foundational studies, Randal Johnson's 1982 *Literatura e cinema: Macunaíma: do modernismo ao Cinema Novo* and Heloísa Buarque de Hollanda's 1978 *Macunaíma: da literatura ao cinema*, discuss translation as a potential mode for analyzing transformations that unfold in the shift of *Macunaíma* from page to screen. Referring to the film as the novel's "tradução fílmica" (filmic translation) allows Johnson to draw on theories of translation in an analysis that foregrounds the differences between how literature and cinema communicate (22). Divergences exist between the novel and the film given that, as Johnson rightly contends, "o cineasta radicalizou e levou a suas últimas consequências determinados elementos do romance, notadamente o canibalismo" (the filmmaker radicalized and carried to their ultimate consequences certain elements of the novel, notably cannibalism; 4). This radicalization involves employing a visually explicit style, concretizing magical elements, and identifying an external impetus for remaining changes, such as Macunaíma's momentary appearance as a prince when smoking marijuana and his permanent transformation into a white man after the enchanted bath. In doing so, Joaquim Pedro removed the tale from a mythical realm and situated it in the political climate of the 1960s.

Scholars as well as the director have turned to a critical grammar of translation to describe the relationship of the text to the film. In his compelling analysis, Johnson claims that the film as "a segunda obra, a tradução, ganha significância autônoma precisamente através de suas inevitáveis e necessárias divergências da obra original" (the second work, the translation, gains autonomous meaning precisely through its inevitable and necessary divergences from the original work; 10). This idea of the film accumulating meaning via creative derivation from the literary work recalls Benjamin's view of translation as the continued life of an original text, as well as approaches from Borges and Campos to translation as a form of rewriting and re-creation. Buarque de Hollanda comments on this tendency to conflate adaptation with translation in studies of the film: "O que significa adaptar? Seria viável, como desejava Mário de Andrade, submeter-se realmente à estrutura do pensamento fabular? Seria desejável que Joaquim Pedro se empenhasse na tradução da rapsódia para o cinema? De qualquer forma, é possível a tradução ou a transposição literal?" (What does it mean to adapt? Would it be viable, as Mário de Andrade desired, to really conform to the thought structure of fables? Would it be desirable that Joaquim Pedro exerted himself in the rhapsody's translation to film? In any case, is translation or literal transposition possible?; 53). In suggesting that both text and film function as adaptations, Buarque de Hollanda presents a comparative analysis drawing on ideas of intersemiotic translation. Similarly, in the undated "Argumento cinematográfico" (Cinematographic argument), Joaquim Pedro de Andrade describes writing and cinematography in terms of translation: "A maior força expressiva do cinema está no que se vê, e a descrição de formas em movimento, feita por meio de palavras, estará sempre longe de poder traduzir a linguagem plástica dos filmes" (The most expressive force of cinema is in what is seen, and the description of forms in movement, made through words, will always be far from able to translate the plastic language of films; Cinemateca Brasileira Archive, GR-SC.12/003 3). The director realizes how cinematographic language exceeds verbal forms and posits that movements between textual and filmic language should test translation's limits.

Following Buarque de Hollanda's observation that the literary work rationalizes the mythical and the film concretizes the text's magical elements (56), it is possible to read each phase in the transcreation of *Macunaíma* as an attempt to render it more legible to a broader public. The shift from Amerindian myths to Koch-Grünberg's ethnographic account to Mário de Andrade's modernist narrative introduced indigenous and popular stories to an elite readership. Substituting the novel's magical transformations for drug-induced shifts in perception make the film more relatable for its likely audience in the 1960s and 1970s. To contextualize the film in the era's sociopolitical landscape, scenes unfold in Rio de Janeiro with Ci, the novel's mother of the forest, engaging in urban guerrilla warfare.[43] By replacing the modernizing São Paulo of the novel with a politically charged Rio de Janeiro, the film responds to the period's political climate and accounts for international viewers' greater recognition of Rio de Janeiro.

These changes result in a more overtly political film that exemplifies and critiques Brazil's ambiguous relationship with the consumption that fuels industrial capitalism. In the text "Cannibalism and Self-Cannibalism," which was initially written to introduce the film at the 1969 Venice Film Festival, Joaquim Pedro de Andrade characterizes the film as "the story of a Brazilian devoured by Brazil" (83). The director emphasizes how acts of consumption shape Macunaíma's filmic trajectory in a capitalist world where one could either eat or be eaten.[44] Similarly foregrounding questions of consumption, Buarque de Hollanda finds the difference between the two works rooted in their political stakes as she notes, "Joaquim, entretanto, transforma o livro afetivo e melancólico de Mário de Andrade num filme incisivo, crítico e pessimista" (Joaquim, meanwhile, transforms the affective and melancholic book by Mário de Andrade into an incisive, critical, and pessimistic film; 72). Her reading corresponds with the film's reception when released in 1969 in a Brazil where the 1964 military coup and the 1968 decree of the Fifth Institutional Act (AI-5), which fortified military control over the country, remained fresh wounds. Critics outside of Brazil, including Johnson and J. R. Molotnik, whose 1976 *Jump Cut* review examines how the film's farcical tone critiques capitalist excess, echo Buarque de Hollanda's interpretation of the film as more explicitly political than the novel. These critics present compelling readings of the film's political stakes, but they tend to minimize or overlook the politics inherent in Mário de Andrade's modernist transcreation of indigenous and popular tales and traditions. In theorizing its own limited translatability, the novel indicates the potential for communicating across cultures and, at the same, the resistance to making cultural difference and local knowledge easily accessible.

Through the use of nonverbal language with visual imagery and musical cues, the film introduced the hero Macunaíma to a broader audience. While film generally remained most available to middle- or upper-class city dwellers in Brazil, *Macunaíma* enjoyed relative commercial success as one of Brazil's top twenty-five box office earners from 1968 to 1973.[45] Stylistically, the film employs vibrant colors, often associated with Brazil's image as a tropical paradise, and playful flourishes, such as the young Macunaíma briefly transforming into a blond prince dressed in a multicolored tunic and tights. These exaggerated aesthetics situate the film in a realm typical of popular genres of chanchadas that contrasts with the relative visual scarcity of realism and earlier phases of Cinema Novo.[46] Casting Grande Otelo, an actor best known for his roles in chanchadas from the late 1930s to the 1950s and in Nelson Pereira dos Santos's *Rio, Zona Norte* (1957), as the young Macunaíma allows the film to engage with popular genres and to question conventional representations of race, age, and gender.[47] The film opens with a white mother, played by Paulo José, giving birth to Grande Otelo's middle-aged, black Macunaíma (see fig. 2.2 on page 94). The actors' roles do not remain fixed throughout the film with Paulo José playing Macunaíma after he emerges from the enchanted bath as a white man. Grande Otelo reappears in the film as the infant son born to white parents, Macunaíma and Ci, in casting that subverts racial assumptions and ignores the logic of aging to read as comical.

Critics Robert Stam, João Luiz Vieira, and Ismail Xavier rightly associate Grande Otelo's multiple roles with the film's tropicalist reuse of earlier forms, noting, "The socially conscious recycling of chanchada actors (Grande Otelo, Zezé Macedo), music, and strategies enabled

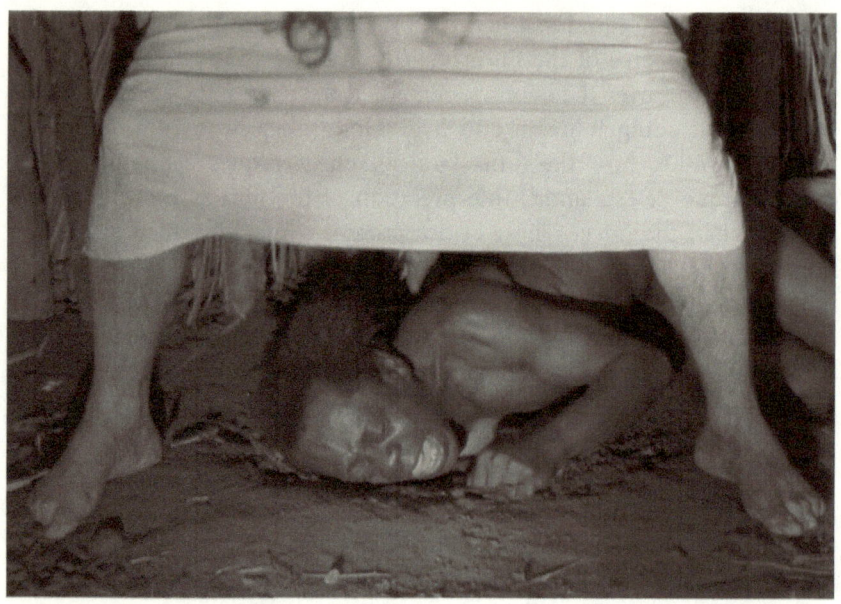

Figure 2.2. Grande Otelo as Macunaíma in the 1969 film *Macunaíma*.

Macunaíma, especially, to realize . . . the reconciliation of political and aesthetic avant-gardism with popular and box-office appeal" (402). The film thus extends *Macunaíma*'s reach to a larger audience in Brazil than had access to the novel. In addition to this relative commercial success in Brazil, *Macunaíma* received critical acclaim in national and international venues. The film won prizes in Brazil in 1969 for best film, best screenplay, best cinematography, best actor for Grande Otelo and for Paulo José, and best director, as awarded by the National Film Institute, the Museum of Image and Sound of Rio de Janeiro, and festivals in Brasília, Manaus, and Marília.[48] The film received the prize for best film at the International Film Festival of Mar del Plata (Argentina) in 1970 and an award for best screenplay at the Cinema Novo Festival in New York in 1972. When the Cinemateca Brasileira created a list in 1988 of the thirty most significant films in the history of Brazilian cinema, *Macunaíma* ranked seventh.[49] These recognitions confirm the film's continued reception as a critical success with relatively widespread distribution that has heightened the national and global visibility of the trickster Macunaíma.

Whereas Mário de Andrade's text never explicitly characterizes Macunaíma as Brazilian, the film foregrounds visually and sonically themes of national identity. Expressions of nationality could help to make the film comprehensible at international film festivals and art-house cinemas as a particular vision of an exotic Brazil. The opening credits roll over an abstract, aerial illustration of a forest composed of shades of green and yellow, the colors of Brazil. Heitor Villa-Lobos's 1936 composition "Desfile aos heróis do Brasil" (Parade to Brazil's heroes), a lively and patriotic *marcha*, accompanies the opening and closing credits that mark the beginning and end of Macunaíma's life.[50] Dedicated to the "heróis desta terra / esta pátria querida que é o nosso Brasil" (heroes of this land / this dear country that is our Brazil), the song underscores, with irony, the themes of Brazilian identity and nationalism in the film. The *marcha* praises the glory of traditional heroes, whereas the film depicts the life of Macunaíma, the hero without any character or, as the film's director suggests, with bad character. After the credits and song end, the film fades to black and then cuts to a red screen as the narrator, in off, recites the novel's opening, beginning the same with "no fundo do mato-virgem" (deep in the virgin forest) before substituting the novel's declarative "nasceu Macunaíma, herói de nossa gente" (Macunaíma, hero of our people, was born) with the more descriptive "houve um silêncio tão grande, escutando o murmurejo do Uraricoeira, que . . ." (there was such a vast silence, listening to the murmuring of the Uraricoeira, that . . .). A guttural scream interrupts the narration as the film cuts to a scene inside of a shack to reveal the source of the sound: a masculine-looking woman giving birth to Macunaíma as a full-grown man.

This sequence introduces Macunaíma as an unlikely hero of Brazilians, a reading that the distribution and reception of the film abroad furthered. In the United States, New Line Cinema first distributed the film in 1972 as a dubbed version titled *Jungle Freaks*. Promotional materials underscored the film's playful and bawdy sensibilities by advertising it as "95 minutes of Brazil nuts" with brightly colored cartoon images of tropical birds, sexualized women, and a ticking time bomb. Situating the film as a fun romp facilitated its distribution in the United States by the same company that released John Waters's films. Viewers were promised an exotic, unserious film that depicted Brazilians as wild and erotic, which contrasted with the political and economic critiques that made the film an astute transmutation of the novel. The comparative accessibility of the film renders it more vulnerable to such exploitative readings. The apparent contradictions between style and content led initial reviewers, like Roger Greenspun in the *New York Times* in 1972, to condemn the film for being "generally more interesting as idea than as achieved image." Despite these negative reviews, the film's initial run paved the way for reviews by Anglo-American film critics Molotnik and Johnson, who recognized *Macunaíma*'s political and aesthetic importance. Whereas Johnson addressed primarily an academic audience, Molotnik's *Jump Cut* essay spoke to a more generalized public of film aficionados in the United States. This short piece helped make the film more accessible to North American viewers by recognizing how categories of race, gender, and age could be "humorously manipulated in a way that seems somewhat arbitrary to a US viewer even though it makes satirical sense in Brazil" (Molotnik 22). With this awareness of reception, Molotnik appreciated *Macunaíma*'s nuances. Identifying the film's essence in its refusal to explain, Molotnik concluded, "The film stands squarely on its own beliefs, as 'Brazilian' to a foreigner's eye as the picture postcard view of Guanabara Bay" (24). The film's foregrounding of distinctly Brazilian elements created a mode of representation that frames its distribution and promotion.

In extending the reach of Macunaíma's tale into other linguistic and spatiotemporal contexts, the film facilitated cultural dialogue yet also generated misinterpretations that suggest the resistance of local knowledges to enter into global circuits of the arts. After its initial dissemination through film festivals in Brazil and abroad, international sales of the film began in 1970, with rights sold to France, Argentina, Mexico, and, as a single market, Peru, Bolivia, and Ecuador. Contracts were signed with distributors in Venezuela and the United States in 1971, Portugal and Lusophone Africa in 1972, England and Poland in 1973, Denmark and Australia in 1974, and Uruguay in 1975.[51] These sales allowed for the circulation of the film primarily in Spanish America, other parts of the Lusophone world, and Anglophone countries. To render its dialogue into other national languages, film requires linguistic translation. An invisible translator, recognized only in the depths of the credit sequence, produces the subtitles critical to a film's international distribution and reception.[52] At times subtitles struggle to convey all of the layered meanings of a phrase like the emblematic "Ai, que preguiça!," which the initial English subtitles rendered as "Gee. Am I tired." This phrase transmits the basic meaning of the hero's refrain without unpacking the pleonastic joke of referring to sloth in Tupi and Portuguese. Since film also communicates through nonverbal language and music, the linguistic and cultural translations of its subtitles are less central to its global distribution than such practices are to literary circulation.[53] In embracing cinema's visual and sonic elements, Joaquim Pedro de Andrade created a work that circulated globally despite potential limitations of linguistic translation in the subtitles.

Even with film's privileging of nonverbal language, cultural references and other specificities remain relatively incomprehensible for audiences outside of Brazil without guides for interpretation. Literary works can include footnotes, glossaries, or other explanatory texts in a practice of thick translation, whereas film does not generally allow for these paratextual measures. Subtitles, in contrast, are spatially and temporally restricted as they must convey the necessary dialogue or narration and keep pace without intervening too much on the screen. *Macunaíma* presents one possible response to a need for cultural translation by including a clip of Joaquim Pedro de Andrade speaking directly to the camera to help contextualize the film for viewers. The director outlines the trajectory of *Macunaíma* from myths and legends collected by a German ethnologist to Mário de Andrade's novel and, subsequently, to his filmic adaptation. The preface emphasizes the irreverent humor and subversive nature of Brazilian popular culture vis-à-vis societal norms as a trait that originated in indigenous tales. He ends his remarks by hoping that "as aventuras bem brasileiras de Macunaíma, herói de nossa gente" (the very Brazilian adventures of Macunaíma, hero of our people), entertain us and make us think. This directorial prelude serves to frame his film as more explicitly Brazilian than the novel, while also placing it in relationship to the modernist novel with its indigenous and popular sources. The introduction fails to mention cannibalism and consumption as key concepts to understanding the film's critical intervention in Brazil's cultural history. As a result, Molotnik rightly characterizes this brief preface as "insufficient for the non-Brazilian viewer" (22). This lack of explanation might be intentional as it leaves foreign viewers with an incomprehension akin to the experience of elite Brazilians when they first encountered Mário's modernist text.

Similar to its source material, the film of *Macunaíma* resisted complete legibility among foreign publics. The film's comparative commercial and critical success, however, created a feedback loop that generated more interest in the modernist novel, as critic Eduardo Escorel astutely contends. He considers the film more political, especially in its explicit critique of consumption as a metaphor for capitalism, than the novel. According to

Escorel, three key filmic elements contribute to this difference: the use of the Villa-Lobos's *marcha*, the addition of scenes where Macunaíma eats dirt, and the final sequence where Macunaíma dies in the water at the hands of Iara rather than transform into a constellation (65). The ending exemplifies what Joaquim Pedro characterized as the film's main theme: a Brazilian being devoured, quite literally, by Brazil. Escorel's essay also considers how censorship impacted the circulation of the film in Brazil and internationally. Censors initially demanded sixteen cuts to the film, which would have drastically altered the director's vision. Following negotiations, an uncensored version was exhibited at the Venice International Film Festival in September 1969, where it was favorably received. International opinion seemed to influence the Brazilian federal police's October 1969 decree of censorship, which consisted of four cuts instead of the initial sixteen. It was not until 1979 that an uncensored, full-length *Macunaíma* was released in Brazilian cinemas. After its digital restoration, the film appeared in a Cinema Novo homage at the Cannes Film Festival and the New York Film Festival in 2004; festivals in London, Paris, Brussels, Boston, Brasília, Rio de Janeiro, and São Paulo in 2005; and the Karlovy Vary International Film Festival and the Venice Film Festival in 2006. This version of *Macunaíma* was commercially released in Brazil and has remained in circulation via DVD releases in Brazil in 2006, France in 2007, with a Blu-ray release by Kino Classics in 2018.[54]

This continued presence of *Macunaíma* on screen has facilitated the ongoing distribution of the novel in Brazil and in translation abroad. When the film was released in 1969, the novel was in its fifth edition. By 2000, the novel was in its thirty-second edition and the critical edition in its second. The first translations of the novel were not published until after the film's debut. Another wave of translations emerged in the 1980s, following the domestic release of the uncensored film, and in the 2010s, after the film's restoration. Patterns of publication, translation, and distribution suggest a correspondence between the film's release and an uptick in the novel's circulation and sales. In the Anglo-American context, the film version is particularly central to the visibility of Macunaíma's tale. Critiqued for its tonal misfires and rigid literalisms, the 1984 English-language translation remains out of print. The film still appears at festivals and retrospectives at the Anthology Film Archive in New York in 2017 and the Austin Film Society in 2018. The film's ongoing relevance in introducing audiences to Macunaíma indicate the necessity of creative adaptations to the dissemination of this Amerindian tale.

Translation as Ventriloquism:
Pauline Melville's Fictional Reimaginings of Macunaíma

Macunaíma circulates within an Anglophone context as a character in translation and also as the narrator of *The Ventriloquist's Tale*, a 1997 novel by Guyanese author Pauline Melville. In this intertextual dialogue with Mário de Andrade's work, Melville foregrounds Macunaima's Amerindian origins between Brazil, Venezuela, and Guyana.[55] *The Ventriloquist's Tale* raises questions about how stories, languages, cultures, and peoples travel in the Amazon and transform in the process. According to Melville, "Guyana, of course, has its own extraordinary reality. It hangs in a sort of limbo. It is South American while not being part of Latin America. Nor is it one of the Caribbean islands. It is a country with a shifting, floating, ever-changing cultural base, difficult to pin down" ("Guyanese Literature" 9). Given this view of her native country, it makes sense that Melville would select a character who transforms to narrate her novel and, thus, exerts apparent agency over his actions and other indigenous voices. As a first-person narrator in the prologue who then vanishes into the narrative, Melville's Macunaima occupies a mediating role as he draws on personal experiences to represent indigenous lives. This narrative practice aims to contrast earlier appropriative gestures of metropolitan writers and foreign ethnographers.

Existing scholarship on *The Ventriloquist's Tale* analyzes the postcolonial stakes of its intertextual relationship to *Macunaíma*, often through the lens of translation. These studies ask what it means for a Guyanese author to access Amerindian tales, in part, through a Brazilian modernist novel. By examining connections between translatability and native informants, April Shemak contends that Macunaima's multiple transformations in Melville's novel "reveal the untranslatability of language and culture," especially when representing indigeneity (369). For Shemak, the ventriloquist narrator camouflages his voice throughout the narrative to prevent readers from accessing a translatable version of indigenous experiences. This refusal to render indigeneity recognizable confirms what Shemak views as Melville's postcolonial gesture when engaging with *Macunaíma*. While her analysis of indigenous representation vis-à-vis questions of translation is intriguing, Shemak does not acknowledge Melville's dependency on Goodland's flawed translation. In fact, as Albert Braz astutely claims, "both Shemak and Melville unquestionably accept Goodland's translation of Andrade's text as if it were Andrade's own work" ("Mutilated Selves" 23). Melville accesses Macunaíma through Goodland's translation instead of discovering him via Koch-Grünberg's German text or Mário de Andrade's Brazilian Portuguese prose. While *The Ventriloquist's Tale* may be, as Miguel Nenevé and Roseli Siepamann argue (307), a rewriting of *Macunaíma*, it passes through Goodland, who dedicated his translation to Melville's relative Edwina Melville for introducing him to the novel. *The Ventriloquist's Tale* cites Goodland's mistranslation of "Ai! que preguiça!" when the narrator claims, "All I ever said was: 'Aw, what a fucking life!'" (4). In distorting Macunaíma's key phrase, Melville perpetuates the character's association in the Anglophone world with vulgarity rather than laziness.

However, as Stephanos Stephanides rightly recognizes, the intertextual link between a Brazilian modernist masterpiece and a Guyanese postcolonial novel would be unlikely without the English-language translator (304). Despite the flaws of Goodland's translation, it fulfills one of the translator's tasks that Benjamin envisioned: extending the reach of a given work into a different time and space. Even though Brazil and Guyana share a border region inhabited by Amerindians who move freely between nations, the literary dialogues established between Portuguese-speaking Brazil and English-speaking Guyana remain infrequent, due to linguistic divides and geographic distance between their coastal cities. Melville's gesture toward Brazilian literature points to a desire to break down linguistic, cultural, and national boundaries that have persisted since the colonial era, an interest shared by comparative Luso-Hispanic scholars and by Hemispheric Americanists.[56] Discovering Macunaima via the translation, rather than the filmic exploration of Brazilian identity, allows Melville to situate her narrator as an indigenous person of the Americas, which corresponds with the character's positioning as American in the 1928 novel. Creating Macunaima as a product of a border region calls attention to how shared hemispheric experiences were already present in the indigenous and popular sources.

The idea of orality is another key entry point to Melville's novel. In an analysis that minimizes the role of Melville's textual dialogues with *Macunaíma*, Stephanides posits, "If Andrade has cannibalized on written texts, Melville cannibalizes orally transmitted history and myth of her border region" (304). Agnel Barron similarly insists that Melville privileges oral traditions as she reworks colonial and postcolonial uses of the kanaima trope to underscore the contributions of women and Amerindians to the creative representations of the region (2). These studies of Melville's novel draw on discussions of translation or orality, which raises questions as to how these two realms interact, especially with respect to ventriloquism. Translation and ventriloquism function as forms of mediation often erroneously dismissed for lack of creative agency and, thus, rendered invisible. The absence of translators' names on publications led Lawrence Venuti to lament the translator's invisibility in 1995. Similarly, the ventriloquist communicates through another's body in an act that negates the corporality of his own voice. What Mladen Dolar identifies as the object voice, a third level of the voice that neither conveys meaning nor receives aesthetic admiration, is obscured in the process of ventriloquism (4).

With the shape-shifting Macunaima as her narrator, Melville frames ventriloquism as an oral form of mediation analogous to written translations. The prologue opens by establishing the intertextual connection and, at the same time, blurring the line between the fictional and the biographical: "Spite impels me to relate that my biographer, the noted Brazilian Senhor Mario Andrade, got it wrong when he consigned me to the skies in such a slapdash and cavalier manner" (*Ventriloquist's* 1). By positioning Mário de Andrade as his biographer, the narrator implies his "realness" as a person worthy of biography. Questioning the veracity of the hero's transformation into a constellation allows the narrator to exert agency over his tale, insisting, "I lay claim to the position of narrator in this novel. Yes, me. Rumbustious, irrepressible, adorable me" (1). The narrator's description of himself as having "black hair, bronze skin and I would look wonderful in a cream suit with a silk handkerchief" (1) corresponds to the traits ascribed to the Amerindian trickster Makunaíma and Andrade's protagonist Macunaíma. To further this link to mischievous types, the narrator imagines himself in a suit, which recalls the Brazilian archetype of a *malandro*.[57] Though the narrator does not state his name, readers familiar with Macunaíma can recognize his identity. The narrator later explains, "My name translated means 'one who works in the dark.' You can call me Chico. It's my brother's name but so what. Where I come from it's not done to give your real name too easily" (1). This comment about the difficulty in revealing one's name evokes what Doris Sommer describes as the "slap of refused intimacy" of particularist texts (*Proceed* ix). Akin to Rigoberta Menchú's public performances of silence, Chico's refusal to reveal his real name reminds readers of his cultural difference.[58] Framing himself as a mediator of indigenous life and oral traditions for Anglophone readers, but refusing to divulge his name, Chico suggests the political stakes of Melville's reworking of *Macunaíma*.

To build on Mário de Andrade's reimagining of the cultural geography of the Americas, the prologue in *The Ventriloquist's Tale* emphasizes links between orality and writing in indigenous memories:

> As for my ancestry, it is impeccable. I will have you know that I am descended from a group of stones in Ecuador. Where I come from people have long memories. Any one of us can recite our ancestry back for several hundred generations. I can listen to a speech for an hour and then repeat it for you verbatim or backwards without notes. Writing things down has made you forget everything. My grandmother distrusts writing. She says all writing is fiction. Even writing that purports to be factual. (*Ventriloquist's* 2)

By way of her narrator's ancestry, Melville insists on the Amerindian roots of her novel. Drawing attention to the fallibility of writing and to the blurred divides between fiction, history, and ethnography recalls the Brazilian modernist's subversion of genre classifications.

The narrator connects his abilities at hunting and camouflage to his preternatural gifts as a ventriloquist, which, he claims, "were spotted as soon as I began to speak" (8). By boasting, "I can do any voice: jaguar, London hoodlum, bell-bird, nineteenth-century novelist, ant-eater, epic poet, a chorus of howler monkeys, urban brutalist, a tapir" (8), the narrator points to the aural and oral components of ventriloquism whereby careful listening allows him to portray a range of voices. After inviting readers to explore his homeland, the narrator ends the prologue by saying goodbye: "That's all for now, folks. The narrator must appear to vanish. I gone" (9). This self-conscious reflection on the paradox of the narrator's visibility resonates with the possible invisibility of translators or ventriloquists, who are rarely acknowledged unless they call attention to themselves. After vanishing as the narrator, Macunaima appears in the novel as part of an origin story in which a rock-colored woman slept with the sun and birthed children known as the Macunaima. The grandmother of Danny, one of the novel's protagonists, explains, " 'The two eldest brothers, Macunaima and Chico, are our heroes' " (105). With this novelistic retelling of an oral tale, Melville indirectly identifies her narrator, introduced in the prologue by his brother's name Chico, as Macunaima. This reference links Melville's narrator to Mário de Andrade's protagonist as the "hero of our people," with "our" referring not to Brazilians, but to an indigenous group or, more broadly, the peoples of the Americas.

The narrator returns in first person in the epilogue, proclaiming, "I am busy lying in my hammock, warming my behind over the embers" (353). Without stating his name, Melville's narrator establishes parallels between himself and earlier novelistic and filmic Macunaímas in terms of laziness. This image also recalls how outsiders exploring the Amazon have represented Amerindians, a connection made explicit by the narrator: "Travellers come across them lying in their hammocks preening themselves, decked with feathers from humming-birds and macaws" (354). The description traffics in exotic and tropical images stereotypically associated with indigenous characters. Moreover, the narrator insists, "We are also brilliant at divining what you would like to hear and saying it, so you can never be really sure what we think. Another art suited to politics. Ventriloquism at its zenith" (354). The narrator underscores how prone he and his fellow Amerindians are to transformations due to desires of European and North American readers and interlocutors.

Though Melville's novel and its Brazilian antecedent differ in terms of their indigenous characters' narrative agency, I consider their similarities more critical to understanding their intertextuality as literary works of the Americas. Both employ Macunaíma's tales to question the existence of borders and the validity of narrow constructs of nationality. Whereas the Brazilian rhapsody privileges writing over orality with its narrator preserving the hero's tale in writing, Melville's novel foregrounds oral storytelling through a first-person narrator in the prologue and epilogue. *The Ventriloquist's Tale* ends with the narrator's return from Europe, explaining, "I decided to give up my quest for the parrot, temporarily, and head for home—sweet irony—to my own people" (356). Rather than remain among his people, he opts to "take up residence once more in the stars." He continues, "Now that I'm leaving I will let you into the secret of my name. It is Macun . . . No. I've changed my mind" (357). In referencing the parrot and the stars, the narrator solidifies the intertextuality with Mário de Andrade's work. Their conclusions emphasize similarities as literary works that transform Amerindian myths and extend their reach to new readers and contexts. Melville's narrator refuses to state his name in a performative gesture of secrecy, since readers familiar with the tale's antecedents know that he is Macunaima. The character Macunaíma, however, can circulate between languages and cultures in various mythical, modernist, and postcolonial iterations, without becoming flattened into homogeneous forms of world literature and culture. By guarding his name as a performative secret, Melville's ventriloquist narrator asserts his own creative agency through naming and, moreover, questions the politics of translatability.

Reading the origins and afterlives of *Macunaíma* through the lens of translation, as I illustrate in this chapter, draws attention to intertextual and cultural dialogues that traverse linguistic and national borders. In focusing on intersections of travels and translations, I trace the trajectory of Macunaíma's story from Amerindian tales documented by German ethnologist Theodor Koch-Grünberg to their creative transpositions into Mário de Andrade's modernist narrative and, subsequently, into interlingual translations and filmic and fictional transmutations. The heightened degree of linguistic and cultural specificity in the 1928 text posed a challenge to translators of the Brazilian Portuguese narrative into English and other national languages. Despite its thematic relevance to the Americas, the novel's circulation within Brazil, Spanish America, and the United States remained quite limited for over forty years after its original publication. Joaquim Pedro de Andrade's film, with its vibrant colors, shocking and, at times, grotesque visuals, and distinctive soundtrack, allowed for the tale of the "hero of our people" to reach a broader public in the hemispheric Americas and Europe. While the film frames itself as a commentary on Brazilian national and cultural identity, its continued reception outside of Brazil points to the staying power of Macunaíma's story with its roots in Amazonian tales and its examination of the incongruities structuring life in the Americas. Pauline Melville's fictional reimagining of Macunaíma as the first-person narrator of *The Ventriloquist's Tale* both indicates and contributes to the hemispheric importance of this character and his adventures. Her ventriloquist narrator uses naming to assert creative agency and to question the politics of translatability, which resembles to a degree the work of critic and writer Silviano Santiago that I examine further in the next chapter.

Chapter 3
Silviano Santiago's Translational Criticism and Fiction

In 1971, Brazilian professor, cultural critic, and writer Silviano Santiago stepped up to a podium at a university in Montreal and gave a lecture titled "L'entre-lieu de discours latino-américain." The speech resituated the global position of Latin American literature and anticipated developments of postcolonial studies and border studies. Speaking in French, he declared that, for Latin Americans, "to speak, to write, means to speak against, to write against" (Santiago, *The Space In-Between* 30–31). Although Santiago did not directly state his reasons for this combative stance, his lecture reacted to the political climate of the era. By critiquing colonializing dynamics that considered Latin America a lesser copy of either Europe or its neoimperial analogue, the United States, Santiago questioned privileging originality and recognized the creative potential of the copy in Latin America. He explored how to negotiate between local cultures and global influences akin to the earlier modernist views of cultural cannibalism. In Santiago's argument, Latin American writers consume, digest, and creatively transform concepts from Europe and North America to generate distinctive texts and artistic works. With this touchstone speech, Santiago emerged as an exemplary Latin American intellectual for the late twentieth century: a Brazilian citizen who has lived and studied abroad and who translates with relative ease between languages, cultures, and nations in his scholarly and fictional writing.

Born in Brazil in 1936, Santiago spent the 1960s and early 1970s as a professor at universities in New Mexico, New Jersey, and New York before returning to Brazil in 1974. His doctoral training at the Sorbonne in French literature and critical theory informed his approach to Latin American literature on display in his essay on the space in-between. His experiences moving between Brazil, Europe, the United States, and the rest of Latin America and between distinct languages, cultural influences, and written genres resemble the trajectories of contemporaries, including Argentine critics Sylvia Molloy and Beatriz Sarlo, Argentine novelist and critic Ricardo Piglia, and Brazilian literary scholar Leyla Perrone-Móises. Santiago is unique among his generation of Latin American artists and intellectuals due to his combination of French training, work experiences in North American universities, residence in Brazil, and fictional exploration of theoretical concepts. In his fiction, especially the 1985 novel *Stella Manhattan*, Santiago echoes Spanish American novelists like Argentine Manuel Puig in *El beso de la mujer araña* (1976, *Kiss of the Spider Woman*) or Chilean José Donoso in *El lugar sin límites* (1968, *Hell Has No Limits*). These novels depict popular culture, queer voices, and intersections of the personal and the political that shape paths of exile and migration. Like Puig and Donoso, Santiago lived in voluntary exile for personal and political reasons. These experiences abroad put him in contact with avant-garde art and ideas as he found his critical and fictional home in translation as a scholar trained in French theory who studies the cultures of the Americas and writes in Portuguese from Brazil.

By reading his criticism and fiction through the lens of translation, rather than frames of postcolonial and postmodern thought often associated with his work, I will locate his agency as a creative transformer who develops a translational aesthetic between languages and nations. Santiago recognizes the creative transformations inherent in the copy via his analysis of how Latin American writers engage in forms of resistance that question established hierarchical binaries. He further emphasizes the innovation generated from the so-called periphery in his later essay on the cosmopolitanism of the poor, which claims that cosmopolitanism in the current era of heightened globalization is no longer only a privilege of elites. His concept of the space in-between dialogues with Machado de Assis's idea of the national instinct as a writer's intimate sense of being Brazilian regardless of subject matter and Oswald de Andrade's call for cultural *antropofagia* in Brazil. Santiago considers how Latin Americans continue to negotiate European and North American influences when creating innovative works that respond to new geopolitical realities and capture the range of experiences comprising the nation in heterogeneous time.[1] Fitting for a reevaluation of the role of the nation, the idea of the space in-between reached a North American audience in French and English before finding a public in Brazil and the rest of Latin America. An English translation of the Montreal lecture was published in 1973 by the Council on International Studies at State University of New York at Buffalo, where Santiago taught at the time. He later expanded and published the essay as "O entre-lugar do discurso latino-americano" in his 1978 book *Uma literatura nos trópicos* (A literature in the tropics), which served as the basis for translations into Spanish in 2000 and English in 2001.[2] With the essay's comparisons of colonial and national literatures, Santiago explores how travel and translation impact language, individual subjectivity, and collective identities.[3]

Unlike Brazilians Antonio Candido and Roberto Schwarz, who tend to prioritize the place of the nation in their comparative literary studies, Santiago uses Latin America as the frame for his cultural analysis in a gesture similar to Piglia, Molloy, and Sarlo.[4] Santiago's writings illustrate how nationality persists as an intimate experience of being Brazilian, even as he engages with global influences. In exemplifying this approach, his idea of the space in-between parallels Emily Apter's translation zone as a realm where linguistic and cultural hierarchies become destabilized. Both concepts represent fields of possibility, but they are not free from geopolitical dangers or psychological repercussions. Santiago's criticism and fiction explore what Apter terms "translational transnationalism," which invites "a comprehensive sense of the politics of literacy, literariness, and reading publics" ("On Translation" 5). Discursive constructs and spatial relations of power preoccupy Santiago's critical thought. His fiction set in the United States further examines how relationships between perceived centers and peripheries impact Brazilians and other Latin Americans living abroad. Moreover, the relatively limited distribution of his writings in translation indicates imbalances in publishing circuits.[5]

While Santiago's essays address the role of literature in a country with historically high rates of illiteracy, his fiction engages with a politics of language and literacies. In *Stella Manhattan*, characters move through New York with varying ease due to linguistic abilities and educational backgrounds that allow them to navigate unfamiliar terrain. For the Brazilian protagonist traversing the southern United States in the 1960s in "Borrão," knowing English is not enough to understand the social dynamics encountered on the trip. These characters experience how being literate abroad is a question of both language and culture. Critical essays showcase Santiago's ability to move between Portuguese prose, Spanish American literary examples, and French theory, whereas his fiction captures the codeswitching of Brazilians living in the United States. By not always glossing the meaning of English and Spanish words in his Portuguese, Santiago creates a prose attuned to the slips within and between languages. This fascination with language recalls Jacques Derrida's ideas, but does not result in dense and dry prose, as one might expect. Instead, he renders Derrida's complex thought and convoluted phrases into an accessible and playful style of Portuguese prose.

This chapter approaches Santiago's work through the framework of translation in order to underscore the possibilities for and limitations of cross-cultural exchange between Brazil and the United States. Recognizing the critical and artistic potential of the space in-between, Santiago challenges existing power dynamics that often relegate Latin Americans to a secondary position. His interest in language's creative transformations and infidelities extends to the translational aesthetic of his fiction about Brazilians and other Latin Americans in the United States. I analyze *Stella Manhattan* and his short story collections *Keith Jarrett no Blue Note (Improvisos do jazz)* (1996) and *Histórias mal contadas* (2005) as fictional manifestations of the space in-between. To explore how language and identity transform as Brazilians live in the United States, his fiction employs a translational prose that pushes back against assumptions of translatability that often flatten cultural specificity and negate difference.[6] After following the trajectory of Santiago's thought from the in-between to the cosmopolitanism of the poor, I conclude with a brief reflection on the relationship between his writing and translatability.

The Space In-Between: From Deconstructive Origins to the Translation Zone

Santiago grew up in a Brazil increasingly under the influence of the United States due to the Good Neighbor Policy, Hollywood, popular culture, and advertising. As a child in a small town in Minas Gerais, he experienced the world beyond Brazil via mass culture from the United States. In a 2000 interview, he noted that comics, war films, and musicals "proporcionaram-me também minhas primeiras *viagens*. Traduzi essa experiência do cosmopolitismo provinciano num livro de poemas que se chama *Crescendo durante a guerra numa provinciana ultramarina*" (also granted me my first *travels*. I translated this experience of provincial cosmopolitanism in a book of poems titled *Growing Up during the War in an Ultramarine Province*; qtd. in Coelho 87). Published in 1978 and dedicated to Brazilian artist Hélio Oiticica, this collection combined personal memories with research on links between politics and culture during the war years.[7] The poems blend his recollections with archival research to create a collage-like aesthetic. The opening poem, "O rei dos espiões" (The king of spies), ponders what happens behind the masks of superheroes Batman and Superman.[8] In contrast, the next poem, "Um valor mais alto se alevanta" (A higher value rises up), refers to events surrounding World War II as "um torpedo alemão avança contra Wall Street" (a German torpedo advances against Wall Street; 17). "Dois poemas em prosa sobre os quadrinhos" (Two prose poems about comics) cites Carlos Lacerda's 1945 condemnation of the influence of comics: "A verdade é que nós estamos importando veneno para as nossas crianças" (The truth is we are importing poison for our children; 19). Placing Lacerda's critique next to a similar quote from a psychiatrist creates a prose poem that generates unexpected meaning. Another poem highlights São Paulo's cosmopolitanism based on a 1942 article in *O Estado de São Paulo*. The titles "South of the Border" and "Self-Made Man" for poems written in Portuguese indicate Santiago's incipient transnational and translational aesthetic. This creative process of citing and rewriting puts his ideas about language and the in-between into practice to render his childhood's "provincial cosmopolitanism" into poetry.

After completing his undergraduate studies at the Federal University of Minas Gerais, Santiago traveled to Paris to pursue his graduate degree in literature. In 1962, before finishing his dissertation, he received an offer to teach Portuguese language and Luso-Brazilian literature at the University of New Mexico.[9] He encountered in Albuquerque a United States roiled by civil rights struggles and conservative fears of encroaching communism. Living in the southwestern United States, he grappled with what it meant to be Brazilian in an area with a large Hispanic population that was often forced to work in harsh conditions. His experiences as a Brazilian in the United States differed from the late nineteenth-century interactions of Rodrigues and Sousândrade with elite Spanish Americans in New York as it became a center of global economic and cultural capital. Though Santiago worked with educated Latin Americans at the university, he also met Spanish-speaking New Mexicans whose familial roots stretched back to the colonial period and others who had arrived more recently as migrant laborers. Exposure to discriminatory practices and different constructs of race while living in the United States later informed *Histórias mal contadas*. As the de facto representative of Brazil at the university and social gatherings, Santiago conveyed a subjective understanding of nationality. By teaching language and surveys of Portuguese and Brazilian literature, he developed comparative readings across historic periods that helped to generate his reflections on the space in-between.

Before returning to Brazil, Santiago taught at Rutgers University in New Jersey and State University of New York at Buffalo. Living in relatively close proximity to New York City granted Santiago access to cultural innovations, political movements, and communities of Latin American artists and intellectuals, which proved essential to his formation as a critic and writer.[10] While a professor of French literature in Buffalo, he strengthened his understanding of French critical theory through personal encounters with Jacques Derrida, Michel Foucault, and Julia Kristeva. When Santiago returned to Brazil in 1972 as a visiting scholar, he imparted recent trends of deconstructionism in French theory to a Brazilian public. In a lecture at Pontifícia Universidade Católica, Rio de Janeiro (PUC-Rio) in 1975, which was later published in his 1978 collection, he outlined principles of literary analysis and interpretation according to Roland Barthes, Claude Lévi-Strauss, Gérard Genette, Jacques Derrida, and Michel Foucault.

Although Santiago did not dedicate himself to translating the entire deconstructionist corpus into Portuguese, he served as a key mediator for the introduction of French theory to Brazil. His lectures and publications during the 1970s synthesized theoretical readings and translated essential concepts and quotes into Portuguese. Two of Derrida's seminal works, *Writing and Difference* and *Of Grammatology*, had been published in Brazil as *A escritura e a diferença* and *Gramatologia* in 1971 and 1973, respectively. In 1976, Santiago helped to make Derrida's ideas more accessible to Brazilian readers by supervising the creation of *Glossário de Derrida* (Glossary of Derrida), a collective project with literature students at PUC-Rio.[11] The glossary's introduction stresses the difficulties in understanding Derrida's ideas due to his baroque prose and shifting meanings of his lexicon. According to Santiago and his students, Derrida's texts operate under a basic principle of "um agressivo questionamento dos pressupostos históricos sobre que se apoia o discurso da metafísica ocidental. Tal gesto se traduz por uma constante violência contra a interpretação clássica de certos livros, contra o uso indiscriminado de certos conceitos" (an aggressive questioning of the historical presuppositions upon which the discourse of Western metaphysics is supported. Such a gesture is translated by a constant violence against the classical interpretation of certain books, against the indiscriminate use of certain concepts; Santiago, *Glossário* 5). They read, annotated, and interpreted Derrida's work to create a glossary consisting of sixty-two entries contextualizing, synthesizing meaning, and translating French terms into Portuguese. This project served to convey complex concepts like *différance*, grammatology, and *pharmakon* in a more intelligible manner for Brazilian readers.

For Santiago, deepening his knowledge of Derrida's ideas contributed to his intellectual development as he analyzed Brazilian and Spanish American literature through a lens of French theory. He conceives of his work in terms of translation and dialogue, noting, "meus escritos traduzem sempre, de uma forma ou de outra, as minhas relações com o pensamento europeu" (my writings always translate, in one form or another, my relations with European thought; qtd. in Coelho 92), even as "dialogo tanto com a vertente europeia como com a americana" (I dialogue as much with the European aspect as with the American; qtd. in Coelho 96). By combining interests in continental philosophy with personal reflections on dislocation, he crafted an essay on the space in-between that carried traces of travel and translation. He later attributed the Montreal locale, in part, to the favorable reception of his combative perspective, given the province's status as a linguistic and cultural minority within Canada (Santiago and Ramos 199).[12] In other words, speaking in French from Quebec allowed Santiago to better address the peripheral position of Latin American discourse.

Departing from Eugenio Donato's invitation to speak on *antropofagia*, Santiago proposed a deconstructionist analysis of the discursive relationship between Latin America's colonial past and current marginalization. He subsequently characterized his talk in Montreal as a reading of Lévi-Strauss, Derrida, and Foucault in relation to a Latin American politics of resistance (Santiago and Ramos 195). Epigraphs from Antonio Callado's 1967 novel *Quarup* and Foucault's *The Archaeology of Knowledge* point to the duality of Brazilian culture and European ideas informing the essay (Santiago, *The Space In-Between* 25). The quote from *Quarup* about a land turtle making a shell out of the head of a dead jaguar that had previously bitten him captures a creative process of resistance and transformation. The body of the vanquished enemy becomes retooled as an object of self-defense and protest in a gesture that exemplifies the oppositional stance of the space in-between. The epigraph from Foucault emphasizes the need for negation and questions whether continuity and influence can serve as the basis for communication.

Santiago's indebtedness to Foucault also appears in the essay's title and theoretical approach, namely, the appearance of "discourse" as a key term with multiple meanings. In a general sense, discourse denotes a group of verbal performances. It also refers to the series of sentences and sequences of signs that create a discursive formation. Synthesizing these ideas, Foucault explains, "The term discourse can be defined as the group of statements that belong to a single system of formation" (*Archaeology* 107). He outlines the development and differentiation of discursive regimes into science, literature, philosophy, religion, politics, and history. Though Foucault privileges European examples and Santiago focuses on discourse in Latin America, both favor discontinuities and moments of rupture over permanence. Santiago situates Latin American discourse in the space in-between, a position analogous to what Foucault identifies as "this blank space from which I speak, and which is slowly taking shape in a discourse that I still feel to be so precarious and so unsure" (17). Foucault considers his text "an attempt to define a particular site by the exteriority of its vicinity," given that, "at every turn, it denounces any possible confusion. It rejects its identity, without previously stating: I am neither this nor that" (17). This aim to delimit a position of enunciation similarly motivates Santiago's essay.

Asserting that "the major contribution of Latin America to Western culture is to be found in its systematic destruction of the concepts of *purity* and *unity*," Santiago conceives of the space in-between as a combative zone of enunciation for Latin American intellectuals (*The Space In-Between* 30–31). However, as Denílson Lopes accurately claims, "the space in-between does not just relate to the experience of intellectuals: it implies a redefinition of the national" ("From the Space" 360). This reconsideration of the national develops out of a comparative analysis of Latin American texts through a deconstructionist lens. Focusing on discursive constructs of power allows Santiago to consider how speaking and writing from the space in-between could challenge hierarchical relationships. His essay opens with the colonial moment as a prime example of interactions between the oppressed and the oppressor. Santiago claims that European victory over the indigenous in the Americas resulted primarily from "the brutal imposition of an ideology that produced a recurrence of words such as 'slave' and 'beast' in the writings of both Portuguese and Spanish alike" (*The Space In-Between* 27). According to João Camillo Penna, Santiago remains indebted to European thought and thus continues in the intellectual tradition of Brazilian ethnology. By situating his critical concepts within frameworks of dependence and colonialism, Penna carefully unpacks Santiago's varied influences, including Roland Barthes, Edward Said, and Antonio Candido. In particular, he frames Derrida's idea of the supplement, which refers to writing that adds to or substitutes something already complete, as essential to Santiago's textual apparatus (Penna 302). The supplement's analogue in translation studies is the remainder, which Lawrence Venuti theorizes based on the work of Jean-Jacques Lecercle. The remainder consists of variations on current standard dialect such as slang, anachronisms, and loan words that underscore language's heterogeneity. According to Venuti, the remainder is "the most visible sign of the domesticating process that always functions in translating," yet it "can also be a significant point of foreignizing effects" (*Translation Changes Everything* 37). Santiago expresses a similar interest in language's supplements and remainders.

To examine the linguistic production of domination, Santiago draws on Derrida's work, especially *Writing and Difference* with its recognition of speech and writing as distinct practices. Santiago suggests that oral transmission of the European word among indigenous peoples of Latin America prevented "positing, indivisibly, in *writing* [*écriture*] the name of the divinity" (*The Space In-Between* 28). Colonizers relied on theatrical representation and imitation of gestures by indigenous peoples to link religious and linguistic codes. Santiago cites Derrida's formulation in *Of Grammatology* that the divine sign and name are born at the same time and place to support his claim that the colonial project privileges, above all, a singular God, sovereign, and language (29). This insistence on singularity implies resituating European dynamics of language and power on the other side of the Atlantic. Santiago begins to unravel the discursive construct of church and state in the Americas as an imitation of European "originals" without acknowledging that his own analysis exists within a textual system of production and reproduction. Though it maintains a Eurocentric worldview that cites Foucault and Derrida, Santiago's essay represents an essential step toward a postcolonial reading of Brazil's origins.

For Santiago, duplication is the defining trait of the Americas, but a perfect copy is impossible. The colonial process thus entails repeating European origins with a difference:

> America is transformed into a copy, a simulacrum that desires to be increasingly like the original, even though its originality cannot be found in the copy of the original model, but rather in an origin that was completely erased by the conquerors. Through the constant destruction of original traces, together with the forgetting of the origin, the phenomenon of duplication establishes itself as the only valid rule of civilization. (29)

Transferring people, ideas, and institutions from one continent to another, which Santiago terms a "phenomenon of duplication," could also be framed as forms of creative transformation. Cultural models from Europe undergo changes in the Americas, resulting in misquotations, rewritings, and unfaithful translations. This process raises questions about where to situate originality within creative efforts to "civilize" the hemisphere. Rather than focus on Latin America's indebtedness to Europe, Santiago contests unidirectional power relationships by encouraging a reframing of the conceptual lens "to highlight the elements of the work that establish its difference" (31). Valorizing imperfections and variations in their "copies" of European originals recognizes the potential for creative agency and transformation among Latin American writers. Santiago cites literary examples from Argentine writers Julio Cortázar and Jorge Luis Borges that question the very concept of originality and the related idea of perfect reproducibility. In an interview with Argentine critic Jorge Wolff, Santiago explains that the space in-between must have emerged from his "schizophrenic" situation of teaching French literature, attending meetings in English, and talking with friends in Spanish (219). Wolff astutely characterizes Santiago's essays from 1970 onward as transnational interpretations of Latin American literature and culture through the lens of French theory.

Santiago's emphasis on the potential of the space in-between as a realm where Latin American writers playfully devour and reinterpret European literature anticipates later trends that highlight the creative possibilities of transculturation and hybridity, including the theories of Gloria Anzaldúa's Borderlands, Mary Louise Pratt's contact zone, Néstor García Canclini's hybrid cultures, or Homi Bhabha's third space.[13] The concept of the space in-between exhibits a concern with language, originality, and duplication that also interests scholars of translation. Although published nearly three decades before the translational turn in the humanities, the essay's theoretical concepts and supporting examples suggest parallels between the tasks of the Latin American critic and the translator.[14] Per Santiago, the Latin American critic "will study what s/he gets out of it and will end with a portrayal of the technique that the same writer constructs in her/his aggressive resignification of the original model: thus s/he will dismantle the principles that posited it as an unreproducible and wholly unique object" (*The Space In-Between* 34). These comments could also refer to the translator's task of dismantling a source text and recreating it in another language in a process that considers its translatability. Unlike reproducibility, which describes creating an exact copy often via mechanized systems, translatability explores a text's aesthetic and linguistic qualities that invite or resist translation. Santiago discards tired constructs of originality by claiming that Latin American writing "should affirm itself as a writing *upon* another writing" where the writer reads, interprets, transforms, and "plays with the signs of another writer and another work" (34). The Latin American writer creates "a kind of global translation, a pastiche, a parody or a digression rather than a literal translation" (34). In differentiating Latin American modes of translation from literal translations, Santiago stresses how the region's writers utilize their creative agency to transform texts, subvert literary hierarchies, and question the associated geopolitical dynamics of power.

To support his claim about Latin American creativity, Santiago positions Cortázar and Borges as writers who playfully engaged with European literatures. Their work surprised Santiago when he first read it in the mid-1960s because he knew of nothing comparable in Brazilian literature at the time (Wolff 218). Santiago has noted that the linguistic games in their fiction, "son tan 'verdaderos' como los ensayos escritos a partir de conceptos. Este tipo de ensayismo también ha posibilitado una visión que escapa de las contingencias nacionalistas" (are as "real" as the essays written based upon concepts. This type of essay writing also has facilitated a vision that escapes nationalist contingencies; Santiago and Ramos 200). These texts escape nationalist discourses and genre categories to explore possibilities of interpretation from a space in-between. According to Penna's astute analysis, these literary examples indicate the operation of the supplement by illustrating how certain words or texts, like Pierre Menard's *Quixote* in Borges's short story, substitute and add to the original (302). The supplement allows Santiago to question originality through destabilizing acts of reading, translating, and rewriting.

The fictional examples also indicate the centrality to the literatures of the Americas of translation as an aggressive and creative act of appropriation, consumption, and transformation.

By closely analyzing the opening scene of Cortázar's *62: A Model Kit*, Santiago posits that, "during the process of translation, the imaginary of the [Latin American] writer is always on stage" (*The Space In-Between* 34). An embodiment of how transnational experiences intersect with translations, Cortázar lived in Paris as he wrote in Spanish, translated stories by Edgar Allan Poe, and served as an interpreter for UNESCO. His essay "Translate, traduire, tradurre: traducir" explains that these experiences left him with "an appreciation for the subtle transmigrations and transgressions that take place in the translation of any text when its meaning goes beyond the bridges of language" (qtd. in Balderston and Schwartz 21). In his analysis of Cortázar's novel, Santiago focuses on language and translation to uncover layers of significance imbued in the protagonist's words and actions. For Santiago, the French sentence "I would like a bloody castle," which the protagonist found on a mirror in a Parisian restaurant, evokes the name René de Chateaubriand, the author of *René* and *Atalá*. This association raises the question of how to read texts in the Americas modeled on European romanticism. Santiago advances the in-between as "this space in which, although the signifier may remain the same, the signified disseminates another inverted meaning" (35). Ideas of translation and deconstruction inform his development of a theory attuned to dynamics of power between national languages and cultures.

The importance of translation to Santiago's rethinking of the position of Latin American discourse becomes more apparent with the example of Borges's "Pierre Menard, Author of the *Quixote*." The story interrogates how the original relates to the copy by examining Menard's visible and invisible work. A French symbolist working in the early twentieth century, Menard does not want to write another *Don Quixote* but rather to compose, word for word, the *Quixote* itself. Menard dismisses the attempt to be Cervantes by forgetting historical events from 1602 to 1918 as too simple; instead, he aims to arrive at the *Quixote* while remaining Pierre Menard. Borges's analysis of the two *Quixotes* notes that, even though they contain the same words in the same order, their meanings differ due to their distinct eras of publication. "Pierre Menard" has deservedly become a cornerstone of translation studies given its examination of relationships between a source text and subsequent readers, writers, and translators who render the work into other languages, spaces, and times.

As George Steiner argues in *After Babel*, "'Pierre Menard, Author of the *Quixote*' (1939) is the most acute, most concentrated commentary offered on the business of translation" (73). Steiner contends that subsequent works on translation exist as responses to this piece. Sergio Waisman similarly emphasizes Borges's key role in translation studies as a writer who "destabilizes the concept of a 'definitive text' and challenges the supposed primacy of the center from where it comes" (11). For Waisman, Borges's interest in translation's creative infidelities facilitates a rethinking of center-periphery relations.[15]

Santiago's analysis of "Pierre Menard" underscores the transgressive and transformative possibilities of reading, interpreting, and writing:

> Menard's presence—difference, writing, originality—inscribes itself within the transgression of the model, within a subtle and imperceptible movement of conversion, perversion, and inversion. The originality of Pierre Menard's project, its visible and written aspect, derives from the fact that he refuses to accept the traditional notion of artistic invention since he himself denies the total freedom of the artist. . . . The Latin American artist accepts prison as a form of behavior, and transgression as a form of expression. (*The Space In-Between* 37)

Both Menard and the Latin American writer refuse to accept existing hierarchies privileging the original over the copy and instead locate originality in subtle subversions and creative transformations of the model. By analyzing these literary examples from Cortázar and Borges, Santiago suggests how such works can help to change cultural dynamics that tend to relegate Latin America to peripheral positions.

Santiago insists that Latin Americans write back from an "apparently empty space" that exists "somewhere between sacrifice and playfulness, prison and transgression, submission to the code and aggression, obedience and rebellion, assimilation and expression" (38). This positioning "demonstrates that we should free ourselves from the image of smiling carnival and fiesta-filled holiday haven for cultural tourism" (38). With the phrase "empty space," Santiago references the idea of "blank space" from Foucault's introduction to *The Archaeology of Knowledge*. He proceeds to contest the space's emptiness by consecrating it as a zone from which Latin American writers subvert European and North American models and challenge stereotypical visions of the region. To conclude, the essay frames the space in-between as "where the anthropophagous ritual of Latin American discourse is constructed" (38). Recalling the initial epigraph from *Quarup* where the land turtle transforms the jaguar's head into a protective shell, this closing sentence stresses the centrality of creative transformation in Latin American culture.

Characterizing Latin American discourse as an "ritual antropófago" (cannibalistic ritual) alludes to Oswald de Andrade's ideas of *antropofagia*. Through his literary references, Santiago more fully situates his space in-between in dialogue with concepts of translation. Translation scholar Edwin Gentzler notes the affinities between Brazilian modernism's cultural cannibalism and the translator's creative agency to embark on a "new devouring process" that incorporates and transforms foreign words and ideas (86). These connections pass through the work of Haroldo de Campos and his theory and practice of transcreation.[16] Parallels to Santiago's concept of the space in-between are more apparent in Haroldo de Campos's 1981 text "Da razão antropofágica: A Europa sob o signo da devoração" ("Anthropophagous Reason: Dialogue and Difference in Brazilian Culture"). Both critics describe a practice of cultural cannibalism as central to how Brazilians and, more generally, Latin Americans negotiate their relationships to metropolitan influences. Campos and Santiago return to the colonial moment to highlight how contesting hierarchies and embracing creative infidelities have long defined Latin American cultural practices. Santiago's idea of the space in-between manifests itself in his fiction's geography and his characters' psychologies, as I will now examine further.

Transamerican Tales in the Translation Zone: The Spaces In-Between of Santiago's Fiction

Santiago explores creative implications of the cultural cannibalism of Latin American discourse with narratives that address experiences of dislocation and interpretation. For Santiago, interpretation is an essential task for critics, readers, and writers of fiction. He stresses that "o intérprete é, em suma, o *intermediário* entre texto e leitor, fazendo ainda deste o seu próprio leitor. Procura formalizar e discutir, para o curioso, os problemas apresentados pela obra" (the interpreter is, in short, the intermediary between text and reader, still making from this his own reader. He seeks to formalize and to discuss, for the curious, the problems presented by the work; Santiago, *Uma literatura nos trópicos* 7). Santiago often occupies this role of interpreter or intermediary, but I would contend that the term "translator" more accurately captures the creative agency involved in mediating between languages, ideas, and peoples. Though he rarely translates texts from one national language to another, he embarks on linguistic and cultural translations in fiction set in the United States by inserting Spanish, English, and French phrases into his prose and alluding to political, cultural, and geographic specificities.[17]

Stella Manhattan, *Keith Jarrett no Blue Note*, and *Histórias mal contadas* draw on and fictionalize Santiago's experiences of dislocation while living in the United States in the 1960s and 1970s.[18] In the 1980s, while his criticism focused on concerns of national literature, his fiction began to examine how people and cultures transform as they cross geopolitical and linguistic borders.[19] His characters' trajectories and affiliations suggest how the intimate sense of being Brazilian that Machado de Assis identified in 1873 as a writer's "national instinct" persists, even with the proliferation of transnational lives in this moment of heightened globalization. As Machado rightly contended over a century ago, depictions of "local color," such as tropical landscapes and folkloric celebrations, fail to capture the complexity of Brazil as a large nation of varied peoples. Individual feelings of nationality do not necessarily correspond with commonplace markers of being Brazilian, nor is nationality an exclusive all-encompassing identity. As Marshall Eakin incisively argues in *Becoming Brazilians*, a sense of being Brazilian exists alongside other forms of local, regional, racial, ethnic, gender, sexual, and professional identities (266–69). Brazil's diverse peoples and cultures do not all conform to images of an exotic land that foreign publics desire.[20] Although regionalist works still occupy an important place in Brazilian letters, urban spaces beyond Brazil have become more frequent settings for recent Brazilian literature.[21] Santiago's stories about Brazilians in metropolitan New York, provincial New Mexico, and other parts of the United States indicate how dislocation has become more common in the late twentieth and early twenty-first centuries due to expanded access of foreign travel and the rise of political and economic conditions that necessitate emigration. The question of how to express a personal sense of being Brazilian in literary works remains a pressing one as Santiago and his characters inhabit multiple identities simultaneously.

For Santiago and his Brazilian characters, the "national instinct" is above all an intimate feeling not contingent upon location or content. In conveying how displacement affects migrants and exiles in his fiction, Santiago informs his readers in Brazil of the difficulties of migrating and adjusting to life in the United States as Portuguese-speaking Brazilians. According to his former student Evelena Hoisel, in his novels and stories, "migração inscreve-se através de diversos signos—migrações discursivas, geográficas, culturais, metafóricas—e está associado ao tema da viagem, da mudança no comportamento, na localização geográfica, no interesse pelo outro" (migration is inscribed through diverse signs—discursive, geographic, cultural, metaphoric migrations—and is associated with the theme of travel, of changes in behavior, in geographic location, in interest in the other; 147). His fiction captures how estrangement generates personal transformations, namely, greater self-awareness and empathy. What Machado framed as "intimate sentiment" of being Brazilian thus becomes more personal in Santiago's work as a realm between languages and cultures that allows for self-reflection, expression, escape, and protection. People long excluded from the national project as queer, alternative, or even sexually "deviant" can exist openly and belong in the form of characters who express sexual and homoerotic desires in *Stella Manhattan* and *Keith Jarrett no Blue Note*. Far from their native Brazil, these characters explore their sexuality in ways that deepen experiences of inhabiting spaces between nations, languages, cultures, and sexualities. As Karl Posso compellingly argues, Santiago's fiction establishes connections between homosexuality and exile, which recalls the writings of Cuban Severo Sarduy.[22]

The linguistic and cultural spaces in-between that Santiago's characters occupy have physical manifestations in apartments, restaurants, and other private realms. Underscoring the multiplicity of the in-between, Denílson Lopes succinctly states, "The space in-between is a concrete and material space: at the same time, it is political and existential, local, mediated and transnational. It is the space of affect and memories" ("From the Space" 362). These iterations at the intersection of nations, languages, cultures, and sexual identities populate the New York of *Stella Manhattan*. The main events of the novel unfold in Manhattan on October 18th and 19th, 1969, a temporal frame that coincides with one of Santiago's stays in New York. It was also a year of dislocation for many Brazilians due to the increased repression and censorship in Brazil after the military dictatorship implemented the Fifth Institutional Act (AI-5) in December 1968. The regime hardliners exerted their power with the decree, which closed Congress, suspended habeas corpus, and implemented other restrictions intended to suppress the political agency of oppositional voices. The novel's protagonist Eduardo da Costa e Silva arrives in New York in April 1968, prior to AI-5, after fleeing Brazil for more personal reasons—a homosexual relationship that brought disgrace to his family. Exiled in New York, Eduardo meets Brazilians involved in underground resistance to the dictatorship, cosmopolitan intellectuals like Professor Aníbal Paes Leme and his wife Leila, Spanish-speaking exiles from Cuba, migrants from Puerto Rico, and other citizens of the United States. Political forces and sexual desires structure the lives of residents of this multilingual and multinational city.

Eduardo works in the Brazilian consulate processing visas, a job he secured thanks to his father's friend Colonel Valdevinos Vianna. Eduardo and Vianna reside in a fictional Manhattan where characters with multiple identities and code names or nicknames circulate.[23] Cuban immigrant Francisco Ayala, more commonly known as Paco or La Cucaracha, lives next door to Eduardo. Marcelo Carneiro da Rocha, a visiting lecturer at New York University and Eduardo's friend from college, also goes by his guerrilla code name Caetano or his female persona Marcela, the Marquesa de Santos. Similarly, the protagonist first appears in the novel as his alter ego Stella Manhattan. Stella, the star of Manhattan, drifts through her small apartment, joyfully singing after a blissful night with her new lover Rickie. In addition to feminine Stella and professional Eduardo, the protagonist transforms into Bastiana, the maid from his childhood home, when cleaning the apartment and remembering the past. The character uses the code name Rosebud with the underground militia. With the fluid and multiple identities of his characters, Santiago explores previously theorized ideas about contesting the fixity of texts, languages, and identities.

The colonel similarly embodies a dual identity as the married military official Vianna and the sexually adventurous Viúva Negra, the Black Widow. He publicly projects an image of a family man with conservative values and, according to underground guerilla members, fascist affiliations. Vianna's "other" emerges privately in an apartment at 75th and Amsterdam that he rents using Eduardo's name, solely for sexual encounters with other men. In this uptown apartment and Eduardo's Greenwich Village walk-up, Vianna, Eduardo, and other characters feel free to express sexual desires as they seek refuge from the foreignness of the public sphere. These private realms provide solace by allowing identities to intermingle and transform and by isolating these experiences to intimate spaces of transaction and translation. Posso keenly observes that homosexual exile in the novel "makes manifest the idea that society's regulation of the sexual and political is a process of exclusion" (35). The abject experience of homosexuality generates vulnerability among characters leading multiple lives. The security and the protection that private realms supposedly offer become dismantled when the underground militia group raids Vianna's Manhattan apartment. The attack exemplifies how the political and the sexual intersect in a physical manifestation of the space in-between.

Private realms occupy a similar place of importance in *Keith Jarrett no Blue Note*, which consists of five interconnected short stories featuring the same nameless protagonist and other recurring characters. The tales transition smoothly between geographic spaces of past memories and recent events in a form of movement that parallels the improvisational style of jazz. The protagonist's apartment offers him protection as a furnished space bereft of personal touches, yet situated between his memories of Rio de Janeiro and the estrangement he faces during daily life in this anonymous North American town. One fall day, when purchasing an album, he responds affirmatively when asked if it was cold outside. The shopkeeper laughs and warns that it will only get worse in the next months. This exchange prompts a realization: "Você já se sentia fora do espaço da cidade, agora você se sente fora do tempo dela. Um estrangeiro, inconveniente além do mais" (You already felt outside of the space of the city, now you feel outside of its time. A foreigner, inconvenient besides everything else; Santiago, *Keith Jarrett* 29). Direct address in the second person implicates readers in experiences of dislocation and loneliness. Without a name, the tale's *você* (you) emerges as an everyman clouded by his thoughts. Recollections of the Rio he left three years ago blend with images of his current home: "Você fica pensativo e reflete que a imagem dupla sonhada nessa noite—espelho da cidade onde você está nos Estados Unidos e reflexo do bairro onde você mora no Brasil—no máximo poderia ser o encontro desencontrado da neve aqui embaixo . . . com o sol tropical lá em cima" (You remain pensive and reflect that the double image dreamed that night—mirror of the city where you are in the United States and reflection of the neighborhood where you live in Brazil—at the most could be the missed encounter of snow here below . . . with the tropical sun up above; 95). The dream visually renders the protagonist's position in a liminal space between the Brazilian sun of the past and the North American snow of the present.

These fictional in-between spaces point to how intersections of race, ethnicity, and class in the United States differ from experiences in Brazil, which Santiago continues to explore in *Histórias mal contadas*. The collection opens with an epigraph from Clarice Lispector's 1940 letter to Lúcio Cardoso lamenting that "as coisas são iguais em toda parte" (things are the same everywhere; 1). Based on her international travels, Lispector observed the homogeneity of cinemas and posited that women abroad with shoes in the style of Carmen Miranda longed to consume an exotic image of Brazil, even though Brazilians did not wear such shoes. The epigraph foreshadows the book's thematic explorations of Brazilians abroad and comparisons between Brazil and the United States. The first five stories draw from Santiago's experiences while teaching at the University of New Mexico.[24] Most notably, "Borrão" portrays a fictionalized version of his 1963 bus trip from New Orleans to Albuquerque. The bus is a microcosm of race and class relations in the southern United States, which differ from those of Brazil.[25]

To navigate daily life in the United States, the protagonist must engage in forms of linguistic and cultural translation. He resorts to a common technique in travel narratives by describing foreign landscapes in terms of analogous places in Brazil. Years after his travels, he remembers "as terras alagadas e úmidas da Louisiana e as planícies sem fim do Texas. Depois de ter deixado uma região subtropical e úmida tornava-se insidiosa a secura do ar no ônibus advinda da calefação. . . . Secura digna de Brasília, que só vim a conhecer uma década mais tarde" (Santiago, *Histórias* 37; "the flooded, humid lands of Louisiana, and the endless Texas prairies. After having left a subtropical and humid region, the air inside the bus turned insidiously dry. . . . A dryness worthy of Brasília that I only came to know some ten years later," Santiago, "Blot" 202–03). Santiago makes the scenery more accessible for his Brazilian readers by comparing the landscapes of Texas and Brasília. Curiously, the protagonist first discovered the dry plateau of the Brazilian capital in Texas and only later in Brazil. Narrative descriptions of physical surroundings fade as the protagonist's relationship with fellow passengers becomes central to his experience of the region. These exchanges force him to examine his position as a foreigner and a racially coded subject within the segregated southern United States of the 1960s.

When describing his conversation with a black man on the bus, the protagonist stresses his difficulty communicating in English: "Disse *conversei*, devia ter dito *tentei* conversar. Meu inglês era fraco, fraquíssimo, mal dava para compor algumas frases convencionais. . . . Endurecidas pela voz, deviam soar sem sentido para qualquer ouvinte mais exigente"

(39; "I said 'spoke,' I should have said, I tried to 'speak with.' My English was poor, really poor, I could barely compose the most conventional sentences. . . . Stiffened by my voice, they must have sounded like nonsense to any exacting listener," 204). With this self-reflective gesture, the protagonist verbalizes the linguistic limitations that people face when they attempt to discuss more complex ideas in a foreign language. Moreover, he acknowledges that his voice in English must have sounded strange due to his lack of fluency and his French-inflected accent, noting, "O *broken english* justificava a falta de diálogo no clima cordial e umas placas com dizeres repetidos e sinônimos, lidas na rodoviária de Baton Rouge, esquentavam a imaginação frustrada, deixando-me desperto e cismarento" (42; "My broken English was responsible for this lack of cordial dialogue and, also, there were those signs I had read in the Baton Rouge bus terminal, with their repeated and synonymous meanings, that enflamed my already frustrated imagination, and left me awake and apprehensive," 206). By not translating the idiom "broken English" into Portuguese, Santiago underscores the communication gaps and isolation felt when living in a foreign language. Though the protagonist understands the signs' linguistic meaning, he struggles to grasp their implications of racial segregation and socioeconomic divides.

The narrator sympathizes with the plight of the black men on the bus, even though he does not fully comprehend their situation. He wants to discuss their parallel experiences of marginalization and oppression, but his limited linguistic ability and his fellow passenger's lack of familiarity with Brazil impede such dialogue:

> A sofrida experiência dele e do seu povo no vale do Mississíppi-Missouri contrastada com a minha experiência de imigrante recém-chegado dum outro sul—*south of the Mexican border*. . . . Não sei se significava alguma coisa dizer a ele que eu era brasileiro. Pelé ainda não existia no país que desconhecia o futebol, o *soccer*. . . . Para todos os efeitos Carmem Miranda era mexicana ou cubana, irmã ou sobrinha de Xavier Cugat. O mago das rumbas. (39–40)

> The suffering he and his people in the Missouri-Mississippi valley had experienced, in comparison with my own experiences as a recently arrived immigrant from another south—"south of the Mexican border." . . . I don't know if it meant anything to

say that I was Brazilian. Pelé didn't exist yet in this country; they were clueless about "futebol," rather, soccer. . . . As far as Americans were concerned, Carmen Miranda was Mexican or Cuban, the sister or niece of Xavier Cugat, the King of Rumbas. (204)

Linguistic and cultural barriers prevent the narrator and his bus companion from fully relating to one another. References to soccer and Carnival, which are now synonymous with Brazil's global image, barely registered in the southern United States of the early 1960s. In Santiago's fictional account, Brazil and Brazilians suffered from relative invisibility and mistranslations. Even Carmen Miranda, the Portuguese-born Brazilian star of Hollywood musicals, lost her constructed Brazilianness to emerge as a transnational Latina bombshell.[26] While remembering how he attempted to connect with fellow passengers, the protagonist also cites the similarities between their pre-Lenten celebrations Carnival and Mardi Gras.

The narrator realizes the limitations of applying Brazilian concepts of race to other contexts when he encounters the institutionalized segregation organizing life in the southern United States in the mid-twentieth century. The story thus points to the difficulties of translating race as a construct and a lived experience. Upon entering the Jim Crow South, the protagonist's self-perceived whiteness disappears since understandings of race are embedded within institutions, social norms, and cultural expressions of a given space and time. His racial classification differs due to distinct histories and discursive constructions within Brazil and the United States.[27] Traveling by bus separates him from the white middle class, who opt to travel by plane or car, and situates him among blacks and Mexicans. He remembers: "eu era o único de pele clara dentro do banheiro, dentro do ônibus" (43; "I was the only fair skinned person in the bathroom, on the bus," 206), but, due to his tan and black, curly hair, "era branco, mas não era caucasiano—para usar o termo de que se valem os gringos" (43; "I was white, but I wasn't Caucasian—to borrow a term used by gringos," 206-07). His light skin and education afford him privilege in Brazil, but he is seen as a "non-Caucasian" passenger in the United States.[28]

With the progression of the trip from New Orleans into Texas, black people leave the bus and people of Mexican descent climb aboard. Segregation persists as the race and ethnicity of the bus passengers change. The bathroom doors for "coloreds" encode segregation linguistically by including the words *hombres* and *mujeres* below "men" and "women," thus ensuring that Spanish-speakers know their place within a divided society. This relative lack of distinction across marginalized peoples conveys to readers in Brazil a compacted misreading of prejudice in the United States, whereby blacks, Mexicans, and South Americans are often grouped together. Santiago includes the epithet "wetbacks" in English to express the hatred directed toward Mexican migrants. Rather than leave the term untranslated, Santiago defines it for his Brazilian readers in a parenthetical aside as "costas molhadas em virtude da travessia noturna e clandestina do Rio Grande" (45; "wet from clandestine, nocturnal crossings of the Rio Grande River," 208). This description communicates the phrase's meaning but fails to capture its derogatory valences for readers unfamiliar with the context. Using terms in English like "wetbacks" in his Portuguese prose invites readers to embark on their own cultural and linguistic translations in order to better understand the text. Susan C. Quinlan attempts to create a similar effect in her translation into English with the supplementary phrase "the 'bóias frias,' as referred to in Brazil" (208). This compensation approximates the specificity of "wetbacks" as a marker of hatred, but the layered meanings of *bóias frias* (lunch-pail lads) in the Brazilian context remain unknown to readers of the English. This codeswitching distances readers by challenging their comprehension of culturally specific terms.

Due to his "broken English" and his physical appearance, the narrator moves through the United States as racially and ethnically other. His experience at a restaurant in Fort Worth exemplifies this shift in how others perceive his race. Before continuing on to Albuquerque, he wants to have a good lunch, so he takes a cab from the station to a restaurant recommended by the driver. He enters the restaurant, selects a table, and sits down, imagining the ribs he will soon be eating as he waits. After half an hour, the waiters have attended all of the customers without stopping by his table, so he leaves the restaurant. The protagonist comes to realize that the restaurant had refused to acknowledge his presence due to his non-Caucasian traits, which differentiate him from the other patrons. With his body as racially other in this context, he no longer enjoys the privileges granted to him in Brazil as a member of the educated elite. This journey forces him to confront hierarchies of race and class in the United States of the 1960s. At the tale's conclusion, he realizes that being ignored in the restaurant leaves a scar on his psyche that would remain buried for years to come: "A dor não se reconheceu ferida, por isso deve ter sido tão rápida a cicatrização" (47; "The pain did not recognize the wound—which is why I scarred over so fast," 209). Telling the story allows him to acknowledge the pain of personal exposure to racism and to recognize that, "apesar das aparências, não esqueci aquela viagem de ônibus" (39; "despite appearances, I have not forgotten that bus trip," 203). The incident also illustrates the difficulty in translating racial constructs and lived experiences across linguistic, cultural, and national borders. By transforming an individual anecdote into a compelling narrative about a Brazilian's racial interpellation in the land of Jim Crow, Santiago serves as a mediator and translator of historical approaches to race in the United States for readers in Brazil.

To better depict the linguistic and cultural translations that shape the lives of his Brazilian characters in the United States, Santiago crafts a translational aesthetic via foreign words and specific allusions. This style of prose requires readers to engage in personal processes of translation to make meaning out of terms often unknown to Brazilians. *Keith Jarrett no Blue Note* references the jazz improvisations of the eponymous album in story titles and themes. *Stella Manhattan*'s metafictional gestures and intertextuality emphasize the key role of creative transformations in this fictional world. Santiago finds inspiration for his novel in visual arts: "Narrador e personagens dobradiças, homenagem aos 'Bichos', de Lygia Clark, e a 'La Poupée', de Hans Bellmer" (Narrator and flexible characters, homage to "Bichos," by Lygia Clark, and "La Poupée," by Hans Bellmer; Santiago, *Stella* 276). Similar to Brazilian artist Clark's metal "animals" or German photographer Bellmer's images of life-sized dolls, the novel's characters and narrator contain folds and layers of appearances and identities. Epigraphs from Pierre Bonnard, Franz Kafka, and Gaston Bachelard provide further insight into the theories and artists influencing Santiago. Understanding these references requires a high degree of cultural capital, which Santiago possesses as one of Brazil's cultural and intellectual elites.

Incorporating foreign words in *Stella Manhattan* helps to represent the linguistic reality of an immigrant New York and replicate for readers the linguistic and cultural displacement that Brazilian characters experience as foreigners in the United States. The novel opens with Stella singing in English: "*Wonderful morning! what a wonderful feeling!*" (11). The English translation loses this mark of foreignness as the song and the narration unfold in the same language: " '*Oh what a beautiful morning! I've got a beautiful feeling!*' " (3). The English-language translator George Yúdice employs italics to indicate that, for the character singing, English is a foreign language. The shift from wonderful to beautiful loses the alliteration of "what a wonderful feeling!" in the original. The translation removes the ambiguity of gender granted by the absence of a subject pronoun in the Portuguese "cantarola em silêncio" (11). English grammar requires the use of a subject pronoun, so the neutral *cantarola* becomes "she sings quietly" (3). Specifying gender for grammatical necessity minimizes the protagonist's greater fluidity between the female Stella and the male Eduardo.

Santiago captures the misunderstandings and mistranslations that can happen between English, Spanish, and Portuguese in New York. For instance, Stella's neighbors observe her morning theatrics through the open window before the woman "conclui: 'He's nuts.' 'Who's nuts?' 'The Puerto-rican who lives in the building across the street'" (12). The translation includes the same exchange without shifting between the Portuguese narration and the couple's English. The passage in translation compensates for the absence of codeswitching through other transitions and transformations that suggest the fluid nature of gender and national identity. The neighbors' dialogue uses "he," which contrasts with the pronoun "she" in the opening paragraph of the translation. Describing Stella as Puerto Rican instead of Brazilian indicates the tendency to not differentiate between Latin Americans and instead assume, given demographics, that they are all Puerto Ricans. The assumption of Stella's Puerto Rican identity points to what Antonio Luciano Andrade de Tosta and Rodolfo Franconi describe as the "in and out" movement of Brazilians in the Latinx community in the United States. *Stella Manhattan* explores themes akin to those addressed by Brazilian American or Brazuca writers, but Tosta and Franconi rightly distinguish it from Brazuca works since Santiago wrote the novel in Portuguese and published it in Brazil. Critical praise for its narrative multiplicity and postmodern reflection on the role of the author further differentiate *Stella Manhattan* from Brazuca fiction.[29]

The novel's opening pages reveal Stella's bilingualism as a Brazilian living in New York who alternates with ease between Portuguese and English. The narration and dialogue similarly switch between English and Portuguese with fluidity as Stella attempts to cheer herself up: "'Sorria, Stella, sorria, vamos sorrir. . . . A vida é bela. Life is beautiful. Gorgeous! New York is beautiful! You're beautiful. Here comes the sun. It's all right'" (13; "Smile, Stella, come on, let's have a smile. . . . Life is beautiful. Maravilhosa!," 5). Halfway through her pep talk, she switches from Portuguese to English with the phrase "life is beautiful," which she says in both languages in the original. The remaining sentences in her motivational speech appear in English without a Portuguese gloss. Santiago leaves readers to grasp their meaning from context or their own knowledge of the language. Yúdice attempts to create a similar bilingualism by inserting "maravilhosa" in between "life is beautiful" and "New York is beautiful," but the inclusion of an isolated Portuguese word does not force readers to confront a less familiar language to the same degree (5). Portuguese phrases in the translation, such as Stella's exclamation of "Merda!" in the opening scene, serve to remind readers of the character's status as a foreigner (4). Santiago depicts Stella's linguistic fluidity by alternating between Portuguese and English without glosses, which serves to internalize processes of translation and to foreground immigrant characters' linguistic and cultural multiplicities. This prose style anticipates Doris Sommer's later invitation to play bilingual games. In claiming bilingualism as beneficial for democracy, Sommer notes that "even illiterate bilinguals can slip from one language to another to circumvent power and win points" (*Bilingual Aesthetics* xiv). Santiago's immigrant characters illustrate this potential of moving between languages and cultures, even when they lack formal education.

Fluent codeswitching exists between Portuguese and Spanish with the introduction of Paco, Eduardo's Cuban neighbor. Santiago often portrays Paco's speech in Spanish without a gloss into Portuguese to depict the mutually intelligible conversations that unfold between speakers of Spanish and Portuguese. When Eduardo meets Paco on the elevator, the prose shifts from Portuguese to Spanish even before Paco begins to speak:

> Vizinho de andar de Eduardo deu de cara umas vezes com ele no elevador, e na terceira ou quarta vez que toparam um com o outro le saludó muy simpaticamente en español porque yo lo sentía aquí (e batia com o dedo no peito, ali no lugar do coração) que tú eras latino. "Brasileiro? ay, no me lo digas!" . . . Ficaram conversando charlando no corredor por alguns minutos, e aí Paco resolveu chamar o amigo para um drinque en mi casa que es la tuya por supuesto. Eduardo aceitou. (30)

> He lived on the same floor as Eduardo and from time to time they'd meet face to face in the elevator. On their third or fourth encounter La Cucaracha greeted him in Spanish because I knew it all along (tapping his heart with this forefinger) that *you could only be a Latino*. "Brazilian? You don't say" . . . They chatted for a little while longer and Paco asked his new friend

in for a drink, telling him make yourself at home, my house is yours. Eduardo accepted the invitation. (18)

The exposition in Portuguese blends seamlessly into Paco's spoken Spanish, capturing the flow of a cross-lingual exchange between two Latin Americans. The English translation flattens the fluid multilingualism of Santiago's original text, which contributes to representing diverse linguistic and cultural identities within a Latinx New York. Tosta cites their encounter, specifically, Paco's exaggerated gestures, as an example of cultural difference that points to common stereotypes among Brazilians of Spanish Americans as loud, exaggerated, and impolite ("Latino, eu?" 581). He fails to sufficiently highlight the linguistic and cultural affinities between these groups, even while accurately noting the discrimination that Brazilians and other Latinos face in the United States and the prejudices that exist between the communities.

Paco and Eduardo understand each other despite linguistic differences, which suggests the possibilities of situating Brazilians in the United States as part of a broader understanding of the Latinx community. Inter-Latin American friendships that unfold in fictional cities in the United States, as I will further discuss in relationship to Adriana Lisboa's work in the next chapter, illustrate how experiences of displacement and longing for community transcend divisions of language and nation. In *Stella Manhattan*, it is only when Paco adds a side comment in English while preparing drinks that Eduardo realizes that "todo esse tempo ele falara português e Paco uma mistura de espanhol macarrônico bem diferente do aprendido na Nacional" (Santiago, *Stella* 32; "all along he had been speaking Portuguese and Paco a macaronic Spanish quite different from what he had learned at the National University," 19). The dialogue between Eduardo and Paco switches between Portuguese, Spanish, and, occasionally, English to illustrate the dynamic of their friendship. Beyond the linguistic connection, they share a similar worldview as Latinos with comparable musical tastes whose homosexual desires force them into underground realms of the city's hidden gay scene. Their friendship illustrates how linguistic, national, and sexual identities intersect in the in-between spaces of New York.

The novel's English translation cannot capture the fluid shifting between Portuguese and Spanish to the same extent, but Yúdice compensates with descriptors of speech, like "intoned in a heavy Cuban accent," and occasional Spanish words to convey Paco's mode of speaking (19). The translation portrays Paco's expressive nature with exclamations such as, "'You'd have to see it to believe it, chico, qué macho!'" (18) and "'Without music, no hay alegría'" (19). Though Yúdice opts to blend English and Spanish when quoting Paco to more fully express his personality, the translation cannot recreate the feeling of bilingual Spanish-Portuguese communication in Santiago's original. In seeking to introduce Santiago's novel to a broader reading public, Yúdice verges on flattening the linguistic and cultural specificities of in-between experiences that make *Stella Manhattan* such a compelling representation of New York as a global Latinx city. His integration of occasional Spanish and Portuguese words prevents the English translation from being reduced to a homogeneous and easily accessible text for a broad readership. The resulting translation is admirable, especially given the limitations that Yúdice faces when translating into another national language a text that already exhibits a translational aesthetic.

Eduardo and Paco find solace in the shared spaces and languages of *Stella Manhattan* yet not all interactions unfolding in Santiago's fictional interiors possess a similar sense of mutual support. The apartment of the protagonist in *Keith Jarrett no Blue Note* represents a zone of isolation between "qualquer resquício de memória do passado longínquo e de lembranças dos dias atuais" (whatever remnant of memory of the distant past and of remembrances of current days; 116–17). Lacking direct contact with others, his intimate exchanges unfold through telephone calls, voice mails, letters, and memories. The protagonist's phone conversations with an increasingly frantic woman in "You Don't Know What Love Is / *Muezzin*" capture the jealousy and suspicion that can surround affairs and clandestine homosexual encounters. The female caller Catarina, who speaks Spanish, questions the protagonist about whether he knows the whereabouts of her lover Michael. Her interrogations become more personal in subsequent calls as she reveals her knowledge of his name (Carlos), nationality (Brazilian), and his apartment's location. Fragmented memories return of an encounter in New York the summer before with a couple, a gringo Michael and a Puerto Rican Catarina. Similar to Eduardo and Paco, Carlos and Catarina communicate in Portuguese and Spanish. Their bilingual conversation, however, appears solely in Portuguese in Santiago's prose. Without codeswitching, the text fails to capture their cultural connection as Latin Americans in the United States that cuts across linguistic divisions. In contrast, fluid codeswitching between Eduardo's Portuguese and Paco's Spanish make their exchanges more palpable and expressive.

Pauses and static punctuate the stilted phone conversation of Carlos and Catarina. Readers experience the dialogue without embarking on personal acts of translation, which results in a more distant engagement with the story that parallels its characters' detached isolation.

Santiago complements codeswitching in *Stella Manhattan* with descriptive markers of speech in languages other than Portuguese. Comments like "falava muito bem mesmo, sem sotaque" (*Stella* 59; "he really spoke well, without an accent," 41) indicate Vianna's capacity to move fluently between Portuguese and English. Maintaining the prose in Portuguese allows readers to move through the passage with similar ease, which is less possible in sections with more codeswitching. Accent, as conveyed through extra-dialogical descriptors, emerges as a key determinant of linguistic competency in the novel. Speaking without an accent denotes fluency and, more importantly, the opportunities afforded to specific characters to move deftly between languages and nations. While Eduardo and Vianna easily switch between languages, immigrants like Paco with less education navigate linguistic exchanges with more difficulty. When praised for his linguistic skill, Vianna explains that he served as the liaison between the Brazilian military and the US embassy for several years and that he also had "cursos de especialização com militares gringos no Texas e no Panamá" (59). The word "gringo," which Yúdice maintains in his translation, "special courses with gringo officers in Texas and Panama" (41), captures the colloquial, often pejorative way of referring to people, goods, and ideas from the United States. Vianna alludes to the US military training of Latin American officers and other forms of intervention during the 1960s and 1970s that brought about dictatorships in the region. Without explicitly condemning interventionist actions, the novel presents a skeptical view of US influence in Latin America that contrasts with *O Novo Mundo*'s nineteenth-century optimism regarding hemispheric exchanges that I examine in the first chapter.

The Brazilians in the fictional New York of *Stella Manhattan*, the anonymous apartment of *Keith Jarrett no Blue Note*, and the transcontinental bus of "Borrão" share a trilingual space with other Latin Americans and Latinos in the United States. Santiago's Brazilian characters both identify with and differentiate themselves from these Spanish Americans and Latinos, due to their distinct geopolitical reasons for migrating and traveling. To examine the emotional and political stakes of these in-between lives, Santiago employs a prose style that demands more sustained attention from his Brazilian readers as they encounter foreign terms and cultural references akin to migrants' experiences in the United States. Santiago's literary works that unfold within the space in-between of an immigrant United States invite consideration of the place of Brazilian people and cultures in the increasingly global context at the end of the twentieth century and the start of the twenty-first.

Rethinking Brazilian Letters in the Translation Zone: Toward a Cosmopolitanism of the Poor

Santiago continues to explore what it means to write in Portuguese as a Brazilian by moving beyond the Latin American space in-between to examine the "cosmopolitanism of the poor" in the titular essay of his 2004 book, *O cosmopolitismo do pobre: Crítica literária e crítica cultural* (The cosmopolitanism of the poor: literary and cultural criticism). The collection opens with a 1995 essay about how an "atração do mundo" (attraction for the world) marks expressions of Brazilian national identity and culture that intersect with forms of globalization. In his study of Latin American cosmopolitan intellectuals, Mariano Siskind frames this fascination as a "deseo de mundo" (desire for the world). He notes that "cosmopolitan intellectuals invoked the world alternately as a signifier of abstract universality or a concrete and finite set of global trajectories traveled by writers and books" (Siskind 3). Based on this archival usage, Siskind conceives of the world as a "cosmopolitan discursive space . . . represented, invoked, challenged, and inhabited" by Latin American writers (7) as they "work through the traumatic aspects of the question of modernity" (10). Santiago similarly traces claims of an "attraction for the world" in Brazilian literature, from nineteenth-century formative memoirs through twentieth-century concepts of Antonio Candido's "dialect of *malandragem*" and Roberto Schwarz's "misplaced ideas."[30] In doing so, he examines how an impulse for the world relates to a rootedness in the local within Brazilian culture. Members of Santiago's generational cohort embrace a comparable mode of criticism, as Leyla Perrone-Moisés exemplifies by analyzing Brazilian literature in a Latin American framework through the lens of French theory.[31]

These critics place Latin American thought in dialogue with recent critical debates about cosmopolitanism, world literature, and translation. Their essays directly address Machado de Assis's concept of a "national instinct" in Brazilian letters, which I have discussed in more detail in the first chapter. In his 1995 essay, Santiago succinctly reminds readers: "Para Machado, a cultura brasileira não reside na exteriorização (ficcional ou poética) dos valores políticos da nossa nacionalidade. . . . A tarefa da geração contemporânea de Machado de Assis . . . seria a de transformar o instinto de nacionalidade em força e forma conscientes pelo 'influxo externo'" (For Machado, Brazilian culture does not reside in the (fictional or poetic) exteriorization of the political values of our nationality. . . . The task of Machado de Assis's generation . . . would be that of transforming the instinct of nationality into force and form aware of "external influence"; *O cosmopolitismo* 17). Santiago charges other Brazilian writers with rendering what Machado identified as an intimate feeling of being Brazilian into narrative forms. Perrone-Moisés goes further by claiming that Machado realized this goal in his own fiction: "Nesse famoso artigo, ele afirma que o nacionalismo estreito empobrece as obras literárias, que a nacionalidade não reside na temática ou na cor local. . . . Afirmação teórica cuja justeza ele provou com sua obra romanesca, nacional e universal" (In that famous article, he affirms that strict nationalism impoverishes literary works, that nationality does not reside in themes nor in local color. . . . Theoretical affirmation whose fairness he proved with his national and universal novelistic work; 64).[32] Machado's novels elegantly demonstrate how Brazilian literature can address both national specificities and more global concerns.[33] With their critical readings, Santiago and Perrone-Moisés underscore the foresight of Machado's 1873 essay about the continued relevance of the national alongside the universal.

Recent debates about world literature raise questions about cosmopolitanism's meaning and relevance today, as critics consider how an "attraction for the world" manifests itself in the current moment of heightened globalization and resurgent nationalisms. Moreover, how does a desire for cosmopolitan recognition of Brazilian literature and criticism affect politics and practices of translation? These concerns are central to my study of the travels and translations of Brazilian writers and texts in the early twenty-first century, as I further analyze in the remaining chapters. For now, I would like to posit these queries as a way to approach Santiago's trajectory as an artist and intellectual speaking from the in-between. Santiago's essays and fiction invite us to consider how cosmopolitanism has changed since the nineteenth century by returning to one of his main intellectual concerns: the relationship between the center and the periphery. Recognizing the sophistication of supposedly marginalized peoples and place, Santiago proposes the "cosmopolitanism of the poor" as an ideological heir to the space in-between that accounts for the expanded, global circulation of people, ideas, and goods.

By pondering to whom cosmopolitanism belongs, Santiago destabilizes existing hierarchies in a gesture that resonates with James Clifford's concept of "discrepant cosmopolitanisms."[34] Understanding cosmopolitanisms in the plural emphasizes the range of historical experiences and cultural structures that result in differing degrees of involvement with local and global systems. For Clifford, "a focus on *discrepant* cosmopolitanisms also allows us to hold on to the idea that whereas something like economic and political equality are crucial political goals, something like cultural similarity is not. It gives us a way of perceiving, and valuing, different forms of encounter, negotiation, and multiple affiliation" ("Mixed Feelings" 365). This expanded understanding of cosmopolitanisms values difference as it positions educated elites as well as often-marginalized individuals as citizens of the world with equal claims to political and economic rights. Clifford and Santiago both recognize discrepancies in claims to cosmopolitanism that emerge from different societal realms. These disparities are features of cosmopolitanisms that resist cultural homogenization for Clifford, whereas Santiago frames socioeconomic status as a defining trait of his cosmopolitanism of the poor.

To conceive of the cosmopolitanism of the poor, Santiago opens his essay with a close analysis of Portuguese director Manoel de Oliveira's 1997 film *Viagem ao começo do mundo* (*Voyage to the Beginning of the World*). This cultured selection indicates Santiago's distance from lived experiences of poverty, even as he theorizes a cosmopolitanism specific to the poor. The movie contains two films in one: the director's film, which explores well-trodden artistic terrain of individual memory and nostalgia, and another film, which centers on Afonso, a French actor and son of Portuguese emigrants, as he attempts to reconnect with his familial origins. This second film interests Santiago because it dramatizes two distinct types of poverty: one existing before the Industrial Revolution and another after. The film's romantic representations of a man working his own land exemplify preindustrial poverty in an anachronistic Portuguese village. A new form of poverty emerges within the "postmodern *global village* constituted in transit by the economic circuits of the globalized world" (Santiago, "The Cosmopolitanism" 25). With the concentration of people and capital in urban areas, rural workers move to cities in their native countries and foreign ones. In these centers of economic and cultural capital, people can access food and shelter but lose ties to traditional ways of life.

Linking this contemporary movement to earlier cycles of poverty and immigration, Santiago notes, "Today Brazil's *retirantes*, many of them natives of Brazilian states that are relatively rich, follow the flow of transnational capital like a sunflower" (28). Unlike the *retirantes* of Brazil's past, who moved between impoverished, drought-ridden rural towns and richer, coastal cities, Brazilian migrants now seek opportunities in the global cities of London, New York, or Paris. They may move from the comparatively rich states of São Paulo or Rio de Janeiro but nevertheless enter the global system of postindustrial capitalism from the relative margins. Oliveira's film serves as Santiago's point of departure for commenting on poverty in relationship to language, culture, and nation in the face of heightened globalization. His analysis centers on questions of language and translation with specific attention to Afonso's inability to communicate with his family in Portuguese. For Santiago, this missed linguistic connection suggests that poor cosmopolitan immigrants, like Afonso's father Manoel, should not have to choose between successes in the global village and ties to local communities. Instead, Santiago argues that "each nation-state in the First World can provide them . . . the possibility of not losing touch with the social values that sustain them in the cultural isolation they must endure in the postmodern metropolis" (29). This claim recalls Clifford's justification for discrepant cosmopolitanisms.

Complementing these ideas, Santiago proposes distinct forms of multiculturalism. The first type refers to an older concept seen in Brazil and throughout the Americas, where "multicultural action is the work of white men so that everyone, without exception, will be Europeanized in a disciplined way like them" (30). This cordial multiculturalism informed the work of folklorists, anthropologists, and artists in the late nineteenth and early twentieth centuries. Gilberto Freyre's view of a supposed "racial democracy," created through the fraternal and patriarchal mixing of Brazilian races and cultures, exemplifies how elites used multicultural rhetoric to construct a unified national identity.[35] Santiago cites José de Alencar's *Iracema* (1865), Aluísio Azevedo's *O cortiço* (1888), and Jorge Amado's *Gabriela, cravo e canela* (1958) as novels depicting romanticized multiculturalism, which purportedly celebrates the nation's diverse peoples but, in reality, reduces this diversity to a homogenizing construct of "Europeanized" people.[36] Grounded in elite desires to elide difference in the name of hegemonic identity, this multiculturalism tends to maintain hierarchies as former colonies continue to reproduce themselves in images of the metropolis. Santiago's critique of this type of multiculturalism resonates with his idea of the space in-between, since both concepts interrogate the relationship of the copy to the original and, thus, question the very existence of originality.

To respond to shifts in the global circulation of people and capital, Santiago calls for a new form of multiculturalism that "seeks to first take into account the influx of poor migrants in the postmodern megalopolises . . . and second to take in poor ethnic and social groups marginalized by the marked process of multiculturalism in the service of the nation-state" (34). This vision of multiculturalism allows for difference, unlike the cordial multiculturalism that attempted to transform diversity into hegemonic constructs of nationality. In the current era of heightened globalization, the nation is no longer a utopian ideal upheld by elites but rather a heterogeneous construct that allows for divergent cosmopolitanisms. Commenting on how transnational flows of capital impact marginalized individuals, Santiago suggests that "the national culture would be, or rather should be, newly configured in a way that would lead to the unprecedented manifestation of a cosmopolitan attitude among economically disadvantaged cultural actors" (35). Shifts in technology and the global economy have expanded cosmopolitan ideals and experiences beyond a limited group of elites to include marginalized people from supposedly peripheral nations. Santiago cites Afro-Brazilian cultural organizations, the Nós do Morro film projects in Rio de Janeiro's favelas, and the multilingual website of the Movimento Sem Terra (MST, Landless Workers' Movement) as examples of this cosmopolitanism of the poor. Despite limited material resources, these groups gain international attention due to the social and cultural capital of their websites, performances, and dialogues with scholars and journalists. For Santiago, foreigners' visits to favela organizations and global performances by marginalized artists illustrate how exchanges between "center" and "periphery" now unfold in both directions. He rightly links these interactions to expanded cosmopolitanisms, but, as I have established in the previous two chapters, bilateral exchanges between Brazil and foreign countries are not a new phenomenon. *O Novo Mundo*'s transnational trajectory and *Macunaíma*'s routes of creation and circulation exemplify such interactions in the late nineteenth and early twentieth centuries.

Cosmopolitanism has long belonged to Brazil as an elite privilege and continues to exist primarily for politicians, diplomats, business leaders, artists, and intellectuals. From his elite position, Santiago discursively extends access to cosmopolitanism to historically marginalized peoples of Brazil. Given its inclusive definition, the cosmopolitanism of the poor resonates with philosopher K. Anthony Appiah's reflections on cosmopolitanism. Tracing the concept back to the Cynics' claims of being "kosmopolites," that is, "citizens of the world," Appiah insists that cosmopolitanism implies an obligation to others as understood in an ideal of global citizenship. He reminds us that "the well-traveled polyglot is as likely to be among the worst off as among the best off" (*Cosmopolitanism* xviii). New technologies, which facilitate forms of virtual and real travel that demand translations, have contributed to an expansion of cosmopolitanisms. These citizens of the world have an obligation to others, regardless of national origin, racial or ethnic background, and socioeconomic status. Santiago frames language as vital to this new understanding of cosmopolitanism with his examples of linguistic misunderstandings in Oliveira's film and the emergence of multilingual websites. His essay comments on the need for and limitations of translation in establishing communication across disparate cultures and nations. In underscoring the dimensions of transnational exchange and translation that constitute the cosmopolitanism of the poor, Santiago expands his critical vision beyond Latin America to observe how increased global mobility has impacted cosmopolitanisms. Now that poor migrants exist as cosmopolitans alongside global elites, the principle of understanding one another as citizens of the world is more pertinent. Appiah insists that the ability to live together is possible through conversation, especially between people from different ways of life (xxi). Translation facilitates such exchanges among people with distinct national and linguistic backgrounds.

The idea of a cosmopolitanism of the poor helps us to think about how tropical images and other easily consumable visions of Brazil circulate in an international sphere. Do the favela dwellers, struggling artists, and nonprofit organizations that Santiago cites as examples of this new form of cosmopolitanism achieve global prominence primarily by representing an exotic otherness that markets desire? This form of cosmopolitanism, unfortunately, still trades on elite perceptions of the poor as inferior and other. Although Santiago rightly acknowledges that transnational experiences of travel, migration, culture, and consumption no longer belong only to elites, he fails to recognize that his construct of the cosmopolitanism of the poor perpetuates hierarchical divisions on a socioeconomic basis. Throughout his career, he has attempted to complicate such binaries by questioning the validity of oppositions between original and copy, center and periphery, and the cosmopolitan and the poor. While Santiago has created productive terms for rethinking these relationships, he continues to acknowledge the existence of the poor or the peripheral, marking these categories as "other" in the process. This tendency, though problematic, does not differentiate his work from practices of other Latin American intellectuals who mediate between languages, nations, theoretical influences, and formational experiences to comment on cultural dynamics of a globalized world. In fact, Santiago embodies Siskind's view of the Latin American cosmopolitan intellectual as a male writer "who derives his specific cultural subjectivity from his marginal position of enunciation and from the certainty that this position has excluded him from the global unfolding of a modernity articulated outside a Latin American cultural field" (Siskind 9).

Santiago responds to shifting global dynamics in his recent essays to recognize how cosmopolitanisms have expanded to include all echelons of society. The question remains whether acknowledging their cosmopolitanism grants impoverished people access to elite lettered realms associated with what Pascale Casanova describes as the "world republic of letters." Perhaps it would be more accurate to suggest that they enter into the "world republic of culture" by employing their cultural capital for social, political, and economic expediency within a global capitalist system.[37] These cosmopolitan poor, as Santiago's examples suggest, have learned to capitalize upon the value of their cultural works through circulation, display, performance, and sales. They respond to market demands with goods and artworks that often conform to the desires of global consumers for an exotic and impoverished land. Images of poverty suggest one possibility for translating Brazil that reinforces stereotypical visions and misperceptions. A contrasting impulse points to the potential of translation policies and practices to secure Brazil's place alongside other cosmopolitan nations within the world republic of letters.

These approaches reveal the necessities and the difficulties of translating and circulating Brazilian literature in a global market. Preferences for translatable works, in the sense of being easy to translate, among publishers, readers, and even translators have a tendency to either commodify otherness or flatten difference. Translating the nation for cultural consumption at home and abroad is inevitably a partial and flawed process. While neither comprehensive nor ideal, the options that I have outlined here raise key considerations about how to translate heterogeneous experiences and intimate feelings of nationality into forms of art and literature for national and global publics. Translation into other national languages allows for works written in Brazilian Portuguese to circulate in a global market, beyond Portugal and other Lusophone nations. Rather than continue to select literary works for translation according to an assumption of translatability, I consider how embracing a politics of untranslatability would affect representations capturing the diverse experiences of Brazil and its peoples. The next chapter delves further into these questions through Adriana Lisboa's hemispheric fictions as exemplary of broader trends in the current literary landscape of Brazil in the Americas.

Chapter 4

Testing Translatability

Adriana Lisboa's Hemispheric Brazilian Novels

As a contemporary novelist from Brazil who lives in the United States and writes in Portuguese, Adriana Lisboa grapples with the question of what it means to write Brazilian literature in the twenty-first century. Writers like Lisboa often engage with local particularities as they address concerns that speak to readers beyond national and linguistic borders. According to Héctor Hoyos, an interest in "consolidating, simultaneously, both the world *and* Latin America as their chambers of resonance" has contributed to the emergence of global Latin American novelists, such as Roberto Bolaño, Diamela Eltit, Chico Buarque, César Aira, and Mario Bellatín (7).[1] Although grouped together by Hoyos for their engagement with both the global and the Latin American, these writers are not homogeneous given the varied degree to which they experiment in their prose, interact with regional or national specificities, and are innovative in their linguistic formulations. The resulting texts differ in terms of their perceived ease of translation and, relatedly, their circulation within a global literary market. Anglo-American trade presses are more likely to translate Latin American works with representational narratives, whereas texts that problematize language and critique the very possibility of representation tend to be published by university or small independent presses when they appear in translation.[2]

In many respects, Lisboa embodies the profile of a global Brazilian writer as a native of urban Rio de Janeiro who pursued formal musical and literary education; lived in France, Japan, and the United States; and now represents Brazil at conferences, literary festivals, and universities or research exchanges. Recipient of the 2003 José Saramago Prize in honor of literary works by young authors in Portuguese, she was one of the Bogotá39 in 2007, a recognition of the top thirty-nine writers under the age of forty from Latin America.[3] Her novels have been translated into fifteen languages, including English, Spanish, French, German, Italian, and Arabic. Her most translated novel, *Sinfonia em branco* (2001), has versions in English (*Symphony in White*, 2010) and eleven other languages. *Azul-corvo* (2010) enjoys a relatively large global presence with translations in six languages, including *Crow Blue* (2013). Both *Rakushisha* (2007) and *Hanói* (2013, Hanoi) have been translated into three languages, but only the earlier novel has appeared in English as *Hut of Fallen Persimmons* (2011). There are also translations of *Um beijo de colombina* (2003, Columbine's kiss), *Contos populares japoneses* (2008, Popular Japanese stories), and *O coração às vezes para de bater* (2007, The heart sometimes stops beating). Her writing has appeared in anthologies of Brazilian prose in Portuguese, Spanish, English, Italian, French, German, and Swedish.[4]

As a global Brazilian novelist, Lisboa combines the dual impulses that Hoyos identifies with plots that situate Brazilian characters in unfamiliar foreign settings, which, in turn, reveal how experiences of dislocation affect language and identity. She crafts a translational prose that recalls Santiago's style by inviting readers to experience the linguistic and cultural displacements that characters must navigate in foreign surroundings. These gestures toward translation resonate with Rebecca Walkowitz's concept of a "born-translated novel," where "translation functions as a thematic, structural, conceptual, and sometimes even typographical device" (4). While Walkowitz foregrounds an interest in the global literary market in studying novels either written for or as translation, I posit that thematic and aesthetic approximations of translation best capture the complexities of transnational travels and lives, as Lisboa's recent novels *Rakushisha*, *Azul-corvo*, and *Hanói* exemplify. She exudes a twenty-first-century version of what Machado de Assis described as a Brazilian writer's instinct of nationality as not being limited to depictions of local color. Akin to Santiago, she addresses geographic, linguistic, and cultural displacement from a space in-between Brazil and other nations, most pertinently, the United States. In doing so, she creates *Azul-corvo* and *Hanói* as hemispheric Brazilian novels that reflect on, exist in, and engage with Brazil and the rest of the Americas simultaneously. Depicting how Brazilians negotiate complex linguistic, cultural, racial, and ethnic identities as they interact with Spanish Americans in the United States indicates the relative marginality of Brazilians within Latinx and Latin American communities. Lisboa's novels continue the work of *O Novo Mundo*'s articles, Sousândrade's epic, and Santiago's fiction of rendering observations and experiences of Brazilians living in the United States into Portuguese for a primarily Brazilian readership.

Lisboa finds her home, figuratively, in translation as she moves between languages and nations through her work as a literary translator and her fiction's thematic and stylistic explorations. Her narratives feature seemingly simple prose, clear plot developments, and well-defined characters, which publishers associate with translatability in the market sense of being easy to translate. Even though she employs linguistic codeswitching and cultural allusions that resist facile translation, translators and publishers in the English-language market praise the relative accessibility of her narratives and language, which contributes to the small trade press Bloomsbury publishing *Crow Blue*. After considering how dynamics of translatability impact the publication and circulation of Brazilian literature in hemispheric and global markets, I focus on Lisboa's recent novels as case studies for analyzing how to represent linguistic and cultural forms of translation that Brazilian characters encounter when living abroad. Despite their apparent translatability, *Azul-corvo* and *Hanói* resist flattening the specific experiences of their first- and second-generation immigrant characters from Brazil, El Salvador, Mexico, and Vietnam now living in the United States. Lisboa captures how frames of racial, ethnic, national, and other identity markers change as characters travel and migrate in order to consider whether it is possible to translate contextualized constructs of identity and belonging.

Theorizing Translatability and the Place of Brazilian Literature

Lisboa's work serves as an ideal space to examine how theories of translation and translatability intersect in the production and circulation of contemporary Brazilian literature within hemispheric and global realms. Her recent novels depict how traveling or living abroad generates feelings of displacement that require characters to engage in linguistic and cultural translations. These narratives may initially seem easy to translate from Brazilian Portuguese as they correspond to a narrative style typical of global Latin American novels that circulate with greater frequency among North American and European audiences.[5] Closer attention to her prose, however, reveals an aesthetic particular to the multilingual and multicultural context between Brazil and other nations in which her novels unfold. By manifesting a form of translatability that both resonates with Walter Benjamin's concept and responds to editorial interests, her novels since *Rakushisha* suggest how Brazilian literature can circulate globally without flattening linguistic and cultural specificity. Represented by the German-based Mertin Literary Agency and published by prestigious Alfaguara and Iluminaras in Brazil, Lisboa aims to utilize her privileged position in the global literary sphere to represent exiles, immigrants, and refugees often rendered invisible or marginalized within society, especially in elite realms of literature and culture.

This literary project differs from earlier projections of Brazil for foreign audiences through displays at world's fairs, Hollywood films of the Good Neighbor years, and the musical styles of samba and bossa nova, which often reinforced stereotypes of Brazil as a tropical nation primed for global prominence given its wealth of natural resources and its diversity of cultures.[6] As the largest nation in Latin America and the only Portuguese-speaking one, Brazil's cultural and linguistic insularity has contributed to the relatively limited circulation of its literary works in a global market. In calling for a "poetry for export" in 1924, Oswald de Andrade celebrated the distinctive quality and technical innovation of Brazilian writing while recognizing the literary trade imbalances that relegated Brazil to the peripheries. Realizing his vision of a greater global prominence for Brazilian literature remains a work-in-progress connected to the geopolitical and sociocultural dynamics of translation and the economics of publication. Brazil's literature became more visible in the United States from the 1960s to 1980s, when hemispheric politics of the Cold War contributed to the establishment of incentives for publishing Latin American literature in translation, such as the American Association of University Presses program funded by the Rockefeller Foundation and the Center for Inter-American Relations translation program.[7] While Spanish American texts dominated this publishing phenomenon of the Boom, works by Brazilians Machado de Assis, Graciliano Ramos, Rachel de Queiroz, Jorge Amado, and Clarice Lispector, among others, were translated into English in this period.[8]

Critics, publishers, and government agencies observe the imbalances that continue to structure Brazilian literature's position in a global market in the early twenty-first century. Lawrence Venuti rightly contends that asymmetries in the field of translation correlate with global socioeconomic, political, and cultural inequities, whereby English is the most translated language but the one least translated into worldwide. For instance, in 1994, translations into Portuguese accounted for 60 percent of new titles in Brazil, with up to 75 percent coming from English (*Scandals* 160).⁹ Claire Williams and Carmen Villarino Pardo claim that international focus on Brazil during its preparations for the 2014 World Cup and the 2016 Olympic Games provided an opportunity to heighten the global standing of Brazilian literature and, ideally, to combat stereotypical visions of the nation via literature.¹⁰ To capitalize on this moment, Brazil announced in 2011 a reformulation of the National Library's program started in 1991 to support the translation and publication of Brazilian writers abroad.¹¹ The National Library also promoted, in collaboration with the Ministry of Foreign Affairs, national arts and literature by supporting Brazil as the honored nation at the 2011 Europalia International Arts Festival and the 2013 Frankfurt Book Fair. Due to these efforts, as well as heightened reader interest, Anglo-American publishers have expanded their offerings of Brazilian literature in translation.¹²

It is critical to consider which Brazilian texts circulate within the global literary market given that, as Venuti reminds us, "translation wields enormous power in constructing representations of foreign cultures" (*Scandals* 67). Ideally, translating Brazilian literature would allow for diverse views of the nation's geography, people, cultures, and history to reach an audience beyond national and linguistic borders. While translations can reinforce stereotypical images and commonplace representations of Brazil, they can also introduce readers to voices that revise and expand understandings of the nation. In advocating for "a translation ethics of difference," Venuti calls on translators to straddle foreign and domestic cultures in order "to produce a text that is the potential source of cultural change" (87). Embracing an ethics of difference would invite a wider range of voices, styles, stories, and experiences to populate translations of Brazilian literature into English. Translators and publishers have begun to embark on this task, resulting in the publication of Conceição Evaristo's *Ponciá Vicencio* (2006), Davi Kopenawa's *The Falling Sky: Words of a Yanomami Shaman* (2013), Marcelo d'Salete's *Run for It: Stories of Slaves Who Fought for Their Freedom* (2017) and *Angola Janga: Kingdom of Runaway Slaves* (2019), and Geovani Martins's *The Sun on My Head* (2019). These narratives, memoirs, graphic novels, and short stories by

Afro-Brazilian and Amerindian writers challenge assumptions and misconceptions about Brazil held by Anglophone readers and, in the process, complicate and deepen their knowledge of the nation and its peoples.

Translation initiatives and editorial projects grant foreign readers access to Brazil's literary landscape but, given the small percentage of Brazilian works translated from Portuguese into other languages each year, the resulting vision remains inevitably limited. In recent years, publications from small publishing houses, university press imprints, and websites like Words Without Borders have helped to diversify the profile of Brazilian literature in translation.[13] Works selected for translation in trade presses, however, still largely correspond to the perceived desires of a global audience by highlighting Brazil's exotic difference or its cosmopolitanism. Novels by Jorge Amado and Paulo Lins, for example, depict visions of "local color" that feature tropical sensuality and stylized favela violence, respectively.[14] On the other hand, works included in English-language anthologies of Brazilian literature, such *Granta*'s best young Brazilian writers, portray educated and well-traveled characters whose professions, worries, consumption patterns, and cultural preferences parallel those of urban residents in other nations.[15]

Addressing the politics and economics of translation helps to understand Brazil's profile in this current publishing landscape and, more specifically, Lisboa's place within it. Though guided by financial concerns and market incentives, selecting Brazilian literature for translation and publication abroad often involves aesthetic considerations about a work's perceived translatability in terms of its relative accessibility for foreign readers. While independent, nonprofit, and university presses have started to carve out a space for a more diverse profile of Brazilian literature translated into English, larger trade presses and even some translators opt to work primarily with novels and stories that they deem translatable.[16] According to market-driven definitions, a literary work's translatability resides in its ease of translation due to accessible language and style. Publishing in translation mostly works that meet these criteria generates a homogeneous view of the nation's literature where novels predominate, which does not reflect the full range of voices, styles, genres, and experimental forms in Brazil. Practicing what Venuti terms an "ethics of difference" and what Emily Apter describes as a "politics of untranslatability" would help the publishing industry to contest narrow visions of foreign cultures when selecting and translating literary works for a global market.

Both concepts point to the need for resistance in translation and other forms of cross-cultural communication, which recalls Gayatri Spivak's postcolonial stance. Drawing on her experiences as a translator of Bengali women's writing, Spivak posits that deeply engaging with a text through intimate acts of reading is critical to translation. Unfortunately, she notes that "the politics of translation from a non-European woman's text too often suppresses this possibility because the translator cannot engage with, or cares insufficiently for, the rhetoricity of the original" (Spivak 313). Following Spivak's politics of translation requires recognizing the comparative global status of languages, especially when imbalances of political and cultural power exist between source and target languages. She also acknowledges that translation unfolds in a global system of languages and literatures with varying degrees of academic and editorial prestige and prominence. A critical question for Spivak and other translators working with underrepresented languages and marginalized voices is how to retain a text's cultural specificity without homogenizing it to conform to market demands and foreign readers' presumed interests. To illustrate this challenge, Spivak refers to examples of cultural translation in English-language novels by J. M. Coetzee, Toni Morrison, and Wilson Harris. She contends that these texts suggest the difficulties of translating specific forms of knowledge in a postcolonial context as they "ask us to attend to the rhetoric which points to the limits of translation" (326). Paying close attention to both linguistic and cultural specificity as potential marks of untranslatability allows "readers-as-translators" to discover "what books we can forage, and what we must set aside" (329). In acknowledging that certain books resist translation almost completely due to their particularisms while others invite more engagement, Spivak provides one model of how to approach with greater cultural awareness and ethical commitment the selection of Brazilian literary works for translation and publication in an English-dominated global market.

Spivak's vision of a politics of translation intersects with ideas from Venuti and Apter about how translation from one national language into another poses the danger of inflicting violence upon the text by flattening out local particularities in the name of the universal. In his 1995 treatise on translation, Venuti proposed combatting the translator's invisibility, especially within the Anglo-American literary market, by advocating for a foreignizing, rather than domesticating, practice of translation. This mode would manifest itself primarily by preserving marks of foreignness in the translated text but would also involve selecting source works that do not conform to existing canons of literature in translation. Moreover, he urged translators to embrace experimental tactics that would draw attention to linguistic and cultural difference in the translated text (*Translation Changes* 2–3). His instrumental approach argued for forms of resistance that resonate with Spivak's postcolonial politics of translation but without acknowledging the critical role of readers. In revising his earlier theories, Venuti has moved closer to the political and ethical stance of a Spivakian reader-as-translator. Conceiving of translation as a variable personal act of interpretation allows for "an ethical reflection that acknowledges the inevitable loss of source-cultural difference as well as the exorbitant gain of translating-cultural difference, a trade-off that exposes the creative possibilities of translation" (4). This recognition of translation's ethical complexities and creative potential resembles earlier interventions of Latin American writers, most notably Jorge Luis Borges and Haroldo de Campos, into debates on translation theory and practice. Venuti proposes ethics of translation that stress how the selection, translation, and subsequent circulation of literary works in a global market constitute an event capable of facilitating cross-cultural communication and generating misunderstandings.

Ethics also concern Apter's approach to questions of translatability and world literature. While she rightly commends translation's role in expanding the global literary landscape beyond a traditional Western canon, she also condemns how "many recent efforts to revive World Literature rely on a translatability assumption" (*Against* 3). A reliance on seemingly translatable works within world literature and global literary markets minimizes the diversity of literature circulating between languages and nations. Apter astutely criticizes how world literature as an idea and a practice either reflexively endorses cultural equivalence or celebrates racial, ethnic, and national differences as commercialized identities primed for circulation in commodity culture. She questions the dependence on translatability, understood here as a given text's perceived readability and accessibility, in elevating works to the category of world literature through translation and publication. With a politics of untranslatability, she posits an ethical stance against these trends that she disdains.

To better understand how translatability structures the place of contemporary Brazilian literature, including Lisboa's works, in a global literary market, it is necessary to consider definitions of this concept in connection to editorial preferences. One of the critical touchstones remains Benjamin's classic 1923 essay "The Translator's Task." Drawing on his experiences translating Charles Baudelaire's poetry into German, Benjamin articulated ideas about translation in relation to a source text that dialogued with his metaphysical understandings of language. He claimed, "If translation is a form, then translatability must be essential to certain works . . . this does not mean that their translation is essential for themselves, but rather that a specific meaning inherent in the original texts expresses itself in their translatability" (76). The quality of translatability guarantees that a translation preserves its ties to the original, even as it releases the text into another language through a liberating process of recreation. Locating translatability within the source text, rather than the translation itself, paralleled Benjamin's ideas about the aura of an artistic work and pure language.[17] By insisting on the importance of the original, he minimized his creative role as a translator when he posited that "the extent to which a translation can correspond to the essence of this form is determined objectively by the translatability of the original" (82). Benjamin subsequently granted the translator a degree of agency when he defined his task as "to set free in his own language the pure language spellbound in the foreign language, to liberate the language imprisoned in the work by rewriting it" (82). In framing translation as rewriting, he anticipated later developments in translation studies that emphasize the creative possibilities of translating.[18]

Benjamin's essay continues to serve as a point of departure for discussing translatability with an attention to how the distinctiveness of language determines the potential for translation. He posited that "the less value and dignity the original's language has, the more it is the communication of sense, the less is to be gained from it for translation . . . makes the latter impossible. The more distinctive the work, the more it remains translatable, in the very fleeting nature of its contact with sense" (82–83). If publishers were to follow Benjamin's understanding of translatability, works that foreground distinctive language would be recognized as translatable and, as such, translated with greater frequency. For translators, the task of rewriting linguistically innovative texts would be creatively and critically rewarding. However, in the contemporary global marketplace, this vision of translatability rarely guides the selection, translation, and subsequent distribution of literary works. Benjamin overlooked the role of the market and readers in proposing translatability as essential to the connection between an original text and its translation. His vision of translatability does not coincide with its usage by contemporary translators and publishers, who tend to praise accessible works for being translatable.

In today's global literary market, a work is more likely considered translatable in the sense of easy to translate when it features a narrative told in a fairly straightforward manner via comparatively simple prose. For instance, translator Alison Entrekin cites Lisboa's accessible prose and relatable narrative as key to *Azul-corvo*'s translatability, explaining, "The first thing that struck me about *Crow-Blue* . . . was its cross-cultural appeal and translatability. . . . In it, Lisboa writes from the in-between world of migrants, who teeter on the cusp of belonging but who are forever outsiders at the same time. Perfect, I thought, for a book about to be translated, as its characters—and writer—are themselves in an ongoing process of self-translation" (272). Guided by market preferences, Entrekin assesses that Lisboa's prose would pose minimal challenges in translation. At first glance, Lisboa's novel exemplifies this market-driven vision of translatability. However, codeswitching and cultural references challenge translators to reveal a prose style that, despite its initial appearances, is not completely translatable. Gestures of resistance in her prose point to the potential for a politics of untranslatability, even as the narrative's relative accessibility situates the novel in the market realm of translatability. To navigate these divergent views, I propose reading Lisboa's novel as illustrative of Benjamin's approach to translatability as grounded in the distinctive language and quality of a source text.

Lisboa's entrenchment in literary, academic, and editorial institutions differentiates her from Afro-descendant, Amerindian, LGBTQ+, feminist, immigrant, landless or homeless, or otherwise marginalized writers in Brazil who have started to circulate more within global literary realms. Despite recent editorial advances, these voices remain relatively underrepresented in the Anglo-American literary marketplace. This comparative lack of representation corresponds to publishing dynamics in Brazil that allow artistic and intellectual elites like Lisboa and Santiago to continue to prevail within editorial economies of prestige.[19] These preferences extend into the editorial market in the United States, where works by marginalized voices or experimental writers appear in smaller nonprofit or university presses in the occasional instances that they do get published. Unlike publishers who discount the creative potential of the untranslatable, Apter foregrounds a politics of untranslatability within her vision for an alternative global literary landscape. She explains that her "aim is to activate untranslatability as a theoretical fulcrum of comparative literature with bearing on approaches to world literatures" (*Against* 3). This approach draws on Derrida's translation theories and Barbara Cassin's philosophical work on untranslatables.

In turning to the untranslatable as a political possibility, Apter delves into debates surrounding translatability and untranslatability. Lydia H. Liu ponders "what theoretical assumptions about *difference* between languages" these discussions generate (*Translingual* 11). To respond to this question, Liu situates earlier theories of translation by Benjamin, Derrida, and George Steiner in relation to religious concepts of language. In contrast, Apter follows a more philosophical approach by dialoguing most closely with Derrida before focusing on the construct of the Untranslatable. With this capitalization, Apter and her colleagues distinguish their philosophical approaches from commonsense understandings of the term. Their *Dictionary of Untranslatables*, which Barbara Cassin edited in French and Emily Apter, Jacques Lezra, and Michael Wood edited in the English translation, responds to the difficulty of translating certain concepts, such as "saudade" or "kitsch," with essays about their philosophical specificities and theoretical nuances. In their introduction to the translation, Cassin and Wood explain, "To speak of *untranslatables* in no way implies that the terms in question, or the expressions, the syntactical or grammatical turns, are not and cannot be translated: the untranslatable is rather what one keeps on (not) translating" (n.p.). The untranslatable intrigues readers and translators due to a distinctiveness that resists facile comprehension and invites ongoing interpretations.

Apter's view of the Untranslatable centers on its relative resistance to understanding and circulation. She characterizes it as "that x-factor that disqualifies presumptive knowability in matters of linguistic definition" (*Against* 121). In staking claim to a politics of untranslatability, she expands upon Derrida's view of the slippages inherent to language that complicate processes of meaning-making. She also dialogues, indirectly, with Benjamin's idea of the translator's task to envision translation as "a form of creative property that belongs fully to no one" (15). By noting the void of direct ownership over a translation, she recognizes that the "translational author—shorn of a singular signature—is the natural complement . . . to World Literature understood as an experiment in national sublation that signs itself as collective, terrestrial property" (15). With this gesture toward the collective, Apter aims to minimize translation's imbrication within commercial systems of the global literary market. For Pieter Vermeulen, this move away from understanding translation as a proprietary commodity represents a fundamental flaw in her proposal. He aptly criticizes Apter's misreading of how literature interacts with the market and, relatedly, her underestimation of the market's power to "convert singularities into marketable differences" (Vermeulen 80). As Vermeulen contends, overlooking market complexities contributes to Apter's overly simplistic politics of untranslatability.

The issues that Apter's work and its critical reception raise are relevant to analyzing the place of contemporary Brazilian literature in global and hemispheric literary markets. What would happen if selections of Brazilian literature for translation privileged experimental works attuned to localized specificities of language and culture, instead of prioritizing an assumption of translatability? This hypothetical shift would invite writers, translators, publishers, editors, and government agencies to consider how a politics of untranslatability, guided by an awareness of market dynamics, could unfold in the Brazilian context. Currently, however, mainstream trade presses tend to deem linguistic and stylistic experimentations untranslatable. Such texts employ language in a distinctive manner to create literary works that, decades earlier, Benjamin likely would have praised for their intrinsic translatability. Their linguistic and cultural specificities invite us, as readers, translators, and critics, to continue unpacking their nuances and interpreting them for ourselves and others. These works and phrases are, to evoke how Cassin and Wood characterize the untranslatable, "what one keeps on (not) translating." A politics of untranslatability is thus best understood not as a rejection of translatability itself, but rather as a move away from its commercial affiliation with facile understanding in favor of approaches to translation that value literary works for their linguistic innovation and cultural distinctiveness, as I will explore further in the conclusion. For now, I turn to Lisboa's novels to consider how her narratives tease out these complex interactions between translatability, translational aesthetics, transnational subjectivities, and market demands.

Adriana Lisboa's Transnational Tales

Lisboa's novels explore how undocumented Salvadorans, Vietnamese refugees, and lower- to middle-class Brazilians navigate complexities of migration, community, and citizenship in the United States. In contrast to the struggling travelers and migrants of her narratives, Lisboa occupies a privileged realm, alongside Santiago and others, of cosmopolitan Brazilian writers. After growing up in Rio de Janeiro during the military dictatorship and transition to democracy, she studied music and lived in France as a jazz singer before returning to Brazil to complete a PhD in comparative literature. She worked as a translator from English and French for eleven years until she decided in 2012 to dedicate herself full-time to her own writing.[20] Lisboa credits translation with making her a better writer since it forced her to pay close attention to the selection of words and their syntax.[21] She moved to Colorado in 2006 and continues to live in the United States, now in Austin. Feelings of displacement due to travel and migration animate her characters' affective experiences in *Rakushisha*, *Azul-corvo*, and *Hanói*. The novels' protagonists attempt to establish connections to new landscapes by rendering them into more familiar terms from past memories and locales. In doing so, Lisboa represents how personal constructs of home and nation change over time as links to one's birthplace or ancestral homeland become increasingly tenuous.

Lisboa's narratives circulate in translation to contribute to her prominence as a global Brazilian writer. She further enhances her international profile at literary festivals, readings, writers-in-residence programs, and other events. Lisboa and her contemporaries Bernardo Carvalho, Carola Saavedra, and Daniel Galera, among others, craft global Brazilian novels that simultaneously engage with Brazil and the world via the experiences of characters while abroad.[22] Their literary works indicate an interest in depicting otherness or, at times, recall, in an indirect and fictionalized manner, their authors' trajectories.[23] Existing scholarship on contemporary Brazilian fiction highlights how writers explore the porosity between experiences of the global and the national and representations of the real and the fictional. For Karl Erik Schøllhammer, the term "contemporary Brazilian fiction" raises the question of what "Brazilian" means in a postcolonial and globalized landscape where the nation occupies a less central role. Even as impulses toward the global substitute the earlier centrality of the nation, the regional and the national persist as constructs in contemporary Brazilian novels. Schøllhammer also observes how authors integrate themselves into their work with metafictional reflections and autofiction. Beatriz Resende identifies *presentificação*, which she defines as an insistence on the present, as contemporary Brazilian fiction's most notable characteristic (27–28). This temporal urgency coincides with a fragmentation of urban space and, more pertinently, allows for new voices to speak for themselves without mediation.

Other critics ascertain common themes that traverse Brazilian literature from earlier movements to contemporary fiction. In establishing travel as essential to Brazilian literature and culture, Maria Isabel Edom Pires identifies three main types of travelers: the nineteenth-century romantic naturalist, the twentieth-century immigrant, and the twenty-first-century traveler aware of exile or in contact with the clandestine. Lisboa similarly recognizes a thematic recurrence of travel in her novels as a search for art, a form of migration or exile, an act that creates dislocation, and a metaphor for life ("Navegar" 157–58). Clandestine experiences and spaces distinguish twenty-first-century travels and migrations in Brazilian fiction, according to José Leonardo Tonus. He refers to Celina in *Rakushisha* as a traveler who, while in Kyoto, inhabits realms like plazas, buses, metro stations, and libraries associated with clandestine activities (Tonus 146). I contend that the characters in *Azul-corvo* and *Hanói* more fully resemble what Pires defines as the twenty-first-century traveler. In the fictional worlds of Denver in *Azul-corvo* and Chicago in *Hanói*, first- and second-generation immigrants from Brazil, El Salvador, Mexico, or Vietnam are in close proximity to exile and other clandestine journeys. Unlike nineteenth-century travelers who embarked on geographic explorations of remote lands or early twentieth-century immigrants who established a life of upward mobility in a new country, these contemporary characters confront the hardships of being an immigrant in a United States increasingly marked by xenophobic attitudes and resurgent nationalisms.

Before shifting her focus to immigrant lives, Lisboa addresses in *Sinfonia em branco* through *Rakushisha* how literal travels in Brazil and to Japan and figurative ones via poetry impact personal relationships and connections to place.[24] In *Sinfonia em branco*, sisters Clarice and Maria Inês travel between the family farm of their 1960s childhood near Frioburgo in the interior of Rio de Janeiro state and the coastal capital city, where they study, struggle with loss, and attempt to establish their own familial ties as adults.[25] Travels in *O beijo de colombina* unfold in the streets of Rio de Janeiro and the verses of Manuel Bandeira as the narrator traverses a palimpsestic landscape of personal memories and poetic references.[26] When researching and writing *Rakushisha* in 2006, Lisboa traveled to Kyoto with a Japan Foundation fellowship. She investigated how the Japanese wabi-sabi aesthetic cultivates imperfection and transience as expressions of existence in line with Buddhist principles ("Navegar" 156). With *Rakushisha*, Lisboa aimed to transfer and, in the process, creatively transform the wabi-sabi aesthetic from its classical Japanese context into the stylistic and narrative realm of contemporary Brazilian prose. The title refers to Kyoto's Hut of Fallen Persimmons, a retreat that seventeenth-century Japanese poet Matsuo Bashō visited and one of his disciples built. Rakushisha exists in the novel as a space for reflection and a symbol of tranquility where ideas from Bashō's travel diary intermingle with experiences of Lisboa's Brazilian protagonists. To emphasize how figurative travels via reading depend upon linguistic translations, the novel adopts a collage format featuring excerpts of Bashō's diary translated into Brazilian Portuguese and haikus printed in romanized Japanese with their Portuguese translation.

The main narrative arc of *Rakushisha* consists of Haruki, a Japanese Brazilian illustrating the Portuguese translation of Bashō's diary, and Celina, a *carioca* still mourning the death of her two-year-old daughter six years earlier, traveling to Kyoto to escape their daily realities.[27] Displaced from familiar surroundings, Haruki begins to process his failed relationship with Yukiko, the translator of Bashō's diary, and his tenuous connection to his Japanese Brazilian identity. Celina, meanwhile, comes to terms with her sadness by remembering earlier personal tragedies while Bashō's words guide her meanderings through Kyoto. The idea of belonging haunts both Haruki and Celina. In a diary entry that opens the novel, Celina addresses her geographic displacement: "Sou do outro lado do planeta. Pode-se dizer que vim escondida dentro da bagagem de outra pessoa. É como se eu tivesse entrado clandestina, apesar do visto no meu passaporte . . . Não pertenço a este lugar" (Lisboa, *Rakushisha* 9; "I'm from the other side of the planet. You might say that I came hidden in another person's luggage. It's as if I had entered illegally, in spite of the visa in my passport . . . I don't belong in this place," *Hut of Fallen Persimmons* 3).[28] As she reflects on her lack of personal connection to Japan, Celina notes her proximity to the clandestine realms that Pires associates with twenty-first-century travelers. Bashō's writings lead Celina to the more profound realization that "a viagem nos ensina algumas coisas. Que a vida é o caminho e não o ponto fixo no espaço . . . aquilo que possuímos de fato, nosso único bem, é a capacidade de locomoção. É o talento para viajar" (125; "traveling teaches us a few things. That life is a path and not a fixed point in space . . . that the one thing we do indeed possess, our only asset, is our capacity of locomotion. It is our talent for traveling," 142). This idea brings to mind Lisboa's account of travel as a metaphor for life. Celina recognizes that travel, though it has a widespread pedagogical function, remains mainly a privilege for people who want to discover other places and cultures and can afford to do so.

In this unfamiliar setting, Celina wanders through the city accompanied by Bashō's verses and her memories of happier times before her daughter's death. When faced with a shopkeeper or another person who does not speak English, her lingua franca in Japan, Celina attempts to make herself understood with limited knowledge of Japanese through creative forms of linguistic and cultural translation. For instance, the clerk at an incense store accompanies the saying "Mukashi mukashi" with a hand gesture to suggest its meaning (41). Celina glosses the phrase with its Portuguese equivalent "há muito tempo" ("a long time ago"), rather than leave it untranslated, and notes that many stories in Japan begin with this repeated word (41; 43). Lisboa captures how efforts to compensate for not knowing another language facilitate cross-cultural communication yet also maintain distance. To craft a linguistic landscape that resembles experiences of traveling in Japan, the novel includes lines in English without glosses, such as, "*Welcome to Tokyo-Handy guide. Tokyo Metropolitan Government*" (67). These untranslated phrases point to the status of English as a shared language among Lisboa's Brazilian characters and other cosmopolitan travelers to Japan. Since her characters and other educated Brazilians can read and communicate in English, Lisboa opts to not translate the brochure language into Portuguese nor include explanatory glosses. By leaving traces of foreignness in her Portuguese prose via the sonic reverberations of repeating Japanese words and untranslated English phrases, the text begins to develop a translational aesthetic that becomes further refined in her subsequent novels about migrants and refugees. *Rakushisha*, however, still follows editorial conventions that facilitate readability by placing foreign words in italics and including glosses for most foreign phrases.

In *Azul-corvo* and *Hanói*, the prose moves more freely between Portuguese, Spanish, and English without glosses to indicate the forms of multilingual conversation that exist among immigrants in the United States. While intelligible for Lisboa's immigrant characters and, most likely, her educated readership in Brazil, this movement between languages suggests the potential limitations of translating into another language a novel with translation as a constitutive thematic and stylistic element. Lisboa perfects a translational prose to represent more completely the linguistic nuances and cultural misunderstandings that unfold between peoples from different countries living in cities and suburbs of the United States. Unlike

Santiago, who transformed events from his years living in United States into autofiction in *Histórias mal contadas*, Lisboa draws on her familiarity with immigrant life without directly fictionalizing her experiences. Her ability to compare the distinctive geographies of the American Southwest and Brazil informs the descriptions of landscape in *Azul-corvo*. Her volunteer work with refugees in Denver inspires the Vietnamese characters in *Hanói*. To capture the varied experiences of Brazilians in the United States, she depicts immigrant characters of distinct backgrounds, ages, genders, nationalities, and legal statuses. Her fictional representations reflect the heterogeneity of race, gender, socioeconomic status, and educational background of the estimated eight hundred thousand to 1.5 million Brazilians currently living in the United States.[29]

In depicting the lives of fictional Brazilians in the United States, Lisboa navigates a realm of immigrant literature that borders on categories of Brazuca and Brazilian American culture.[30] Antonio Luciano Andrade de Tosta identifies colloquial language, characters based on real people, a thematic focus on immigration, and an attempt to represent reality as traits of Brazuca novels ("Latino, *eu*?" 577). This definition allows for categorizing works written in Portuguese and published in Brazil as Brazuca literature if Brazilian immigration in the United States is their primary theme. By exploring a broader range of themes, *Azul-corvo* and *Hanói* resist classification as Brazuca literature to instead emerge as hemispheric Brazilian novels. Though written in Portuguese, Lisboa's recent novels about Brazilians in the United States dialogue more generally with depictions of how immigration impacts familial bonds, linguistic practices, national identities, and conceptions of home in contemporary US ethnic literature. Her multilingual characters of diverse nationalities and ethnicities exist in fictional landscapes that illustrate how geographic, linguistic, and cultural displacement demands personal gestures of translation as migrants and exiles navigate new surroundings. Akin to tales of family and migration that emerge as the basis for a *Bildungsroman* in Latinx literary works by, among others, Junot Díaz and Sandra Cisneros, Lisboa explores how Vanja in *Azul-corvo* and Daniel in *Hanói* come of age as they develop their own relationships to home, family, and language.[31] Their journeys and negotiations of multiple identities, languages, and cultural ties transcend national particularities, yet they grapple with what it means to be Brazilian and to live in the United States.

For characters in *Azul-corvo* and *Hanói*, what was once a foreign landscape becomes increasingly familiar as memories of their ancestral homes begin to fade. These hemispheric Brazilian novels acknowledge the distinct political, socioeconomic, cultural, and familial motivations for migrations even as the narratives focus more on how the characters establish roots in Colorado and Chicago. As ties to biological families and native lands unravel with distance and time, they form new support structures in their adopted home. These alternative networks bring together friends and colleagues from varied backgrounds who now reside in displaced realms of borderlands and in-between spaces. Her novels construct a vision of home that transcends linguistic divides and national identities by depicting how Brazilian characters interact with other migrants and residents in the United States through textual forms of linguistic and cultural translations. Lisboa thus illuminates how transamerican and transnational dynamics can facilitate cross-cultural communication and generate misunderstandings that hint at the limitations of presumed translatability.

Differentiated Latinx Immigration and Citizenship in *Azul-corvo*

Azul-corvo, the first novel that Lisboa wrote after moving to the United States, depicts the life of the thirteen-year-old protagonist Evangelina, who goes by Vanja, as she moves from Rio de Janeiro to the Denver suburb of Lakewood after the death of her mother Suzana. Vanja lives with Fernando, another Brazilian previously married to her mother and listed as her father on her New Mexico birth certificate, who helps her search for her biological father. The journey takes them to the outskirts of Santa Fe, where they meet Florence, the mother of Daniel, Vanja's biological father, who now lives in the Ivory Coast. The trajectories of Vanja, Suzana, and Fernando indicate how living between Brazil and the United States has extended to a wider range of Brazilians since the late nineteenth century, when elites Joaquim Nabuco, José Carlos Rodrigues, and Sousândrade constituted the small community of Brazilians in New York that I discussed in the first chapter. With Fernando, a former militant now exiled, as one of the novel's Brazilian characters in the United States, Lisboa demonstrates how political necessity, rather than a cosmopolitan impulse for the world, can instigate migration.

Fernando's tale recalls *Stella Manhattan*'s representation of how repressive machinations of the military dictatorship forced a generation of Brazilians into exile. Living in Europe and North America in the 1960s and 1970s, Brazilian exiles and migrants, like Silviano Santiago and his characters, interacted with other Latin Americans. The reasons for exile vary in *Stella Manhattan*, with protagonist Eduardo fleeing his family's shame about his homosexuality and his friend Marcelo, who participates in the New York–based cell of an underground guerrilla group, escaping Brazil for political reasons. In the fictional New York of the late 1960s, Eduardo interacts with other exiles from Spanish America, most notably his Cuban neighbor Paco. *Azul-corvo* focuses on experiences of exile and migration decades after Brazil's 1964 military coup and subsequent dictatorial regime. Lisboa's novel depicts a landscape that Santiago previously examined in *Histórias mal contadas*: the southwestern United States. These fictional portraits of the region stress how Brazilians negotiate shifting linguistic, national, racial, and ethnic identities. In the borderland of the Southwest, residents have for centuries translated between English, Spanish, and indigenous languages and their associated cultures in daily lives, official records, and personal identity constructs.[32] By introducing Brazilians into an existing translation zone of the southwestern states of Colorado, Texas, and New Mexico, Lisboa follows Santiago's lead to further complicate ideas and representations of Latinx and Latin American identities.

Living in this realm of linguistic and cultural exchange, the novel's Brazilian characters exemplify how their transnational experiences necessitate an engagement with translation at an individual level. For Suzana, this realization began as a child when her family moved from Brazil to Texas, where her father worked for Shell Oil. The dynamics of global capital, namely, the increased role of multinational corporations in Brazil during the second half of the twentieth century, brought Suzana and her family to the United States. After growing up in Texas, she traveled to England where she met and later married Fernando, a militant in the Araguaia Guerrilla movement who fled Brazil after deserting the armed resistance to the dictatorship.[33] Fernando abandoned the struggle before military interventions destroyed the movement and killed the majority of the guerrillas. As an exiled foreigner, he lived with Suzana in Albuquerque until their divorce, when he moved to Colorado. Suzana stayed in New Mexico, taught Spanish, Portuguese, and English, and later gave birth to Vanja. When Vanja was two, they moved to Rio de Janeiro, where Suzana ensured that they maintained linguistic contact with the rest of the Americas by teaching her daughter English and Spanish. In creating a trilingual home in New Mexico that served as "uma confluência de mundos" ("a confluence of worlds") and later in Brazil, Suzana exemplified how living between languages, cultures, and nations demands personal acts of translation (Lisboa, *Azul-corvo* 185; *Crow Blue* 191).[34] They also transited between the two nations as dual citizens of Brazil and the United States. Suzana became a naturalized US citizen who maintained her Brazilian citizenship and Vanja was born in New Mexico to a Brazilian mother. With state-granted citizenship in two nations, both characters are transnational citizens of the Americas, a concept that recognizes other forms of rights and participation.[35]

As a dual citizen, Vanja can return to the United States following her mother's death without navigating the complexities of the immigration system. Since neither state violence nor abject poverty prompt her journey, her story is an exception to the usual patterns of migration from Latin America and other parts of the Global South to the United States. Her status as a young, legal citizen who knows English does not pose a threat to schoolmates and adults she meets in Colorado and New Mexico. Vanja is the ideal translator of Brazilian migrant experience for the novel's educated readers in Brazil and the United States given her perceived innocence and her privileged position within migrant networks due to her citizenship status, socioeconomic and educational background, and linguistic abilities. Though her dual citizenship allows her to enter the United States without filing specific documents or facing heightened scrutiny, she still feels out of place geographically, culturally, and linguistically when arriving in Colorado after living in Rio de Janeiro for eleven years.

Upon encountering an alien landscape of dry air and empty suburban streets at the confluence of the Great Plains and the Rocky Mountains, Vanja attempts to comprehend these surroundings by describing them in language more commonly associated with Rio de Janeiro. In contrast to Rio's warm and humid air incubating insects and dampness, Colorado's dry summer heat leaves her skin dehydrated and makes her wonder if "não era um lugar feito para os seres humanos, não mais do que para as baratas" (12; "it wasn't a place made for humans, any more than it was for cockroaches," 2). According to Fernando, she will eventually adjust to this seemingly inhospitable climate. After spending several months in Colorado, Vanja observes, "Depois que você passa tempo demais longe de casa, vira uma interseção entre dois conjuntos, como naqueles desenhos que fazemos na escola. Pertence aos dois, mas não pertence exatamente a nenhum deles" (72; "After you have been away from home for too long, you become an intersection between two groups, like in those drawings we do at school. You belong to both, but you don't exactly belong to either," 67–68). By situating herself and other immigrants in the center of a Venn diagram, Vanja emphasizes how multiple identities interact within the lived experiences of transnational migrants and citizens. Her sense of belonging to both countries without fully being a part of either differs from the place of the traveler who, like Celina in *Rakushisha*, always feels out of place abroad.

The analogy that Vanja employs to characterize her own identity and societal position also applies to the classification of *Azul-corvo* as a hemispheric Brazilian novel. The narrative belongs to the Americas and to Brazil without being relegated fully to one or the other. While the characters typify the common experiences across immigrant lives in this current moment of heightened globalization, the novel also represents specificities of Brazilian history, languages, and cultures that can impede foreign readers' abilities to fully understand the text without paratextual materials. Fernando's backstory as an underground Maoist revolutionary in the Amazon exemplifies how Lisboa integrates Brazilian history into her prose. To completely grasp the meaning of this reference and, by extension, Fernando's narrative arc, readers must either draw on previous familiarity with the Araguaia Guerrilla or seek additional sources to complement the information dosed out in the narrative. *Crow Blue*, Entrekin's English-language translation, lacks a critical introduction and explanatory footnotes to contextualize the broader era and the specific historical details of the armed resistance to the Brazilian military dictatorship. Lisboa's seemingly translatable narrative thus contains moments of cultural and historical specificity that impede the easy legibility of the translated narrative.

Through the character of Fernando, Lisboa crafts a fictionalized version of the complex internal warfare and ideological conflicts that shaped the armed guerrilla struggle in Brazil against the military dictatorship in the early 1970s. With storylines about underground political resistance, both *Azul-corvo* and *Stella Manhattan* serve to translate Brazilian experiences of exile in the United States for Portuguese-language readers in Brazil and, subsequently, to other hemispheric and global readerships through literary translations. Whereas Santiago's novel concentrates on events of the late 1960s and leaves the characters' futures open, Lisboa approaches Fernando's political militancy via flashbacks that help to characterize the man currently living in Lakewood. Under the code name Chico Ferradura, Fernando trained with Maoists for ten months in China before returning to Brazil via Bolivia to arrive in Acre prior to delving into the depths of the Amazon. This creation of a dual identity for protection parallels the pseudonyms and multiple names within the political and sexual underground worlds of *Stella Manhattan*. While in the movement, Fernando heard of comrades being captured and tortured. He also fell in love with Joana, a fellow guerrilla known as Manuela. Fernando decided to abandon the movement, rather than follow Joana and other comrades into an ongoing battle with a military intent on destroying them. After saying goodbye to his mother in Goiânia, he left Brazil forever. By interweaving Fernando's memories with Vanja's accounts of his current life, Lisboa renders Brazil's painful political past into a personal narrative that proves more accessible to members of the next generation.

Although Fernando and Vanja left Brazil for distinct reasons, both now reside in Colorado at an intersection of nations, languages, and cultures that characters similarly occupy in works by Latinx and other multicultural, immigrant, or ethnic writers.[36] Lisboa's characters follow the proclamation of Chicana feminist Gloria Anzaldúa: "To survive the Borderlands / you must live *sin fronteras* / be a crossroads" (217). Even though the political and cultural stakes differ, the act of embodying what Anzaldúa envisions as a linguistic, cultural, and geopolitical crossroads parallels the experiences of Lisboa's immigrant characters. For Anzaldúa, the Borderlands function as a visceral idea and a lived experience of the Southwest as Tejanos, Chicanos, and Mexican Americans straddle borders between Mexico and the United States. This region formed a part of Mexico until 1848 when an arbitrary line extending from the Rio Grande demarcated the division between the two nations. Movements of the border and the positioning of border control checkpoints have separated Anzaldúa and residents of the southwestern United States from their ancestral and cultural homelands of greater Mexico. Lisboa's Brazilian characters living in this space of encounter lack the proximity to their native land and language that defines the experience of Anzaldúa's Borderlands. Instead, a continental span separates these Brazilians from their home country. They must negotiate racial and ethnic categories and sociolinguistic practices that tend to foreground the shared inheritance of Spanish as a defining trait of Hispanic or Latinx communities.[37] Similar to Brazilian immigrants living in New York, Boston, Los Angeles, and Florida that populate anthropological and sociological studies, Lisboa's Brazilian characters inhabit a realm of linguistic and cultural intersections with social, political, and psychological ramifications resembling Apter's translation zone.[38]

Azul-corvo examines similarities and differences between Brazilians and other Latin American immigrants through Vanja's friendship with her nine-year-old neighbor Carlos, an undocumented immigrant from El Salvador. As neither Mexicans nor Chicanos, Vanja and Carlos do not correspond to the images most associated with the Latinx community in the Southwest. They belong to the realm of "other Latinos" that represent different waves of immigration to the United States.[39] Many Salvadorans arrived, most prominently in the greater Los Angeles and Washington, DC, regions, in the 1980s due to the Salvadoran Civil War. A surge in Brazilian immigration also occurred in the late 1980s and early 1990s during a period of hyperinflation in Brazil.[40] Carlos and Vanja, however, migrate to the United States for distinct reasons and at a later date. Familial ties brought Vanja to Colorado, whereas Carlos and his family arrived on tourist visas that they then overstayed. The narrative does not explicitly state his family's reasons for migrating but, given El Salvador's recent history, they were most likely fleeing from violence and poverty exacerbated by natural disasters. Vanja's dual citizenship and linguistic abilities afford her relative privilege as a Brazilian in the United States, especially in comparison to Carlos as a poorer and undocumented immigrant with limited English skills. The novel defines Carlos's immigration status with the phrase "Carlos não tinha *papeles*" (102; "Carlos didn't have *papeles*," 101). Spanish-speaking immigrants tend to characterize their precarious status in terms of an absence of *papeles*, or papers, by which they mean proper documentation. Inserting this term in italicized Spanish into the Portuguese indicates how codeswitching can convey significant sociocultural and political meanings within the multilingual realm of Latin Americans in the United States.

Due to his family's immigration status, Carlos fears the police and other governmental authorities. He also struggles to speak, read, and write in English, the official language of his new home. Even though age, gender, and immigration status could easily distance Vanja and Carlos, they develop a friendship reminiscent of the playful interactions of older and younger siblings. Vanja helps Carlos with his reading, lets him play on the computer, and watches television with him. The similarity between their native languages of Portuguese and Spanish also helps to facilitate this dynamic. When Carlos spends time with Vanja and Fernando, he overhears them speaking Portuguese and proudly claims, "¡*Yo entiendo un poco el portugués!*" (106).⁴¹ Carlos speaks in a mixture of Spanish and broken English, a trait that Lisboa renders through codeswitching. She does not normalize codeswitching in her prose in the way that Junot Díaz does by peppering his English prose with Dominican slang and Spanish words without placing them in italics.⁴² Her use of italicized Spanish and English words resembles Santiago's approach to codeswitching as both writers indicate a word's foreignness through italics but minimize glosses of its meaning.

Lisboa captures the trilingual codeswitching of conversations between Vanja, Fernando, and Carlos as Latin American immigrants in the United States. For instance, on Fernando's birthday, Carlos tells him, "*I like you así mismo. I not care you are velho. Eres mi amigo. My friend. How say friend in português?* Amigo, respondi. Ah! ele era pura felicidade. Ele sempre era pura felicidade quando descobria palavras iguais na sua língua e na nossa. Quando se deparava com mais uma de nossas muitas interseções latinas. *Amigo en português, amigo en español. Qué bueno*" (115). Carlos alternates between his native Spanish and his somewhat stilted English as he tries to learn new words in Portuguese. Though the English-language translation includes Spanish phrases and the Portuguese words *velho* and *amigo*, it minimizes this multilingual aesthetic by privileging English: "I like you *así mismo*. I not care you are *velho*. *Eres mi amigo*. My friend. How say friend in *português*? *Amigo*, I said. Ah! He was pure happiness. He was always pure happiness when he discovered words that were the same in his language and ours. When he came across yet another of our many Latin intersections. *Amigo en português, amigo en español. Qué bueno*" (115). Recognizing linguistic similarities between Spanish and Portuguese situates Carlos, Vanja, and Fernando within a broader Latinx community of the Americas. Both the original passage and its translation mark words as foreign, with Spanish and English italicized in the Brazilian text and Portuguese and Spanish phrases in italics in the English translation. In the translated dialogues, the text no longer differentiates the act of speaking in English as foreign, even though English is not the native language of these three characters. By removing this distinction of foreignness in conversation, the translation does not convey entirely the nuances and complexities of how language and identity intersect among Latin American immigrants in the United States. This attempt to translate a trilingual dialogue illustrates how Lisboa's novel pushes up against limits of linguistic and cultural translation, despite editorial assumptions of the text's translatability.

These interactions illuminate how Brazilian and Salvadoran characters over time acclimate to the linguistic and cultural codes in the United States. These immigrants integrate what were once incomprehensible foreign terms into their vocabularies to codeswitch with relative ease between Portuguese, Spanish, and English. Commenting on this adaptive function of language, Vanja notes, "Outra coisa que acontece quando você passa tempo demais longe de casa é que se depara com certas novidades no lugar novo através do idioma novo e daqui a pouco a língua que fala é uma estranha combinação de sintaxe em sua língua nativa mais um léxico de duas caras. Eu não dizia labirinto no milharal, dizia *corn maze*" (106; "Another thing that happens when you have been away from home for too long is that you learn about new things in the new place via the new language and soon the tongue you speak is a strange combination of your native syntax and a two-faceted vocabulary. I didn't say *labirinto no milharal*, in Portuguese. I said 'corn maze,'" 106). As she adjusts to her previously unfamiliar surroundings, Vanja becomes more likely to use terms in English, like "corn maze," that correspond to specific cultural phenomena that she encountered in the United States. She draws parallels between the position of immigrants and other displaced peoples and the linguistic experiences that accompany such dislocations.

To highlight the commonalities of immigrant lives across the Americas, Vanja claims, "Minha história não é só minha. É sua também. Nosso *American dream*" (71; "Your story isn't just yours. It's mine too. Our American dream," 67). This identification with a collective American dream suggests that desires to pursue education and to achieve financial success belong to a community of hemispheric Americans that transcends the borders of the United States. Attempting to reach this shared American dream represents a continuation of Brazilians' propensity since the mid-nineteenth century to look toward the United States as a model of "progress." At the turn of the twenty-first century, elite efforts to modernize their nations no longer serve as the primary reason to bring together Latin Americans in the United States. Instead, similar histories of political repression, dictatorial regimes, violence, abject poverty, and inequality unite immigrants of different linguistic, national, ethnic, and socioeconomic backgrounds as they aspire for a better life. Vanja recognizes this camaraderie through her use of the personal pronoun *nosso* to describe the American dream. On a more intimate level, her friendship with Carlos allows her to identify their shared experiences as Latin Americans while she also acknowledges her privileged position as a transnational citizen.

Moreover, Vanja recognizes the complexities of immigrant identity as it pertains to the particularities of the Brazilian experience in the United States:

> Não somos imigrantes *hispânicos*. Pode olhar para o nosso rosto, a gente inclusive é bem diferente em termos de biotipo e não falamos espanhol, falamos português. POR. TU. GUÊS. (Na escola, eu tinha que preencher um papel com o meu grupo étnico. As opções eram: CAUCASIANO. HISPÂNICO. AMERICANO NATIVO. ASIÁTICO. AFRO-AMERICANO. Onde é que eu ficava nessa história?) (70–71)
>
> Hold on, we are not Hispanic immigrants. Take a look at our faces. We're actually quite different in terms of biotype and we don't speak Spanish. We speak Portuguese. POR. TU. GUESE. (At school, I had to put my ethnic group on a form. The options were: CAUCASIAN. HISPANIC. NATIVE AMERICAN. ASIAN. AFRICAN-AMERICAN. Where was I in all that?) (67)

While this passage could be interpreted as Lisboa's ironic criticism of how Brazilians position themselves abroad, I instead read the link of physical appearance to language and ethnicity as an example of racial theories that a young Brazilian like Vanja might resort to without critical awareness when attempting to find her place in the United States. Her comments on language, appearance, and identity parallel perspectives of Brazilian immigrants to the United States documented in recent sociological and ethnographic studies.[43] These migrants encounter established categories on census forms and other official documents that do not correspond to their racial, ethnic, or linguistic profiles. As Vanja laments, she does not fit neatly into a single ethnic group, leaving her questioning where she belongs. Her uncertainty over how to classify herself echoes the racial misunderstandings in Santiago's "Borrão" as the protagonist traveled by bus across the southern United States in the 1960s. In these narratives, race as a social and linguistic construct emerges as an untranslatable in the sense that Cassin and Apter propose.

By positing concepts of race and ethnicity as untranslatables, I do not intend to claim that these terms cannot be translated, but rather I aim to underscore how they invite sustained analysis and comparison. As readers, students, and citizens of the Americas, we continue returning to specific racial constructs and (not) translating them. Vanja faces this difficulty of translating her self-conception in Portuguese as a Brazilian into the racial and ethnic options given in English on forms in the United States. In academic studies, Brazilian immigrants voice a similar need to navigate linguistic and sociocultural particularities in order to position themselves in the racial and ethnic landscape of the United States. These migrants often feel at a loss given that they tend to identify primarily as Brazilians or, on the basis of their home state, as *paulistas, cariocas, mineiros*, or *baianos*. Rendering such identities bound by geography and culture into census categories proves challenging, especially since race unfolds in Brazil as a spectrum instead of subscribing to the "one-drop rule" that prevails in the United States.[44] However, migration between Brazil and the United States causes ideas of race to transform, which influences people's racial self-identification. Sociologist Tiffany Joseph studies how living in the United States impacts Brazilian migrants' views of race after they return to Brazil. Her concept of the Brazilian migrants' "transnational racial optic" accounts for how intertwined constructs of race, nationality, and ethnicity change as Brazilians migrate between the two nations. Some Brazilians in the United States self-identify as Latinos, even as they recognize specificities of Brazil's language, culture, history, and geopolitical stance that differentiate their experiences from those of Spanish American migrants and their descendants (Joseph 6–7). They reject the label Hispanic due to its association with the Spanish language. Official forms that equate Hispanics and Latinos or omit Latina/o as a category end up negating the presence of Brazilians in the United States. Vanja thus struggles to situate herself as a dual US and Brazilian citizen whose racial, ethnic, and linguistic backgrounds do not easily conform to the rigidity of these classifications in English.

As Vanja's experiences in the United States suggest, constructs of race cannot translate directly from the context of one nation into the sociocultural and linguistic realms of another. Finding equivalent words between Portuguese and English may solve the linguistic question of translation, but it fails to respond to the more pressing cultural and contextual concerns. Vanja confronts the comparative untranslatability of her fluid identity as a transnational Brazilian citizen when attempting to make herself legible according to the narrow constructs that classify her fellow schoolmates and neighbors in suburban Denver. To translate *Azul-corvo* as *Crow Blue*, Alison Entrekin renders what she considers Lisboa's readable Portuguese into similarly accessible English without commenting on or compensating for the cultural specificities and transnational racial optics that define Vanja's status as a migrant and a dual citizen. Entrekin's translation initially brings to mind the English-language writings by Sandra Cisneros, Zadie Smith, or Chimamanda Ngozi Adichie about how migration affects familial bonds and creates multilayered identities. However, conveying exchanges of Brazilian and Spanish American characters in the United States surrounding complex questions of race, ethnicity, and language proves challenging for translators of *Azul-corvo* into other national languages.

Despite the commonalities that shape migrant lives, varied literary and linguistic traditions respond to and comment on adapting to unfamiliar surroundings in different ways. *Azul-corvo* portrays, with nuance, how Brazilian and Spanish American migrants, namely, dual citizen Vanja, aging political exile Fernando, and undocumented Salvadoran boy Carlos, navigate shifting constructs of race, ethnicity, and nationality. Though Lisboa's language seems straightforward at first, her prose develops complex ideas and layered identities through occasional trilingual dialogues, historical allusions, and affective musings. Intimate experiences of her Brazilian characters in the United States cannot be easily translated into another linguistic or national context, even though her prose's perceived translatability attracts attention from translators and publishers in the global literary market. With its distinctive language and cultural specificity that invite continued analyses, *Azul-corvo* maintains degrees of translatability, in Benjamin's sense of the term, and untranslatability, in Cassin's approach. The novel resists conforming to homogeneous visions of world literature that Apter fears and instead captures how migrants engage in transamerican negotiations while struggling to translate themselves into the languages and cultures of their new surroundings.

Refugees, Immigrants, and a New Politics of Translation in *Hanói*

Lisboa's hemispheric Brazilian novels illustrate how older immigrants preserve stronger ties to their home countries while younger generations adjust more easily to new surroundings. Their differentiated adaptations relate to characters' abilities as linguistic and cultural translators. Generational disparities, which inform how Vanja and Carlos interact with Fernando and Carlos's parents in *Azul-corvo*, emerge more prominently in the fictional Chicago of *Hanói*. The novel centers on the unlikely friendship and, later, romance between Alex, a clerk at a corner store in Little Vietnam, and David, who shops at the market. Through Alex, whose mother Huong was born to a Vietnamese woman Linh and an American sergeant Derrick, Lisboa explores how linguistic, cultural, and national identities overlap among a non–Latin American immigrant community. Living in Chicago with her son Bruno, Alex's ties to her Vietnamese origins are fairly tenuous as she struggles to speak Vietnamese with her mother and grandmother. By inserting transliterations of Vietnamese words for food and proper nouns into her Portuguese prose, Lisboa adds texture to her depictions of Alex's maternal family and their culture without rendering the text inaccessible to readers. David, a jazz musician recently diagnosed with a terminal illness, represents the synthesis of two prevalent groups of Latin American immigrants as the son of Luiz, "o brasileiro de Capitão Andrade descendia de italianos" (Brazilian from Capitão Andrade descended from Italians) and Guadalupe, "a mexicana de Hermosillo, até onde se sabia, descendia do povo que Hernán Cortés praticamente dizimou" (Mexican from Hermosillo who, as far as we knew, descended from the people that Hernán Cortés practically decimated; Lisboa, *Hanói* 164). To differentiate David from other Latinos in the United States, the narrative emphasizes his Brazilian father's Italian heritage and his Mexican mother's indigenous origins.

Similar to Vanja, David is the product of cross-cultural encounters of an earlier generation of migrants. He exists between the languages and cultures of Brazil and Mexico as a hemispheric American born and raised in the United States. Unlike Vanja's mother, who moved with relative ease between Brazil and the United States as a dual citizen, David's parents struggled to survive as undocumented Latin Americans in the United States. His father attempted to arrive in the country on a tourist visa but did not receive one. Entering the country illegally through Mexico, he followed a path common for Brazilian migrants not granted the required documents.[45] Luiz and Guadalupe occupied a clandestine position as undocumented immigrants who could never return to their native countries with their son.[46] David remembers the story of his parents' first encounter three months after his father arrived in Framingham, a city twenty miles west of Boston where Brazilians account for up to 20 percent of the sixty-eight thousand residents.[47] Meeting on a bus, Luiz haltingly said to Guadalupe the few expressions he knew in English: "*Good morning, miss . . . Cold today, yes? . . . I go work. You go work too?*" (217).[48] Through this dialogue in italicized English without glosses, Lisboa renders for readers in Brazil the awkward experiences and stilted speech of a recently arrived Brazilian who lacks the education and linguistic skills of more privileged migrants. Codeswitching with imperfect English conveys how Luiz remembers his initial sense of displacement in an unfamiliar language and land.

The resulting relationship would provide Luiz solace amid the inhospitable surroundings of his new country. He recalls that, when first living in the United States, "achava tudo estranho. Achava a comida estranha. Dormia mal à noite, e tinha pesadelos" (I found everything strange. I found the food strange. I was sleeping poorly at night, and I was having nightmares; 217). Falling in love with Guadalupe, saving up for an engagement ring, and marrying her allowed Luiz to come to peace with this strangeness. The couple rented a home in Framingham and created a family as Latin Americans in the United States that transcended barriers of language, nation, and culture. When talking with relatives in Brazil, English emerged as a source of pride, even though Luiz erred in his vocabulary and mispronounced words. Once he called his family to brag: "Minha noiva trabalha como *baby sister*. . . . Sua família não sabia o que fazia uma *baby sister*, mas soava importante" (My fiancée works as a *baby sister*. . . . His family did not know what a *baby sister* did, but it sounded important; 134). Though his use of "baby sister" instead of "babysitter" did not register with his family, the linguistic slip is humorous for readers who know the meanings of the two phrases. Understanding the implied humor of this miscommunication requires that readers know English, the power dynamics between languages, and the sociocultural contexts of both countries. These nuanced interactions illuminate how even seemingly translatable prose contains linguistic specificities and cultural references that resist direct interlingual translations.

Through individual gestures of linguistic and cultural translation, Luiz facilitated cross-cultural exchanges and also generated misunderstandings due to his difficulties learning English and Spanish, which resulted in Portuguese being the family's default language (40). Luiz's struggles to adapt to the United States after leaving Minas Gerais resemble a common trajectory among Brazilian migrants. The novel recounts this shared history:

Os imigrantes de Minas Gerais, da região de Governador Valadares (onde ficava a cidade de Luiz), tinham começado a chegar aos Estados Unidos nos anos sessenta. Instalavam-se na Nova Inglaterra. Viravam funcionários de salões de beleza, lanchonetes, lavandeiras. Alguns se instalavam em Miami também. Em Nova York. Mandavam dinheiro de volta para casa. . . . O plano era ir para os Estados Unidos, juntar um dinheiro, voltar para casa e abrir um negócio. A terra do Tio Sam era uma terra de possibilidades. Em dólares. (102)

Immigrants from Minas Gerais, from the region of Governador Valadares (where Luiz's city was), had started to arrive in the United States in the sixties. They settled in New England. They became employees at beauty salons, diners, laundries. Some also settled in Miami. In New York. They sent money back home. . . . The plan was to go to the United States, save up money, return home and open a business. The land of Uncle Sam was a land of possibilities. In dollars.

Lisboa's sketch of Brazilians in the service industry concentrated in certain US cities with the hopes of returning home wealthy corresponds with sociological and anthropological accounts of migration flows between Brazil and the United States. Studies identify Governador Valadares as a central node in networks of migration dating back to the 1960s, when a group of young men migrated to Boston and, later, urged their family members to follow (Martes 46–47). With hyperinflation in the 1980s, *valadarenses* began to arrive in larger numbers in Boston and, more specifically, Framingham. According to Maxine Margolis, "Brazilians in Brazil who typecast Governador Valadares as *the* archetypal immigrant-sending community need look no further than Framingham to confirm this stereotype" (*Goodbye* 85). Luiz embodies this archetype as a fictional Brazilian from Capitão Andrade who settled in Framingham and whose dream of returning to Brazil faded as years passed and he established his life in the United States.

The narrative extends beyond Luiz's experiences to examine multigenerational effects of migration through his son David's existence between nations, languages, and cultures. To capture the complex identities of immigrants and their descendants in *Hanói*, Lisboa explores how language use varies between generations of migrants. Older Brazilians, like Luiz, have difficulty pronouncing *th* in English, a sound that does not exist in Portuguese. This impediment becomes evident when Luiz comments in English on his abandoned plan to return to Brazil:

> *Things change* . . . embora ele não conseguisse fazer aquele som do *th* e dissesse *tings change*, mas ninguém deixava de entender por causa disso (no caso do número três era mais delicado, ele dizia *tree*, árvore, em vez de *three*, então às vezes relatava, por exemplo, ter visto *tree people* em vez de *three people*. David, pequeno, rolava de rir, com afetuoso deboche e um toque de superioridade arrogante. *Meu pai viu o povo das árvores!* (103)

> *Things change* . . . however he never managed to make that sound of the *th* and said *tings change*, but nobody misunderstood him because of this (in the case of the number three it was more delicate, he said *tree*, instead of *three*, so at times he reported, for example, to have seen *tree people* instead of *three people*. David, little, rolled over laughing, with an affectionate tease and a touch of arrogant superiority. *My dad saw the tree people!*

Luiz recognizes that "things change," even as he fails to pronounce the phrase correctly. Though resigned to stay, he cannot fully adapt to the United States given, in part, the barrier of English pronunciation. David does not face these difficulties since he grew up studying English in school and speaking it with friends. While David laughs at his father's miscommunications, he faces his own limitations when speaking in Portuguese and Spanish. His varied competency in multiple languages typifies the linguistic practices of second-generation immigrants or immigrants who arrive in the United States as children. The use of English in this passage illustrates how simple mispronunciations can result in changed meanings and more serious misunderstandings. Here Lisboa opts to provide a gloss for Luiz's mispronunciation of three as tree through David's response. Clarifying the reason for the confusion and the resulting humor makes the exchange more legible for her readers in Brazil.

In other instances, Lisboa preserves a degree of unfamiliarity when depicting experiences of migrants and their descendants in the United States for her novel's primary Brazilian readership. Characters exist in *Hanói* between their native and adopted lands as they craft a home for themselves through embodied experiences of linguistic and cultural translation. At times, they adapt to traditions of the new country, as when David and his immigrant parents celebrated Independence Day by watching fireworks together. Luiz thought that "a independência era sempre algo louvável. . . . Então ele ia ver os fogos de artifício no dia quatro de julho, e aquilo lhe enchia os olhos, aquela beleza de filme" (independence was always something laudable. . . . He therefore went to see the fireworks on the Fourth of July, and that filmlike beauty filled his eyes; 227). The fireworks enthralled Luiz as a symbol of freedom, which he interpreted through the comparatively familiar realm of Brazilian history where "um rei ou um príncipe . . . tinha puxado a espada . . . e dito independência ou morte" (a king or a prince . . . had drawn his sword . . . and said independence or death; 227). Framing independence as commemorated in the United States through the lens of Brazil's past granted Luiz emotional access to a collective celebration. For readers familiar with these histories, Luiz's vague recollection suggests that both nations established independence from colonial powers yet did so in distinct ways. While a revolutionary struggle and a 1776 declaration freed the United States from colonial rule of the British monarch, Brazil experienced continuity as Pedro I, the son of Portuguese king João VI, stayed in Brazil, rather than return to Portugal with the rest of the royal family, and declared the nation's independence in 1822.[49] Despite his limited historical knowledge, Luiz enjoyed the festivities in his adopted country and venerated ideas of freedom as crucial to the life that he envisioned for his family in the United States.

The characters in Lisboa's narratives long to engage with the broader world and, at the same time, remain connected to the specificities of their homes. They form new bonds in their adopted country without completely severing ties to their past to exemplify the cross-cultural exchanges and potential misunderstandings characteristic of hemispheric Brazilian novels. While translators and publishers tend to praise these works for their translatability in the trade sense of relatively accessible prose and conventional narrative structure, characters' experiences between languages, cultures, and nations uncover the philosophical untranslatability of certain elements of immigrant life. Constructs of race and ethnicity prove difficult to translate from one realm into another given linguistic specificities of certain terms and their imbrication with historical, sociocultural, and geopolitical contexts. Though Entrekin may find equivalents when translating Vanja's commentary on US ethnic categories from Lisboa's Brazilian Portuguese into English, the translation fails to fully capture the strangeness of these terms for the characters and, more generally, within the Brazilian context. Like her characters, Lisboa keeps on returning to culturally specific concepts and understandings of race to continue pondering how to render them into another language and context. To preserve the untranslatable nature of these terms and experiences, Lisboa crafts a translational prose through codeswitching and cultural allusions that, in turn, hinders facile understanding of her subtly nuanced narratives.

In my reading of Lisboa's novels within the contemporary landscape of global Brazilian literature, I propose that Apter's ideas of the translation zone and the politics of untranslatability function best in dialogue with one another. While a degree of market translatability allows literary works to circulate within the translation zone of global publishing, a politics of untranslatability prevents these narratives from becoming reduced to homogenized visions of world literature or commercialized expressions of national difference. Lisboa's hemispheric or global Brazilian novels reside within the translation zone, rather than engage in an explicit politics of untranslatability. *Rakushisha*, *Azul-corvo*, and *Hanói* follow narrative conventions to represent transnational travels to Japan and hemispheric and global migrations to the United States. Fictional encounters of Brazilians with peoples from Japan, El Salvador, the United States, Mexico, and Vietnam reveal the limitations of cross-cultural communication during the contemporary moment of heightened globalization, even when characters have impressive linguistic abilities. The novels, by extension, suggest the untranslatable nature of specific linguistic expressions and cultural allusions. Recognizing the linguistic, cultural, geopolitical, and philosophical potential of untranslatability allows for a resistance to the demands of the global literary market, which facilitates publishing in translation of a wider range of literary voices from Brazil. Embracing an alternative politics of translation and publication would invite retranslations and ongoing returns to the untranslatable in Brazilian literature and culture, as I discuss further in the conclusion.

Conclusion

Translating Brazil Today

Retranslations and Untranslatability

The idea of translating Brazil in the contemporary moment no longer serves as a synonym for constructing and circulating a romanticized vision of nationality, as it often did in the mid-nineteenth century. What, then, does it mean to translate Brazil in the twenty-first century? Who translates what, and for whom? How do these translations resonate with earlier moments of translating Brazil in the Americas? For the Brazilian artists and intellectuals that I study in the previous chapters, translations unfold in a figurative sense and as a linguistic, cultural, and epistemological practice. Since the late nineteenth century, these elites have traveled throughout Brazil and the Americas and migrated to the United States. Their encounters with unfamiliar settings, languages, and peoples generated feelings of displacement that demanded various forms of translation as creative transformation in order to negotiate new surroundings, to render experiences abroad to readers at home, and to represent Brazil for a hemispheric public. Rather than directly copy foreign models of industrialization or reproduce the language of indigenous myths, José Carlos Rodrigues and Mário de Andrade embraced their agency as translators to creatively rewrite and transform original texts. Similarly, Silviano Santiago and Adriana Lisboa found their homes in translation as they transformed their academic training and personal experiences living abroad into a translational prose that represents the linguistic and cultural negotiations of their Brazilian characters who travel and migrate.

My study approaches intersections of travel and translation of Brazil in the Americas through a limited focus on Brazilian artists and intellectuals whose works, including periodicals, narratives, films, and critical essays, have engaged in linguistic and cultural acts of translation. Rather than restrict my approach to interlingual translations of literary works from Brazilian Portuguese into English, I conceive of translation in a more capacious sense to examine responses to and representations of displacement. Existing studies by Irene Rostagno, Piers Armstrong, Elizabeth Lowe and Earl Fitz, and Deborah Cohn provide insight into the dynamics of translating Brazilian and, more generally, Latin American literature into English and the reception of these works. Brazilian literature in English translation began to receive more prominence in the mid-twentieth century with the work of Samuel Putnam, who wrote *Marvelous Journey: A Survey of Four Centuries of Brazilian Writing* and translated, among others, Jorge Amado's 1943 novel *Terras do sem-fim* as *The Violent Land* for Alfred A. Knopf in 1945, Gilberto Freyre's 1933 essay *Casa-grande e senzala* as *The Masters and the Slaves: A Study of the Development of Brazilian Civilization* in 1946, also for Knopf, and Euclides da Cunha's 1902 masterpiece *Os Sertões* as *Rebellion in the Backlands* in 1944 for the University of Chicago Press. Publisher Alfred A. Knopf also played a critical role in heightening the profile of Brazilian literature in the United States, beginning with his publication of Isaac Goldberg's 1922 study *Brazilian Literature*. During the Good Neighbor years, Knopf's wife Blanche traveled to South America on a "literary roundup," where she discovered the work of Jorge Amado and Graciliano Ramos. The press published Ramos's *Angústia* (1936) as *Anguish* in a 1946 translation by Lewis C. Kaplan. In subsequent decades, Knopf continued to publish critical works of Brazilian literature, including Amado's *Gabriela, Clove and Cinnamon*, translated by James L. Taylor and William L. Grossman in 1962, and *Dona Flor and Her Two Husbands*, translated by Harriet de Onís in 1969; João Guimarães Rosa's 1956 novel *Grande Sertão: Veredas*, translated by Harriet de Onís and James L. Taylor in 1963 as *The Devil in the Backlands*; and Clarice Lispector's 1961 novel *A maçã no escuro*, translated by Gregory Rabassa in 1967 as *The Apple in the Dark*.[1]

Knopf's commitment to translating and publishing Brazilian literature in the 1960s coincided with Cold War–era initiatives to support the publication of Latin American literature in the United States, including the American Association of University Presses (AAUP) translation program from 1960 to 1966 and the Council for Inter-American Relations (CIAR) literature program from 1967 to 1983.² With support from the AAUP program, the University of California Press published *Modern Brazilian Short Stories*, translated by Grossman, in 1967; Machado de Assis's *Esau and Jacob*, translated by Helen Caldwell, in 1965; and *The Psychiatrist and Other Stories*, translated by Grossman and Caldwell, in 1963. California also published Caldwell's translations of Machado's novels *Dom Casmurro* in 1966 and *Memorial de Aires* as *Counselor Ayres' Memorial* in 1972. The University of Texas Press received support from the AAUP program to publish, as part of its Texas Pan American series, Graciliano Ramos's 1938 novel *Vidas secas* in 1965 as *Barren Lives*, translated by Ralph Edward Dimmick, and Rachel de Queiroz's 1939 novel *As três Marias* in 1963 as *The Three Marias*, translated by Fred P. Ellison. In the late 1960s, the Rockefeller Foundation shifted its funding for translations from the AAUP program to the CIAR program, which granted translators opportunities to publish in *Review*, the council's magazine of literature and arts of the Americas, and provided funding to trade presses like Avon, Pantheon, Harper and Row, Farrar, Straus and Giroux, and New Directions. Among others, the Bard imprint of Avon Books contributed to the profile of Brazilian literature in the United States with the publication of Márcio Souza's 1976 novel *Galvez, imperador do Acre* in 1980 as *The Emperor of the Amazon* and his 1980 novel *Mad Maria* in 1985, both translated by Thomas Colchie, and Amado's 1937 *Capitães da areia* in 1988 as *Captains of the Sand*, translated by Rabassa.

In the first decades of the twenty-first century, university presses, most notably Oxford's Library of Latin America series, and trade imprints, like Penguin Classics, have demonstrated a renewed interest in publishing Latin American literature in translation. Key works from nineteenth-century and early twentieth-century Brazilian literature appear in the Library of Latin America series, including José de Alencar's 1865 prose poem *Iracema*, translated by Clifford E. Landers in 2000; Machado de Assis's *Posthumous Memoirs of Brás Cubas* in Rabassa's 1998 translation, *Esau and Jacob* in Lowe's 2000 translation, *Dom Casmurro* in John A. Gledson's 1998 translation, and *Quincas Borba* in Rabassa's 1998 translation; and Aluízio Azevedo's 1890 naturalist masterpiece *O cortiço*, translated by David H. Rosenthal in 2000 as *The Slum*.³ These translations, with paratextual essays by esteemed literary scholars and historians, represent a key initiative in the reevaluation of Brazilian letters and their role in the Americas. Penguin Classics has reprinted Amado's *The Violent Earth* (2013) and *Captains of the Sea* (2013), along with new translations by Rabassa of Amado's novels, *The Double Death of Quincas Water-Bray* (2012) and *The Discovery of America by the Turks* (2012). To contribute to the circulation of Brazilian literature in English, Penguin has published works by canonical writers, including Lima Barreto's 1915 novel *Triste fim de Policarpo Quaresma* in Mark Carlyon's 2015 translation *The Sad End of Policarpo Quaresma*, and younger voices, such as Alison Entrekin's 2015 translation *Blood-Drenched Beard* of Daniel Galera's 2012 novel *Barba ensopada de sangue*.

This brief summary outlines key periods, figures, institutions, and presses in the translation and publication of Brazilian literary works since the mid-twentieth century but by no means provides a comprehensive account of Brazilian literature in translation into English. While this Anglo-American editorial landscape, especially in trade presses, has tended to privilege publishing novels in translation, university presses and other smaller independent presses have contributed critical translations of Brazilian poetry, most notably *An Anthology of Twentieth-Century Brazilian Poetry*, edited by Elizabeth Bishop and Eduardo Brasil and published by Wesleyan University Press in 1972. The Wesleyan Poetry series also published a bilingual edition of João Cabral de Melo Neto's *Selected Poetry, 1937–1990*, edited by Djelal Kadir. Drama has been more overlooked as a genre for translation but, since 2000, Nelson Rodrigues's work has garnered attention in translation into English with *The Theater of Nelson Rodrigues*, published in 2001 by the Brazilian Ministry of Culture, and *Nelson Rodrigues: Selected Plays*, featured in the Oberon Modern Playwrights series in 2019. The project of translating Brazilian literature into English remains far from finished, as a closer look at recent retranslations and approaches to untranslatability will illuminate.

Elite artists and intellectuals no longer serve as the only translators of Brazil. Historically marginalized and underrepresented peoples, such as favela residents, immigrants, Afro-descendants, Amerindians, and LGBTQ+ communities, contribute increasingly to the diversity and complexity of the visions of the nation that circulate abroad. The representations of Brazil from voices like Geovani Martins, Oscar Nakasato, Conceição Evaristo, Davi Kopenawa, and Natalia Borges Polesso aim to resist the facile translatability of homogenized literary forms primed for consumption in a global literary market. They suggest the need for embracing a politics of untranslatability that invites readers and translators to return to difficult ideas, phrases, and texts and to continue on interpreting and (not) translating them. Smaller presses with a commitment to translation, such as New Directions, Dalkey Archive Press, Open Letter Books, Two Lines Press, and Deep Vellum, have contributed to the translation and circulation in English of Brazilian literature, particularly its often-overlooked voices. Online platforms, like Words Without Borders and Asymptote, or print journals with online features, such as *Granta*, *World Literature Today*, *Two Lines: World Writing in Translation*, and *Wasafari: International Contemporary Writing*, provide additional possibilities for the circulation of literature translated into English. Thanks to a heightened interest in Brazil among English-reading publics and renewed investment of the Brazilian government in its national letters, Brazilian literature translated into English has enjoyed an expanded profile in independent, university, and trade presses, as well as online venues, over the past decade.

Considering the market's role in the circulation of Brazilian literature allows me to ponder why certain voices and visions remain excluded from this partial process of translating Brazil while others have received renewed attention. In doing so, I turn my focus to retranslation and untranslatability as dilemmas of translation that impact the profile of Brazilian letters in the Americas. By retranslation, I refer to new translations of previously translated works for distinct editorial and creative reasons. Examining retranslations of Brazilian literature into English raises the question of why a translator would return to an already translated text and, subsequently, why a press would publish that retranslation. A desire to improve upon a bad translation or an interest in updating the translation in order to introduce a canonical writer to a new generation of readers often motivate decisions to retranslate. The forthcoming versions of Mário de Andrade's *Macunaíma* and João Guimarães Rosa's *Grande Sertão: Veredas* in English respond to the first impulse. Returning to novels whose experimental prose style, linguistic invention, and heightened cultural specificity challenge translators points to the potential intersections between practices of retranslation and a politics of untranslatability. The new translations of novels and stories by Clarice Lispector and Machado de Assis corroborate the second rationale for retranslations, given that their previous translations into English were published mainly by university presses or small presses with relatively limited distribution.

The new translations of Lispector's work best exemplify this phenomenon of retranslation. Benjamin Moser's 2009 biography *Why This World: A Biography of Clarice Lispector* ignited greater interest in Lispector among Anglophone readers. His narration of her life and writing emphasizes details of her Jewish ancestry, her family's escape from the Ukraine, and the seeming foreignness of her Portuguese, even though she arrived in Brazil as a toddler and grew up in Recife and later Rio de Janeiro. Scholars in Brazil, most notably Benjamin Abdala Junior, have rightly critiqued Moser's biography for insufficiently acknowledging his indebtedness to the earlier research of Nádia Battella Gotlib's 1995 biography *Clarice, uma vida que se conta* and Teresa Cristina Montero Ferreira's 1999 study *Eu sou uma pergunta: Uma biografia de Clarice Lispector*.[4] Despite these well-founded criticisms, Moser's biography has nonetheless introduced Lispector as an intriguing and larger-than-life figure to a broader Anglophone readership. Her work circulated prior to Moser's intervention in English-language translations published by university or small presses, but she was relatively unknown outside the academic circles of Latin American literature or feminist thought.[5] Given her distinctive prose and personality, Lispector was long a household name in Brazil, known simply as Clarice. By framing Clarice as an enigma, a foreigner, a Jew, and, almost secondarily, a writer, Moser heightened her profile among Anglo-American readers and within the global literary market.

As an agent of translation, Moser furthered Lispector's prominence by retranslating *The Hour of the Star* in 2011 and serving as the general editor for New Directions' series of her works in translation. Since 2011, New Directions has published retranslations of *The Hour of the Star*, *Água Viva*, *Near to the Wild Heart*, *The Passion According to G.H.*, and *The Besieged City*, and translations of *A Breath of Life*, *The Complete Stories*, and *The Chandelier*.[6] These translations have generated interest in Lispector's work among an English-reading public and have received favorable reviews in venues such as *Bookforum* and the *New York Times Book Review*. In 2016, Katrina Dodson won the esteemed PEN Translation Prize for *The Complete Stories*. Due to the critical acclaim and relative commercial success of these English translations, Lispector has gained greater visibility in the United States. This publishing phenomenon, which Dodson has described as "Clarice-mania," analogous to "Ferrante fever," raises questions concerning the literary marketplace and why translators and publishers decide to retranslate works by certain literary figures when they do.[7] In her review of the recent New Directions translations, Elizabeth Lowe acknowledges that Lispector's writings invite multiple interpretations and, relatedly, retranslations for varied reasons. Market factors inform publishers' determination of whether a given text would generate sales in retranslation. For New Directions, stylistic concerns motivated their decision to translate Lispector's works with Moser as the general editor responsible for rendering her works into a uniform voice in English. Lowe recognizes that, since translations age more quickly than originals, retranslations are needed to account for changes in language and context. She questions how the New Directions project dismisses previous translators' work as it insists on the need for a singular voice in translation with Moser as the stylistic arbiter.

Drawing on her analysis of the New Directions project and her experience retranslating Euclides da Cunha's *Os Sertões* as *Backlands: The Canudos Campaign* for Penguin Classics in 2010, Lowe observes the necessity of retranslation, especially as a mode of historic revision. She concludes that "there is no final, perfect, right or wrong translation. If conditions are right, a 'great translation' will emerge, resonant in the literary heritage of the receiving culture, and thus reaffirming the place of the original in the source culture canon" ("Revisiting Re-translation" 423). Her view of translation's infinite possibilities as grounded in historical and cultural contexts resonates with Borges's idea that a work gains in meaning as interpretative readings, rewritings, and translations create multiple versions in the absence of a definitive text. Retranslations, per Lowe, enhance the meaning of a specific text by situating it in relationship to other spatial and temporal contexts. For Lawrence Venuti, retranslations draw attention to the translator's agency and intentionality as they attempt to differentiate themselves from an earlier translation (*Translation Changes* 100). In framing the retranslator as a figure who aims "to interpret the source text according to a different set of values" (100), Venuti highlights that retranslations often respond to shifts in the translating culture, even as "they can also produce such changes by inspiring new ways of reading and appreciating the source texts" (107). Multiple translations enhance the literary and cultural significance of a text within both its source and target contexts. Translation and, by extension, retranslation contribute to what Benjamin described as the afterlife, or extended life, of a particular work, a process that proves particularly important when dealing with the circulation of canonical literary figures in translation.

Retranslating Lispector's work into English in the first decades of the twenty-first century responds, in part, to an interest of Anglophone readers for women's voices from comparatively peripheral nations and languages. Translators and publishers are more open to embracing and maintaining the distinctiveness and, at times, strangeness of her prose. Moser and his team of translators avoid domesticating her writing by maintaining her punctuation, approximating her tone, and aiming for consistency in translating specific terms. For instance, near the end of *A hora da estrela*, Lispector links a series of interconnected ideas about death with commas. In his 1986 translation, Pontiero changes the structure of Lispector's longer sentence to align with preferences in English for shorter sentences and more direct language. In contrast, Moser's translation maintains the rhythm of the original sentence and its use of commas.[8] By following Lispector's punctuation to recreate her prose's distinctive rhythm in English, Moser crafts a retranslation that presents her novella to a broader readership without minimizing its stylistic and tonal specificity.

This approach to retranslating guides Moser's work as the general editor of the New Directions series. Dodson similarly comments on the challenges of rendering Lispector's strange language and distinctive style into English. Unlike previous translators, who often minimized the oddness of her prose, Dodson aims to convey its strangeness in English. In her translator's note, she astutely observes, "My advantage in translating the *Complete Stories* nearly forty years after their author's death, as her international fame and readership rise, is that a growing familiarity with her style enables its peculiarities to be understood as more than arbitrary" (631). Dodson, Moser, and the other translators working on the New Directions retranslations can hew more closely to the specificities of Lispector's prose since they do not face editorial pressure to smooth out the irregularities of her language nor the possibilities of scathing critiques for what an earlier readership might have considered accidental mistranslations. These recent versions of Lispector's novels, stories, and *crônicas* into English heighten Brazil's profile in the global literary market, especially in the Americas.

"Clarice-mania" has extended to the Spanish-speaking world since 2000 with Ediciones Siruela's Biblioteca Clarice Lispector and Ediciones Corregidor's Vereda Brasil series.[9] Her writing has been available in Spanish translation since the 1970s, with the publications of Juan García Gayo's translations *Un aprendizaje o el libro de los placeres* in 1973 and *Legión extranjera* in 1974, Haydée Yofre Barroso's translation *El via crucis del cuerpo* in 1975, and Basilio Losada's translation *Cerca del corazón salvaje* in 1977. Siruela, a Madrid-based press, has published the most comprehensive catalog of Lispector in Spanish with their Biblioteca Clarice Lispector of reprinted translations, retranslations, or new translations of ten novels, a selection of *crônicas*, an interview, her complete stories, and Moser's biography. Corregidor's Lispector catalog features many of the same works but with different translators, thus indicating possibilities for multiple translations and interpretations. Prominent Argentine critics of Brazilian literature Gonzalo Aguilar, Paloma Vidal, and Florencia Garramuño have translated, respectively, *La hora de la estrella*, *La legión extranjera* and *Un soplo de vida (pulsaciones)*, and *La ciudad sitiada*. These editions also include supplemental texts by Brazilian scholars Vilma Arêas, Ítalo Moriconi, Benedito Nunes, and Silviano Santiago, as well as by Moser and Cixous. With these retranslations accompanied by critical essays, Corregidor's Vereda Brasil collection has heightened Lispector's editorial profile among Argentine readers. In doing so, the project complements the New Directions series to affirm Lispector's position in the Americas and, by extension, the global literary market as one of Brazil's most renowned writers.

As both Lowe and Venuti note in their pieces on retranslation, translators and publishers often retranslate works of canonical writers as their prominence helps to guarantee a continued readership in the target language. Retranslations update and refresh the language, tone, and cultural references of the translated text, given that translations have a half-life of roughly thirty years, according to Lowe ("Revisiting Re-translation" 416). Returning to Lispector's works now makes sense temporally, since the first wave of translations of her writings into English unfolded roughly thirty years ago, in the late 1980s and early 1990s. A similar amount of time has elapsed between earlier translations of Machado de Assis's work and more recent renderings of his writings into English. William L. Grossman translated Machado's 1881 masterpiece *Memórias póstumas de Brás Cubas* in 1952 as *Epitaph of a Small Winner*. Three years later, Percy Ellis translated the novel as *Posthumous Reminiscences of Braz Cubas*. Over forty years later, Rabassa retranslated the text as *The Posthumous Memoirs of Brás Cubas* for Oxford's Library of Latin America. Now, after another twenty years have passed, Flora Thomson-DeVeaux and the team of Margaret Jull Costa and Robin Patterson have returned to Machado's text and created new translations for Penguin Classics and Liveright, respectively.[10]

Machado's work has also received renewed attention with Karen Sotelino's 2013 translation of *Resurrection*, his previously untranslated first novel, and various short story collections, most notably *The Collected Stories* translated by Costa and Patterson and published by Liveright in 2018.[11] Similar to the reception of Lispector's *Complete Stories* a few years earlier, the publication of Machado's *Collected Stories* has garnered critical praise. The *New York Times* included the collection as one of its one hundred notable books of 2018, an honor granted to Dodson's translation in

2015. Moser favorably reviewed *The Collected Stories of Machado de Assis* in his article "He's One of Brazil's Greatest Writers. Why Isn't Machado de Assis More Widely Read?," published in a July 2018 issue of the *New Yorker*. Moser positions himself yet again as an arbiter of Brazilian literature for Anglophone readers. His *New Yorker* article introduces Machado as an icon by blending biographical details with elements from his literary works, an approach that resembles, but on a smaller scale, his earlier narration of Lispector's life and work.

Both Machado de Assis and Clarice Lispector emerge as evergreen literary figures who continue to invite retranslations of already translated works and new translations of previously untranslated novels, stories, and essays. Translators, publishers, and other agents of translation who shape the profile of Brazilian literature that reaches foreign readers return to these writers given their canonical place in national and, increasingly, world literature. Brazil's federal government continues to incentivize translating and publishing works by these iconic writers, with forty-two works by Lispector and forty by Machado published in translation worldwide with National Library support from 1991 to 2017. Translating and retranslating their writings into English and Spanish, among other languages, contributes to the enhanced profile of Brazilian literature within a world literary system. Like Borges in Argentina, Machado de Assis and Clarice Lispector remain writers rooted in Brazilian specificities, even as their texts explore philosophical and metafictional concerns that transcend national and linguistic borders to generate interest among a broader readership.

These writers, however, represent only two figures within the various experiences that constitute Brazilian literature. Investments in retranslating their writings into English suggest, in part, an increasing interest in women writers and Afro-Brazilian voices. Lispector's tales often meditate on the quotidian domestic life of middle-class women, while Machado, a self-taught, Afro-Brazilian bureaucrat, addressed slavery only briefly in his work.[12] Their recent success in retranslation also reveals a potential interest among translators, publishers, and readers for modes of literary cosmopolitanism instead of preferences for exoticism associated with Jorge Amado's prominence in translation.[13] Besides Lispector and Machado, poet, novelist, and playwright Hilda Hilst; feminist poet and translator Ana Cristina César; novelists of Lebanese descent Raduan Nassar and Milton Hatoum; and writer Moacyr Scliar, who depicts the Jewish diaspora; among others, can expand Anglophone readers' perceptions of

Brazil's people, history, culture, and language. These now-canonical figures of Brazilian letters represent perspectives of gender, sexuality, race, class, religion, and ethnicity often excluded or rendered marginal in romanticized, nineteenth-century constructs of Brazil and their twentieth-century parallels in images of an exotic nation. In selecting works by more experimental or underrepresented Brazilian writers, translators and publishers can aim to balance market demands with a desire to embrace a politics of untranslatability.

By a politics of untranslatability, I posit a move away from translating only texts that presses deem translatable for their accessibility. Following a politics of untranslatability would involve returning to works that challenge on linguistic, cultural, and philosophical levels in order to recognize more completely the diversity of Brazilian voices and styles. Rather than dismiss the experimental prose of Mário de Andrade and João Guimarães Rosa or the underrepresented voices of Afro-Brazilian Conceição Evaristo and former favela resident Geovani Martins as untranslatable or strange, translators following a politics of untranslatability would embrace the challenge of rendering the text into another language through processes of creative rewriting and transformation. Julia Sanches, who translated Martins's 2018 debut story collection *O sol na cabeça* as *The Sun on My Head* in 2019, adopted such an approach to convey the slang and rhythm of spoken, colloquial language among boys growing up in Rio's favelas. For these works and translators, the untranslatable, in line with the ideas of Emily Apter and Barbara Cassin, exists as a word, concept, or phrase that allows for continued returns and interpretations. Untranslatability and retranslation thus exist as intertwined concepts since texts considered untranslatable, in the market sense of being difficult to translate, invite close readings, multiple interpretations, and, therefore, retranslations. Rather than conceive of translatability and untranslatability as opposites, I recognize their similarities and symbioses since literary works deemed untranslatable in commercial terms are often translatable according to Benjamin's vision of translatability governed by the original's distinctive language and quality. Embracing a politics of untranslatability would involve maintaining the linguistic and cultural specificities of texts, rather than conforming to the homogeneous aesthetics of world literature.

Instead of accepting market translatability as the predominant aesthetic, I suggest that we consider what a politics of untranslatability would look like for the circulation of Brazilian literature in Anglophone and global literary markets. Smaller publishing houses and university presses indicate a shift toward this vision of untranslatability with the Brazilian literary works that they have recently translated into English. The trajectory of Hilst, one of the most important and controversial Brazilian writers from the second half of the twentieth century, in English translation illustrates the incremental inroads of such a politics of untranslatability. Her work first appeared in English in 2012, nearly a decade after her death in 2004, with the translation by Nathanaël and Rachel Gontijo Araújo of the 1982 novel *A obscena senhora D* as *The Obscene Madame D*. Since introducing Anglo-American readers to Hilst's experimental prose with its idiosyncratic language and erotic themes, Nightboat has published *Letters from a Seducer*, John Keene's 2014 translation of her 1991 novel *Cartas de um sedutor*, and *Fluxo-Floema*, Alexandra Joy Forman's 2018 translation of her debut 1970 novel. Melville House published in 2014 *With My Dog-Eyes*, Adam Morris's translation of her 1986 novella *Com meus olhos de cão*, and co.im.press published in 2018 *Of Death: Minimal Odes*, a collection of poetry translated by Laura Cesarco Eglin. Critics and translators often frame Hilst in connection to Lispector, drawing on readers' comparative familiarity with Lispector to make Hilst's experimental and erotic, verging on pornographic, prose more legible to Anglophone readers. Renewed critical attention to Hilst in Brazil and the United States has paralleled her circulation in English translation.[14]

Hilst is not the only respected twentieth-century Brazilian writer to have emerged from relative obscurity as English translations heighten their hemispheric and global profiles. Raduan Nassar has entered into the spotlight of Brazilian literature translated into English after decades of remaining comparatively unknown due to minimal circulation abroad of his limited literary corpus. As the child of Lebanese immigrants raised in Pindodrama, a small town in rural São Paulo state, Nassar represents a distinctive voice in Brazilian letters who published *Lavoura arcaica* in 1975 and *Um copo de cólera* in 1978. After these acclaimed novels, he retired from writing in 1984 to tend crops on a medium-sized farm until 2011.[15] Now living in the capital of São Paulo, he has returned to the literary limelight with English versions of his debut, translated as *Ancient Tillage* by Karen Sotelino, and *A Cup of Rage*, translated by Stefan Tobler, published in the United Kingdom by Penguin Classics in 2015 and in the United States by New Directions in 2017. In 2016, he received the prestigious Camões Prize in honor of the entirety of his work. Since 1989, Portuguese and Brazilian governments have awarded this prize to living authors in the Portuguese language, recognizing thirteen Portuguese writers, twelve Brazilians, and two writers each from Angola, Mozambique, and Cape Verde. In the same year, Tobler's translation *A Cup of Rage* appeared on the longlist for the Man Booker International Prize.

Translation and the economy of prestige associated with certain literary prizes have enhanced Nassar's status as a Brazilian writer in the Anglo-American market.[16] Publishing Nassar in English translation indicates a reevaluation of his experimental, sensual, and psychological prose and, potentially, shifts in market demands and economics of translation. Earlier translators and publishers would have likely shied away from the experimentation of *Um copo de cólera*, which consists of extended, stream-of-consciousness sentences that last for entire paragraphs, pages, and chapters. His seemingly never-ending sentences with baroque flourishes present an affront to the syntactical preferences of English, with its shorter sentences that clearly mark the relationship between subject, verb, and predicate. These stylistic choices contribute to his depiction of the sexually charged, psychologically complex, and borderline violent encounter between two lovers of disparate ages. Maintaining this symbiosis of style and content in English translation is difficult. While a range of factors, including market interests, personal preferences, or academic needs, inform which works get published in translation, the publication of *A Cup of Rage* suggests how such decisions can generate what Venuti terms a foreignizing translation practice (*The Translator's Invisibility* 23–24). Specific linguistic and cultural practices in a foreignizing translation resist dominant values of the target language and resonate with the potential of a politics of untranslatability to expand understandings of Brazilian literature.

In interpreting with care texts long considered untranslatable, these translations of works by Hilst and Nassar showcase the possibilities of untranslatability as a critical practice and creative tool that draws attention to Brazilian writers previously overlooked in national and global literary markets.[17] Translating difficult texts and underrepresented voices can expose readers beyond national and linguistic borders to a more nuanced and comprehensive understanding of the complexities of Brazilian literature. The publication of Davi Kopenawa's *The Falling Sky: Words of a Yanomami Shaman* in 2013 and Wilson Bueno's 1992 *Mar paraguayo* as *Paraguayan Sea* in Erín Moure's 2017 translation exemplify how such an approach to translation can introduce a broader reading public to voices historically relegated to the margins of Brazilian letters or completely forgotten. *The Falling Sky* emerges as a collaboration of

Amerindian philosopher and ecological advocate Kopenawa with French anthropologist Bruce Albert, who recorded Kopenawa in his indigenous language and then transcribed, edited, and translated his story into the textual version in French, which was subsequently translated into English and Portuguese. This blend of life story, autoethnography, and ecological manifesto translates the spoken language of the Yanomami, an indigenous Amazonian group, into written languages of former imperial powers that colonized the Americas. This book engages in epistemological translations by rendering ideas about interactions between humans, animals, and the forest and other ecological concepts from a complex Amerindian tradition into terms that "white people" could understand. Shifting from the Amazon to southern Brazil, *Mar paraguayo* depicts the movements of people and languages in a border region. With its invented blending of Portuguese, Spanish, and Guaraní, Bueno's challenging poetic text invites readers and translators to continue interpreting and (not) translating it, as Moure did when creatively transforming the work into a mixture of English, French, and Guaraní.[18] By carrying across voices often ignored or marginalized within Brazilian letters to Anglophone readers, translations of Amerindian and migrant texts indicate the ethical and political potential of creative and critical practices that activate the untranslatable.

The English-language market is one barometer for the dissemination of Brazilian literature in the Americas, which does not necessarily correspond to the dynamics unfolding in the Spanish-language context given the linguistic similarities between Portuguese and Spanish. Works by more experimental writers, including Nuno Ramos, Santiago Nazarian, Veronica Stigger, Ana Cristina César, and Augusto and Haroldo de Campos, have been published in Spanish, while their works rarely circulate in English. Of these writers, only Ana Cristina César and Haroldo de Campos have had book-length translations into English. In 1997, Boulevard published *Intimate Diary*, a selection of César's poetry and prose translated by Patricia E. Paige, Celia McCullough, and David Treece. More recently, poet Brenda Hillman and her mother Helen Hillman, a native speaker of Portuguese, collaborated with Brazilian poet and critic Sebastião Edson Macedo and, in the role of editor, Katrina Dodson to translate César's poetic and prose collection *A teus pés* into English. Parlos Press published their version, *At Your Feet*, in 2018. César's enigmatic and experimental writing provides fertile ground for future translations. Poems and critical essays by another key figure of the Brazilian avant-garde in the second half of the twentieth century, Haroldo de Campos, have appeared in English translation in *Novas: Selected Writings*, edited by Antonio Sergio Bessa and Odile Cisneros and published by Northwestern University Press in 2007. Embracing a politics of untranslatability would allow more of these experimental Brazilian writers to reach a broader readership in the Americas via translation into Spanish and English.

The current projects of contemporary translators from Brazilian Portuguese into English demonstrate a greater adherence to a politics of untranslatability that expands ideas of Brazilian letters within the English-speaking Americas. Zoë Perry received the 2015 PEN/Heim Translation Fund grant for her unpublished translation of Stigger's innovative 2013 novel *Opisanie świata*. In an essay about translating the novel, Perry observes that, despite the increased interest in translating contemporary Brazilian literature, many of the modernist writers to which Stigger alludes remain untranslated or their translations are out of print. Brazilian works that engage in modernist experimentation or diverge from stylistic or thematic preferences within institutions of world literature often do not enter the Anglo-American and, by extension, global literary markets via translation. Following a politics of untranslatability could allow for more avant-garde texts, including Stigger's novel and the works of Oswald de Andrade and Raúl Bopp that it praises, to circulate beyond Brazil in translation. The in-progress retranslations of *Macunaíma* by Katrina Dodson and *Grande Sertão: Veredas* by Alison Entrekin similarly illustrate the aesthetic and editorial potential of embracing untranslatability. In preparing her translation, Dodson has delved into archives in Brazil, studied Tupi, and embarked on a reading of the novel attuned to its linguistic experimentation and cultural specificities. She has received a travel grant from the Brazilian National Library and a translation fellowship from the National Endowment for the Arts to support her work on this retranslation. These government investments in her project indicate the text's importance to both Brazilian national literature and the broader sphere of world literature.

Based on a competitive evaluation of her sample translation, Entrekin received a contract from Guimarães Rosa's estate to retranslate his modernist masterpiece into English. Entrekin estimates that the translation will take five years to complete, in comparison to the usual six months required to translate more straightforward, contemporary Brazilian novels. In an essay about recreating the novel in English, Entrekin compares the experience of first reading Guimarães Rosa's Portuguese prose to "setting foot in a foreign country where the people speak a dialect similar to your own language, but with such a different accent and turns of phrase that you struggle to make sense of it" ("When in Hell"). This strangeness of the novel's language, with invented words prioritizing aural qualities of rhythm, rhyme, and alliteration, poses a challenge to translators. Entrekin acknowledges these difficulties but refuses to view *Grande Sertão: Veredas* as literally untranslatable. Since its neologisms do not have dictionary equivalents, the novel invites the creativity of translators who delve into the arduous task of rendering the Portuguese prose into another language. In claiming that she considers Guimarães Rosa's masterpiece "to be translatable in that it is 'reproducible,'" Entrekin emphasizes her own agency as a translator ("When in Hell"). She states the ethos guiding her attempt to translate this modernist marvel: "If I am to do him justice, I will have to recreate his idiolect in my native tongue in a kind of poetic workshop, seeking compensatory rhythms, archaisms, exotic words, and syntax for all that is inevitably lost in the crossing" ("When in Hell"). Dismissing the domesticating approach that the previous translators into English employed, Entrekin vows to read and interpret the original text with care in a mode of translation that resonates with a politics of untranslatability.

Rather than avoid translating difficult texts, Dodson and Entrekin commit themselves to a politics of untranslatability as they constantly return to the experimental language and amplified cultural specificity of *Macunaíma* and *Grande Sertão: Veredas*. The fact that their projects have already received critical attention illustrates the shifting realities of translating Brazil, whereby animating the potential of the untranslatable can diversify the range of Brazilian voices and experiences that circulate within the Americas. Over the course of this book, I have examined how hemispheric travels of Brazilian artists and intellectuals have generated feelings of displacement, which demand linguistic, cultural, and epistemological translations involving creative transpositions and transformations. In the 1870s, José Carlos Rodrigues's periodical projected a "new world" outlook of economic progress, diplomatic relations, and cultural exchange that foregrounded ties between Brazil and the United States. By reporting on events and experiences in the United States for a Brazilian readership, *O Novo Mundo* exemplified a form of hemispheric translation that Silviano Santiago and Adriana Lisboa would later employ in fictional tales about Brazilian characters living in the United States. While never visiting the United States, Mário de Andrade posited another way of belonging to the Americas with his Amerindian trickster Macunaíma, whose tales reached a hemispheric public through filmic and fictional afterlives. These varied forms of translation underscore the creative agency of artists, intellectuals, writers, and translators as they encounter new ideas and confront unfamiliar surroundings. Translating Brazil, as a heterogeneous nation with a polyphony of voices and experiences, within the hemispheric Americas emerges as a difficult, but urgent, task in our current era of heightened globalization with its darker underside of resurgent xenophobic nationalism.

NOTES

Introduction. Theorizing Travels and Translations of Brazil in the Americas

1. See Cribelli for a study of the emperor's visit to the United States that emphasizes his interest in technology. For more on Pedro II and his travels, see Barman's *Citizen Emperor*, especially chapter 9, and Schwarcz's *The Emperor's Beard*, in particular chapter 14. I return to Pedro II's travels in the United States in the first chapter.

2. All translations from Portuguese and Spanish into English, unless otherwise noted, are my own.

3. I examine the relevance of Longfellow's poetry for Latin American writers more in the first chapter. See Gruesz's article "*El Gran Poeta* Longfellow and a Psalm of Exile" for more on Longfellow's reception in Spanish America.

4. Roraima's governor Suely Campos asked the federal government to close the border with Venezuela in April 2018, but the Supreme Court ruled against the closure in August 2018. Tensions between Brazilians and Venezuelan migrants escalated in Pacaraima, a town of ten thousand inhabited by three thousand to four thousand homeless refugees, resulting in violence and the return of some refugees to the other side of the border (Adamo Idoeta n.p.). As indigenous peoples and Spanish-speaking Venezuelans cross into Brazil, they must communicate across languages without translators. This contested border exists in a region where indigenous peoples roam relatively freely, and where Macunaíma, Mário de Andrade's hero and Pauline Melville's narrator, was born. I return to this region in the second chapter.

5. The details of this story appear in a July 23, 2018, article by Estelita Hass Carazzai in the *Folha de São Paulo*.

6. See the final section of chapter 3 for more on Santiago's concept of the cosmopolitanism of the poor.

7. Gustavo Pérez Firmat similarly asked *Do the Americas Have a Common Literature?* in his 1990 study.

8. Roland Greene's proposal of New World studies as a comparative and collaborative enterprise resembles Fitz's idea of Inter-American studies. Whereas Fitz frames inter-American literary studies as a true comparatist project where scholars work in three, or more, languages, Hemispheric American studies has developed in English and American studies departments in an effort to correct the US-centric nature of the disciplines. This emerging field recognizes what Latin Americanists have long known: that America refers not only to the United States, but also to the continental span. See Levander and Levine's edited volume for an overview of Hemispheric American studies. For an outline of the links between these concepts and disciplines, see Antonio Barrenechea's entry to the ACLA State of the Discipline Report on "American Literature." Justin Read frames Hemispheric studies as "'in translation' between the extant cultural-scholarly institutions of Anglo-American and Latin American Studies" (xvii).

9. Notable interventions from scholars with the United States as their primary focus include Gruesz's *Ambassadors of Culture*, Brickhouse's *Transamerican Literary Relations and the Nineteenth-Century Public Sphere*, and Saldívar's *Trans-americanity: Subaltern Modernities, Global Coloniality, and the Cultures of Greater Mexico*.

10. Robert Patrick Newcomb and Richard A. Gordon expand efforts to read and analyze across linguistic and cultural divides to the Iberian Peninsula and other parts of the global Hispanic and Lusophone worlds with their edited volume *Beyond Tordesillas: New Approaches to Comparative Luso-Hispanic Studies*.

11. These works include, among others, Jossianna Arroyo's *Travestismos culturales: literatura y etnografía en Cuba y Brasil* (2003), Luís Madureira's *Cannibal Modernities: Postcoloniality and the Avant-Garde in Caribbean and Brazilian Literature* (2005), Paulo Moreira's *Literary and Cultural Relations between Brazil and Mexico: Deep Undercurrents* (2013), Sergio Delgado Moya's *Delirious Consumption: Aesthetics and Consumer Capitalism in Mexico and Brazil* (2017), and Adam Shellhorse's *Anti-Literature: The Politics and Limits of Representation in Modern Brazil and Argentina* (2017).

12. For studies that frame interactions between Brazil and the United States in geopolitical or historical terms, see Britta Crandall's *Hemispheric Giants: The Misunderstood History of U.S.-Brazil Relations* and Micol Seigel's *Uneven Encounters: Making Race and Nation in Brazil and the United States*. Crandall focuses on diplomatic relations while Seigel proposes a transnational vision of cultural history of the early twentieth century.

13. Rachel Price emphasizes the experiences of Sousândrade and Martí in New York as critical to their views about materialist excess and capitalist consumption. As I explore in chapter 1, Sousândrade expressed his critiques in poetry rather than journalism, whereas Martí articulated his ambivalence in journalistic texts and essays.

14. For more on Pan-Americanism and twentieth-century literature, see Stephen M. Park's study of networks of North American and Spanish American artists and intellectuals. Claire F. Fox examines how Pan-American thought influenced cultural policy during the Cold War.

15. Crandall characterizes the two nations as "hemispheric giants" in her study of their diplomatic relationships. Richard M. Morse recognizes the critical roles of Brazil and the United States in his study *O espelho de Próspero: Cultura e ideias nas Américas* but frames his comparison in terms of Ibero-America and Anglo-America.

16. For more detailed histories, see Thomas Skidmore's *Brazil: Five Centuries of Change*, which focuses on political and socioeconomic developments, and Darlene Sadlier's cultural history *Brazil Imagined: 1500 to the Present*.

17. See Izecksohn for a comparative study of the two wars that examines links between tactics of enlistment in the Union and Brazilian armies, emancipation, citizenship, and national unification. His analysis emphasizes how these distinct countries experienced war similarly in terms of military recruitment, centralization, and hierarchies (2).

18. In *Brazil: Essays on History and Politics*, Leslie Bethell draws parallels between abolition and its aftermath in Brazil and the United States with "The Decline and Fall of Slavery in Brazil (1850–88)."

19. See Gouveia's *The Triumph of Brazilian Modernism: The Metanarrative of Emancipation and Counter-Narratives* for an extensive study of Brazilian modernist movements from 1920 to 1945, their inscription into literary history, and later reevaluations of this narrative. Painters Anita Malfatti and Tarsila do Amaral and writers Menotti Del Picchia, Oswald de Andrade, and Mário de Andrade, collectively known as the Group of Five, were key in the early stages of *modernismo*. I return to Oswald's ideas of *antropofagia* and Mário's multilayered project in chapter 2.

20. Though Gilberto Freyre never used the phrase "racial democracy" in his 1933 masterpiece *Casa-grande e senzala*, the concept is often attributed to his study of the supposedly benevolent nature of slavery in Brazil when compared to the practices in the United States. See Marshall Eakin's *Becoming Brazilians: Race and National Identity in Twentieth-Century Brazil* for a study of Freyre's ongoing influence in Brazilian thought.

21. Zita Nunes's analysis of this poem helps frame Brazilian modernism in relation to US racial politics of (59–62).

22. For more on the dictatorship, see Thomas Skidmore's *The Politics of Military Rule in Brazil, 1964–1985*.

23. See Perrone's *Masters of Contemporary Brazilian Song: MPB, 1965–1985* for more on intersections of music and politics in the work of Buarque, Veloso, and Gil. See Dunn's *Brutality Garden* for a study of Tropicália that frames Veloso,

Gil, and their collaborators as continuing a trajectory of innovation started with Oswald's *antropofagia*. For more on Veloso's exile in London and his life, see his essays in *Alegria, alegria* and his memoir *Tropical Truth*.

24. See Cohn, Franco, Lowe and Fitz, and Rostagno for more on how Cold War cultural politics impact literature.

25. The acronym BRIC refers to Brazil, Russia, India, and China as nations of the Global South poised to exert political and economic power globally in the early twenty-first century. See Larry Rohter's 2010 *Brazil on the Rise: The Story of a Country Transformed* for a fairly optimistic vision of Brazil's recent trajectory and Michael Reid's 2014 *Brazil: The Troubled Rise of a Global Power* for a more nuanced view of the nation's global position.

26. According to the Pew Research Center, the number of unauthorized immigrants in the United States has declined since its peak at 12.2 million in 2007 to a population of 10.7 million undocumented immigrants in 2016.

27. For more on how Brazilian migration to the United States has changed after 9/11, see Martes's economic sociology of Brazilians in Massachusetts and Margolis's ethnography of Brazilian émigrés in *Goodbye, Brazil*.

28. In her study of José Martí as a translator of empire and a migrant subject, Laura Lomas considers translation a mode of transculturation. She contends that Pratt's contact zone is indebted to Santiago's space in-between and frames Martí as an ancestor of Santiago, given their transnational position as translators who carry across ideas from North America to Latin America and vice versa (63–65, 70–76). I see similarities between the space in-between and the contact zone, but I do not agree with Lomas's conjecture that Pratt followed in Santiago's intellectual path. Their ideas, as I explicate in the introduction and the third chapter, developed out of distinct genealogies.

29. See Gayle Rogers's *Incomparable Empires: Modernism and the Translation of Spanish and American Literature* for another transatlantic approach to poetics and translation. Rogers conceives of translation in relationship to shifting imperial dynamics of Spain and the United States in the early twentieth century. Infante considers how poets writing in Spanish and Portuguese from Iberia and Latin America influenced Anglo-American ideas of modernism.

30. I return to Cassin's ideas and their translation into the *Dictionary of Untranslatables* in my fourth chapter's discussion of translatability, the untranslatable, and Adriana Lisboa's fiction. I will discuss Apter's approach to untranslatability later in the introduction and again in the fourth chapter.

31. See Shellhorse for a careful reading of baroque poetics, experimentation, and expressions of anti-literature in Haroldo and Augusto de Campos that draws parallels to the works of Brazilian prose writers Clarice Lispector and Osman Lins and Argentine writer David Viñas. The *Princeton Encyclopedia of Poetry and Poetics*' entry on Noigandres outlines the concrete poetry in the 1950s and 1960s of the Campos brothers and Décio Pignatari and recommends other relevant bibliography.

32. For an overview of Haroldo de Campos as a translator, poet, and critic, see the introduction to *Novas*, an anthology of his writings translated into English. See *Transcriação* for a collection of Haroldo's writings on translation. Augusto de Campos comments on his translation practice and theory in *À margem da margem* and *Invenção*. Haroldo creates the neologism transcreation (*transcriação*) to describe his translation practice, while Augusto de Campos prefers *arte-tradução* or *intradução*. I opt for Haroldo's term, given its suggestion of the movement and the innovation involved in creative transpositions or, in other words, transcreations.

33. See Kristal's *Invisible Work: Borges and Translation* for a study of Borges and translation that focuses on language and aesthetics. Kristal aims to render Borges's work as a translator visible and thus proposes a relatively limited view of translation that contrasts with Waisman's more political and capacious approach to the term.

34. See Vieira's 1999 chapter for more on Haroldo de Campos's poetics of transcreation in relation to Oswald de Andrade's metaphor of cultural *antropofagia*. See Jackson's 2010 chapter for a study of how Brazilian concrete poets Décio Pignatari, Augusto de Campos, and Haroldo de Campos approach translation as part of their project of verbivocovisual poetry. In his 2008 study *Translation and Identity in the Americas*, Gentzler dedicates his fourth chapter to ties between Oswald de Andrade's cultural cannibalism and Haroldo de Campos's transcreation. After linking Campos, Benjamin, and Derrida as theorists of translation, Gentzler outlines how critics Roberto Schwarz, Else Vieira, and Randal Johnson have interpreted the São Paulo–based critic-poet's work on translation.

Chapter 1. The New World Travels and Translations of O Novo Mundo

1. They did not envision the exploitative attempts to implement capitalist modernity during the Amazonian rubber boom. See Hardman and Beckman for more on this "export age," a period of extraction ranging from 1875 to 1925.

2. See Rydell (9–16) for an overview of the exhibition's opening. For more on this exchange from Brazil's perspective, consult Schwarcz's "Os trópicos" (208–10), chapter 15 of her *The Emperor's Beard*, and Barman (275–80).

3. Schwarcz frames Brazil's scientific codification of race from 1870 to 1930 in terms of nineteenth-century racial theories of determinism, positivism, and social Darwinism developed in Europe (*The Spectacle of Races*, 44–70). See Costa's comparisons of liberalism, land policies, and slavery in Brazil and the United States.

4. Although Haiti had two short-lived periods of monarchal rule from 1804 to 1806 and from 1849 to 1859, Brazil's empire was unique in the hemisphere for its temporal span from 1822 to 1889 and its continuity with the Portuguese

monarchy. For more on how Brazil's colonial and imperial histories differentiate it from other Latin American nations, see sections on colonial and nineteenth-century literature in Fitz's *Inter-American Literary History* and the discussions of Brazil's insularity in the introduction and first chapter of Perrone's *Brazil, Lyric, and the Americas*.

5. Revolutionary ideas from the United States and France inspired Brazilians who sought freedom from Portugal. In 1792, José Joaquim de Maia e Barbalho, a Brazilian student writing as Vendek, wrote to Thomas Jefferson, in his role as ambassador to France, for advice for independence movements (Maxwell, *Conflicts and Conspiracies* 80–82). *O livro de Tiradentes* compiles early versions of the US Constitution translated into Portuguese, which played a role in uprisings against the Portuguese. After the end of the US Civil War, Southerners expressed interest in Brazil, where slavery remained legal. The Brazilian government facilitated immigration from the United States to Brazil between 1865 and 1869. In "Confederates and Yankees," Silva contends that Southerners' experiences in the Reconstructionist South and their desire to remain slaveowners resulted in two thousand to four thousand ex-Confederates forming colonies in São Paulo, Pará, Bahia, and Rio de Janeiro; Northerners only migrated due to incentives of the immigration agent Quintino de Souza Bocaiúva (383). See Horne for a brief overview of *confederados* in Brazil.

6. See Foner (1–35) for more on the Emancipation Proclamation, the Thirteenth Amendment, and Reconstruction.

7. Foner situates the Fourteenth Amendment in the political context of the failure of presidential Reconstruction and Johnson's vetoing of the Civil Rights Bill (257). The Reconstruction Act organized Confederate states into regions of military oversight and laid out steps for them to complete in order to receive congressional recognition (276).

8. See chapter 14 of Schwarcz's *The Emperor's Beard* for more on Pedro II's foreign travels.

9. See Izecksohn for comparisons of race, citizenship, and state-building in the Civil War and the Paraguayan War, or War of the Triple Alliance. Recruitment of black soldiers in both wars resulted in manumission and abolition.

10. Experiences in New York; Washington, DC; and London shaped Nabuco's views on abolition under monarchy. He later served as Brazilian ambassador to the United States from 1905 to 1910. Dennison examines links between Nabuco's monarchism and Pan-Americanism, and Ganzert studies his support of US-Brazil connections.

11. See Chalhoub for more on the ambiguity of freedom in the last decades of slavery in Brazil due to conditional manumission, labor contracts, and increased emancipation. See Needell for an overview of how historiographies vary in their approach to the factors shaping Brazilian abolitionism.

12. See Skidmore for more on Brazilian intellectual thoughts on race from 1870 to 1930.

13. In *Constituição política do Império do Brasil seguida do Acto Addicional, da lei da sua interpretação e de outras*, Rodrigues outlined his liberal republicanism by noting the constitution's preference for Catholicism as the state religion (65), the benefits of free trade (88), and the need for a free press (144–45).

14. See Boehrer and Cardim for more on Rodrigues's biography and historical relevance. Boehrer dismisses claims from biographers that Rodrigues worked for the American Tract Society and the American Bible Society when first in New York due to the lack of documentation, instead highlighting his literary and journalistic career (128–29).

15. See Pap for more on *Jornal de Notícias* (1877–1884, Erie, PA), *Voz Portuguesa* (1880–1887, CA), and *União Portuguesa* (1887–1942, Oakland, CA) as periodicals that catered to Azorean and Portuguese immigrants, and Freitas for a study of contradictions of modernity in *Aurora Brasileira*. Hardt and Miller rightly note that Park's categories from 1922 conflate the immigrant and foreign-language press. Miller opts for the term "ethnic press" since it implies duration beyond first-generation immigrants.

16. See Sílvia Maria Azevedo for an analysis of Brazilian illustrated journals and Telles's *Desenhando a nação* for a comparative study of illustrated periodicals in Rio de Janeiro and Buenos Aires.

17. The exact number of subscribers is difficult to determine. According to Rodrigues's entry in the *Dicionário Biobibliográfico de Historiadores, Geógrafos e Antropólogos Brasileiros*, his May 10, 1915, retirement speech from *Jornal do Comércio* and Cardim's biographical article, *O Novo Mundo*'s circulation reached eight thousand. Rodrigues's letter establishing the Novo Mundo Association estimated that, by 1877, 6,500 volumes would be sold in Brazil ("Dear Sir . . ." 2). Letters to Rodrigues, archived at Brazil's National Library, indicate that prominent Brazilian writer and politician Visconde de Taunay, Republican journalist and politician Quintino Bocaiúva, and intellectual Francisco Inácio Marcondes Homem de Melo, as well as Portuguese writer and politician Teófilo Braga and Swiss American geologist Arnold Guyot read and collaborated with the journal. Among others, Homem de Melo praised Rodrigues for the "eficaz serviço, que está prestando a vossa pátria com a publicação do *Novo Mundo*" (effective service, that you are lending your country with the publication of *O Novo Mundo*; letter dated June 17, 1873). As Marisa Lajolo and Regina Zilberman cogently examine, readers in Brazil have historically belonged to elite classes.

18. O Novo Mundo Association's bylaws and Rodrigues's February 14, 1875, letter establishing the joint stock company ("Dear Sir . . .") are accessible through the *American Broadsides and Ephemera* series.

19. Gruesz mentions this merged "J.C. Rodrigues publication" without discussing Rodrigues further (*Ambassadors* 191). She insightfully reads *El Mundo Nuevo*'s cover image of a globe with a feminine muse linking "Norteamérica" and "Sudamérica" as expressing "an integrated América as an inspirational ideal is not a political reality" (189). This image did not appear on the merged periodical,

but its message resonates with *O Novo Mundo*'s cover image of a ship linking New York and Rio de Janeiro.

20. Letters and articles included in Rodrigues's personal papers at the Brazilian National Library in Rio de Janeiro.

21. Rodrigues's personal views cannot be conflated with those of *O Novo Mundo*. Publications emerge within what Robert Darnton terms the "communications circuit," the dialogue between a print community and a reading public.

22. See Robert Patrick Newcomb's *Nossa and Nuestra América: Inter-American Dialogues* for a comprehensive comparative study of essayistic constructs of "our" America among Spanish American and Brazilian writers.

23. Martí lived primarily in New York from 1881 to 1895 and contributed writings on North American life, compiled as *Escenas norteamericanas* (North American scenes), to twenty Latin American newspapers. His 1891 essay "Nuestra América" (Our America) depicted the United States as a monster to the north, yet earlier pieces admired the nation's work ethic and integration of immigrant labor. The bibliography on Martí is extensive given his importance for the fields of Latin American, Latinx, and Hemispheric American studies. For studies of Martí's writings from his years in the United States, see the collection *José Martí's Our America: From National to Hemispheric Studies* edited by Jeffrey Belnap and Raúl Fernández. Anne Fountain, in *José Martí, the United States, and Race*, similarly focuses on how Martí's experiences in the United States informed his thoughts on race. Julio Ramos, in the second half of *Divergent Modernities*, proposes an insightful reading of Martí's ambivalent writings about life, modern technology, and politics in the United States. Lomas analyzes Martí as a Latino migrant subject whose writings translate, in a figurative sense, US modernity for Spanish readers.

24. Campos also claims that, for *O Novo Mundo*, the United States supplanted Europe as an ideal model for Brazil. See my articles in *Luso-Brazilian Review* and *Hispanic Review* for more on *Correio Braziliense* and *Nitheroy*.

25. See chapter 1 of Sadlier's *Brazil Imagined* for more on Cabral's mission and colonial representations of Brazil.

26. In *Local Histories/Global Designs*, Mignolo develops the modern/colonial world system as a concept that traces continuities and distinctions between the sixteenth-century colonial world structured on religious affiliations and the modern world organized by racial and national divisions, starting in the late nineteenth century (30–36).

27. Gruesz explains that nineteenth-century Latino writers often occupied official ambassadorial positions since "translation and ambassadorship are closely related functions, as both mediate between linguistic and cultural systems" (19). As a Brazilian exile in New York, Rodrigues filled the role of an unofficial diplomat.

28. This act legislated land grants to establish public universities and colleges for "the benefit of agriculture and the Mechanic arts." Schools praised in the journal, most notably Cornell, received support from federal land grants.

29. J. C. Fletcher and Daniel P. Kidder wrote *Brazil and the Brazilians* in 1857 based on twenty years of experience in Brazil and consultation of Instituto Histórico e Geográfico Brasileiro archives. They attempted to correct exotic misconceptions of Brazil common in the United States and other foreign countries, but their language echoed discourses of colonists or naturalists depicting the tropics as Eden. See Buarque de Holanda's *Visão do paraíso* for a classic Brazilian study of the paradisiac in Iberian colonial representations of the Americas. Greenblatt identifies wonder as a unifying feature in European responses to the New World (22). The language of marvel and wonder shaped colonial depictions of the Americas and persists today in what Mignolo characterizes as the ongoing links of coloniality and modernity.

30. Orton quoted from earlier writings about Brazil's geology, such as *A Journey in Brazil*, written by Louis Agassiz and his wife Elizabeth Cabot Agassiz after spending nineteen months in Brazil in 1865 and 1866. Their account of Brazil's land, people, and culture attempted to make the nation more familiar to a North American reading public.

31. See Freitas's *Charles Frederick Hartt, um naturalista no império de Pedro II* for more on his life and work.

32. The ad for Rodrigues's *Chrestomathia* featured a quote from the *Evening Post* applauding its versatility for classroom instruction. The reader compiled excerpts of literary works in English to provide a broad overview of literature for students of English, indicating another level of Rodrigues's work as a translator between the United States and Brazil. A copy of this book is available at the Institute of Brazilian Studies at the University of São Paulo.

33. See Soares Inácio et al. for more on corollaries between progress and public elementary education in nineteenth-century Brazil. Elites viewed access to basic education among free people key to Brazil becoming modern.

34. Education in imperial Brazil was predominately private in religious or military schools, with public primary and secondary schools relatively scarce until the first half of the twentieth century. Brazilian higher education consisted of separate law, medical, and polytechnic schools until they joined in Rio de Janeiro in 1920 to create what would become in 1937 the University of Brazil. The ideas on education that Manuel Bergström Lourenço Filho articulated in a 1951 government publication resemble the views that *O Novo Mundo* supported roughly seventy years earlier.

35. Branner's publications include *Geographical and Geological Exploration in Brazil* (1886), *Geologia elementar: preparada com referencia especial aos estudantes brasileiros e à geologia do Brazil* (1915), and *Outlines of the Geology of Brazil to Accompany the Geologic Map of Brazil* (1920). See Champlin for a brief biography of Branner.

36. The Oliveira Lima Library at the Catholic University of America holds Branner's letters to Oliveira Lima, spanning from 1905, when Oliveira Lima sent Branner a copy of his book *Nos Estados Unidos*, until 1920.

37. Branner shared his ideas for the lecture series in a March 13, 1911, letter. On November 15, 1912, he noted that the Limas "left many saudades at our house." Letters from February 26, March 17, and December 18, 1913, outlined Martin's plans for the textbook on Brazilian history and noted the growing interest in Brazilian history at Stanford.

38. Freitas draws parallels between *Aurora Brasileira* and *O Novo Mundo* in terms of style, content, and mission. Cornell's noncirculating stacks hold the only complete copy of the periodical, but it can be consulted via a CD included with Freitas's book. Brazil's National Library has a few issues of the journal, which suggest its limited circulation in Brazil, though neither the periodical nor Freitas publish statistics about the number of subscribers.

39. See my article in the *Journal of Lusophone Studies* for an earlier version of this section.

40. According to Plum's statistics of exhibition size, the 1851 London exhibition covered 8.4 hectares with 13,937 exhibitors and 6,039,195 visitors, the Philadelphia exhibition was 30.3 hectares with 60,000 exhibitors and 10,165,000 visitors, and the 1900 Parisian fair was 46 hectares with 83,000 exhibitors and 50,800,801 visitors (63).

41. See Rydell, Plum, and Giberti for more on the significance of the Centennial Exhibition as an intersection of nationalism, modernity, and industrial capitalism. Studies by Brazilian scholars Hardman, Turazzi, and Schwarcz note the importance of world's fairs for constructing Brazil as a modern nation dependent upon tropical resources.

42. A scan of the catalog confirms that Brazil's most significant contribution was agricultural, with eight pages listing coffee, medicinal plants, and tobacco, while machinery received one page. Plant and animal products included land animals, sugar, and liquor. The fine arts section listed twenty-two items such as portraits, landscapes, and historic scenes. Brazil had seventy-nine items in mining and metallurgy, outpacing Mexico's twenty-seven. Argentina and Mexico had a larger presence in manufacturing than Brazil, whose manufactured goods included chemicals, ceramics, furniture, silk, yarns, and medicine. Brazil contributed sixty-four entries to education and science, compared to the 372 items of the United States.

43. *O Novo Mundo* began its coverage after the initial planning phases, so its reports did not include earlier conflicts over designs, installation, and classification system. See Giberti for more on these disagreements.

44. The *New York Herald* contained special reports, likely written by James O'Kelly, about Pedro II's journey as the first monarch to visit the United States. The emperor received press coverage reserved for celebrities as evidenced in *Dom Pedro in the United States*, a volume at the Oliveira Lima Library that contains more than one hundred articles documenting his 1876 travels. Articles described him as the "American emperor" and claiming to be "proud to note in him the

go-ahead American traits" ("Our Yankee Emperor"). See Cribelli for a detailed account of press coverage of Pedro II's visit to the United States.

45. See Said's classic 1978 study for more on how Western culture employs orientalist practices and aesthetics. Latin American scholars note the use of orientalist discourses to conceive of and represent the unknown, as Altamirano observes with Sarmiento's analogy between the pampas and the deserts of Arabia (83–89). This description rendered the pampas both exotic and familiar, a gesture similar to the pavilion's architecture.

46. Besides Brazil, ten other nations, including Spain and Portugal, built structures at the Centennial Exhibition. The Spanish American participants Argentina, Bolivia, Chile, Colombia, Ecuador, Guatemala, Honduras, Mexico, Nicaragua, Peru, and Venezuela shared sections of the main exhibition hall. Uslenghi analyzes how Argentina, Brazil, and Mexico entered the visual economies of capitalism at the 1876, 1889, and 1900 universal exhibitions. See Andermann, "Tournaments of Value," for a comparative reading of Brazil and Argentina at exhibitions in the late nineteenth century. See Tenorio-Trillo for more on curating Mexico as modern at the Paris 1889 Universal Exposition and other fairs.

47. A complete listing of these awards and the honored Brazilians appeared in the subsequent issue (6.72, 258–59).

48. A year after this lecture, the Royal Geographical Society published Burton's translation of *The Lands of Cazembe: Lacerda's Journey to Cazembe in 1798*, and two other translations of Portuguese narratives of travel to Africa.

49. See Garcia for more on Burton as a translator of Brazilian literature. Isabel Burton explained in a May 21, 1872, letter to Rodrigues archived at the Brazilian National Library that she was the sole translator of *Iracema*. She identified challenges in translation since certain things "come off splendid in Portuguese and crass in English."

50. *O Novo Mundo* explains that most Brazilian readers accessed Cooper's books in French. Marlyse Meyer observes, "Translation from English to French and then, in abridged form, to Portuguese was the trajectory of these cultural transmigrations" (268). Cooper's frontier narratives address themes relevant for Brazilian readers, like the interactions of indigenous people with "civilization." See Fitz, *Rediscovering the New World* (80–94), and Wasserman, *Exotic Nations* (154–87), for parallels between the writings of Cooper and Alencar.

51. Gruesz analyzes Longfellow's ties to the Spanish-speaking world in the nineteenth century by noting the existence of at least twelve different Spanish translations of *Evangeline* ("El Gran Poeta Longfellow" 396–99). The poem's account of the Acadian removals of 1755 depicts hemispheric history of interest to translators of Longfellow into Spanish (402).

52. According to Brazilian critic Afranio Peixoto's 1935 reflection on North American influence in Brazilian literature, "*Evangeline* touched us with pity and there are many Evangelines among us—living tributes to the North American

poet; besides being widely read it was translated to my certain knowledge four times" (127).

53. Pedro II noted in his diary that he ate lunch with Longfellow on June 10, 1876, and went to Longfellow's house the same day for dinner, where he received two books from Longfellow (vol. 17, 47–50). See Jaksić for more on Longfellow's significance in the Luso-Brazilian world (100–01).

54. See Jerome's "Letter to Pammachius" for his defense of sense-for-sense translation. Venuti frames these divisions as equivalence and function, or a translation's connection to the source text and relation to the target language (5).

55. As of 1879, the novel had been translated in Germany, France, Armenia, Belgium, Bohemia, Brazil, Denmark, Finland, Wales, Greece, Holland, Hungary, Spain, Italy, Poland, Portugal, Russia, Serbia, and Sweden.

56. The periodical first mentioned Sousândrade in a November 24, 1871, note about his daughter's education paired with an image of her school (2.14, 25). In 1875, the periodical cited his new administrative role (5.57, 238). See Gabriela Vieira de Campos for more on Sousândrade's role in *O Novo Mundo*, which expands upon Williams's *Sousândrade: Vida e obra*. Campos identifies Sousândrade as the author of two pieces on politics and four on literature (41).

57. Lobo claims Sousândrade did not receive financial support from Pedro II and opted for exile in New York (*Épica e modernidade* 22).

58. See Schwarcz's *The Spectacle of Races* for a comprehensive study of racial theories, including positivism, naturalism, determinism, and social Darwinism, and their implementation in Brazil from 1870 to 1930.

59. Mizruchi notes that the cultural diversity of the United States from 1865 to 1915 emerged as a source of anxiety and fascination, resulting in anti-immigrant attitudes that fueled resistance to a fully developed welfare system.

60. I follow Campos's scholarship on Sousândrade's authorship of articles in *O Novo Mundo* (41). While the poet signed political articles as J. Souza de Andrade, his literary notes remained anonymous or were signed S. A., as with "Anchieta ou o Evangelho nas Selvas" on February 23, 1876, and "Literatura" in the August 1877 issue.

61. See Alonso's study of Spanish American regional novels for more on the "autochthonous" as a "discursive mode based on a rhetorical figure encompassing three elements: spoken language, geographical location and a given human activity" (76). See Wasserman for more on how elites used exotic tropes to create Brazil's national literature.

62. Perrone elucidates how *O Guesa* expresses an inter-American outlook in the poet's preface, the poetic subject's wanderings, the verses' multilingualism, and the poem's intertextuality (*Brazil, Lyric* 103–17). He positions the Brazilian poem as a continuation of Alonso de Ercilla's sixteenth-century epic *La Araucana* and an antecedent of the works of Spanish American poets Vicente Huidobro and Pablo Neruda. Contemporary Brazilian writers and artists, like Adriano Espínola,

Salgado Maranhão, and Caetano Veloso, also engage in intertextual dialogues with the poem.

63. Price analyzes Sousândrade's poem as a critique of global capitalism (83–93). She underscores how the poem's aesthetic innovation and fragmentation facilitate criticisms of the dangers of speculation and market forces. Uslenghi situates the poem in the context of the 1876 Centennial Exhibition to claim that visions of Latin American and US modernities on display in Philadelphia enabled "Sousândrade's satirical dialogue between republic and monarchy as well as the parade of allegorical figures who embody a culture of capitalist extraction" (50).

64. Infante departs from the Campos brothers' re-vision to situate Sousândrade as a precursor to Pound in his study of translation and transatlantic poetics (117–38). Lobo proposes a study of the entire poem. See Rocha for an astute analysis of Sousândrade's work as a bridge between Brazil and the United States (*Maranhão-Manhattan* 21–60). Williams offers a biographical account of Sousândrade and published translations of stanzas one to twenty, 106 to 108, and 176 of "The Wall Street Inferno" in *Latin American Literary Review* in 1973. Robert E. Brown's translation of twenty-six stanzas from "The Wall Street Inferno" appeared in 1986 in the *Latin American Literary Review*, accompanied by notes from Augusto and Haroldo de Campos, and also almost in its entirety in the Campos brothers' *ReVisão de Sousândrade*. Odile Cisneros's more recent translation in *Luso-American Literature* renders the first six stanzas, then 100 to 110, 117, 118, and the final four stanzas. Her version covers much of the material previously translated by Williams or Brown with an attention to sound and a greater embrace of experimentation.

65. The poem employs twelve different languages, including Greek, Latin, Tupi, Quechua, English, French, Spanish, and Portuguese. These languages correspond to the classical, Amerindian, and European influences that Sousândrade integrated into his verses to create a lyrical epic of the Americas.

66. Brown's translation of the forty-fifth stanza was included in his *Latin American Literary Review* piece.

67. See Torres-Marchal's three-part article for a detailed analysis of the references and source materials for the epic's depiction of Pedro II's travels in the United States. Price underscores Sousândrade's critique of capital in her study of concrete aesthetics and the history of empire, slavery, and media technologies (77–93).

68. Critics tend to divide Machado's novels into a romantic phase and a realist one, which begins with *Memórias póstumas de Brás Cubas* in 1881. Schwarz describes the first phase as "somewhat colorless fiction" but notes continuity across Machado's work (*Master* 149). Rocha attributes the different periods to an increasing recognition of the author as a reader questioning originality. Daniel views the division as a shift from romantic-realism to literary impressionism, suggesting that the synthesis of these sensibilities resulted from experiences of multiraciality

(*Machado de Assis* 238). See Jackson's *Machado de Assis* for a comprehensive study of his life and writings. Abel Barros Baptista views Machado's work as inaugurating a cosmopolitan spirit in Brazilian letters that does not negate nationality (177).

69. Hélio de Seixas Guimarães's study of the critical reception of Machado de Assis's work is an exception to this tendency as he situates the essay's publication in *O Novo Mundo* and references Machado's correspondence with Rodrigues. His contextualized reading highlights New York as a center of print capitalism in the shifting political, cultural, and economic landscape of the late nineteenth century (56–59).

70. In "The Argentine Writer and Tradition," Borges argued that Argentine writers were not restricted to the local to create national literature. See Lowe and Fitz for more on how these writers questioned the idea of originality (15).

Chapter 2. Modernism for Export: The Translational Origins and Afterlives of *Macunaíma*

1. Schwartz's introduction illuminates how Brazilian modernist manifestos dialogue with national and cosmopolitan expressions, including surrealism and cubism. Following the convention in Brazilian scholarship, I refer to Mário de Andrade and Oswald de Andrade by their first names or their full names.

2. See the first chapter of Perrone's *Seven Faces: Brazilian Poetry Since Modernism* for more on the manifestos in relationship to Oswald's poetry and the period's poetic trends. Perrone links the idea of "poetry for exportation" to the work of Brazilian popular musicians in chapter 6 of *Brazil, Lyric, and the Americas*. Dunn also establishes a link between Brazilian modernism, specifically Oswald's radical perspective, and Tropicália in *Brutality Garden*.

3. See Schwartz's introduction for comparisons of the creative and scholarly responses of Oswald and Mário to the question of a Brazilian language and way of writing. Mário's "Prefácio Interessantíssimo" ("Extremely Interesting Preface") to *Paulicéia desvairada* (*Hallucinated City*) comments on the sonority, pronoun usage, and other neologisms of Brazilian Portuguese. He attempted to develop a *Gramatiquinha da Fala Brasileira* (Grammar of Brazilian speech), but the project was never completed. I return to these questions of language in relationship to *Macunaíma* later in this chapter.

4. See the introduction accompanying Leslie Bary's 1991 translation of Oswald de Andrade's "Cannibalist Manifesto" for a succinct and informative English-language overview to the text and its context with relevant bibliography. I cite Bary's annotated translation, but the "Manifesto Antropófago" has been translated into English a total seven times, with versions by, among others, Stephen Berg, and Adriano Pedrosa and Veronica Cordeiro. These translations indicate the

staying power of the 1928 manifesto. See Carlos Jáuregui's entry in the *Dictionary of Latin American Cultural Studies* for more on *antropofagia* as a "heterogeneous and often contradictory aesthetic venture" in Brazilian culture and thought (22). Jáuregui delves further into ideas of cannibalism, cultural *antropofagia*, colonial dynamics, and counter-colonial discourses in Latin America in his book-length study *Canibalia*.

5. In 1550, German explorer Hans Staden was captured by the Tupinambá, an indigenous group known for a practice of ritualized cannibalism. Staden escaped after nine months, returned to Germany, and wrote about his capture. The manifesto cited another event of cannibalism with Bishop Sardinha's death in 1556 at the hands of the Caltis people. For more on the figurative repercussions of *antropofagia* in Brazil, see Johnson's "Tupy or not Tupy: Cannibalism and Nationalism in Contemporary Brazilian Literature and Culture."

6. This English version is the working title for Katrina Dodson's forthcoming translation for New Directions.

7. Existing studies examine *Macunaíma* and its source materials. In his 1955 study M. Cavalcanti Proença referred to Koch-Grünberg, Barbosa Rodrigues, Couto de Magalhães, Capistrano de Abreu, Francisco Augusto Pereira da Costa, and Lindolfo Gomes as potential sources. Haroldo de Campos reads the novel's myths and legend through Vladimir Propp's morphology of folktales. Lúcia Sá questions in *Rain Forest Literatures* earlier critical tendencies to dismiss "indigenous texts as unworked raw materials" (40). Lopez notes parallels between the travels of Macunaíma and those of Mário's maternal grandfather, Joaquim Almeida de Leite Moraes, from São Paulo to Goiás and Pará via the Araguaya and Tocantins Rivers, as documented in *Apontamentos de viagem* from 1882 (338).

8. José de Paula Ramos Jr.'s dissertation *A fortuna crítica de Macunaíma: Primeira onda (1928–1936)* analyzes *Macunaíma*'s critical reception. The first, unsigned review in the *Diário Nacional* was positive. Critics and writers friendly with Mário, including Antonio de Alcântara Machado, Oswald de Andrade, and Ronald de Carvalho, published favorable reviews. In contrast, João Ribeiro's review in the *Jornal do Brasil* considered the text's use of real Tupi words alongside invented ones, discordant regionalisms, and other incongruous elements defects.

9. Lopez's introduction to the critical edition summarizes the main ideas that Mário de Andrade articulated in the first preface from December 19, 1926 (xxxviii–xxix), and the second one dated March 27, 1928 (xliv–xlvi). The edition also includes facsimile reproductions of the prefaces in Mário's handwritten drafts (351–59, 363–77).

10. I discuss Borges's views of translation in the introduction. See Rodríguez Monegal for possible dialogues between Mário and Borges in the 1920s and Assunção for a study of orality and urban space in their poetry.

11. See Antelo's "Macunaíma: Apropriação e originalidade" in the critical edition for a more extensive comparisons of how the ethnographic and the

avant-garde intersect, especially in the parallels of Mário and Carpentier as writers and musicologists interested in indigenous and Afro-descendant cultures, and popular folklore (257–61).

12. She first published her findings in *Mário de Andrade: Ramais e caminho* in 1972, revised them in the 1974 *Macunaíma: A margem e o texto*, and expanded in the critical edition's "Vínculos: Makunaima/Macunaíma."

13. See the introduction for a more complete discussion of transcreation and other theories of translation and travel.

14. At the end of his life, Mário was working on a book on poetic translation, which he had roughly outlined in notes and annotations of published translations gathered in his archive (IEB-USP Archive, MA-MMA-112-014-101).

15. I use my own translations here and thank Katrina Dodson, who is currently completing her translation of the novel, for sharing linguistic insights.

16. Thomas O. Beebee observes "an extraordinary cycle of translation" of Arekuná and Taulipang legends from Akulí and Mayulaípu into Portuguese, then from Portuguese to German by Koch-Grünberg, and later "transadapted" from German into Portuguese in *Macunaíma* (101). Though he did not directly translate *Macunaíma*'s source materials, Mário translated an essay by Erich M. Von Hornbostel on the music of the Makushi, Taulipang, and Yakuaná people. Drafted in 1930, this unpublished translation is archived at the IEB-USP Archive (MA-MMA-111).

17. According to Silviano Santiago's "A trajetória de um livro" in the critical edition of *Macunaíma*, there were eight hundred copies printed of the novel's first edition in July 1928, one thousand copies of the second in 1937, and three thousand copies of the third in 1944 (184). Italian, French, and Spanish translations in the 1970s made the narrative more accessible outside of Brazil (191).

18. In "(De-)Latinizing America," Melo analyzes the novel's struggle with Europe as key to its parody of myths of national foundation (308–11). See Wasserman for more on how *Macunaíma* blurred traditional boundaries to subvert cultural hierarchies that privileged Europe as established in Alencar's "Indian" novels (*Exotic Nations* 186–242).

19. I opt to include my own translations of *Macunaíma* rather than cite Goodland's translation, given its limitations.

20. By synthesizing the Arekuná tale, where Macunaíma is the youngest and Jiguê the oldest, with the Taulipang version with Maanape as the oldest, Mário positions Macunaíma as the youngest brother, Maanape as the oldest, and Jiguê as the middle child (312–13).

21. See Azevedo's *Portuguese: A Linguistic Introduction* for more on the linguistic reasons for devoicing, shortening, or dropping vowel sounds in the popular pronunciation of *córregos* as *corgos* (41–43).

22. The 1922 "Prefácio interessantíssimo" to *Pauliceia desvairada* examines differences in formal writing and colloquial speech in Brazil. Mário de Andrade attempted to write Brazilian and compile a study of spoken Brazilian Portuguese, as I discuss in "Translating Humor" (47–48).

23. Apter praises world literature for its attempts to deprovincialize the canon through translation but fears its tendencies toward either endorsing cultural equivalence or celebrating commercialized difference (*Against* 2–3).

24. See Nancy Díaz's *The Radical Self: Metamorphosis to Animal Form in Modern Latin American Narrative* for more on transformations in *Macunaíma* and other Latin American novels.

25. In *Dance of the Dolphin*, Candace Slater astutely distinguishes *feitiço* and its translation as witchcraft by noting its origins in the past participle of *fazer* and by commenting on how people in the Brazilian Amazon use the term (43).

26. The novel explains that "a água era encantada" (the water was enchanted; 37), suggesting a linguistic link to *encantados*, or Enchanted Beings in Amazonian tales who can take human or dolphin form. See Slater for more on *encantados*. Macunaíma transforms into a white man after bathing in the enchanted water but is not an *encantado*.

27. Mário de Andrade's Cuban contemporary Lydia Cabrera (1899–1991) similarly drew on oral tales of origin in her story "Taita jicotea y taita tigre" in *Cuentos negros de Cuba*, published in French translation in 1936 and in Spanish in 1940. The story explains how one man became the first black man after he got too close to the sun and burned, and how another man went to the moon and whitened himself to be the first white man (Cabrera 41–43). In the Spanish edition's preface, Fernando Ortiz characterized Cabrera's stories as "una colaboración, la del folklore negro con su traductora blanca" (a collaboration of black folklore with its white translator; qtd. in Cabrera 8).

28. The bibliography on Afro-Brazilian religions continues to expand, yet the classic *The African Religions of Brazil* by French sociologist Roger Bastide provides a comprehensive overview of the topic and its forms of syncretism.

29. This passage refers to samba's origins in the encounters of cross-sections of Brazilian society at the house of Bahian Hilária Batista de Almeida (1854–1924), or Tia Ciata, near Praça Onze in Rio de Janeiro's "Little Africa." Musicians such as Donga, Pixinguinha, and Sinhó and artists and intellectuals like Manuel Bandeira and Gilberto Freyre went to her house. See Vianna's *The Mystery of Samba* (67–85) for more on Tia Ciata and samba.

30. See Azevedo for more on the pronunciation of unstressed vowels in Brazilian Portuguese (39–40).

31. According to Luíz Madureira, "*Tem mais não*, Andrade's version of the pleonastic, formulaic ending of Tupi oral narratives, is the colloquial (or 'popular') form of the grammatically correct *não tem mais* (there is no more)" (94).

32. Wasserman views the move from parrot to narrator to text as "transposing language from the realm of culture into that of nature so that the story can be told to us" in a gesture of independence from the former colonial power (*Exotic Nations* 242).

33. Ulises Petit de Murat was arrested by Estado Novo police in 1944 while transporting the translation and art from Argentina to Brazil. Mário's influential friends managed to secure his release. While Mário received the translation and began reading it, he died before finishing his annotations. The illustrations were published in a 1957 edition by Cem Bibliófilos and the 1978 *Macunaíma—illustrações do mundo do herói sem nenhum caráter de Carybé*. See Newton Freitas's letters to Mário de Andrade in the IEB-USP Archive (MA-C-CPL3168, 69, 70) for more on the translation.

34. For more on the novel in translation, see "Traduções de *Macunaíma*" in the critical edition (429–35). I use the term "transcreation" to describe Olea's translation given his engagement with Haroldo de Campos's ideas. Campos wrote the preface to the translations by Olea and Thiériot. See Gómez's "Brazilian Transcreation and World Literature" for an astute study of the incompatibility of Olea's transcreation and Biblioteca Ayacucho's thick translation.

35. The notes describe "a gente" (the people) as a "expressão brasileira mais ou menos significando 'nós'" (Brazilian expression meaning more or less "we") before citing similar use in a North American song (Andrade, *Macunaíma* 387). A lexical entry defines "saúva" as "formiga" (ant; 387), and a note identifies Vei as "na mitologia ameríndia do norte do Brasil, é uma mulher velha, o sol" (in the Amerindian mythology of northern Brazil, she is an old woman, the sun; 388).

36. Referencing a scene where Macunaíma "plays" or, less euphemistically, has sex with Ci, Mário claimed, "Acho milhor não traduzir todo este trecho por ser excessivamente imoral" (I find it better to not translate this whole passage for being excessively immoral; 388). The author described a scene with the term "sim-sinhô" for buttocks as "muito rabelaisiana e difícil por isso" (very Rabelaisian and therefore difficult; 391). Hollingsworth also used Rabelaisian in a note accompanying her sample translation to justify why she did not include certain elements.

37. An excerpt of her translation of chapter 6 is included in the 1988 critical edition (431). Though Hollingsworth referred in an April 16, 1936, letter to sending Mário a copy of the translated novel via her father (IEB-USP Archive, MA-C-CPL3692), neither chapter 6 nor the complete translation can be located in the IEB-USP Archive.

38. These adaptations of *Macunaíma* included, in addition to the 1969 film version, Antunes Filho's 1978 theatrical version and G.R.E.S. Portela's performance of a *samba-enredo* at the 1975 Carnival. Earlier, Mário de Andrade had envisioned an unrealized adaptation of his novel into an opera-dance of six movements (IEB-USP Archive, MA-MMA-087). Historian Richard M. Morse wrote the parody "McLuhanaíma: The Solid Gold Hero; or, O Herói com Bastante Caráter,"

which alludes to media studies scholar Marshall McLuhan and *Macunaíma*. Morse commented playfully on the transformations involved in *Macunaíma*'s creation and ongoing reception by noting, "This book may be, and surely will be, reproduced, translated, deformed, and plagiarized in all the lingua francas" (*New World Soundings* 228). More recently, Iara Rennó released *Macunaíma Ópera Tupi*, a 2008 album inspired by the novel that incorporated a range of styles and the participation of sixty musicians.

39. Translation into English was fundamental for the success of authors associated with the Boom, as Elizabeth Lowe and Earl Fitz argue in *Translation and the Rise of Inter-American Literature*. See Gregory Rabassa's memoir for his experiences as a key translator of the Boom. Cohn identifies translation as essential to the Boom by focusing on how translation and publishing incentives contributed to US cultural policy during Cold War. César Braga-Pinto discusses the relationship of Brazilian literature to the Spanish American Boom via the case of Clarice Lispector.

40. Gómez uses Appiah's concept of thick translation, which applies Geertz's thick description to translations that employ explanatory notes, as she rightly contends, "Instead of presenting the smooth assumption of translatability, the Ayacucho edition performs the untranslatability of localized cultural practices" (333).

41. For a more detailed explication of the refrain, its sonority, and meanings, see note 10 of the critical edition (Andrade, *Macunaíma* 6), which references Maria Augusta Fonseca's analysis of Tupi-Portuguese amalgamation.

42. I comment on Goodland's translation of *Macunaíma* in "Translating Humor, Nationalisms, etc.," 49–50. See Braz's "Traducing the Author" for an astute critical evaluation of (in)fidelity in the English-language translation.

43. According to Madureira, the film criticizes the consumerist self-cannibalism of Cinema Novo's allegorical turn to modernism. The urban guerrilla Ci neither embraces radical politics nor undermines the patriarchy. Her unequal relationship with Macunaíma "replicates the elitism proper to most avant-gardes, both poetic and political" (122).

44. Ismail Xavier highlights this dichotomy in his analysis of the film as a commentary on how Brazilian identity, often coded as rural, interacts with technological modernization and capitalist consumption (143–44).

45. Another classic of Cinema Novo, Nelson Pereira dos Santos's 1971 *Como era gostoso o meu francês* (How tasty was my little Frenchman), appeared on the National Film Institute list that Molotnik cited (23).

46. For Stam, Vieira, and Xavier, *Macunaíma* exemplifies Brazilian film's recuperation of the chanchada in the 1960s and 1970s as "a fount of a cinema once nationalistic, pragmatic, and popular" (404). Per Shaw's astute analysis, chanchadas dominated Brazilian film production from the 1930s to 1950s as popular musical comedies modeled on Hollywood films in a parodic form that integrated elements of national identity.

47. See Stam's *Tropical Multiculturalism* for an insightful analysis, informed by Mikhail Bakhtin's theories of the carnivalesque, of racial constructs and representations in the film version of *Macunaíma* (238–47).

48. See the film's entry in the filmography database of the Cinemateca Brasileira for a detailed list of its awards: bases.cinemateca.gov.br/cgi-bin/wxis.exe/iah/?IsisScript=iah/iah.xis&base=FILMOGRAFIA&lang=p&nextAction=lnk&exprSearch=ID=000102&format=detailed.pft.

49. Joaquim Pedro de Andrade's archive at the Fundação Casa de Rui Barbosa includes a June 30, 1988, letter from the Cinemateca's executive director Carlos Augusto Calil sharing the news about *Macunaíma*'s inclusion on the list.

50. Chris McGowan and Ricardo Pessanha define *marcha* as a festive Afro-Brazilian genre strongly accented on the downbeat and influenced by ragtime and one-step (210). It was often used in Carnival in the 1920s and 1930s.

51. See Box 7.5 of Joaquim Pedro de Andrade's archive at the Fundação Casa de Rui Barbosa for more information on the international sales of the film, including copies of signed contracts and correspondence about the sales.

52. Abé Mark Nornes insightfully analyzes subtitling as a form of translation often rendered invisible as he argues that abusive, rather than corruptive, subtitling would challenge conventions and call attention to the practice.

53. Box 7.6 of Joaquim Pedro de Andrade's archive at the Fundação Casa de Rui Barbosa includes details about *Macunaíma*'s circulation and profits, as well as copies of the English and French subtitles produced in Brazil.

54. For this new release by Kino Classics, Katrina Dodson updated the English-language subtitles for *Macunaíma*.

55. I follow the accent use in the novels, with the modernist protagonist as Macunaíma and Melville's narrator as Macunaima. Intertextuality in Melville's novel also includes reference to Evelyn Waugh, thematic similarities to works by Joseph Conrad and Mario Vargas Llosa, and dialogues with oral traditions of the kanaima trope. See articles by Verónique Bragard, Geneviève Fabry, and Agnel Barron for more on these intertextual connections.

56. See the 2017 volume *Beyond Tordesillas*, edited by Newcomb and Gordon, for new approaches to Iberian and Latin American studies that respond to the call of Jorge Schwartz to transcend the linguistic and imperial divisions of the Treaty of Tordesillas (1494). See Levander and Levine for more on Hemispheric American studies.

57. Anthropologist Roberto DaMatta characterizes the *malandro* as a trickster and rogue who operates through the *jeitinho*, or favor, in the now-canonical study *Carnavais, malandros e heróis* (*Carnivals, Rogues, and Heroes*).

58. Sommer describes how Rigoberta opened her 1994 speech at the Political Forum of Harvard University with an incantation in Quiché that she refused to translate because it would lose its poetic quality in translation (*Proceed* 122). This incident points to the potential untranslatability of cultural difference.

Chapter 3. Silviano Santiago's Translational Criticism and Fiction

1. I refer here to Partha Chatterjee's critique of Anderson's formulation of nations as imagined communities existing within empty homogenous time as inadequate for the postcolonial moment. Chatterjee accurately identifies the model's limits when addressing multiple temporalities and experiences that coexist within the spaces of nations in the late twentieth and early twenty-first centuries.

2. For more on its publication history, see the notes to Gazzola and Williams's translation in *The Space In-Between*, a 2001 collection of Santiago's essays. I quote from their translation. Favorable reviews in *Luso-Brazilian Review*, *Foreign Affairs*, and *Latin American Research Review* highlight the book's importance to border and postcolonial studies. In 2000, Garramuño and Amante published the essay in Spanish in the volume *Absurdo Brasil*.

3. His 2006 *As raízes e o labirinto da América Latina* identifies roots and labyrinth as ways of understanding identity in Latin America based on his reading of Buarque de Holanda's *Roots of Brazil* and Paz's *The Labyrinth of Solitude* in Mexico. He continues to interpret essays in his introduction as editor of the 2002 three-volume *Intérpretes do Brasil*.

4. Santiago challenged the insular tendencies of Brazilian literary criticism with references to Cortázar and Borges in "The Space In-Between," a text that Garramuño frames as one of the first comparative readings of Latin American literature. See Wolff for more on Santiago's connections to Piglia, Sarlo, and the *tel quel* group.

5. Of his novels, *Stella Manhattan* has been translated into English in 1994, French in 1993, and Spanish in 2004 and *Em liberdade* and *Mil rosas roubadas* into Spanish in 2003 and 2016, respectively. Two short stories have appeared in English: "You Don't Know What Love Is / Muezzin," from *Keith Jarrett no Blue Note*, translated by Susan C. Quinlan in *Urban Voices*, and "Blot" from *Histórias mal contadas*, also translated by Quinlan, in *Luso-American Literature*. Select essays have also appeared in English, Spanish, French, German, and Polish.

6. I view translational prose as one that demands readers to translate, whereas Vieira sees "postmodern translational aesthetics" as linked to the Campos brothers' translation theories. She notes that Santiago translated Jacques Prévert's poems modeled on Bandeira and Drummond, leading him to view the translator as "a double plagiarist. He plagiarizes the text to be translated and plagiarizes the national poets that he selected as models" (qtd. in Vieira 71).

7. Living in New York from 1970 to 1978, Oiticica overlapped with Santiago, who spent time in New York while working at State University of New York at Buffalo from 1969 to 1973. The two first met in 1970, and Santiago later visited Oiticica's loft in the East Village. They exchanged ideas on psychoanalysis, Nietzsche, photography, language, and new political alternatives, developing a

friendship that Santiago honors by dedicating of his 1978 poetry collection to Oiticica. According to Santiago, these conversations "worked very well for me and it seems they worked for him as well" ("*Loft* 4" n.p.). Small and Zelavansky provide overviews of Oiticica's work. See Santiago's "Hélio Oiticica em Manhattan" for more on his life in New York.

8. See Perrone's *Brazil, Lyric, and the Americas* for a reading of Santiago's poems as a "lyrical response to increased USAmerican presence in Brazil" (67).

9. See *Envisioning Brazil: A Guide to Brazilian Studies in the United States*, edited by Eakin and Almeida, for more on university courses and research on Brazilian literature, culture, history, and politics. The introduction and first part on the origins of Brazilian studies in the United States are particularly relevant.

10. A 2013 interview with Julio Ramos underscores the simultaneity of Santiago's time in New York, his contact with deconstructionism, and the political movements in the United States around 1968. Santiago characterizes this trip to New York as critical for intellectual, artistic, and personal development, recalling, "por primera vez yo sentí una sensación muy plena, de gran libertad" (for the first time, I felt a very clear sensation, of great freedom; 192).

11. Twenty-one students participated. Only two, Evelina de Carvalho Sá Hoisel and Sônia Régis Barreto, remain active professors at the Universidade Federal da Bahía and PUC-São Paulo, respectively.

12. In addressing a Canadian and, more specifically, Quebecois public, Santiago integrated another key region of the Americas into his repertoire. Although his speech did not directly comment on Canadian literature, the fact that it resonated with the audience's linguistic and cultural experiences of difference suggests the importance of including Canada in discussions of inter-American literature, according to Fitz's conceptualization of the field.

13. Lopes suggests that comparing Santiago to Édouard Glissant as writers of the Americas could prove fruitful, even though Glissant's French Caribbean origins imply a distinct colonial past and present repercussions. See Bassnett's 1998 essay for an earlier reflection on how translation could contribute to cultural studies.

14. See Bachmann-Medick's introduction to a 2009 special issue of *Translation Studies* for an overview of these intellectual turns. She explains that "a 'translational turn' in the humanities relies on concrete and critical sensitivity to cultural translation processes in their political dimensions and underlying structures" (16). I suggest that Santiago has displayed this "critical sensitivity" to the geopolitical implications of linguistic and cultural translation.

15. See Kristal for another study of Borges and translation.

16. Translation theorist Serge Gavronsky also employed the metaphor of cannibalism to question the assumed relationship between the translator and the text. His 1977 essay traces the dominant mode of translation from that of word-for-word fidelity to one that recognizes translation's limitations and difficulties and

opts to cannibalize the text by first absorbing the original and then reconciling it with the historical and cultural context of the translated text.

17. As supervisor of the *Glossário de Derrida*, Santiago helped to translate deconstructionist concepts into Portuguese. He introduced, selected, and translated poems from French to Portuguese for the 1986 bilingual edition of Jacques Prévert's poetry. In 1995, he translated from French to Portuguese Alain Robbe-Grillet's *Por que amo Barthes*.

18. Though Santiago's 1995 novel *Viagem ao México* explores playwright Antonin Artaud's travels, I exclude it from my analysis to focus on his works about Brazilians in the United States. See Marcus Brasileiro's dissertation for a reading of *Viagem ao México* and *Stella Manhattan*. Brasileiro analyzes characters' dislocation to argue that João Gilberto Noll, Silviano Santiago, and Bernardo Carvalho question singular views of Brazilian national identity. See chapter 7 of Moreira's *Literary and Cultural Relations between Brazil and Mexico* for an astute analysis of *Viagem ao México* in relationship to the essays "Why and for What Purposes Does the European Travel?" and *As raízes e o labirinto da América Latina*. Moreira warns against reading Santiago's fiction as an application of his criticism.

19. Essays in *Nas malhas da letra*, written from 1982 to 1988, explore, among other topics, Brazilian modernism.

20. With translations into more than forty languages, Jorge Amado's literary depictions of an exotic Bahia illustrate the commercial success of regional color with foreign readers. See Piers Armstrong for more on Amado's favorable international reception (133–45). In recent decades, foreign fascination with violence and poverty in Brazilian films like *City of God* points to an interest in what Beatriz Jaguaribe terms the "shock of the real" (67).

21. The prominence of the Amazon and the *sertão* in the fiction of Milton Hatoum and Ronaldo Correia de Brito indicates the ongoing importance of the region to national imaginaries, even as they differ from Graciliano Ramos's social realism or João Guimarães Rosa's experimental prose. Daniel Galera and Michel Laub, among other writers from southern cities, focus their literature on the urban middle class. Works like Bernardo Carvalho's *Mongólia* (2003), Regina Rheda's *First World Third Class and Other Tales of the Global Mix* (2005), and João Gilberto Noll's *A solidão continental* (2012) depict forms of dislocation similar to Santiago's fiction.

22. Posso reads the relationships in *Stella Manhattan* and *Keith Jarrett no Blue Note* through a lens of gender and queer theory (24–116). He situates the tale of Eduardo/Stella and Vianna in 1969, a critical year for gay rights with the Stonewall Riots, and touches on relevant social issues. Lopes underscores the ties to and influences of LGBTQ+ studies on Santiago's work ("Silviano Santiago" 950–54). Quinlan reads transvestism as an alternate way that Santiago describes Brazilian culture and sexuality to underscore the masks and questions of identity

that characterize his attempt to find a space in-between (210–14). Both Santiago and Sarduy drew on knowledge of French theory to interrogate forms of doubling and slippage that exist within and between identities. The topic of homosexual exile is at the forefront of Sarduy's 1972 novel *Cobra* about a transvestite of the same name. I thank John Ochoa for suggesting the connection between Santiago and Sarduy.

23. Santiago uses plays on words when naming characters: Eduardo shares a last name with Brazilian president Artur da Costa e Silva, and Valdevinos Vianna suggests wretchedness and chivalry (Posso 28–29).

24. These stories could be classified as "autofiction" since they fictionalize the autobiographical, as Santiago notes in his 2016 essay "Meditação sobre o ofício de criar" with reference to Serge Doubrovsky's definition of the term (Loc 481). Santiago's work in these stories, as well as *Em liberdade* (1981) and *O falso mentiroso* (2004), questions divisions between the fictional and the biographical. See Diana Klinger (19–56) and Maria Andréia de Paula Silva (176–207) for more on writing the self and autofiction in Santiago's work and contemporary Brazilian literature.

25. See Telles for a sociological approach to the conceptions of race in Brazil and the United States. Racial constructions have tended to be less rigid in Brazil, due to miscegenation and more fluid identities, than in the United States, where the "one-drop" rule prevails. Daniel's *Race and Multiraciality in Brazil and the United States* outlines this historical foundation before indicating recent convergences in approaches to race in both countries.

26. To minimize identification with a single nation, Miranda proposed a translational aesthetic that crafted pan-Americanism into a commodity. For more on Miranda, see Bishop-Sánchez's *Creating Carmen Miranda*.

27. Studies by Skidmore and Telles insist on the exceptionality of Brazil's myth of racial democracy, especially when contrasted to strict binaries framing race in the United States. More recent transnational approaches to race reveal how racial constructs shift with travels, migration, and cultural exchange. Zita Nunes studies how the metaphor of cannibalism and the myth of racial democracy circulate with discourses of race and democracy in and between the United States and Brazil (15). Tiffany D. Joseph demonstrates, from a sociological perspective, how racial views of Brazilian migrants shift with their residence in the United States. Joseph notes that "the United States became a new reference point for assessing Brazilian race relations post-migration" (6) given that a "transnational racial optic is social-psychological and influenced by various factors that in turn shape migrants' racial conception" (7).

28. The narrator's realization of his racialized body in the United States resembles the experience of Brazilian poet Cecília Mereiles, who was told in 1940 to go to the back of the bus when traveling in New Orleans and other parts of the southern United States. This experience inspired her to write the socially committed poem "USA—1940," which was published posthumously. For

an insightful reading of the poem and Mereiles's travels in the United States, see chapter 4 of Peña's *Poetry and the Realm of the Public Intellectual*.

29. Franconi notes the stylistic traits that distinguish Santiago's novel from literary works by and about Brazilians in the United States emphasizing identity construction (728). For Tosta, *Stella Manhattan* is not a Brazuca novel since immigration is not its primary theme, even though it provides insights into the relationships between Brazilians and other Latinx communities in the United States ("Latino, *eu*?" 581–83).

30. Published in 1970, Candido's essay proposes a dialectic of "malandragem" (hustler craft) between order and disorder as characteristic of Brazilian culture based on his analysis of *Memórias de um sargento de milícias*, by Manuel Antônio de Almeida. This 1854 novel has been translated twice into English as *Memoirs of a Militia Sergeant* by Linton L. Barrett in 1959 and Ronald W. Sousa in 2000 as part of Oxford's Library of Latin America series edited by Jean Franco. Schwarz's 1973 essay on "misplaced ideas" argues, through a reading of Machado de Assis's work, that the idea of liberalism is misplaced in Brazil as a slave-holding society.

31. Wolff includes Perrone-Moisés in his study of the *tel quel* group. In *Vira e mexe, nacionalismo*, Perrone-Moisés reflects on how studies of French theory influence her work on globalization and literary nationalism in Brazil.

32. Perrone-Moisés draws parallels between Machado's 1873 commentary on Brazilian literature and Jorge Luis Borges's 1956 essay "El escritor argentino y la tradición," translated by Esther Allen as "The Argentine Writer and Tradition," in their questioning of privileging local color and their defense of universalizing practices. Fitz and Lowe similarly link Machado and Borges given that both writers envisioned a new, creative role for the reader in, respectively, the 1880 novel *Memórias póstumas de Brás Cubas* and the 1939 fiction "Pierre Menard, autor del *Quijote*" (91–93).

33. Santiago has also examined Machado in his fiction with *Machado* (2016), which imagines the author near the end of his life in early twentieth-century Rio de Janeiro. It received the 2017 Jabuti Prize for Best Novel in Brazil.

34. Clifford first developed the idea of discrepant cosmopolitanisms a 1992 essay "Traveling Cultures," later included in his 1997 book *Routes*. The piece distinguished between dwelling and traveling in relation to the cosmopolitan. In his 2015 essay "Deslocamentos reais e paisagens imaginárias," Santiago recognizes the parallels between his concept of the cosmopolitanism of the poor and Clifford's vision of discrepant cosmopolitanisms (21).

35. Based on his comparisons of race relations in his native Pernambuco and the southern United States, Freyre viewed racial miscegenation as a positive force in Brazil. His *Casa-grande e senzala* (1933), as noted by Skidmore, reversed positivist views that saw Brazil's racial mixture as causing "irreparable damage" (191). See Eakin's *Becoming Brazilians* for more on how Freyre shaped concepts of race and nation in twentieth-century Brazil.

36. These novels have all been translated into English. Isabel Burton translated *Iracema, The Honey-Lips: A Legend of Brazil* in 1886. Clifford E. Landers's translation of *Iracema* was published in the Oxford University Press Library of Latin America in 2000. *O cortiço* also appeared in 2000 in the Oxford series as *The Slum*, translated by David Rosenthal. Amado's novel was first published in English as *Gabriela, Clove and Cinnamon* translated by James L. Taylor and William L. Grossman, in 1962 by Knopf. Its first Vintage International edition appeared in 2006. It is worth noting that a university press published translations of nineteenth-century novels with introductions and afterwords by esteemed scholars, while Amado's novel has circulated in trade presses without the paratextual apparatus.

37. See Yúdice for a theoretical conception of "culture as a resource" that "circulates globally with ever increasing velocity" (3–4). Moving beyond the common, negative connotations of expediency as a form of self-interest, Yúdice proposes a "performative understanding of the expediency of culture [that], in contrast, focuses on the strategies implied in any invocation of culture, any invention of tradition, in relation to some purpose or goal" (38).

Chapter 4. Testing Translatability: Adriana Lisboa's Hemispheric Brazilian Novels

1. Hoyos concentrates his study of Latin American literature after 1989 on novels, the preferred genre in Anglophone publishing, especially for translations. Stories and poetry occupy more space in Spanish American and Brazilian markets than in the Anglo-American one, but they are less frequently translated into English than novels. The success of Clarice Lispector's *The Complete Stories* is a notable exception. Hoyos cites one Brazilian novel, Chico Buarque's *Budapeste* (2003), as an example of south-south escapism. This novel's tale of a *carioca* ghostwriter who reestablishes his life as a successful writer in Hungary explores travel, migration, language, and displacement. Translated by Entrekin in 2004, *Budapest* circulates globally due to its themes and its author's fame as a musician.

2. See Rostagno for more on the reception of Latin American writers in the United States. She stresses the role of North American literary tastes, Alfred A. Knopf as a publisher, and hemispheric politics in shaping the translation and circulation of João Guimarães Rosa and Jorge Amado (31–45). Translations of Latin American fiction during the Cold War years indicated trade preferences for authors like García Márquez and Amado, as Armstrong discusses in his first chapter about the different international receptions of Spanish American and Brazilian works in the Boom. Cohn highlights the role of university and small presses in publishing Latin American literature as connected to Cold War politics. See Lowe and Fitz for a broader overview of Latin American literature in translation.

3. In 2007, the Hay Festival created the Bogotá39, which the city government welcomed as part of its Bogotá World Book Capital 2007 initiative. The selected authors, including Lisboa and fellow Brazilians Joaõ Paulo Cuenca, Santiago Nazarian, and Veronica Stigger, participated in events and contributed to an anthology published that year. Ten years later, the festival released another list, the Bogotá39—2017, featuring two Brazilian writers: Natália Borges Polesso and Mariana Torres. See the Hay Festival's website (www.hayfestival.com/bogota39/home) for further details.

4. See Lisboa's website (www.adrianalisboa.com) and page at the Mertin Literary Agency (www.mertin-litag.de/authors_htm/Lisboa-A.htm) for an overview of her work. Three of her novels have appeared in English, with Sarah Green translating *Sinfonia em branco* in 2010 and *Rakushisha* in 2011, and Alison Entrekin translating *Azul-corvo* in 2013. Lisboa's writings have been published in Croatian, Norwegian, Polish, Romanian, Serbian, Slovenian, Swedish, Turkish, and Ukrainian, and translations into Macedonian, Mandarin, and Albanian are forthcoming.

5. Hoyos recognizes the role of critics, scholars, literary markets, and translation in creating, promoting, and maintaining the "world literary standing" of global Latin American novels (6).

6. See Sadlier's *Brazil Imagined*, especially chapters 4 through 7, for an overview of the cultural constructs and expressions of national identity from the late 1800s through the early 2000s. See Stam's *Tropical Multiculturalism* for additional examples of how Brazilian film represents race and racial stereotypes. See Wood's edited volume for more on stereotypes, myths, and imaginaries of Brazil in global film, television, media, and politics.

7. See Franco for an insightful overview of how US political interests in Latin America intersected with hemispheric cultural policies and practices during the Cold War (1–56). According to Cohn, twenty university presses, most prominently California and Texas, participated in the AAUP program, which approved eighty-three books for translation (113–22). The CIAR program supported translators and incentivized mostly trade presses, including New Directions, Pantheon, and Knopf, to publish more than fifty books (170–76). See Rostagno for more on how mid-twentieth-century hemispheric politics guided the actions of Knopf, other editors, and institutions like the Center for Inter-American Relations, and contributed to the more prominent place of Latin American literature in the United States.

8. See Braga-Pinto for more on Brazilian writers and the Boom. Rabassa's memoir reflects on translating Brazilian writers Lispector (70–74), Amado (132–37), and Machado (157–61), besides key figures of the Boom. The dearth of Brazilian authors in the Boom motivates Armstrong's study of the international reception of Brazilian literature (11).

9. Venuti also notes that, in 1987, Brazilian publishers released 1,500 translations and British and American publishers produced only fourteen translations of Brazilian works (*Scandals* 161).

10. See Pardo for more on these initiatives in her analysis of how government agencies and academics use the language of exportation and internationalization to characterize Brazilian literature in 2011 and 2012.

11. See the Biblioteca Nacional site (www.bn.gov.br/explore/programas-de-fomento/programa-apoio-traducao-publicacao-autores) for more on its support of Brazilian literature abroad. From 1991 to 2019, the program gave 1,065 grants and 950 works by Brazilian writers had been published by September 2018. Through 2017, funds were granted to works by 355 Brazilian authors with Lispector and Machado garnering the most support. In descending order, the other most translated authors are Jorge Amado, Rubem Fonseca, Alberto Mussa, Moacyr Scliar, Adriana Lisboa, Luiz Ruffato, Daniel Galera, and Ferreira Gullar. The grant supported sixteen translations of Lisboa's work.

12. For more on recent trends of translating Brazilian literature, see my article in *Comparative Critical Studies* and the appendix to Cimara Valim de Melo's article "Mapping Brazilian Literature Translated into English."

13. Words Without Borders has dedicated three issues to Brazil: the August 2013 issue *Brazil*, the July 2016 issue *Brazil Beyond Rio*, and the December 2018 issue *Another Country: Afro-Brazilian Writing*. The magazine features fiction, poetry, and nonfiction by Afro-Brazilian, queer, regional, and female writers who diversify the voices of Brazilian literature in translation beyond more canonical works. Presses focused on translation, like New Directions, Dalkey Archive, Two Lines, Nightboat, and Open Letter, as well as university presses such as The Americas imprint at Texas Tech and the Brazilian Literature in Translation series of Tagus Press at the University of Massachusetts, contribute to broadening the range of Brazilian literature in English.

14. Neil Larsen examines how Amado's style and themes shift from his earlier "cacao cycle" to the 1958 *Gabriela, cravo e canela* with exotic and erotic depictions of Bahian people and culture that defined his subsequent novels. Larsen contends that these transformations contribute to Amado's popularity in Brazil and internationally (64–78). See Armstrong and Rostagno for more on the international reception of Amado's novels. Since the 1990s, urban violence has supplanted tropical landscapes and folkloric visions as the "local color" that foreign readers expect of Brazilian works. The success of Lin's 1997 novel *Cidade de Deus*, with its 2002 filmic adaptation and its 2006 translation into English as *City of God* by Alison Entrekin, illustrates this preference. For more on the novel and the film in the context of other representations of Rio's favelas, see Peixoto's 2007 article.

15. For Williams, works in anthologies of Brazilian literature published in the United Kingdom, including special issues of *Granta*, *Litro*, and *Wasafari*, exemplify a literary form intended for an English readership.

16. Harvard University Press published Amerindian Kopenawa's collaboration with Bruce Albert. The nonprofit press Nightboat published recent translations of Hilda Hilst's prose and poetry. Host Publications, which has a mission of "creating a seat at the table for marginalized groups," published Afro-Brazilian Evaristo in translation. Publishing conglomerate Penguin Random House, under its imprints Vintage and Penguin Classics, released Amado's novels, while medium-sized publisher Grove Atlantic, under the imprint Black Cat, published Lins's novel.

17. In the same essay, Benjamin claimed that pure language "no longer means or expresses anything but is instead, as the expressionless and creative word, what is meant in all languages" (82). The concept of pure language reappears in his essays, including "On Language as Such and on the Language of Man," where he conceived of translation as "removal from one language into another through a continuum of transformations" (325) until reaching "in ultimate clarity the word of God" (332). Though Benjamin never explicitly defined pure language as sacred, his vision of language evolving toward a more universal meaning hints at an affinity between pure language and God's word.

18. Besides Borges and the Campos brothers, whose ideas I discussed in the introduction, scholar-translators Gregory Rabassa and Suzanne Jill Levine have commented on their creativity as translators of Latin American literature in memoirs *If This Be Treason* and *The Subversive Scribe*, respectively. André Lefevere further develops the idea of translation as rewriting in his 1992 study *Translation, Rewriting, and the Manipulation of the Literary Frame*.

19. See English for an intriguing study of the cultural capital and economic value of literary prizes and awards. Lisboa and Santiago accumulate literary prestige due to the prominent presses Alfaguara and Companhia das Letras that publish their books and the awards received, including the Saramago Prize for Lisboa and the Prêmios Jabuti, Oceanos, and Machado de Assis for Santiago. Smaller and more recent independent presses, like Polén Livros, Editora Veneta, Lote 42, and Todavia, have helped to diversify the voices and styles of national literature circulating within Brazil. The emergence of presses committed to underrepresented writers and social causes in Brazil and the United States has contributed to more variety of Brazilian writers within national and global literary systems.

20. Lisboa has translated, among others, the works of Dai Sijie, Maurice Blanchot, Amy Bloom, Tom Perrotta, Robert Louis Stevenson, and Jonathan Safran Foer.

21. See my article on Lisboa's reading at Berkeley for more about her thoughts on translation. In her hybrid interview "Navegar," she comments on how her familiarity with the precision of English impacts her use of Portuguese (156).

22. Carvalho's *Mongólia* (2003, Mongolia) features a Brazilian diplomat traveling through the Altai Mountains in search of a lost photographer, while *O filho da mãe* (2009, The mother's son) unfolds in St. Petersburg. Saavedra's novels *Toda terça* (2007, Every Tuesday) and *Com armas sonolentas* (2018, With

drowsy arms) depict the exile and solitude of Brazilian and German characters moving between languages and nations. Saavedra has similarly experienced such displacements as a native of Chile who moved to Brazil at the age of three and subsequently lived in Spain, France, and Germany. Galera's *Cordilheira* (2008, Mountain range) narrates the experiences of a Brazilian writer who becomes involved with one of her fans on a trip to Buenos Aires. Contemporary Spanish American writers, including Bolaño, Mexican Guadalupe Nettel, Chilean Alejandro Zambra, and the writers that Hoyos studies, have enjoyed success abroad with similar tales of travel and migration.

23. Diana Klinger identifies this trend in contemporary Latin American fiction as the "escrita de si" (writing of oneself), associated with the return of the author, and the "escrita do outro" (writing of the other) identified with the ethnographic turn. Klinger cites Carvalho, Santiago, and João Gilberto Noll as writers who negotiate between exploring the self and depicting the other.

24. Lisboa published her first novel, *Os fios da memória* (The threads of memory), in 1999. It is her only novel that has not been rereleased with her editorial move from Rocco to Alfaguara. The novel depicts the tale of a family in connection to key moments in Brazilian history, which Lisboa described as "muito inocente por um lado, mas ambicioso demais por outro" (very innocent on the one hand, but overly ambitious on the other; "Navegar" 152). This novel and her most recent one, *Todos os santos* (2019, All saints), are not translated. With its plot unfolding in Rio de Janeiro and New Zealand, *Todos os santos* explores themes of displacement and transoceanic connection that resonate with other recent novels.

25. Ideas of home and family are essential to the analyses of *Sinfonia em branco* in Denílson Lopes's "A volta da casa" and Rex P. Nielson's "Patriarchy's Traumatic Afterlives."

26. Eurídice Figueiredo claims that Lisboa creates novel-palimpsests by impressing one artistic genre over another (196). This image is particularly apt for the poetic dialogues with Bandeira and Bashō in *O beijo de colombina* and *Rakushisha*, respectively, and short fictions resembling haikus in *Caligrafias* (Calligraphies). See the introduction to Bruno Carvalho's *Porous City* for more on how to read Rio de Janeiro as a palimpsest (1–15).

27. Haruki's characterization as a Japanese Brazilian who feels no linguistic or cultural connection with Japan points to the multifaceted nature of Brazil's identity by recognizing the demographic specificity of Japanese Brazilians. Japanese immigrants first arrived in Brazil in 1908 as contract laborers for coffee plantations through an agreement between the Japanese Empire and the Brazilian First Republic. Currently 1.5 million people in Brazil define as Nikkei, or Japanese descendants. See Lesser for more on the history of Japanese immigration to Brazil.

28. Sarah Green translated *Rakushisha* as *Hut of Fallen Persimmons* for The Americas imprint of Texas Tech University Press. Green also translated *Sinfonia*

em Branco as *Symphony in White* for the same series. These translations, though published by a university press, do not include introductions, a translator's note, or other paratextual material to supplement the translation. Per WorldCat, the circulation of *Hut of Fallen Persimmons* is limited, with copies of the English translation at fewer than one hundred university or national libraries worldwide.

29. The exact population of Brazilians in the United States is difficult to determine since undocumented migrants tend to underreport in official census surveys. For more on Brazilians abroad, see Maxine Margolis's ethnography of Brazilians in New York in *An Invisible Minority* and her broader study *Goodbye Brazil: Émigrés from the Land of Soccer and Samba*. Ana Cristina Braga Martes's economic sociology of Brazilians in Massachusetts contends that Brazilian immigrants, despite their heterogeneity, experience fairly consistent forms of cultural baggage (163).

30. I previously refer to the ideas of Franconi and Tosta on literature about and by Brazilians in the United States when analyzing *Stella Manhattan* in chapter 3. See the section on Brazilian writers in Moser and Tosta's edited volume *Luso-American Literature* for more on their role in the United States, which remains understudied in realms of literature and culture. Tosta emphasizes the in-betweenness of Brazuca to refer to Brazilians living and working in the United States, often without proper documentation ("Between Heaven" 715). Tosta notes that, whereas Brazuca authors "clearly write from the perspective of Brazilians in the United States, Brazilian-American authors write as Americans with a compelling Brazilian heritage" ("The Other as Self" 317). Angela Bretas's *Sonho Americano* is an example of Brazuca literature, while Kathleen de Azevedo's 2006 *Samba Dreamers* is a Brazilian-American novel.

31. Dominican American Junot Díaz narrates the struggles of Oscar and Yunior as they navigate linguistic codes, societal expectations, and cultural norms while coming of age in New Jersey in the 2007 Pulitzer Prize–winning novel *The Brief Wondrous Life of Oscar Wao* and the short story collections *Drown* (1996) and *This Is How You Lose Her* (2012). Sandra Cisneros draws on her Mexican heritage and childhood in Chicago to craft the *bildungsroman* of Esperanza in *The House on Mango Street* (1984) and a multigenerational family saga in *Caramelo* (2002). See McCracken for a comparative study of Díaz and Cisneros with particular attention to questions of paratext.

32. Framing the Southwest as the Borderlands evokes Anzaldúa's theorization of the region as a psychological, linguistic, and personal space of combat. See Lozano for a historical study of the policies and politics of language and interlingual translation in the region.

33. The Araguaia Guerrilla began in 1966, when armed militants of the Partido Comunista do Brasil (PCdoB, Communist Party of Brazil), the Maoist counterpart of the Brazilian Communist Party, occupied the Araguaia river basin in efforts to establish a rural stronghold against the military dictatorship. A series

of military operations from 1972 to 1975 defeated the movement and killed sixty guerrillas, of the estimated eighty participating militants. Their bodies were never found, and they were labeled as disappeared, which led families to bring the case to federal courts and then to the Inter-American Court of Human Rights. See Studart for a detailed study of the Araguaia guerrillas.

34. Published by the trade press Bloomsbury in 2014, with printings in the United Kingdom and the United States, *Crow Blue* has reached a broader audience than the two translations published by a university press. A WorldCat search indicates that over two hundred libraries, split between university and public libraries, hold copies of *Crow Blue*.

35. See Fox's "Unpacking 'Transnational' Citizenship" for an overview of the term and examples of multi-layered citizenship. Concepts of citizenship now include constructs that emerge from below, such as Holston's "insurgent citizenship." See Lehnen's introduction for more on citizenship in Brazilian society and literature.

36. The field of ethnic American literatures encompasses African American, Asian American, Latinx, and Amerindian literary traditions. Multilayered identities and hybrid experiences characterize these literary works written in English. Introductory studies to this field, such as *Ethnic American Literature: An Encyclopedia for Students*, fail to mention Brazilian or Portuguese American literary works. With their anthology *Luso-American Literature*, Moser and Tosta correct this oversight by compiling Portuguese, Brazilian, and Cape Verdean voices from the United States. Luso-American writers exist in the contact zone as their works depict linguistic experiences of transnational migrants and citizens through uses of codeswitching, cultural exchanges, and "Portinglês" (Moser and Tosta xxx).

37. The question that often emerges is whether Brazilians are Latinos. The debate hinges on differences in language and colonial inheritance, and, as noted by Tosta in "Latino, *eu*?," shifting positionalities. Distinguishing oneself as Brazilian may be beneficial when Latinos suffer from discrimination, but detrimental for being counted in official statistics and eligible for grants or opportunities. Bernadete Beserra claims that Brazilians in Los Angeles come to identify as Latinos through interactions with other Latin American immigrants and Spanish-speaking populations.

38. The ethnographies of Margolis and Beserra and the sociological studies of Fritz, Joseph, and Martes shed light on Brazilian experiences in the United States, especially in New York, Los Angeles, Boston, and Florida. For diverse approaches to the study of Brazilian immigration to the United States, see Clémence Jouët-Pastré and Leticia Braga's edited volume *Becoming Brazuca*.

39. José Luis Falconi and José Antonio Mazotti title their edited volume *The Other Latinos* to underscore the distinct experiences of immigrants from the Andes, Central America, and Brazil to the United States. These immigrant communities differ from the more dominant groups of Mexicans, Cubans, and Puerto Ricans.

40. Another factor influencing the migration of Brazilians, Salvadorans, and other Latin Americans to the United States was the Immigration Reform and Control Act of 1986, which legalized most undocumented immigrants who had arrived in the country prior to 1982 and established penalties for employing undocumented workers. See Margolis's *Goodbye, Brazil* for more on why Brazilians emigrate and why they go where they do.

41. The English-language translation leaves this sentence, meaning "I understand Portuguese a bit!," in Spanish.

42. Díaz's use of unmarked Spanish and New Jersey Dominican slang has received attention for innovating modes of codeswitching in Latinx literature. In *Weird English*, Evelyn Nien-Ming Ch'ien praises Díaz for his "overtly courageous use of Spanglish" (10). His fluid movement between English, Spanish, and Spanglish without glosses or translations reveals the linguistic violence that Spanish or English inflict on the other language. Lourdes Torres compares Díaz's radical literary language to more conservative uses of codeswitching in Latino/a literature. His use of codeswitching and Spanglish challenges his Spanish-language translators Eduardo Lago and Achy Obejas. See Kingery for an astute analysis of Obejas's translation of *The Brief Wondrous Life of Oscar Wao*.

43. Sociologist Catarina Fritz interviews first- and second-generation Brazilian Americans between eighteen and twenty-four who speak English and have at least seven years of schooling. Her research highlights the uncertainties of racial and ethnic classification among these young adults, especially with respect to the census categories. Joseph similarly employs interviews to examine how residence in the United States impacts the constructed racial identities of Brazilians from Governador Valadares, a Minas Gerais city that has sent the most immigrants to the United States for the past sixty years. She identifies these shifts by interviewing people who have never left Brazil, Brazilian migrants in the United States, and returnees to Governador Valadares after living in the United States.

44. See my analysis of Santiago's "Borrão" in chapter 3, where I refer to the work of Telles and Daniel, for more on differences in racial constructs between Brazil and the United States.

45. Martes notes that, especially after 9/11, it became increasingly difficult for migrants from Governador Valadares to receive tourist visas, so they could only access the United States via a long, dangerous trip through Mexico, which does not require visas of Brazilians. At the time of her fieldwork in the 1990s and early 2000s, financing agents in Minas Gerais facilitated these trips for a fee between $5,000 and $15,000 per person (48–49).

46. See Neves for an analysis of clandestine travels and migratory spaces in *Hanói*. She claims that Alex and David's experiences facilitate an understanding of collective histories of the Vietnam War and Brazilian migration (140). She considers the ethical limitations of Lisboa representing solitude and melancholy

as immigrants' main emotions, which prevent critical reflection on migration's political and socioeconomic consequences.

47. Margolis estimates in *Goodbye, Brazil* that Framingham's Brazilian population ranges from ten thousand to fifteen thousand, with 40 percent from Governador Valadares (86).

48. Though Entrekin has prepared a sample translation, *Hanói* has not yet been published in English translation.

49. See the first chapter of Costa's *The Brazilian Empire: Myths and Histories* for more on Brazilian independence in comparison to the United States.

Conclusion. Translating Brazil Today: Retranslations and Untranslatability

1. See Rostagno's second chapter for more on Knopf's investment in publishing Brazilian literature in translation.

2. See chapters 3 and 4 of Cohn's study for more on these translation initiatives, their financial support, and their connections to the hemispheric politics of the Cold War.

3. The series also includes Euclides da Cunha's 1908 *The Amazon: Land without History*, translated by Ronald W. Sousa; João Capistrano de Abreu's *Chapters of Brazil's Colonial History, 1500–1800*, translated by Arthur Brakel; and Almeida's *Memoir of a Militia Sergeant*.

4. Abdala's 2010 review of the Portuguese translation *Clarice*, chides Moser for not giving Brazilian scholars due credit for heavily informing his work and for relegating Lispector's writing to the background in an effort to situate her family's tale within Jewish history. Abdala critiques Moser's speculative narrative that Lispector's mother contracted syphilis when Russian guards raped her, resulting in her illness and early death.

5. US-based scholars dedicated studies to Lispector's work, such as Earl Fitz's *Clarice Lispector: The Nature and Form of the Lyrical Novel*, Marta Peixoto's *Passionate Fictions: Gender, Narrative, and Violence in Clarice Lispector*, and *Clarice Lispector: A Bio-Bibliography*, edited by Diane Marting. In *Reading with Clarice Lispector*, French feminist Hélène Cixous cites Lispector's work as an exemplary form of *écriture féminine*, women's writing.

6. The 1977 novella *A hora da estrela* was translated as *The Hour of the Star* by Giovanni Pontiero in 1986 for Caracarnet Press and retranslated by Moser in 2011 with an introduction by Colm Tóibín. Elizabeth Lowe and Earl Fitz translated *Água-viva* in 1989 as *The Stream of Life* for the University of Minnesota Press and Stefan Tobler retranslated it in 2012. Her debut 1943 novel, *Perto do coração selvagem*, was translated by Pontiero in 1990 prior to Alison Entrekin's 2012 retranslation. Ronald W. Sousa translated Lispector's 1964 *A paixão segundo*

G.H. in 1988 for the University of Minnesota Press and Idra Novey retranslated it in 2012. Her 1948 novel *A cidade sitiada* was translated in 1999 by Pontiero and retranslated in 2019 by Johnny Lorenz. New Directions published Lorenz's translation of her 1978 posthumous work *Um sopro da vida* as *A Stream of Life* in 2012 and her 1946 novel *O Lustre* as *The Chandelier* in 2019, translated by Magdalena Edwards and Moser. Prior to Katrina Dodson's translation of *The Complete Stories* in 2015, New Directions published two of Lispector's story collections: *Soulstorm*, translated by Alexis Levitin in 1989, and *The Foreign Legion*, translated by Pontiero in 1992. University of Texas Press published *Laços de família*, translated by Pontiero as *Family Ties* in 1972, as part of the Texas Pan American series.

7. See Dodson's piece in *The Believer* for reflections on her role as a translator and intermediary of Clarice in this recent Anglo-American publishing phenomenon.

8. Lispector writes, "Não vos assusteis, morrer é um instante, passa logo, eu sei porque acabo de morrer com a moça" (105). Pontiero translates it as: "Do not be frightened. Death is instantaneous and passes in a flash. I know, for I have just died with the girl" (85). Moser renders it as, "Don't be afraid, death is an instant, it passes like that, I know because I just died with the girl" (76). The commas suggest a pause or a silence that reverberates with Marília Librandi Rocha's idea of "writing by ear" in Lispector's aural novels.

9. Translations of Clarice's work into Spanish have also been published in this time period by, among others, Ediciones SM and Conaculta in Mexico; Casa de las Americas in Cuba; Fondo Editorial Fundarte in Venezuela; and El Cuenco de la Plata, Adriana Hidalgo, and Fondo de Cultura Económica in Buenos Aires.

10. See Thomson-DeVeaux's "Reading Machado Through the Looking-Glass" for an analysis of the novel's existing English translations. Her *piauí* article about *calabouço*'s meaning in nineteenth-century Brazil refers to her in-progress dissertation project of translating the novel. Thomson-DeVeaux's translation, which features a foreword by Dave Eggers, and Costa and Patterson's version were released two weeks apart in June 2020.

11. In 2013, Hackett published John Charles Chasteen's translations *The Alienist and Other Stories of Nineteenth-Century Brazil*. Dalkey published *Stories* in 2014, which featured Rhett McNeil's translations of stories previously untranslated into English. New London Librarium published the bilingual Portuguese-English collection of stories *Ex-Cathedra* in 2014 and *Miss Dollar*, translated by Greicy Pinto Bellin and Ana Lessa-Schmidt, in 2016.

12. See G. Reginald Daniel's *Machado de Assis: Multiracial Identity and the Brazilian Novelist* for a study of Machado's life and work that foregrounds his identity as both black and white, yet neither, as key to his aesthetic sensibilities and sociopolitical affinities. For more on questions of race in Machado, see the second section of Lamonte Aidoo and Daniel F. Silva's edited volume *Emerging*

Dialogues on Machado de Assis, dedicated to "Machado on Race, Identity and Society."

13. Armstrong emphasizes a desire for the exotic in the global reception of Brazilian literature, which contributed to Amado's success in translation. See Lowe's "Jorge Amado and the Internationalization of Brazilian Literature" for an account of Amado as the most widely translated Brazilian novelist, with works published in forty languages in fifty-five countries, and "the first Brazilian writer to achieve commercial success in the United States" (120).

14. Hilst was the honored writer at the 2018 international literary festival in Paraty, Brazil. See Adam Morris and Bruno Carvalho's edited volume *Essays on Hilda Hilst: Between Brazil and World Literature* for critical receptions of her work in English from academics and translators.

15. *Lavoura arcaica* received a Jabuti for best debut, a Brazilian Academy of Letters prize, and the São Paulo Art Critics' Association Prize, which *Um copo de cólera* also won. See Chacoff for more on Nassar's life and work.

16. See English's *The Economy of Prestige* for more on the economic value and cultural capital granted by prizes.

17. The *New Yorker* dedicated in January 2017 a feature "persons of interest" piece to Nassar after the publication of his two works in English translation. Titled "Why Brazil's Greatest Writer Stopped Writing," the piece by Alejandro Chacoff renders Nassar's life into an intriguing narrative.

18. See Larkosh for a compelling reading of *Mar paraguayo* that posits the idea of trans-language as a way to translate between border languages and transgender experiences.

BIBLIOGRAPHY

Archives

Biblioteca Nacional (Rio de Janeiro)
Cinemateca Brasileira (São Paulo)
Fundação Casa de Rui Barbosa (Rio de Janeiro)
Instituto de Estudos Brasileiros, Universidade de São Paulo (São Paulo; IEB-USP)
Instituto Histórico e Geográfico Brasileiro (Rio de Janeiro)
Museu Imperial (Petrópolis)
Oliveira Lima Library (Catholic University of America, Washington, DC)
Stanford University, Green Library (Branner Brazilian Collection)

Periodicals

Aurora Brasileira (Ithaca, New York, 1873–1875)
O Jornal (Rio de Janeiro, Fundação Biblioteca Nacional—Periódicos)
Jornal do Comércio
El Mundo Nuevo / La América Ilustrada
O Novo Mundo: Periódico Ilustrado do Progresso da Edade (New York, 1870–1879)
Revista Industrial Ilustrada (New York, 1877–1879)

Books, Essays, and Articles

Abdala Junior, Benjamin. "Biografia de Clarice, por Benjamin Moser: coincidências e equívocos." *Estudos Avançados*, vol. 24, no. 70, 2010, pp. 285–92.
Act of July 2, 1862 (Morrill Act), Public Law 37–108, which established land grant colleges, 07/02/1862; Enrolled Acts and Resolutions of Congress,

1789–1996; Record Group 11; General Records of the United States Government; National Archives.

Adamo Idoeta, Paula. " 'Um vulcão que entrou em erupção': como é a vida em Pacaraima em meio à crise de imigração na Venezuela." *BBC Brasil*, 20 Aug. 2018, www.bbc.com/portuguese/brasil-45228744. Accessed 13 Dec. 2018.

Agassiz, Louis, and Elizabeth Cabot Agassiz. *A Journey in Brazil*. Tinker and Fields, 1868.

Aidoo, Lamonte, and Daniel F. Silva, editors. *Emerging Dialogues on Machado de Assis*. Palgrave Macmillan, 2016.

Alonso, Carlos. *The Spanish American Regional Novel: Modernity and Autochthony*. Cambridge UP, 1990.

Altamirano, Carlos. "El orientalismo y la idea del despotismo en el Facundo." *Ensayos argentinos: de Sarmiento a la vanguardia*, edited by Carlos Altamirano and Beatriz Sarlo, Ariel, 1997, pp. 83–102.

Amante, Adriana, and Florencia Garramuño, editors. *Absurdo Brasil: polémicas en la cultura brasileña*. Editorial Biblos, 2000.

Andermann, Jens. *The Optic of the State: Visuality and Power in Argentina and Brazil*. U of Pittsburgh P, 2007.

———. "Tournaments of Value: Argentina and Brazil in the Age of Exhibitions." *Journal of Material Culture*, vol. 14, no. 3, 2009, pp. 333–63.

Anderson, Benedict. *Imagined Communities: Reflections on the Origin and Spread of Nationalism*. 3rd ed., Verso, 2006.

Andrade, Joaquim Pedro de. "Argumento cinematográfico." Cinemateca Brasileira Archive, BR CB GR-SC.12/003, pp. 1–4.

———. "Cannibalism and Self-Cannibalism." Johnson and Stam, pp. 81–83.

———, director. *Macunaíma*. Condor Filmes/Filmes do Serro, 1969.

Andrade, Mário de. *Amar, verbo intransitivo*. Novo Século, 2017.

———. *Fräulein*. Translated by Margaret Richardson Hollingsworth, Macaulay, 1933.

———. *Hallucinated City*. Translated by Jack Tomlins, Vanderbilt UP, 1968.

———. *Macunaíma*. Translated by E. A. Goodland, Random House, 1984.

———. *Macunaíma*. Translated by Héctor Olea, Seix Barral, 1977.

———. *Macunaíma: o herói sem nenhum caráter*, edited by Telê Porto Ancona Lopez, Alca XX/Ediciones Unesco, 1988.

———. *Obra escogida*, edited by Gilda de Mello e Souza, Biblioteca Ayacucho, 1979.

Andrade, Oswald de. "Cannibalist Manifesto." Translated by Leslie Bary. *Latin American Literary Review*, vol. 19, no. 38, Jul.–Dec. 1991, pp. 38–47.

———. "Manifesto of Pau-Brasil Poetry." Translated by Stella M. de Sá Rego. *Latin American Literary Review*, vol. 14, no. 27, Jan.–June 1986, pp. 184–87.

———. "O Manifesto Antropófago." Schwartz, pp. 140–47.

———. "O Manifesto da Poesia Pau-Brasil." Schwartz, pp. 135–39.

Anzaldúa, Gloria. *Borderlands / La frontera: The New Mestiza*. 2nd ed., Aunt Lute Books, 1999.

Appiah, K. Anthony. *Cosmopolitanism: Ethics in a World of Strangers*. W.W. Norton & Co., 2006.
———. "Thick Translation." Venuti, pp. 331-43.
Apter, Emily. *Against World Literature: On the Politics of Untranslatability*. Verso, 2013.
———. "On Translation in the Global Market." *Public Culture*, vol. 13, no. 1, Winter 2001, pp. 1-12.
———. *The Translation Zone: A New Comparative Literature*. Princeton UP, 2006.
Armstrong, Piers. *Third World Literary Fortunes: Brazilian Culture and Its International Reception*. Bucknell UP, 1999.
Arroyo, Jossianna. *Travestismos culturales: literatura y etnografía en Cuba y Brasil*. Editorial Iberoamericana, 2003.
Assunção, Ronaldo. *Mário de Andrade e Jorge Luis Borges: poesia, cidade, oralidade*. Editora UFMS, 2004.
Azevedo, Kathleen de. *Samba Dreamers*. U of Arizona P, 2006.
Azevedo, Milton M. *Portuguese: A Linguistic Introduction*. Cambridge UP, 2005.
Azevedo, Sílvia Maria. *Brasil em Imagens: Um estudo da Revista Ilustração Brasileira (1876-1878)*. Editora Unesp, 2010.
Bachmann-Medick, Doris. "Introduction: The Translational Turn." *Translation Studies*, vol. 2, no. 1, 2009, pp. 2-16.
Balderston, Daniel, and Marcy Schwartz, editors. *Voice-Overs: Translation and Latin American Literature*. State U of New York P, 2002.
Baptista, Abel Barros. "Ideia de literatura brasileira com propósito cosmopolita." *De espécie complicada: Ensaios de crítica literária*. Angelus Novus Editora, 2010, pp. 171-202.
Barman, Roderick J. *Citizen Emperor: Pedro II and the Making of Brazil, 1825-91*. Stanford UP, 1999.
Barrenechea, Antonio. "American Literatures." *The 2014-2015 Report on the State of the Discipline of Comparative Literature*. ACLA, 3 Mar. 2014, stateofthediscipline.acla.org/entry/american-literature. Accessed 12 Sept. 2019.
Barron, Agnel. "Kanaima and the Oral Tradition in Pauline Melville's 'The Ventriloquist's Tale.'" *Journal of Caribbean Literature*, vol. 7, no. 1, Spring 2011, pp. 1-13.
Bassnett, Susan. "The Translation Turn in Cultural Studies." *Constructing Cultures: Essays on Literary Translation*, edited by Susan Bassnett and André Lefevere, Multilingual Matters, 1998, pp. 123-40.
Bastide, Roger. *The African Religions of Brazil: Toward a Sociology of the Interpenetration of Civilizations*. Translated by Helen Sebba, Johns Hopkins UP, 1978.
Beckman, Ericka. *Capital Fictions: The Literature of Latin America's Export Age*. U of Minnesota P, 2012.
Beebee, Thomas O. "Cultural Entanglements and Ethnographic Refractions: Theodor Koch-Grünberg in Brazil." *KulturConfusão: On German-Brazilian Interculturalities*, edited by Anke Finger, De Gruyter, 2015, pp. 95-115.

Belnap, Jeffrey, and Raúl Fernández, editors. *José Martí's "Our America": From National to Hemispheric Cultural Studies*. Duke UP, 1998.

Benjamin, Walter. "On Language as Such and on the Language of Man." *Reflections: Essays, Aphorisms, Autobiographical Writings*, translated by Edmund Jephcott and edited by Peter Demetz, Schocken, 1986, pp. 314-32.

———. "The Translator's Task." Translated by Steven Rendell. Venuti, pp. 75-83.

Beserra, Bernadete. "From Brazilians to Latinos? Racialization and Latinidad in the Making of the Brazilian Carnival in Los Angeles." *Latino Studies*, vol. 3, no. 1, 2005, pp. 53-75.

Bethell, Leslie. *Brazil: Essays on History and Politics*. School of Advanced Study, University of London, 2018. jstor.org/stable/j.ctv51309x.

Bhabha, Homi K. *The Location of Culture*. 1994. Routledge, 2004.

Bishop-Sanchez, Kathryn. *Creating Carmen Miranda: Race, Camp, and Transnational Stardom*. Vanderbilt UP, 2016.

Boehrer, George C. A. "José Carlos Rodrigues and *O Novo Mundo*, 1870-1879." *Journal of Inter-American Studies*, vol. 9, no. 1, Jan. 1967, pp. 127-44.

Borges, Jorge Luis. "The Argentine Writer and Tradition." Translated by Esther Allen. *On Argentina*, edited by Alfred Mac Adam, Penguin, 2010, pp. 134-42.

———. *Ficciones*. Alianza Editorial, 1997.

———. "Pierre Menard, Author of the *Quixote*." *Collected Fictions*. Translated by Andrew Hurley, Penguin, 1999, pp. 88-95.

———. "Two Ways to Translate." Translated by Suzanne Jill Levine. *On Writing*, edited by Suzanne Jill Levine, Penguin, 2010, pp. 53-56.

Braga-Pinto, César. "Clarice Lispector and the Latin American *Bang*." *Teaching the Latin American Boom*, edited by Lucille Kerr and Alejandro Herrero-Olaizola, MLA, 2015, pp. 147-61.

Bragard, Verónique. "Uncouth Sounds of Resistance: Conradian Tropes and Hybrid Epistemologies in Pauline Melville's *The Ventriloquist's Tale*." *Journal of Postcolonial Writing*, vol. 44, no. 4, 2008, pp. 415-25.

Bragard, Verónique, and Geneviève Fabry. "A Parrot without Feathers? Ventriloquy, Orality, and Nostalgia in Vargas Llosa's *The Storyteller* and Pauline Melville's *The Ventriloquist's Tale*." *Comparative Literature Studies*, vol. 53, no. 3, 2016, pp. 454-77.

Branner, John Caspar. *Geographical and Geological Exploration in Brazil*. American Naturalist, 1886.

———. *Geologia elementar: preparada com referencia especial aos estudantes brasileiros e à geologia do Brazil*. Alves, 1915.

———. *Outlines of the Geology of Brazil to Accompany the Geologic Map of Brazil*. Washington, 1920.

Brasil, Comissão à Exposição Universal. *O Império do Brazil na Exposição Universal de 1876 em Philadelphia*. Typographia Nacional, 1875.

Brasil, Museu Imperial. Setor de Documentação e Referencia. *D. Pedro II na Exposição de Filadélfia em 1876/IBPC*. Museu Imperial, 1993.

Brasileiro, Marcus V. C. *Deslocamento e subjetividade em João Gilberto Noll, Silviano Santiago e Bernardo Carvalho*. Diss. U of Minnesota, 2010.

Braz, Albert. "Mutilated Selves: Pauline Melville, Mário de Andrade, and the Troubling Hybrid." *Mosaic*, vol. 40, no. 4, 2007, pp. 17–33.

———. "Traducing the Author: Textual (In)fidelity in E. A. Goodland's Translation of *Macunaíma*." *Graphos*, vol. 9, no. 1, 2007, pp. 189–94.

Bretas, Angela. *Sonho americano*. Scortecci, 2003.

Brickhouse, Anna. *Transamerican Literary Relations and the Nineteenth-Century Public Sphere*. Cambridge UP, 2004.

Brizuela, Natalia. *Fotografia e Império: Paisagens para um Brasil moderno*. Translated by Marcos Bagno, Companhia das Letras, 2012.

Bruce, Edward C. *The Century: Its Fruits and Its Festival*. J. B. Lippincott & Co., 1877.

Brune, Krista. "The Necessities and Dangers of Translation: Brazilian Literature on a Global Stage." *Comparative Critical Studies*, vol. 15, no. 1, 2018, pp. 5–24.

———. "The Search for Belonging." *Berkeley Review of Latin American Studies*, Spring 2014, pp. 60–63.

———. "Reconceiving Hipólito José da Costa as a Transatlantic Translator." *Luso-Brazilian Review*, vol. 55, no. 1, 2018, pp. 1–26.

———. "Resituating *Nitheroy* in the Translation Zone: Transnational Travels, Creative Transformations, and the Making of a Modern Brazil." *Hispanic Review*, vol. 86, no. 1, 2018, pp. 69–90.

———. "Retranslating the Brazilian Imperial Project: *O Novo Mundo*'s Depictions of the 1876 Centennial Exhibition." *Journal of Lusophone Studies*, vol. 3, no. 2, 2018, pp. 1–23.

———. "Translating Humor, Nationalisms, etc. in Mário de Andrade's Modernist Writings." *Translation Review*, vol. 99, no. 1, 2017, pp. 45–57.

Buarque, Chico. *Budapeste*. Companhia das Letras, 2003.

———. *Budapest*. Translated by Alison Entrekin, Bloomsbury, 2004.

Buarque de Hollanda, Sérgio. *Raízes do Brasil*. 1936. Companhia das Letras, 1995.

———. *Visão do paraíso: Os motivos edênicos no descobrimento e colonização do Brasil*. 6th ed., Brasiliense, 1996.

Buarque de Hollanda, Heloísa. *Macunaíma: da literatura ao cinema*. 1978. Aeroplano, 2002.

Bueno, Wilson. *Mar paraguayo*. Iluminaras, 1992.

———. *Paraguayan Sea*. Translated by Erín Moure, Nightboat, 2017.

Burton, Richard Francis. "Translation." *The Athenaeum*, no. 2313, 24 Feb. 1872, pp. 241–43.

Bushnell, David, and Neil Macaulay. *The Emergence of Latin America in the Nineteenth Century*. 2nd ed., Oxford UP, 1994.

Cabrera, Lydia. *Cuentos negros de Cuba*. Ramos, Art. Gráf, 1972.

Caminha, Pero Vaz de. *Carta ao Rei Dom Manuel*. Crisálida, 2002.

Campos, Augusto de. *À margem da margem*. Companhia das Letras, 1989.

———. *Invenção: de Arnaut e Raimbaut a Dante e Cavalcanti*. Arx, 2003.
Campos, Augusto e Haroldo de. *ReVisão de Sousândrade*. 3rd ed., Nova Fronteira, 2002.
Campos, Gabriela Vieira de. *O literário e o não-literário nos textos e imagens do periódico ilustrado* O Novo Mundo *(Nova Iorque, 1870–1879)*. MA thesis. Unicamp/IEL, 2001.
Campos, Haroldo de. *Haroldo de Campos—Transcriação*, edited by Marcelo Tápia and Thelma Médici Nóbrega, Perspectiva, 2013.
———. *Morfologia do Macunaíma*. Editora Perspectiva S.A., 1973.
———. *Novas: Selected Writings*, edited by Antonio Sergio Bessa and Odile Cisneros, Northwestern UP, 2007.
Candido, Antonio. "Dialética da Malandragem." *Revista do Instituto de Estudos Brasileiros*, no. 8, June 1970, pp. 67–89.
———. *Formação da literatura brasileira: Momentos decisivos*. 2 vol., 2nd ed., Livraria Martins Editoras, 1964.
Cardim, Elmano. "José Carlos Rodrigues: Sua vida e sua obra." *Revista do IHGB*, no. 185, Oct.–Dec. 1944, pp. 126–57.
Cardozo, Manoel John Gange, Harley Notter, and Easton Rothwell. "Percy Alvin Martin 1879–1942: An Appreciation." *The Hispanic American Historical Review*, vol. 22, no. 2, May 1942, pp. 242–44.
Carvalho, Bruno. *Porous City: A Cultural History of Rio De Janeiro*. Liverpool UP, 2013.
Casanova, Pascale. *The World Republic of Letters*. Translated by M. B. DeBevoise, Harvard UP, 2004.
Case, Thomas E. Review of *The Space In-Between: Essays on Latin American Culture*. *World Literature Today*, vol. 77, no. 1, 2003, p. 160.
Cassin, Barbara, and Michael Wood. "Introduction." *Dictionary of Untranslatables*, edited by Barbara Cassin, Emily Apter, Jacques Lezra, and Michael Wood, Princeton UP, 2014.
Cavalcanti Proença, Manuel. *Roteiro de Macunaíma*. Civilização Brasileira, 1969.
César, Ana Cristina. *At Your Feet*. Translated by Brenda Hillman, Helen Hillman, and Sebastião Edson Macedo, Parlor Press, 2018.
———. *Intimate Diary*. Translated by Patricia E. Paige, Celia McCullough, and David Treece, Boulevard, 1997.
Chacoff, Alejandro. "Why Brazil's Greatest Writer Stopped Writing." *The New Yorker*, 21 Jan. 2017, newyorker.com/culture/persons-of-interest/why-brazils-greatest-writer-stopped-writing. Accessed 20 Jan. 2019.
Chalhoub, Sidney. "The Politics of Ambiguity: Conditional Manumission, Labor Contracts, and Slave Emancipation in Brazil (1850s–1888)." *International Review of Social History*, vol. 60, 2015, pp. 161–91.
Champlin, Margaret D. "Branner, John Casper." *American National Biography Online*, Feb. 2000, www.anb.org/articles/13/13-00186.html. Accessed 10 May 2017.

Chatterjee, Partha. "The Nation in Heterogeneous Time." *Futures Beyond Nationalism*, vol. 37, no. 9, 2005, pp. 925–42.
Chiarelli, Stefania, and Godofredo de Oliveira Neto, editors. *Falando com estranhos: O estrangeiro e a literatura brasileira*. 7Letras, 2016.
Ch'ien, Evelyn Nien-Ming. *Weird English*. Harvard UP, 2004.
Cixous, Hélène. *Reading with Clarice Lispector*. Translated by Verena Conley, U of Minnesota P, 1990.
Clifford, James. "Mixed Feelings." *Cosmopolitics: Thinking and Feeling Beyond the Nation*, edited by Pheng Cheah and Bruce Robbins, U of Minnesota P, 1998, pp. 362–70.
———. *Routes: Travel and Translation in the Late Twentieth Century*. Harvard UP, 1997.
Coelho, Federico, editor. *Encontros: Silviano Santiago*. Beco do Azougue, 2011.
Cohn, Deborah. *The Latin American Literary Boom and U.S. Nationalism during the Cold War*. Vanderbilt UP, 2012.
Coli, Jorge. "Primeira Missa e Invenção da Descoberta." *A descoberta do homem e do mundo*, edited by Adauto Noves, Companhia das Letras, 1998, pp. 107–21.
Costa, Emília Viotti da. *The Brazilian Empire: Myths and Histories*. Rev. ed., U of North Carolina P, 2000.
Crandall, Britta. *Hemispheric Giants: The Misunderstood History of U.S.-Brazil Relations*. Rowman & Littlefield, 2011.
Cribelli, Teresa. "A Modern Monarch: Dom Pedro II's Visit to the United States in 1876." *The Journal of the Historical Society*, vol. 9, no. 2, June 2009, pp. 223–54.
Cunha, Eneida Leal, editor. *Leituras críticas sobre Silviano Santiago*. Editora UFMG, 2008.
DaMatta, Roberto. *Carnival, Rogues, and Heroes: An Interpretation of the Brazilian Identity*. Translated by John Drury, U of Notre Dame P, 1991.
Damrosch, David. *What Is World Literature?* Princeton UP, 2003.
Daniel, G. Reginald. *Machado de Assis: Multiracial Identity and the Brazilian Novelist*. Pennsylvania State UP, 2012.
———. *Race and Multiraciality in Brazil and the United States: Converging Paths?* Pennsylvania State UP, 2006.
Darío, Rubén. *Peregrinaciones*. Libreria de la Vda de C. Bouret, 1901.
Darnton, Robert. "What Is the History of Books?" *The Book History Reader*, edited by David Finkelstein and Alistair McCleery, Routledge, 2006, pp. 9–26.
Delgado Moya, Sergio. *Delirious Consumption: Aesthetics and Consumer Capitalism in Mexico and Brazil*. U of Texas P, 2017.
Dennison, Stephanie. *Joaquim Nabuco: Monarchism, Panamericanism and Nation-Building in the Brazilian Belle Epoque*. Peter Lang, 2006.
Derrida, Jacques. *The Ear of the Other: Otobiography, Transference, Translation*, edited by Christie McDonald and translated by Peggy Kamuf, U of Nebraska P, 1985.

---. "Des Tours de Babel." Translated by Joseph F. Graham. *Difference in Translation*, edited by Joseph F. Graham, Cornell UP, 1985, pp. 165–207.
---. *Writing and Difference*. Translated by Alan Bass, U of Chicago P, 1978.
Díaz, Nancy Gray. *The Radical Self: Metamorphosis to Animal Form in Modern Latin American Narrative*. U of Missouri P, 1988.
Dodson, Katrina. "Translator's Note." *The Complete Stories*, by Clarice Lispector and translated by Katrina Dodson, New Directions, 2015, pp. 629–35.
Dolar, Mladen. *A Voice and Nothing More*. MIT Press, 2006.
Dunn, Christopher. *Brutality Garden: Tropicália and the Emergence of a Brazilian Counterculture*. U of North Carolina P, 2001.
Eakin, Marshall C. *Becoming Brazilians: Race and National Identity in Twentieth-Century Brazil*. Cambridge UP, 2017.
---. *Brazil: The Once and Future Country*. St. Martin's Griffin, 1997.
---. "The Emergence of Brazil on the World Stage." *Latin American Research Review*, vol. 48, no. 3, 2013, pp. 221–30.
Eakin, Marshall C., and Paulo Roberto de Almeida, editors. *Envisioning Brazil: A Guide to Brazilian Studies in the United States*. U of Wisconsin P, 2005.
English, James F. *The Economy of Prestige: Prizes, Awards, and the Circulation of Cultural Value*. Harvard UP, 2008.
Entrekin, Alison. "Translator's Note. *Crow-Blue*." *Passageways*, edited by Camille T. Dungy and Daniel Hahn, Two Lines Press, 2012, pp. 272–73.
---. "When in Hell, Embrace the Devil: On Recreating 'Grande Sertão: Veredas' in English." *Words Without Borders*, 1 July 2016, wordswithoutborders.org/dispatches/article/when-in-hell-embrace-the-devil-alison-entrekin. Accessed 21 Jan. 2019.
Escorel, Eduardo. "Macunaíma na tela: Os fracassos e o triunfo de Joaquim Pedro e Mário de Andrade." *Piauí*, vol. 9, no. 106, July 2015, pp. 62–67.
Ette, Ottmar. *TransArea: A Literary History of Globalization*. Translated by Mark W. Pearson, De Gruyter, 2016.
Falconi, José Luis, and José Antonio Mazotti, editors. *The Other Latinos: Central and South Americans in the United States*. Harvard David Rockefeller Center for Latin American Studies, 2008.
Feinsod, Harris. *The Poetry of the Americas: From Good Neighbors to Countercultures*. Oxford UP, 2017.
Figueiredo, Eurídice. *Mulheres ao espelho: autobiografia, ficção, autoficção*. EdUERJ, 2013.
Fitz, Earl E. *Clarice Lispector: The Nature and Form of the Lyrical Novel*. Twayne, 1985.
---. *Brazilian Narrative Traditions in a Comparative Context*. MLA, 2005.
---. *Inter-American Literary History: Six Critical Periods*. Peter Lang, 2017.
---. *Rediscovering the New World: Inter-American Literature in a Comparative Context*. U of Iowa P, 1991.

Fletcher, James C., and Daniel P. Kidder. *Brazil and the Brazilians, Portrayed in Historical and Descriptive Sketches*. Childs & Peterson, 1857.
Foner, Eric. *Reconstruction: America's Unfinished Revolution 1863–1877*. Harper & Row, 1988.
Foucault, Michel. *The Archaeology of Knowledge, and the Discourse on Language*. Translated by A. M. Sheridan Smith, Vintage Books, 2010.
———. *The Order of Things: An Archaeology of the Human Sciences*. Vintage Books, 1994.
Fountain, Anne. *José Martí, the United States, and Race*. UP of Florida, 2014.
Fox, Claire F. *Making Art Panamerican: Cultural Policy and the Cold War*. U of Minnesota P, 2013.
Fox, Jonathan. "Unpacking 'Transnational Citizenship.'" *Annual Review of Political Science*, vol. 8, 2005, pp. 171–201.
Franco, Jean. *The Decline and Fall of the Lettered City: Latin America in the Cold War*. Harvard UP, 2002.
Franconi, Rodolfo A. "Brazilian in the States: Between Fiction and Reality." *Hispania*, vol. 88, no. 4, Dec. 2005, pp. 726–32.
Frederickson, George M. *The Inner Civil War: Northern Intellectuals and the Crisis of the Union*. Harper & Row, 1965.
Freitas, Marcus Vinicius de. *Charles Frederick Hartt, um naturalista no império de Pedro II*. Editora UFMG, 2002.
———. *Contradições da modernidade: o jornal* Aurora Brasileira *(1873–1875)*. Editora Unicamp, 2011.
Freyre, Gilberto. *Casa-grande e senzala: Formação da família brasileira sob o regime da economia patriarcal*. 49th ed., Global Editora, 2004.
Fritz, Catarina. *Brazilian Immigration and the Quest for Identity*. LFB Scholarly Publishing LLC, 2011.
Ganzert, Frederic William. "The Baron do Rio-Branco, Joaquim Nabuco, and the Growth of Brazilian-American Friendship, 1900–1910." *The Hispanic American Historical Review*, vol. 22, no. 3, Aug. 1942, pp. 432–51.
Garcia, Frederick C. H. "Richard Francis Burton and Basílio da Gama: The Translator and the Poet." *Luso-Brazilian Review*, vol. 12, no. 2, Summer 1975, pp. 34–57.
García Canclini, Néstor. *Hybrid Cultures: Strategies for Entering and Leaving Modernity*. Translated by Christopher L. Chiappari and Silvia L. López, U of Minnesota P, 1995.
———. *Imagined Globalization*. Translated by George Yúdice, Duke UP, 2014.
Garramuño, Florencia. "Silviano Santiago e a literatura latino-americana: A literatura depois do modernismo." Cunha, pp. 51–69.
Gavronsky, Serge. "The Translator: From Piety to Cannibalism." *SubStance*, vol. 6/7, no. 16, Summer 1977, pp. 53–62.

Gentzler, Edwin. *Translation and Identity in the Americas: New Directions in Translation Theory*. Routledge, 2008.
Giberti, Bruno. *Designing the Centennial: A History of the 1876 International Exhibition in Philadelphia*. UP of Kentucky, 2002.
Gómez, Isabel. "Brazilian Transcreation and World Literature: *Macunaíma* Journeys from São Paulo to Caracas." *Journal of World Literature*, vol. 1, 2016, pp. 316–41.
González Stephan, Beatriz. "Showcases of Consumption: Historical Panoramas and Universal Expositions." *Beyond Imagined Communities: Reading and Writing the Nation in Nineteenth-Century Latin America*, edited by Sara Castro-Klarén and John Charles Chasteen, Woodrow Wilson Center Press, 2003, pp. 225–38.
González Stephan, Beatriz, and Jens Andermann, editors. *Galerías del progreso: museos, exposiciones y cultura visual en América latina*. Beatriz Viterbo Editora, 2006.
Gouveia, Saulo. *The Triumph of Brazilian Modernism: The Metanarrative of Emancipation and Counter-Narratives*. U of North Carolina P, 2013.
Greenblatt, Stephen. *Marvelous Possessions: The Wonder of the New World*. U of Chicago P, 1991.
Greene, Roland. "Wanted: New World Studies." *American Literary History*, vol. 11, no. 1/2, 2000, pp. 337–47.
Greenspun, Roger. "Screen: A Social Satire of Brazil." *New York Times*, 6 May 1972, p. A3.
Gruesz, Kirsten Silva. *Ambassadors of Culture: The Transamerican Origins of Latino Writing*. Princeton UP, 2002.
———. "*El Gran Poeta* Longfellow and a Psalm of Exile." *American Literary History*, vol. 10, no. 3, Autumn 1998, pp. 395–427.
Guimarães, Hélio de Seixas. *Machado de Assis, o escritor que nos lê: As figures machadianas através da crítica e das polêmicas*. Editora Unesp, 2017.
Haberly, David T. "The Brazilian Novel from 1850 to 1900." *The Cambridge History of Latin American Literature. Volume 3*, edited by Roberto González Echevarría and Enrique Pupo-Walker, Cambridge UP, 1996, pp. 137–56.
———. *Three Sad Races: Racial Identity and National Consciousness in Brazilian Literature*. Cambridge UP, 1983.
Hardman, Francisco Foot. *Trem-fantasma: A ferrovia Madeira-Mamoré e a modernidade na selva*. 2nd ed., Companhia das Letras, 2005.
Hardt, Hanno. "The Foreign-Language Press in American Press History." *Journal of Communication*, vol. 39, no. 2, Spring 1989, pp. 114–31.
Hartt, Charles Frederick. *Geology and Physical Geography of Brazil*. Fields, Osgood, & Co., 1870.
Hass Carazzai, Estelita. "Não faria de novo, diz mãe brasileira separada dos três filhos nos EUA." *Folha de São Paulo*, 23 July 2018, www1.folha.uol.com.

br/mundo/2018/07/nao-faria-de-novo-diz-mae-brasileira-separada-dos-tres-filhos-nos-eua.shtml. Accessed 13 Dec. 2018.
Hoisel, Evelina. "Silviano Santiago e seus múltiplos." Cunha, pp. 143–71.
Holston, James. *Insurgent Citizenship: Disjunctions of Democracy and Modernity in Brazil*. Princeton UP, 2008.
Horne, Gerald. *The Deepest South: The United States, Brazil, and the African Slave Trade*. New York UP, 2007.
Hoyos, Héctor. *Beyond Bolaño: The Global Latin American Novel*. Columbia UP, 2015.
Ianni, Octávio. *A idéia de Brasil moderno*. Brasiliense, 1992.
IHGB. *Dicionário Biobibliográfico de Historiadores, Geógrafos e Antropólogos Brasileiros*. Vol. 3, Instituto Histórico e Geográfico Brasileiro, 1993, p. 136.
Infante, Ignacio. *After Translation: The Transfer and Circulation of Modern Poetics Across the Atlantic*. Fordham UP, 2013.
Izecksohn, Vitor. *Slavery and War in the Americas: Race, Citizenship, and State Building in the United States and Brazil, 1861–1870*. U of Virginia P, 2014.
Jackson, K. David. "Literary Criticism in Brazil." *The Cambridge History of Latin American Literature Vol. 3*, edited by Roberto González Echevarría and Enrique Pupo-Walker. Cambridge UP, 1996, pp. 329–44.
———. *Machado de Assis: A Literary Life*. Yale UP, 2015.
———. "A Statesman in the Academy: Joaquim Nabuco at Yale." *Estudos Avançados*, vol. 22, no. 62, 2008, pp. 335–49.
———. "Transcriação/Transcreation: The Brazilian Concrete Poets and Translation." *The Translator as Mediator of Cultures*, edited by Humphrey Tonkin and Maria Esposito Frank, John Benjamins, 2010, pp. 139–59.
Jaguaribe, Beatriz. "The Shock of the Real." *Space and Culture*, vol. 8, no. 1, Feb. 2005, pp. 66–82.
Jakobson, Roman. "On Linguistic Aspects of Translation." Venuti, pp. 126–31.
Jaksić, Iván. *The Hispanic World and American Intellectual Life, 1820–1880*. Palgrave Macmillan, 2007.
Jáuregui, Carlos. "Anthropophagy." *Dictionary of Latin American Cultural Studies*, edited by Robert McKee Irwin and Mónica Szurmuk. UP of Florida, 2012, pp. 22–28.
———. *Canibalia: canibalismo, calibanismo, antropofagia cultural y consumo en América Latina*. Iberoamericana, 2008.
Jerome. "Letter to Pammachius." Venuti, pp. 21–30.
Johnson, Randal. *Literatura e cinema: Macunaíma: do modernismo ao Cinema Novo*. Translated by Aparecida de Godoy Johnson, T. A. Queiroz, 1982.
———. "Tupy or Not Tupy: Cannibalism and Nationalism in Contemporary Brazilian Literature and Culture." *On Modern Latin American Fiction*, edited by John Kind, Noonday Press, 1989, pp. 41–59.
Johnson, Randal, and Robert Stam, editors. *Brazilian Cinema*. Columbia UP, 1995.

Joseph, Tiffany D. *Race on the Move: Brazilian Migrants and the Global Reconstruction of Race*. Stanford UP, 2015.

Jouët-Pastré, Clémence, and Leticia Braga, editors. *Becoming Brazuca: Brazilian Immigration to the United States*. Harvard David Rockefeller Center for Latin American Studies, 2008.

Kingery, Sandra. "Translating Spanglish to Spanish: *The Brief Wondrous Life of Oscar Wao*." *Translation Review*, vol. 104, 2019, pp. 8–29.

Klinger, Diana. *Escritas de si, escritas do outro: o retorno do autor e a virada etnográfica: Bernardo Carvalho, Fernando Vallejo, Washington Cucurto, João Gilbert Noll, César Aira, Silviano Santiago*. 7Letras, 2007.

Kopenawa, Davi, and Bruce Albert. *The Falling Sky: Words of a Yanomami Shaman*. Translated by Nicolas Elliot and Alison Dundy, Harvard UP, 2013.

Kristal, Efraín. *Invisible Work: Borges and Translation*. Vanderbilt UP, 2002.

Kristal, Efraín, and José Luiz Passos. "Machado de Assis and the Question of Brazilian National Identity." *Brazil in the Making: Facets of National Identity*, edited by Carmen Nava and Ludwig Lauerhass Jr., Rowman & Littlefield, 2006, pp. 17–28.

Lacerda e Almeida, Francisco José de. *The Lands of Cazembe: Lacerda's Journey to Cazembe in 1798*. Translated by Richard Francis Burton, Royal Geographic Society, 1873.

Lajolo, Marisa, and Regina Zilberman. *A formação da leitura no Brasil*. Editora Ática, 1996.

Larkosh, Christopher. "Flows of Trans-Language: Translating Transgender in the *Paraguayan Sea*." *Transgender Studies Quarterly*, vol. 3, no. 3-4, 2016, pp. 552–68.

Larsen, Neil. *Reading North by South: On Latin American Literature, Culture, and Politics*. U of Minnesota P, 1995.

Lee, Benjamin, and Edward LiPuma. "Cultures of Circulation: The Imaginations of Modernity." *Public Culture*, vol. 14, no. 1, 2002, pp. 191–213.

Lefevere, André. *Translation, Rewriting, and the Manipulation of the Literary Frame*. Routledge, 1992.

Lehnen, Leila. *Citizenship and Crisis in Contemporary Brazilian Literature*. Palgrave, 2013.

Lesser, Jeffrey. *Immigration, Ethnicity, and National Identity in Brazil, 1808 to the Present*. Cambridge UP, 2013.

Levander, Caroline F., and Robert S. Levine, editors. *Hemispheric American Studies*. Rutgers UP, 2008.

Levine, Suzanne Jill. *The Subversive Scribe: Translating Latin American Fiction*. Dalkey Archive, 2009.

Lisboa, Adriana. *Azul-corvo*. Rocco, 2010.

———. *Um beijo de colombina*. Rocco, 2003.

———. *Caligrafias*. Rocco, 2004.

———. *Crow Blue*. Translated by Alison Entrekin, Bloomsbury, 2013.

———. *Os fios da memória*. Rocco, 1999.
———. *Hanói*. Alfaguara, 2013.
———. *Hut of Fallen Persimmons*. Translated by Sarah Green, Texas Tech UP, 2011.
———. "Navegar: ensaio literário e discussão metodológica." *Chiricú Journal: Latina/o Literatures, Arts, and Cultures*, vol. 1, no. 2, 2017, pp. 149–67.
———. *Parte da paisagem*. Iluminuras, 2014.
———. *Rakushisha*. Rocco, 2007.
———. *Sinfonia em branco*. Rocco, 2001.
———. *Symphony in White*. Translated by Sarah Green, Texas Tech UP, 2010.
———. *Todos os santos*. Alfaguara, 2019.
Lispector, Clarice. *The Complete Stories*. Translated by Katrina Dodson, New Directions, 2015.
———. *A hora da estrela*. 20th ed., Francisco Alves, 1992.
———. *The Hour of the Star*. Translated by Giovanni Pontiero, Carcanet, 1986.
———. *The Hour of the Star*. Translated by Benjamin Moser, New Directions, 2011.
Liu, Lydia H. *Translingual Practice: Literature, National Culture, and Translated Modernity—China, 1900–1937*. Stanford UP, 1995.
Lobo, Luiza. *Crítica sem juízo*. Francisco Alves, 1993.
———. *Épica e modernidade em Sousândrade*. Presença Edições, 1986.
Lomas, Laura. *Translating Empire: José Martí, Migrant Latino Subjects, and American Modernities*. Duke UP, 2009.
Lopes, Denílson. "From the Space In-Between to the Transcultural." *Journal of Latin American Cultural Studies*, vol. 16, no. 3, Dec. 2007, pp. 359–69.
———. "Silviano Santiago, estudos culturais e estudos LGBTS no Brasil." *Revista Iberoamericna*, vol. 74, no. 225, Oct.–Dec. 2008, pp. 943–57.
———. "A volta da casa na literatura brasileira contemporânea." *Luso-Brazilian Review*, vol. 43, no. 2, 2006, pp. 119–30.
López, Kimberle S. "*Modernismo* and the Ambivalence of the Postcolonial Experience: Cannibalism, Primitivism, and Exoticism in Mário de Andrade's *Macunaíma*." *Luso-Brazilian Review*, vol. 35, no. 1, 1998, pp. 25–38.
Lopez, Telê Porto Ancona. *Mário de Andrade: Ramais e caminho*. Duas Cidades, 1972.
———. *Macunaíma: a margem e o texto*. HUCITEC Secretaria de Cultura, Esportes e Turismo, 1974.
Lourenço Filho, Manuel Bergström. *Education in Brazil*. Translated by John Knox, Imprensa Nacional, 1951.
Lowe, Elizabeth. "Five Books by Clarice Lispector." *Review: Literature and Arts of the Americas*, vol. 46, no. 1, 2013, pp. 143–46.
———. "Jorge Amado and the Internationalization of Brazilian Literature." *Cadernos de Tradução*, no. 31, 2013, pp. 119–40.
———. "Revisiting Re-translation: Re-creation and Historical Re-vision." *A Companion to Translation Studies*, edited by Sandra Bermann and Catherine Porter, John Wiley & Sons, 2014, pp. 413–24.

Lowe, Elizabeth, and Earl E. Fitz. *Translation and the Rise of Inter-American Literatures*. UP of Florida, 2007.
Lowe, Lisa. *The Intimacies of the Four Continents*. Duke UP, 2015.
Lozano, Rosina. *An American Language: A History of the Spanish in the United States*. U of California P, 2018.
Machado de Assis, Joaquim Maria. *Correspondência de Machado de Assis: tomo II, 1870–1889*, edited by Sergio Paulo Rouanet, Irene Moutinho, and Sílvia Eleutério, Academia Brasileira de Letras, 2009.
Madureira, Luís. *Cannibal Modernities: Postcoloniality and the Avant-Garde in Caribbean and Brazilian Literature*. U of Virginia P, 2005.
Margolis, Maxine. *Goodbye, Brazil: Émigrés from the Land of Soccer and Samba*. U of Wisconsin P, 2013.
———. *An Invisible Minority: Brazilians in New York City*. 2nd ed., UP of Florida, 2009.
Martes, Ana Cristina Braga. *New Immigrants, New Land: A Study of Brazilians in Massachusetts*. Translated by Beth Ransdell Vinkler, UP of Florida, 2011.
Martí, José. *Ensayos y crónicas*, edited by José O. Jiménez, Cátedra, 2004.
Marting, Diane E., editor. *Clarice Lispector: A Bio-Bibliography*. Greenwood Press, 1993.
Maxwell, Kenneth. *Conflicts and Conspiracies: Brazil and Portugal, 1750–1808*. Cambridge UP, 1973.
Maxwell, Kenneth, Bruno Carvalho, John Huffman, and Gabriel de Avilez Rocha. *O livro de Tiradentes: Transmissão atlântica de ideias políticas no século XVIII*. Companhia das Letras, 2013.
McCracken, Ellen. *Paratexts and Performance in the Novels of Junot Díaz and Sandra Cisneros*. Palgrave Macmillan, 2016.
McGowan, Chris, and Ricardo Pessanha. *The Brazilian Sound: Samba, Bossa Nova, and the Popular Music of Brazil*. Temple UP, 1998.
Melo, Alfredo Cesar. "(De-)Latinizing America: How Gilberto Freyre and Mário de Andrade Imagined the Global South." *MLN*, vol. 128, 2013, pp. 298–316.
———. "*Macunaíma*: entre a crítica e o elogio à transculturação." *Hispanic Review*, vol. 78, no. 2, Spring 2010, pp. 205–27.
Melo, Cimara Valim de. "Mapping Brazilian Literature Translated into English." *Modern Language Open*, 2007, doi.org/10.3828/mlo.v0i0.124.
Melville, Pauline. "Guyanese Literature, Magic Realism and the South American Connection." *Wasafiri*, vol. 28, no. 3, 2013, pp. 7–11.
———. *The Ventriloquist's Tale*. Bloomsbury, 1997.
Meyer, Marlyse. "The *Feuilleton* and European Models in the Making of the Brazilian Novel." *Literary Cultures of Latin America: A Comparative History*. Vol. 2, edited by Mario J. Valdés and Djelal Kadir, Oxford UP, 2004, pp. 267–77.

Mignolo, Walter. *The Darker Side of Western Modernity: Global Futures, Decolonial Options*. Duke UP, 2011.

———. *Local Histories/Global Designs: Coloniality, Subaltern Knowledges, and Border Thinking*. Princeton UP, 2000.

Miller, Sally M., editor. *The Ethnic Press in the United States: A Historical Analysis and Handbook*. Greenwood Press, 1987.

Milton, John, and Paul Bandia, editors. *Agents of Translation*. John Benjamins, 2009.

———. "Introduction: Agents of Translation and Translation Studies." Milton and Bandia, pp. 4–18.

Mizruchi, Susan L. *The Rise of Multicultural America: Economy and Print Culture 1865–1915*. U of North Carolina P, 2008.

Molotnik, J. R. "*Macunaíma*: Revenge of the Jungle Freaks." *Jump Cut*, no. 12/13, 1976, pp. 22–24.

Monegal, Emir Rodríguez. *Mário de Andrade/Borges: Um diálogo dos anos 20*. Perspectiva SA, 1978.

Moreira, Paulo. *Literary and Cultural Relations between Brazil and Mexico: Deep Undercurrents*. Palgrave Macmillan, 2013.

Morris, Adam, and Bruno Carvalho, editors. *Essays on Hilda Hilst: Between Brazil and World Literature*. Palgrave Macmillan, 2018.

Morse, Richard M. *New World Soundings: Culture and Ideology in the Americas*. Johns Hopkins UP, 1989.

———. *O espelho de Próspero: Cultura e idéias nas Américas*. Translated by Paulo Neves, Companhia das Letras, 1988.

Moser, Benjamin. "He's One of Brazil's Greatest Writers. Why Isn't Machado de Assis More Widely Read?" *The New Yorker*, 9 & 16 July 2018, newyorker.com/magazine/2018/07/09/ hes-one-of-brazils-greatest-writers-why-isnt-machado-de-assis-more-widely-read. Accessed 18 Jan. 2019.

———. *Why This World: A Biography of Clarice Lispector*. Oxford UP, 2009.

Moser, Robert H., and Antonio L. A. Tosta, editors. *Luso-American Literature: Writings by Portuguese-Speaking Authors in North America*. Rutgers UP, 2011.

Nabuco, Joaquim. *O abolicionismo*. 1883. Publifolha, 2000.

———. *Abolitionism: The Brazilian Antislavery Struggle*. Translated and edited by Robert Conrad, U of Illinois P, 1977.

———. *Minha formação*. 1900. Fundação Biblioteca Nacional, Departamento Nacional do Livro, MinC.

Nassar, Raduan. *Ancient Tillage*. Translated by Karen Sherwood Sotelino, Penguin Classics, 2015.

———. *A Cup of Rage*. Translated by Stefan Tobler, Penguin Classics, 2015.

———. *Um copo de cólera*. 2nd ed., Brasiliense, 1984.

———. *Lavoura arcaica*. 3rd ed., Companhia das Letras, 1989.

Needell, Jeffrey D. "Brazilian Abolitionism, Its Historiography, and the Uses of Political History." *Journal of Latin American Studies*, vol. 42, no. 2, May 2010, pp. 231–61.

Nenevé, Miguel, and Roseli Siepamann. "Representation, Translation and Cross-Culturalism in *Macunaíma* and *The Ventriloquist's Tale*." *Caribbeing*, edited by Kristian van Haesendonck and Theo D'haen, Editions Rodopi, 2014. pp. 295–311.

Neves, Júlia Braga. "Um sentido para o fim: espaços migratórios e melancolia em *Hanói*, de Adriana Lisboa." *Estudos de literatura brasileira contemporânea*, no. 45, Jan.–June 2015, pp. 139–57.

Newcomb, Robert Patrick. *Nossa and Nuestra América: Inter-American Dialogues*. Purdue UP, 2011.

Newcomb, Robert Patrick, translator. "Reflections on Brazilian Literature at the Present Moment. The National Instinct." By Machado de Assis. *Journal of World Literature*, vol. 3, 2018, pp. 403–06.

Newcomb, Robert Patrick, and Richard A. Gordon, editors. *Beyond Tordesillas: New Approaches to Comparative Luso-Hispanic Studies*. Ohio State UP, 2017.

Nielson, Rex P. "Patriarchy's Traumatic Afterlives: Adriana Lisboa's Poetics of Silence in *Sinfonia em Branco*." *Chasqui: Revista de Literatura Latinoamericana*, vol. 43, no. 2, Nov. 2014, pp. 48–61.

Nóbrega, Thelma Médici, and John Milton. "The Role of Harold and Augusto de Campos in Bringing Translation to the Fore of Literary Activity in Brazil." Milton and Bandia, pp. 257–77.

Nornes, Abé Mark. "For an Abusive Subtitling." *Film Quarterly*, vol. 52, no. 3, Spring 1999, pp. 17–34.

Norton, Frank H., and Frank Leslie. *Frank Leslie's Historical Register of the United States Centennial Exposition, 1876. Embellished with Nearly Eight Hundred Illustrations Drawn Expressly for This Work by the Most Eminent Artists in America. Including Illustrations and Descriptions of All Previous International Exhibitions*. Introduction by Richard Kenin, Paddington Press, 1974.

Nunes, Zita. *Cannibal Democracy: Race and Representation in the Literature of the Americas*. U of Minnesota P, 2008.

Oliveira Lima, Manuel de, and Percy A. Martin. *The Evolution of Brazil Compared with That of Spanish and Anglo-Saxon America*. Stanford UP, 1914.

Ong, Walter J. *Orality and Literacy: The Technologizing of the Word*. 3rd ed., Routledge, 2012.

O Novo Mundo Association. "By-Laws of 'O Novo Mundo Association' of the City of New York (Incorporated 1875)." *American Broadsides and Ephemera*, series 1, no. 13679. Office of O Novo Mundo, 1875.

Ortiz, Fernando. *Contrapunteo cubano del tabaco y el azúcar*, edited by Enrico Mario Santí, Cátedra, 2002.

"Our Yankee Emperor." *Dom Pedro II in the United States.* Collection of the Oliveira Lima Library, 1876.
Paes, José Paulo. *Tradução: A ponte necessária.* Ática, 1990.
Pap, Leo. "The Portuguese Press." Miller, pp. 291–302.
Pardo, Carmen Villarino. "Literatura brasileira contemporânea: o desafio da exportação." *Romance Notes*, vol. 52, no. 2, 2012, pp. 151–64.
Park, Robert Ezra. *The Immigrant Press and Its Control.* Harper & Brothers, 1922.
Park, Stephen M. *The Pan-American Imagination: Contested Visions of the Hemisphere in Twentieth-Century Literature.* U of Virginia P, 2014.
Pedro, Emperor of Brazil; Lilia M. Schwarcz; and Begonha Bediaga. *Diário do Imperador D. Pedro II: 1840–1891.* Vol. 17, Museu Imperial, IPHAN, MinC, 1999.
Peixoto, Afranio. "American Social and Literary Influences in Brazil." *Books Abroad*, vol. 9, no. 2, Spring 1935, pp. 127–29.
Peixoto, Marta. *Passionate Fictions: Gender, Narrative, and Violence in Clarice Lispector.* U of Minnesota P, 1994.
———. "Rio's Favelas in Recent Fiction and Film: Commonplaces of Urban Segregation." *PMLA*, vol. 122, no. 1, 2007, pp. 170–78.
Peña, Karen. *Poetry and the Realm of the Public Intellectual: Alternative Destinies of Gabriela Mistral, Cecília Meireles, and Rosario Castellanos.* Legenda, 2007.
Penna, João Camillo. "Formações do sujeito colonial." *Alea*, vol. 14, no. 2, 2012, pp. 295–306.
Pérez Firmat, Gustavo. *Do the Americas Have a Common Literature?* Duke UP, 1990.
Perrone, Charles A. *Brazil, Lyric, and the Americas.* UP of Florida, 2010.
———. *Masters of Contemporary Brazilian Song: MPB 1965–1985.* U of Texas P, 1989.
———. *Seven Faces: Brazilian Poetry Since Modernism.* Duke UP, 1996.
Perrone-Moisés, Leyla. *Vira e mexe, nacionalismo: Paradoxos do nacionalismo literário.* Companhia das Letras, 2007.
Perry, Zoë. "A Love Letter to Brazilian Modernism: On Translating Veronica Stigger." *PEN America*, 8 Jan. 2016, pen.org/a-love-letter-to-brazilian-modernism-on-translating-veronica-stigger/. Accessed 21 Jan. 2019.
Pires, Maria Isabel Edom. "Em viagem: sobre outras paisagens e movimentos no romance contemporâneo." *Estudos de literatura brasileira contemporânea*, no. 44, 2014, pp. 389–402.
Plaza, Julio. *Tradução intersemiótica.* Perspectiva, 1987.
Plum, Werner. *World Exhibitions in the Nineteenth Century, Pageants of Social and Cultural Change.* Friedrich-Ebert-Stiftung, 1977.
Porter, Catherine. "Translation as Scholarship." *Association of Departments of Foreign Languages Bulletin*, vol. 41, no. 2, 2009, pp. 7–13.

Posso, Karl. *Artful Seduction: Homosexuality and the Problematics of Exile.* Legenda, 2003.
Pratt, Mary Louise. *Imperial Eyes: Travel Writing and Transculturation.* 2nd ed., Routledge, 2008.
Price, Rachel. *The Object of the Atlantic: Concrete Aesthetics in Cuba, Brazil, and Spain, 1868–1968.* Northwestern UP, 2014.
Programa de Apoio à Tradução e à Publicação de Autores Brasileiros no Exterior. Biblioteca Nacional, www.bn.gov.br/explore/programas-de-fomento/programa-apoio-traducao-publicacao-autores. Accessed 25 Sept. 2019.
Pym, Anthony. *Exploring Translation Theories.* Routledge, 2010.
Quinlan, Susan Canty. "Cross-Dressing: Silviano Santiago's Fictional Performances." *Lusosex: Gender and Sexuality in the Portuguese-Speaking World*, edited by Susan Canty Quinlan and Fernando Arenas, U of Minnesota P, 2002, pp. 208–32.
Rabassa, Gregory. *If This Be Treason: Translation and Its Dyscontents, a Memoir.* New Directions, 2005.
Rama, Ángel. *Transculturación narrative en América Latina.* Siglo XXI, 1982.
Ramírez, Mari C., Luciano Figueiredo, and Hélio Oiticica. *Hélio Oiticica: The Body of Color.* Tate, 2007.
Ramos, Julio. *Divergent Modernities: Culture and Politics in Nineteenth-Century Latin America.* Translated by John D. Blanco, Duke UP, 2001.
Read, Justin. *Modern Poetics and Hemispheric American Cultural Studies.* Palgrave Macmillan, 2009.
Reid, Michael. *Brazil: The Troubled Rise of a Global Power.* Yale UP, 2014.
Resende, Beatriz. *Contemporâneos: Expressões da literatura brasileira no século XXI.* Casa da Palavra, 2008.
Rinaldi Asciutti, Mônica Maria. *Um lugar para o periódico O Novo Mundo (Nova Iorque, 1870–1879).* Diss. USP/FFLCH, 2010.
Robbins, Bruce, and Paulo Lemos Horta, editors. *Cosmopolitanisms.* New York UP, 2017.
Rocha, Marília Librandi. *Maranhão–Manhattan: ensaios de literatura brasileira.* 7Letras, 2009.
———. *Writing by Ear: Clarice Lispector and the Aural Novel.* U of Toronto P, 2018.
Rocha, João Cezar de Castro. "Introduction: Machado de Assis—The Location of an Author." *Portuguese Literary and Cultural Studies*, no. 13/14, 2006, pp. xix–xxxix.
Rodrigues, J. C. (José Carlos). *Chrestomathia da lingua ingleza.* A. S. Barnes, 1870.
———. "Dear Sir . . ." *American Broadsides and Ephemera*, series 1, no. 13698. Office of the Novo Mundo, 1875.
Rogers, Gayle. *Incomparable Empires: Modernism and the Translation of Spanish and American Literature.* Columbia UP, 2016.

Rohter, Larry. *Brazil on the Rise: The Story of a Country Transformed*. Palgrave Macmillan, 2010.

Rosenberg, Fernando J. *The Avant-Garde and Geopolitics in Latin America*. U of Pittsburgh P, 2006.

Rostagno, Irene. *Searching for Recognition: The Promotion of Latin American Literature in the United States*. Greenwood Press, 1997.

Rydell, Robert W. *All the World's a Fair: Visions of Empire at American International Expositions, 1876–1916*. U of Chicago P, 1984.

Sá, Lúcia. *Rain Forest Literatures: Amazonian Texts and Latin American Culture*. U of Minnesota P, 2004.

Sadlier, Darlene J. *Americans All: Good Neighbor Cultural Diplomacy in World War II*. U of Texas P, 2012.

———. *Brazil Imagined: 1500 to the Present*. U of Texas P, 2008.

Said, Edward W. *Orientalism*. Pantheon Books, 1978.

———. "Traveling Theory." *The World, the Text, and the Critic*. Harvard UP, 1983, pp. 226–47.

Saldívar, José David. *Trans-americanity: Subaltern Modernities, Global Coloniality, and the Cultures of Greater Mexico*. Duke UP, 2012.

Santiago, Silviano. "Blot." Translated by Susan C. Quinlan. Moser and Tosta, pp. 202–09.

———. "The Cosmopolitanism of the Poor." Translated by Magdalena Edwards and Paulo Lemos Horta. Robbins and Horta, pp. 21–39.

———. *O cosmopolitismo do pobre: Crítica literária e crítica cultural*. Editora UFMG, 2004.

———. *Crescendo durante a guerra numa província ultramarina*. Francisco Alves, 1978.

———. "Deslocamentos reais e paisagens imaginárias—o cosmopolita pobre." Chiarelli and Oliveira Neto, pp. 15–32.

———. *O falso mentiroso*. Rocco, 2004.

———, editor. *Glossário de Derrida*. Francisco Alves, 1976.

———. "Hélio Oiticica em Manhattan." *Peixe-elétrico #05*, edited by Tiago Ferro, Ricardo Lísias, Mika Matsuzake, e-galáxia, 2016, location 42–214.

———. *Histórias mal contadas*. Rocco, 2005.

———, editor. *Intérpretes do Brasil*. Editora Nova Aguilar, 2002.

———. *Keith Jarrett no Blue Note (Improvisos de Jazz)*. Rocco, 1996.

———. *Em liberdade: uma ficção de Silviano Santiago*. Paz e Terra, 1981.

———. *Uma literatura nos trópicos: Ensaios sobre dependência cultural*. 1978. 2nd ed., Rocco, 2000.

———. "*Loft* 4: A Cave in the Heights." *Call Me Helium*. 2014. www.callmehelium.com/6-3-english-article-silviano.html. Accessed 14 Oct. 2018.

———. "Meditação sobre o ofício de criar." *Peixe-elétrico #05*, edited by Tiago Ferro, Ricardo Lísias, Mika Matsuzake, e-galáxia, 2016, location 432–583.

———. *As raízes e o labirinto da América Latina*. Rocco, 2006.

———. *The Space In-Between: Essays on Latin American Culture*, edited by Ana Lúcia Gazzola, with an introduction by Ana Lúcia Gazzola and Wander Melo Miranda; translated by Tom Burns, Ana Lúcia Gazzola, and Gareth Williams, Duke UP, 2001.

———. *Stella Manhattan*. Nova Fronteira, 1985.

———. *Stella Manhattan*. Translated by George Yúdice, Duke UP, 1994.

———. *Viagem ao México*. Rocco, 1995.

———. "You Don't Know What Love Is / *Muezzin*." Translated by Susan C. Quinlan. *Urban Voices: Contemporary Short Stories from Brazil*, edited by Cristina Ferreira-Pinto, University Press of America, 1999, pp. 225–42.

Santiago, Silviano, and Julio Ramos. "Los viajes de Silviano Santiago: conversaciones con Julio Ramos." Translated by Renata Pontes. *Papel máquina: Revista de cultura*, vol. 4, no. 8, Oct. 2013, pp. 191–211.

Santos, Lidia. Review of *The Space In-Between: Essays on Latin American Culture*. *Luso-Brazilian Review*, vol. 40, no. 1, Summer 2003, pp. 133–34.

Sarmiento, Domingo F. *Facundo: Civilización y barbarie en las Pampas Argentinas*. 1845. Stockcero, 2003.

Schleiermacher, Friedrich. "On the Different Methods of Translating." Translated by Susan Bernofsky. Venuti, pp. 43–62.

Schøllhammer, Karl Erik. *Ficção brasileira contemporânea*. Civilização Brasileira, 2009.

Schwarcz, Lilia Moritz. *The Emperor's Beard: Dom Pedro and the Tropical Monarchy of Brazil*. Translated by John Gledson, Hill and Wang, 2004.

———. *The Spectacle of the Races: Scientists, Institutions, and the Race Question in Brazil 1870–1930*. Translated by Leland Guyer, Hill and Wang, 1999.

———. "Os trópicos como espetáculo: a participação brasileira nas exposições universais de finais do século XIX." González Stephan and Andermann, pp. 195–220.

Schwartz, Jorge. "Abaixo Tordesilhas!" *Estudos Avançados*, vol. 7, no. 17, 1993, pp. 185–200.

———. *Vanguardas latino-americanas: polêmicas, manifestos e textos críticos*. Editora da Universidade de São Paulo, 1995.

Schwarz, Roberto. *A Master on the Periphery of Capitalism*. Translated by John Gledson, Duke UP, 2001.

———. *Misplaced Ideas: Essays on Brazilian Culture*. Translated by John Gledson, Verso, 1992.

———. *Ao vencedor as batatas: forma literária e processo social nos inícios do romance brasileiro*. Duas Cidades, 1977.

Seigel, Micol. *Uneven Encounters: Making Race and Nation in Brazil and the United States*. Duke UP, 2009.

Shaw, Lisa. "The Brazilian Chanchada and Hollywood Paradigms (1930–1959)." *Framework: The Journal of Cinema and Media*, vol. 44, no. 1, Spring 2003, pp. 70–83.

Shellhorse, Adam. *Anti-Literature: The Politics and Limits of Representation in Modern Brazil and Argentina*. U of Pittsburgh P, 2017.

Shemak, April. "Alter/natives: Myth, Translation, and the Native Informant in Pauline Melville's *The Ventriloquist's Tale*." *Textual Practice*, vol. 19, no. 3, 2005, pp. 353–72.

Silva, Célio Antonio Alcantara. "Confederates and Yankees under the Southern Cross." *Bulletin of Latin American Research*, vol. 34, no. 3, 2014, pp. 370–84.

Silva, Maria Andréia de Paula. *Silviano Santiago: uma pedagogia do falso*. Appris, 2016.

Siskind, Mariano. *Cosmopolitan Desires: Global Modernity and World Literature in Latin America*. Northwestern UP, 2014.

Skidmore, Thomas E. *Black into White: Race and Nationality in Brazilian Thought*. Duke UP, 1993.

———. *Brazil: Five Centuries of Change*. 2nd ed., Oxford UP, 2009.

———. *The Politics of Military Rule in Brazil, 1964–1985*. Oxford UP, 1990.

Slater, Candace. *Dance of the Dolphin: Transformation and Disenchantment in the Amazonian Imagination*. U of Chicago P, 1994.

Small, Irene. *Hélio Oiticica: Folding the Frame*. U of Chicago P, 2016.

Soares Inácio, Marcilaine, Carla Simone Chamon, and Luciano Mendes de Faria Filho. "The Invention of the Modern School in Brazil: Methods and Materials in Brazilian Schools in the 19th Century." *Classroom Struggle: Organizing Elementary School Teaching in the 19th Century*, edited by Marcelo Caruso, Peter Lang, 2015, pp. 129–52.

Sodré, Nelson Werneck. *História da imprensa no Brasil*. Civilização Brasileira, 1966.

Sommer, Doris. *Bilingual Aesthetics: A New Sentimental Education*. Duke UP, 2004.

———. *Proceed with Caution, When Engaged by Minority Writing in the Americas*. Harvard UP, 1999.

Sousândrade. *O Guesa*, edited by Luiza Lobo and Jomar Moraes, Ponteio, 2012.

———. "The Wall Street Inferno." Translated by Odile Cisneros. Moser and Tosta, pp. 226–30.

Sousa Andrade, Joaquim de. "The Wall Street Inferno (from *O Guesa*)." Translated by Robert E. Brown. *Latin American Literary Review*, vol. 14, no. 27, Jan.–June 1986, pp. 92–98.

Souza, Gilda de Mello e. *O Tupi e o Alaúde. Uma interpretação de Macunaíma*. Duas Cidades, 1979.

Spivak, Gayatri Chakravorty. "The Politics of Translation." Venuti, pp. 312–30.

Staden, Hans. *Hans Staden's True History: An Account of Cannibal Captivity in Brazil*. Translated by Neil L. Whitehead and Michael Harbsmeier, Duke UP, 2008.

Stam, Robert. *Tropical Multiculturalism: A Comparative History of Race in Brazilian Cinema and Culture*. Duke UP, 1997.
Stam, Robert, João Luiz Vieira, and Ismail Xavier. "The Shape of Brazilian Cinema in the Postmodern Age." Johnson and Stam, pp. 389–472.
Steiner, George. *After Babel: Aspects of Language and Translation*. 2nd ed., Oxford UP, 1992.
Stephanides, Stephanos. "Translation and Ethnography in Literary Transaction." *Studying Transcultural Literary History*, edited by Gunilla Lindberg-Wada, De Gruyter, 2006, pp. 300–09.
Studart, Hugo. *Borboletas e lobisomens: vidas, sonhos e mortes dos guerrilheiros do Araguaia*. Francisco Alves, 2018.
Süssekind, Flora. *O Brasil não é longe daqui: O narrador, a viagem*. Companhia das Letras, 1990.
Telles, Angela Cunha da Motta. *Desenhando a nação: revistas ilustradas do Rio de Janeiro e de Buenos Aires nas décadas de 1860 e 1870*. Fundação Alexandre de Gusmão, 2010.
Telles, Edward E. *Race in Another America: The Significance of Skin Color in Brazil*. Princeton UP, 2004.
Tenorio-Trillo, Mauricio. *Mexico at the World's Fairs: Crafting a Modern Nation*. U of California P, 1996.
Thomson-DeVeaux, Flora. "Notas sobre o calabouço: *Brás Cubas* e os castigos aos escravos no Rio." *Revista piauí*, vol. 140, May 2018, piaui.folha.uol.com.br/materia/nota-sobre-o-calabouco/. Accessed 19 Jan. 2019.
———. "Reading Machado Through the Looking-Glass: Case Studies from the Translations of *Memórias póstimas*." *Machado de Assis em Linha*, vol. 11, no. 25, 2018, pp. 96–111.
Tonus, José Leonardo. "Espaços *na* e *da* clandestinidade." *Espaços possíveis na literatura brasileira contemporânea*, edited by Regina Dalcastagnè and Luciene Azevedo, Zouk, 2015, pp. 139–56.
Torres, Lourdes. "In the Contact Zone: Code-Switching Strategies by Latino/a Writers." *MELUS*, vol. 32, no. 1, 2007, pp. 75–96.
Torres-Marchal, Carlos. "Dom Pedro II no Inferno de Wall Street—I." *Eutomia*, vol. 4, no. 7, July 2011.
———. "Dom Pedro II no Inferno de Wall Street—II." *Eutomia*, vol. 4, no. 8, Dec. 2011.
———. "Dom Pedro II no Inferno de Wall Street—III." *Eutomia*, vol. 5, no. 9, July 2012.
Tosta, Antonio Luciano de Andrade. "Between Heaven and Hell: Perceptions of Brazil and the United States in 'Brazuca' Literature." *Hispania*, vol. 88, no. 4, 2005, pp. 713–25.
———. *Confluence Narratives: Ethnicity, History, and Nation-Making in the Americas*. Bucknell UP, 2016.

———. "Latino, Eu? The Paradoxical Interplay of Identity in Brazuca Literature." *Hispania*, vol. 87, no. 3, 2004, pp. 576–85.

———. "The Other as Self or Other? Latinidade and the Politics of Identification in Brazuca Novels." *Gávea-Brown*, no. 34–35, 2012–2013, pp. 301–18.

Trigo, Abril. Review of *The Space In-Between: Essays on Latin American Culture*. *The Americas*, vol. 60, no. 4, 2004, pp. 638–39.

Turazzi, Maria Inez. "Imagens da nação: a Exposição de História do Brasil de 1881 e a construção do patrimônio iconográfico." González Stephan and Andermann, pp. 117–50.

———. *Poses e trejeitos: A fotografia e as exposições na era do espetáculo (1839–1889)*. Funarte, 1995.

United States Centennial Commission. *Official Catalogue*. 3 vols. J. R. Nagle and Company, 1876.

Uslenghi, Aleandra. *Latin America at the Fin-de-siècle Universal Exhibitions: Modern Cultures of Visuality*. Palgrave Macmillan, 2016.

Veloso, Caetano. *Alegria, alegria: Uma caetanave organizada por Waly Salomão*. Pedro Q Ronca, 1977.

———. *Tropical Truth: A Story of Music and Revolution in Brazil*. Translated by Barbara Einzig, Da Capo Press, 2002.

Venuti, Lawrence. *Scandals of Translation: Towards an Ethics of Difference*. Routledge, 1998.

———. *Translation Changes Everything: Theory and Practice*. Routledge, 2013.

———, editor. *The Translation Studies Reader*. 3rd ed., Routledge, 2012.

———. *The Translator's Invisibility: A History of Translation*. Routledge, 1995.

Vermeulen, Pieter. "On World Literary Reading: Literature, the Market, and the Antinomies of Mobility." *Institutions of World Literature: Writing, Translation, Markets*, edited by Stefan Helgesson and Pieter Vermeulen, Routledge, 2016, pp. 79–92.

Vianna, Hermano. *The Mystery of Samba: Popular Music and National Identity in Brazil*. Translated by John Charles Chasteen, U of North Carolina P, 1999.

Vieira, Else Ribeiro Pires. "Liberating Calibans: Readings of *Antropofagia* and Haroldo de Campos' Poetics of Transcreation." *Post-colonial Translation: Theory and Practice*, edited by Susan Bassnett and Harish Trivedi, Routledge, 1999, pp. 95–113.

———. "A Postmodern Translational Aesthetics in Brazil." *Translation Studies: An Interdiscipline*, edited by Mary Snell Hornby, Franz Pöchhacker, and Klaus Kaindl, John Benjamins, 1994, pp. 65–72.

Vieira, Nelson H. "Fora do Brasil—globalização e deslocamento na literatura brasileira contemporânea: migração transnacional e luto cultural." Chiarelli and Oliveira Neto, pp. 48–63.

Waisman, Sergio. *Borges and Translation: The Irreverence of the Periphery*. Bucknell UP, 2005.

Walkowitz, Rebecca. *Born Translated: The Contemporary Novel in an Age of World Literature.* Columbia UP, 2015.
Wallerstein, Immanuel M. *World-Systems Analysis: An Introduction.* Duke UP, 2004.
Wasserman, Renata R. M. *Exotic Nations: Literature and Cultural Identity in the United States and Brazil, 1830-1930.* Cornell UP, 1994.
———. "Preguiça and Power: Mário de Andrade's 'Macunaíma.'" *Luso-Brazilian Review,* vol. 21, no. 1, 1984, pp. 99-116.
Wiegand, Wayne. A. "Introduction: Theoretical Foundations for Analyzing Print Culture as Agency and Practice in a Diverse Modern America." *Print Culture in a Diverse America,* edited by James P. Danky and Wayne A. Wiegand, U of Illinois P, 1998, pp. 1-13.
Williams, Claire. "'Para inglês ver': Traduções de literatura contemporânea brasileira na época dos megaeventos." *Abriu,* vol. 6, 2017, pp. 105-32.
Williams, Frederick G. *Sousândrade: Vida e obra.* Edições Sioge, 1976.
———. "Sousândrade's 'Wall Street Inferno.'" *Latin American Literary Review,* vol. 1, no. 2, Spring 1973, pp. 143-48.
Wolff, Jorge. *Telquelismos latinoamericanos: La teoría crítica francesa en el entre-lugar de los trópicos.* Editorial Grumo, 2009.
Wood, Naomi Pueo, editor. *Brazil in Twenty-First Century Popular Media: Culture, Politics, and Nationalism on the World Stage.* Lexington Books, 2014.
Xavier, Ismail. *Allegories of Underdevelopment: Aesthetics and Politics in Modern Brazilian Cinema.* U of Minnesota P, 1997.
Yúdice, George. *The Expediency of Culture: Uses of Culture in the Global Era.* Duke UP, 2003.
Zelavansky, Lynn, et al. *Hélio Oiticica: To Organize Delirium.* Carnegie Museum of Art, 2016.

INDEX

Agassiz, Louis, 1, 37
Anderson, Benedict, 21
Andes and the Amazon: Across the Continent of South America, The (Orton), 36, 37
Andrade, Joaquim Pedro de: and "Cannibalism and Self-Cannibalism," 92; and *Macunaíma's* film adaptation, 71, 83, 90, 91, 97, 98, 104
Andrade, Mário de: and African American musicians, 12; approach to language of, 67–68, 74–75, 85, 86; and Brazilian identity, 11, 72; Brazilian travels of, 5, 70, 76; and conversations with translators, 82–84, 87; cultural cannibalism of, 68–69, 71, 72–73; and indigenous myths and tales, 75, 92, 93; and intertextuality, 73, 99, 103; and *Macunaíma*, 10, 17, 23, 70–78, 80–82, 89, 90, 92, 97, 179, 190–91; modernist narrative of, 104; and national identity, 94–95; and novel *The Ventriloquist's Tale*, 101, 102; and oral and folkloric traditions, 5, 70–71, 73, 74–75; and orality, 80–81; and racial identity, 78; and transcreation, 93; as a translator, 77, 80, 175; trip to Peruvian Amazon of, 70. *See also* Koch-Grünberg, Theodor
Andrade, Oswald de: and *antropofagia*, 20, 106, 118; and Brazilian literature, 144, 189; "Cannibalist Manifesto" of, 68; language of, 68; "Manifesto of Pau-Brasil Poetry" of, 67
antropofagia: in Brazil, 106; and "Cannibalist Manifesto" (Oswald de Andrade), 68; and Latin American discourse, 118; and *Macunaíma's* film version, 91, 97; and *Macunaíma: the Hero Without a Character* (Mário de Andrade), 68–69; and "Manifesto of Pau-Brasil Poetry," 67; and Mário de Andrade, 71, 72–73; and *Revista de Antropofagia*, 68, 69f; and Silviano Santiago, 111; and transformation into original works, 20, 68
Apter, Emily: and concept of the nation, 20–21; and literary marketplace, 152; and the translation zone, 20, 28, 107, 163, 174; and untranslatability, 16,

Apter, Emily *(continued)*
  146, 150–51, 166, 185; and world literature, 77, 147–48, 151, 168
Azul-corvo (Crow Blue) (Lisboa): and displacement from travel, 153, 154; and dual citizenship, 160, 167–68; landscape descriptions in, 157–58, 160; languages in, 156, 159–60; and nationality, 167–68; protagonist of, 158; race in, 167–68; and role of Brazilians in US, 25, 143; and space in-between countries, 160–61, 162; and translation, 167–68; and the translation zone, 159, 163; and transnational travel, 142, 174; and undocumented immigrants, 163, 168

Bandeira, Manuel, 84–85, 87, 88
Barthes, Roland, 110, 113
Baudelaire, Charles, 60, 149
Benjamin, Walter: and essay "The Translator's Task," 16, 21, 149; and metaphor of broken vase, 18–19; and pure language, 18, 149; and translatability, 152, 168; and translation, 74, 91, 100, 144, 150, 151, 181
Bhabha, Homi, 21–22, 114
Bolaño, Roberto, 141
Bolívar, Simón, 34
Bolsonaro, Jair, 3, 13
Borges, Jorge Luis: in Argentina, 184; and the copy, 114, 116; and European literature, 115; and intertextuality, 73; and national literature, 65; and "Pierre Menard, Author of the *Quixote*," 115, 116–17; and translation, 19, 20, 24, 74, 91, 117, 148, 181
Branner, John Casper, 39–40

Brazil: and 1876 Centennial Exhibition, 39, 42, 44, 46–50, 52–53, 67; 20th century politics in, 12–13; and abolition of slavery, 11, 22, 30–31, 38; and Adriana Lisboa, 142, 153; and Afro-descendants, 13, 178; and Amazon, 36, 46, 57–58, 59, 70, 72, 73, 76, 79, 85, 99, 104; and Brazilian immigrants, 13, 172–73; and capitalism, 9, 28, 29, 43, 46, 92, 136; and city of São Paulo, 79–80, 109, 136, 186; and colonialism, 29, 36, 50, 52–53; and cosmopolitanism of the poor, 137–38; and display at Vienna Exhibition, 42–43; and economic hierarchies, 68; and education, 36, 38–39; and exchanges in higher education with U.S., 40; and film *Macunaíma*, 93–95, 96, 97, 98; geography of, 36–38; geology of, 39, 39–40; and globalization, 10, 13, 119; and Gonçalves de Magalhães, 36; government of, 33, 42, 46, 47, 93, 120–21, 153, 158, 179, 184, 186, 189; and Guyana, 100; and historically marginalized voices, 178; image of, 144, 145, 146; and immigration, 3–4; and impeachment of Dilma Rousseff, 13; Imperial Constitution of, 31; indigenous people of, 57–58; languages of, 6, 53; and Latin American comparisons, 7; and LGBTQ+ communities, 13; and *Macunaíma's* film adaptation, 83, 92–93; and *Macunaíma: the Hero Without a Character* (Mario de Andrade), 70, 104; migration from, 171; military coups of, 11, 12, 93; minorities in, 13; and modernism,

11–12, 70; and modernity, 9, 10, 22, 29, 42, 43, 46, 50, 52–53, 62, 67, 70–71, 76; and modernization, 38, 42, 50, 70; monarchy of, 1, 29, 173; and national identity, 11, 21, 29, 46, 52, 62, 70, 95, 104, 119; natural resources of, 9, 10, 22, 42, 43, 46, 48, 50, 52, 68; and period of 1870s, 9, 11, 22, 39; Portugal's finding of, 36; postal tariffs in, 34; progress as motto of, 80; race, class and ethnicity in, 7, 13, 122–23; and relationship with US, 2, 3, 5–6, 7–8, 12, 13, 20, 27–29, 31, 34, 36, 46, 60, 105, 108, 190; and Rio de Janeiro, 92, 98, 110, 136, 141, 153, 160–61, 180; and Silviano Santiago, 105, 106, 107, 108–10, 113; slavery in, 30–31, 34, 38, 57; and Sousândrade, 60, 61; and Spanish America, 5–7; and transformation to a republic, 11; and translation, 5, 21, 25–26, 175, 176, 191; travel within, 5, 57–58, 76–77; and War of the Triple Alliance, 11, 30. *See also* Centennial Exhibition of 1876

Brazilian literature: and autofiction, 153; canonical writers of, 178, 183–85; circulation of, 179, 185–86; and Clarice Lispector's work, 180–84; and dislocation, 119, 153; and European writers, 58; and gender and sexuality, 185; and global markets, 139–40, 143–46, 147; and Hilda Hilst, 184, 186, 187; and language, 64, 67–68, 188; and literary marketplace, 152, 182, 188; and "local color," 146; and Machado de Assis, 61–65, 88, 119, 133–34, 144, 177, 183–84; and Macunaíma, 100; and national instinct, 62–63, 133–34; and nature, 54, 67; otherness in, 153; and poetry, 58, 178, 188; and publishers and presses, 176–78, 186; and Raduan Nassar, 186–87; and Silviano Santiago, 110, 111; and Sousândrade, 59–61; themes of, 153–54; and translation of Brazilian writers, 88, 139, 145, 146, 152, 176–90; in the US, 144, 176–79, 178–79. *See also* Andrade, Mário de; Andrade, Oswald de; *antropofagia*; Lisboa, Adriana; Lispector, Clarice; Santiago, Silviano; translation

Buarque de Hollanda, Sérgio, 91, 92–93

Burton, Sir Richard Francis, 53–54

Campos, Augusto de: as agent of translation, 17; and Sousândrade, 60; and translation, 19–20

Campos, Haroldo de: as agent of translation, 17; and analysis of *Macunaíma*, 74; and *antropofagia*, 118; and *Macunaíma's* translation, 89; publishing of, 188–89; and re-creation, 18, 19–20, 90, 91; and Sousândrade, 60; and theory of translation, 17–19, 84, 148; and transcreation, 9, 18, 20, 74, 84, 118

Candido, Antonio, 113

Casanova, Pascale, 16

Centennial Exhibition of 1876: attendance of, 52; and Brazilian art, 52–53; and Brazilian coffee, 44–46; and Brazilian pavilion, 48–50; Brazil's plans for, 39; and capitalism, 41; and coloniality, 42, 52–53; and Corliss engine, 28; countries participating in, 44, 48, 50; coverage of, 9–10, 22, 28, 29,

Centennial Exhibition of 1876 *(continued)* 41–42, 43, 44, 46–47, 48, 53; events and displays of, 29, 41, 47, 48–50, 52–53; and fair's inauguration, 28; illustrations of, 45*f*, 49*f*, 50, 51*f*, 51*f*; and modernity, 42, 50, 52–53, 67; and national identity, 29; new technologies at, 1, 28, 42; and progress, 41, 48, 52; and Spanish American nations, 50

Clifford, James, 14, 135

Columbus, Christopher, 35–36

Cooper, James Fenimore, 54

Cornell University, 38, 39, 40

Cortázar, Julio, 114, 115, 116, 117

Cuban Counterpoint: Tobacco and Sugar (Ortiz), 15

Cushing, Caleb, 34

Damrosch, David, 16

Derrida, Jacques: and *Glossário de Derrida*, 17, 110–11; and *Of Grammatology*, 110, 113; and intertextuality, 73; and Latin American politics of resistance, 111; and Silviano Santiago, 110–11, 113; and translation, 19, 151; and *Writing and Difference*, 110, 113

Dodson, Katrina, 188, 189, 190

Dom Pedro II: European and other travels of, 30; and friendship with Longfellow, 1–2, 54; as a linguistic and cultural translator, 2; and modernity, 42; and modernization, 30; and slavery, 57; and tour of Centennial Exhibition, 28–29; US travels of, 1–2, 3, 22, 28, 29, 30, 47, 54, 60

Doria, Franklin, 54–55; and Portuguese translation, 2

Ette, Ottmar, 10

Evangeline (Longfellow): translations of, 2, 54–55

Evolution of Brazil Compared with That of Spanish and Anglo-Spanish America (Oliveira Lima and Martin), 40

Fitz, Earl, 6–7

Foucault, Michel, 9: and *The Archaeology of Knowledge*, 111, 117; and Silviano Santiago, 110, 111, 112; and term "discourse," 112

Freyre, Gilberto: and "racial democracy," 11, 136

García Márquez, Gabriel, 88

Goodland, E.A., 71, 88, 89, 90, 99–100

Grant, Ulysses S., 1, 28–29

Hanói (Lisboa): and Brazilians in the US, 25, 143, 169; and displacement from travel, 153, 154, 170; and dual citizenship, 169; languages in, 156, 171–72; plot of, 169; and relationship to landscape, 157–58; translations of, 142; and transnational travel, 174; and undocumented immigrants, 169–70; and Vietnamese characters, 157, 169

Hartt, Charles Frederick, 37–38, 39, 40, 58, 72

Hollingsworth, Margaret Richardson, 23, 82–83, 84, 85, 86–88, 90

Imagined Communities (Anderson), 21

immigration, 13, 132–33, 136, 143, 152, 154

Imperial Eyes: Travel Writing and Transculturation (Pratt), 14
inter-American literature: and Canada, 6; and colonialism, 6; and comparisons between Brazil, Spanish America and the US, 7; and immigration, 6; and *Inter-American Literary History: Six Critical Periods* (Fitz), 6; and national origin and expansion, 6, 7; and poetic dialogues, 7, 17; and *Rediscovering the New World: Inter-American Literature in a Comparative Context* (Fitz), 6; and slavery, 6

Jakobson, Roman, 18, 19, 90
Johnson, Randal, 90–91
Journey in Brazil, A (Agassiz), 37
Jump Cut (Molotnik), 93, 96

Knopf, Alfred A., 176
Koch-Grünberg, Theodor: and Amerindians as other, 76; and Amerindian tales, 75, 104; German text of, 100; and indigenous myths and legends, 23, 70, 73–74; as inspiration for Mário de Andrade, 72, 73–74; and *Macunaíma: the Hero Without a Character* (Mário de Andrade), 82, 92
Kopenawa, Davi, 145, 178, 187–88
Kristeva, Julia, 73, 110

La América Ilustrada, 33
language: and Adriana Lisboa's novels, 142; Amazonian languages, 6, 76, 188; Amerindian languages, 89, 188; Arabic, 53; and Brazilian literature, 64, 74–75, 86, 88, 188; Brazilian Portuguese, 4, 17, 64, 67–68, 75, 77, 78, 81, 85, 89, 100, 104, 140, 143, 155, 176; creole languages, 6; dialects of Brazil, 75; and displacement, 165, 175; English, 3, 4, 5, 6, 17, 23, 25, 33, 37, 38, 52, 53, 54–55, 56, 71, 75, 82, 84, 85, 86, 88, 89, 90, 96, 98, 100, 104, 107–8, 114, 119, 123–24, 126, 128, 129, 130, 144, 145, 147, 156, 164, 170, 176; European dynamics of, 113; and foreign-language journals, 31–32; French, 6, 17, 24, 54, 64, 83, 105, 107, 111, 114, 119; German, 17, 76, 82, 83, 87, 100, 149; Greek, 54; and João Guimarães Rosa, 189–90; and identity, 164; indigenous languages, 3, 6, 81, 82, 85; Italian, 17, 83; Japanese, 156; Latin, 53, 54; and Latin American grammars, 7; and linguistic barriers, 124–25; and *Macunaíma*, 83, 86; and "Manifesto of Pau-Brasil Poetry," 67; and Mário de Andrade, 67–68, 74–75, 86; and migrants' languages, 3, 24; nonverbal language, 96–97; and orality, 74; and Oswald de Andrade, 67–68; and poetry, 58–59, 67; Portuguese, 3, 4, 5–6, 9, 24, 31, 33, 34, 37, 38, 40, 48, 53, 54, 55, 56, 58, 59, 60, 67–68, 75, 79, 82, 84, 89–90, 96, 106, 107–8, 109, 110, 111, 120, 126, 128, 129–30, 136, 141, 142, 143, 144, 145, 146, 164, 166, 170, 186–87; Romance languages, 53, 83; and space in-between, 109, 114; Spanish, 3, 4, 6, 9, 17, 24, 25, 33, 53, 54, 82, 83, 88, 89, 90, 108, 114, 116, 119, 128, 129, 164; and translation, 2–3, 17, 18–19, 21–22, 75, 83, 89–90, 116,

language *(contiinued)* 147, 189–90; and translation for film, 96; and travel, 15, 24–25; Tupi, 85, 90, 96, 189; and untranslatability, 21, 147; Vietnamese, 169; vulgar language, 89–90, 100; and *Writing and Difference* (Derrida), 113

Latin American literature: and *antropofagia*, 118, and Brazilian and Spanish American writers, 20–21, 88; and Clarice Lispector, 180; and creative transformations, 114, 118; features of, 15; and global Latin American novelists, 141, 144; and hybridity, 114; and Latin American Boom, 12, 88, 144; and Latin American creoles, 15; and "Latin American Discourse: The Space In-between" (Santiago), 23–24, 105, 106, 112, 114–15; Lisboa's Hemispheric Brazilian novels, 24–25; and literary translation, 20, 24–25, 177; and modern transatlantic poetry, 15; and Silviano Santiago, 105–6, 107, 108–18; and transculturation, 15, 114; in translation for U.S., 144, 176; and translator's role, 19; and US publishers, 176–77; and work of Borges, 19–20, 148

Lincoln, Abraham, 30

Lisboa, Adriana: Brazilian novels of, 10, 13, 24–25, 142–43, 144, 153, 156–74; as a Brazilian writer, 141–43, 150, 153; and codeswitching, 143, 150, 164, 165, 170, 174; and comparative literature, 153; and displacement, 24, 25, 130, 142, 154; global translations of, 142; and inclusive form of Latinidad, 8–9, 25; Japanese aesthetic of, 154–55; and Latinx identities, 159–61, 162–63; and literary marketplace, 150, 152, 174; and race, 174; and *Rakushisha*, 142, 144, 153, 154–56, 161, 174; and representing the marginalized, 144, 157–58; *Sinfonia em branco* of, 142, 154; and tales of migrants, 4, 24, 25, 150, 152, 154, 156, 157–58, 160–68, 170–74, 190; and translatability, 25, 143–44, 148, 150, 152, 168; and translation, 17, 24–25, 140, 143, 153, 159–60, 173–74; translational aesthetic of, 156; as a translator, 24, 143, 153; in the US, 3, 153. See also *Azul-corvo*; *Hanói*

Lispector, Clarice, 25, 88, 123, 144, 176, 179–84, 186

Liu, Lydia H., 14, 151

Longfellow, Henry Wadsworth: epic *Evangeline* of, 2, 54–55; and friendship with Dom Pedro II, 1–2; translation of, 54–55

Machado de Assis, Joaquim Maria: and Brazilian literature, 61–65, 88, 120, 144, 177, 183–84; journalism of, 62; and "local color," 62–63, 64, 65, 119, 142; and national instinct, 62–63, 106, 119, 133–34, 142; and *O Novo Mundo*, 57, 61–62; translation of, 183–84; works of, 183–84

Macunaíma: the Hero Without a Character (Andrade, Mário de): Amazonian tale in, 78; and Amerindian tales as prose, 77, 82, 84, 85, 92; and *antropofagia*, 68–69, 71, 72–73; and Brazilian national identity, 70; and Brazil's colonial origins, 70; and character of Macunaíma, 23, 70,

73, 90; circulation of, 23, 75–76, 90, 98, 104, 137; and creative transformations, 23, 71, 90; film adaptation of, 83, 90–98; film and fictional versions of, 10, 23, 70, 71, 104; genre of, 71–72; and indigenous myths and legends, 23, 70, 71, 73–74, 75, 77, 92; and intertextuality, 103; language of, 75; narration of, 77–79, 81–82, 92; and orality, 72, 80–81; and publication in the US, 84–85, 88; readership of, 75–76, 78, 85, 86, 87, 88, 89, 92; summary of, 70; as transcreation, 23, 74; and translation, 12, 17, 23, 69–70, 71, 74–76, 77, 80–90, 98; and transnationality, 76; and travel, 76–77, 79; and untranslatability, 87

Martí, José, 8, 34

Meirelles, Victor, 52–53

Melville, Pauline: and Brazilian literature, 100; and genre classifications, 102; and Guyana, 99; and *Macunaíma*, 101, 104; and novel *The Ventriloquist's Tale*, 23, 99, 100, 101, 103; and translation, 100–1; and ventriloquism, 101

modernism: and *antropofagia*, 20, 68, 71; and cultural cannibalism, 105, 118; and João Guimarães Rosa, 189–90; and indigenous peoples, 11; and *Macunaíma*, 23, 70–71; and Oswald de Andrade, 70; and Tarsila do Amaral, 70; and Week of Modern Art in 1922, 11. *See also* Andrade, Oswald de; Andrade, Mário de; Melville, Pauline

Nunes, Zita, 7, 8

Olea, Héctor, 83, 88, 89, 90

Oliveira Lima, Manuel de, 40

O Novo Mundo (The new world): and 1876 Centennial Exhibition, 9–10, 22, 28–29, 33, 41–42, 44, 47–50, 51, 52, 53; articles of, 22, 29, 32, 35–36, 41, 46, 47, 48, 50, 52, 53, 143; and Brazilian coffee, 44–46, 50; and Brazilian literature, 53–54, 55, 57–65; and capitalism, 43, 65; circulation of, 32, 35; and colonialism, 36, 43; and creative transformations, 28; and educational reform, 36, 38; end of publication of, 34; first issue of, 35*f*; founding of, 31; and Hartt's work, 37–38, 39; and hemispheric connections, 8, 22–23, 27, 29–30, 33, 57, 132, 190; and idea of the nation, 22; illustrations of, 48–49; inter-American outlook of, 32, 34; and José Carlos Rodrigues, 3, 17, 22, 27, 29, 34–35; and literature, 53–57, 65; and Machado de Assis, 61–63; and modernity, 53; and modernization, 22, 28, 29, 38, 42; Portuguese as language of, 31, 59; and progress, 22, 27, 28, 31, 32, 33, 34, 36, 38, 40, 47, 50, 61, 65; readership of, 22, 27, 30, 32, 33, 34–35, 41–42, 47, 48, 59, 65; and relationship with Brazil, 65; and relationship with US, 33, 34–35, 65, 132; reporting of, 33, 34, 40, 42, 43, 46, 47, 52; scholarship on, 32; and scientific expeditions, 36, 38; and slavery, 36, 55–56; and Sousândrade, 59–61; and translation, 23, 27, 29, 32, 34, 53, 54–55, 57, 59, 65; and transnationality, 76; transnational trajectory of, 34, 137; and travel, 29, 32, 52; and travel writing, 36;

O Novo Mundo (The new world) *(continued)*
women's page of, 34; and world's fairs, 41–43. *See also* Sousândrade
Ortiz, Fernando: and transculturation, 15
Orton, James, 36–37, 38
Otelo, Grande, 93–94

Poe, Edgar Allen, 116
Pound, Ezra, 17, 18
Pratt, Mary Louise: contact zone of, 114; and transculturation, 15; and travel writing, 14, 27–28

race: and 1876 Centennial Exhibition, 43; and African peoples of Brazil, 78; and Amazonian tales, 78; and Amerindians of Brazil, 78; in Brazil, 11–12, 13, 31, 48, 58, 78, 122–23, 125, 136; and Brazilian identity, 142–43; and Brazilian immigrants, 166, 167; and Brazilian literature, 78, 185; and discrimination against Latinos, 130; and Europeans of Brazil, 78; and film *Macunaíma*, 93, 96; and identity, 78, 119, 142–43, 167; and indigenous peoples, 58; and nationality, 167–68; and racial and ethnic constructs, 7, 24, 56, 125, 126, 127, 173–74; and segregation, 125–26; as a social and linguistic construct, 166–68; and translation, 25; and untranslatability, 166–67; in the US, 11, 25, 30, 109–10, 122–23, 125–27, 157, 166–67. *See also* slavery
Rama, Angel: and Latin American literature, 15; and transculturation, 15, 80
Revista Industrial Ilustrada, 33

Rodrigues, José Carlos: as agent of translation, 17, 175; articles of, 31, 34; and *Aurora Brasileira*, 40; and cultural exchange, 32–33; and discussion of slavery, 30; education of, 31; and ideal of modernization, 29; and *O Novo Mundo*, 3, 22, 27, 28, 33, 47, 61–62; and praise for Machado's novel, 61; and progress, 34, 190; in the US, 109
Rousseff, Dilma, 13
Routes: Travel and Translation in the Late Twentieth Century (Clifford), 14

Said, Edward, 14, 113
Santiago, Silviano; artistic influences on, 127; and "Borrão" ("Blot"), 107, 123, 132, 166; and Brazil, 108, 110, 113, 119; and Brazilian and Spanish American literature, 111; and Brazilian identity, 119, 153; and codeswitching, 108, 126, 128, 129–30, 131–32; and the copy, 105, 106, 113–14, 117, 137, 138–39; and cosmopolitanism of the poor, 5, 22, 106, 108, 133–39; and creative transformations, 106, 114, 117; and cultural cannibalism, 118; and deconstructionism, 110; and Derrida's ideas, 17, 108, 110–11, 113; and dislocation, 111, 118, 119, 142; and exile and migration, 4, 12, 106, 119–20, 121, 132–33; and fiction set in the US, 107, 108, 119, 120–33, 143; and *Glossário de Derrida*, 110–11; and inclusive form of Latinidad, 8–9, 130, 131; and *Keith Jarrett no Blue Note*, 108, 120, 122, 127, 131–32; and language, 108, 109, 113, 120, 121,

129–32; and "Latin American Discourse: The Space In-between," 117–18; and Latin America's colonial past, 111, 112–13, 136–37; and literary marketplace, 150; and mistranslations, 24, 128; and multiculturalism, 136–37; and national instinct, 119–20; and nationality, 107, 110, 119; and national literature, 119; novel and short stories of, 24, 108, 119–33; and "Pierre Menard, Author of the Quixote," 117; poetry of, 108–9; as a professor, 105, 110; and sexuality, 120, 121–22, 130, 131, 159; Sorbonne training of, 105–6; and space in-between, 10, 12, 24, 80, 105, 106–7, 108, 110, 111–12, 113, 114–18, 120, 122–23, 130–31, 132–33, 137, 142; and *Stella Manhattan*, 106, 107, 108, 119, 120–22, 127–32, 159; and translatability, 104, 108; and translation, 108, 109, 111, 118, 138, 175, 190; translational aesthetic of, 127, 128–29, 131; travels of, 24, 106, 110; and *Uma literatura nos trópicos* (A literature in the tropics), 107, 118–19; in the US, 3, 12, 105, 106, 107, 109, 110. *See also* Derrida, Jacques; Foucault, Michel

Schwartz, Jorge, 6–7
Silva, Luiz Inácio Lula da, 12–13
Siskind, Mariano, 133, 139
Slavery: and abolitionist Nabuco in Brazil, 30–31; abolition of, 11, 30, 31, 36, 38, 56; Brazil's policy of, 34, 36, 38, 56, 57; in Cuba, 36; Dom Pedro II's position on, 57; and education, 38; and Emancipation Proclamation in the US, 30; and hierarchical relationships, 15; legacies of, 29–30; legality of, 29, 30–31, 55; and Lei Áurea in Brazil, 31; and Machado de Assis, 184; and Rio Branco Law, 30–31; and slave stereotypes, 56; and *Uncle Tom's Cabin*, 55–56; in the US, 36, 55–56

Sousândrade: on Brazilian literature, 58; and critique of capitalism, 60–61; education of, 57; journalism of, 57–58, 61; and *O Guesa*, 57, 59–61, 76, 143; and *O Novo Mundo*, 22–23, 57, 59–61; as pen name of Joaquim de Sousa Andrade, 22; and Spanish American literature, 59; in the US, 109

Spanish American writers, 5–6, 8, 88, 106, 120. *See also* Bolaño, Roberto; Borges, Jorge Luis; Cortázar, Julio; García Márquez, Gabriel; Martí, José

Stowe, Harriet Beecher: and slavery, 29, 55, 56; and translation of *My Wife and I*, 17, 55, 56–57; and *Uncle Tom's Cabin*, 55–56

Tosta, Antonio Luciano Andrade de: and Brazilian-American literature, 128, 157; and *Confluence Narratives: Ethnicity, History and Nation-Making in the Americas*, 7
translation: and act of translating, 16, 18–20, 54–55, 75, 84, 115, 132; and Adriana Lisboa's novels, 142, 164–65, 167–68, 173–74; agents of, 16–17, 180, 184; of Brazilian elites, 26, 27; and Brazilian literature, 53–54, 55, 83, 145–46, 176–90; and Brazil's place in the Americas, 3, 5, 8, 9–10, 14, 17, 20, 25–26, 191; and Borges's work, 19–20, 148, 181;

translation *(continued)*
  and Campos brothers, 60; and
  Clarice Lispector's work, 180–84;
  and comparative scholarship,
  14, 53, 150–51; and concept of
  circulation, 15, 16, 20, 23; and
  creative transformation, 15, 20,
  53, 90, 175; and cultural capital,
  16; and cultural difference, 21–22;
  cultural translation, 21–22, 23,
  24, 32; and deconstructionism,
  116; and displacement, 2, 3, 5,
  16, 24, 79, 85, 176; and drama,
  178; English translation, 54–55,
  107, 145, 189; ethics of, 148;
  and experiences of travelers and
  migrants, 9, 15–16, 24; of French
  works, 54, 111; German translation,
  83; and global markets, 148–50;
  and Harriet Beecher Stowe, 55–56;
  and idea of the nation, 20–21, 22,
  25; and Ignacio Infante's work,
  15; importance of, 2, 16, 23, 29,
  53–54; and Inter-American Studies,
  8, 17; intersemiotic translation,
  90, 91; and intertextuality, 104;
  and language, 14, 16, 17, 18–19,
  24, 25–26, 53–55, 83, 84, 85–86,
  116, 136, 140, 147, 149, 170; and
  Latin American Boom, 12, 88, 144;
  and "Latin American Discourse:
  The Space In-between" (Santiago),
  23–24, 115, 116; linguistic and
  cultural translation, 37, 64–65,
  70, 79, 81, 119, 123, 126, 127,
  143, 165, 168, 170, 172–73, 175,
  176; literal translations, 2–3, 10,
  18, 54–55, 70, 71, 77, 89, 90,
  115, 175; literary translation, 37,
  53–55, 89–90, 99, 173–74; and
  Macunaíma, 100, 189, 190, 191;
  and *Macunaíma*'s film adaptation,
  90–92, 191; and *Macunaíma: the
  Hero Without a Character* (Mário
  de Andrade), 69–70, 74–76,
  80–90, 100, 189–91; and Mário
  de Andrade, 80, 82–84, 86, 89,
  90, 175; and migrants' difficulties,
  3–4; and mistranslations, 24; and
  novel *The Ventriloquist's Tale*,
  99–100; and orality, 80–81; and
  poetry, 7, 15, 17, 18, 19, 54–55;
  Portuguese translation, 2, 3, 4, 56,
  57, 145, 146, 155; and publishers
  and presses, 178–79; and reader-
  as-translator, 148; as re-creation,
  80, 149; and the remainder, 113;
  and retranslation, 25, 26, 27, 174,
  178, 179, 181–82, 183, 184; and
  the sign and signified, 18–19;
  and Silviano Santiago, 105, 106,
  107, 108, 114–15, 118, 175; and
  space in-between, 114–15, 118;
  and Spanish American writers, 88,
  141, 155; Spanish translation, 2, 3,
  17, 107, 182, 189; Spivak's vision
  of, 74, 147, 148; theory of, 17–20,
  74, 84, 87, 89, 91, 148, 149–50,
  151; and "The Translator's Task"
  (Benjamin), 16, 18, 21, 149; and
  transcreation, 9, 18, 20, 23, 70, 74,
  86, 89, 90; and translatability, 115,
  140, 143–44, 146, 148–50, 152,
  173, 178, 185; and the translation
  zone, 20, 28; and translators, 3,
  17, 19, 20, 23, 24, 25, 28, 39,
  53, 54–55, 71, 74, 77, 82–83, 84,
  85–86, 87–88, 89, 96, 100, 101,
  102, 104, 115, 139, 145, 147, 149,
  150, 152, 168, 177, 182–83, 189,
  190, 191; and the transnational
  process, 20–21, 116; and travel, 14,

15–16, 23, 24, 25, 26, 27–28, 104; and untranslatability, 10, 16, 20, 21, 25, 26, 81, 83, 85–86, 99, 140, 146–47, 150–51, 152, 168, 173–74, 178–79, 185–86, 187–89, 190; and ventriloquism, 101; Venuti's approach to, 147–48, 181, 183, 187; and visibility, 32; and world literature, 133, 134, 148. *See also* Benjamin, Walter; de Campos, Augusto; de Campos, Haroldo; language; Liu, Lydia H.; Santiago, Silviano; Walkowitz, Rebecca

travel: and 1876 Centennial Exhibition, 52; and Amazon region, 103; and Branner's expeditions, 40; and Brazilians in the Americas, 15, 22, 27, 47; as central to *Macunaíma*, 79; and colonialism, 15; and condition of translation, 14; and creative transformations, 23; and displacement, 2, 5, 13–14, 15, 79, 154; and Dom Pedro II, 1–2, 22, 29, 30, 47; and essay "Traveling Theory" (Said), 14; ethnographic travels, 69; of European and North American naturalists, 15, 27–28, 154; and experiences of travelers and migrants, 3–4, 9, 15–16, 24, 136, 143, 154; and Hartt's work, 39; and James Orton's work, 36–37; in Japan, 156; and language, 15; and "Latin American Discourse: The Space In-between" (Santiago), 24; and Lisboa's novels, 24, 154; of Mário de Andrade, 70; and migration, 120; and "otherness" of non-Western world, 14; and Peruvian Amazon, 70; and poetry, 7; and scientific explorations, 79; and Silviano Santiago, 106; and slavery, 15; and transculturation, 15; and translation, 8, 13–15, 16, 21, 23, 28, 104, 107; and transnational characters, 76; and travelers' characters, 154; and travel narratives, 5, 10, 70, 123. *See also* Andrade, Mário de; language

Treaty of Tordesillas, 6
Trump, Donald, 3, 13

Uncle Tom's Cabin (Stowe), 55–56
United States: and 1876 Centennial Exhibition, 44, 52; and Adriana Lisboa, 141; Brazilian immigrants, 13, 120, 159–68, 170–71, 175; Brazilians in, 3, 4, 5, 6, 8–9, 12, 13, 21, 22–23, 24, 25, 27, 29, 31–32, 47, 58, 108, 109, 120, 143, 157, 158–59, 166, 168, 169–71, 190; and Brazilian students, 38–39; and capitalism, 27, 28, 29, 60; and the Cold War, 12, 88, 144; and colonialism, 29; and democracy, 46; and Donald Trump, 13; and economic hierarchies, 68; educational system of, 36, 38–39, 40, 47, 50, 52; Emancipation Proclamation in, 30; ethnic literature of, 157; and exchanges in higher education with Brazil, 40; fiction set in, 121; and film *Macunaíma*, 95–96; government of, 46, 60; Great Depression in, 12; and immigration, 3–4, 13, 152, 154, 157, 160, 164, 169–71, 174, 175; Independence Day in, 173; institutionalized racism in, 11; and the Irish, 58; and Latin American interventions, 12, 132; and Latinx identities in Borderlands, 162; and Longfellow's poetry, 54; and

United States *(continued)*
Macunaíma: the Hero Without a Character (Mário de Andrade), 104; as model for Brazil, 47; and modernity, 9, 22, 29; and national identity, 29; neocolonial ambitions of, 10, 27; Pedro II in, 22, 60; and period of 1870s, 9, 11, 22, 39, 60; post-Civil War years in, 11, 29; and progress, 33, 47; race, class and ethnicity in, 122–23, 125–27; Reconstruction era in, 30; and relationship with Brazil, 2, 3, 5–6, 7–8, 13, 20, 27–29, 34, 36, 46, 60, 108, 190; and Silviano Santiago, 105, 106, 107, 109; and slavery, 11, 29, 36, 55–56; and Spanish America, 12. *See also* Centennial Exhibition of 1876; race

Ventriloquist's Tale, The (Melville): and Amerindians, 103; and intertextuality, 99, 100, 101, 103; and *Macunaíma* as a novel, 71, 99, 100, 103; Macunaima as narrator of, 99, 101, 102–4; and orality, 100–1, 102, 103; and ventriloquism, 102; and vulgar language, 100

Waisman, Sergio, 19, 117
Walkowitz, Rebecca, 16, 21, 142

www.ingramcontent.com/pod-product-compliance
Lightning Source LLC
Chambersburg PA
CBHW020643230426
43665CB00008B/292